Creating Powerful Brands

The Chartered Institute of Marketing/Butterworth-Heinemann Marketing Series is the most comprehensive, widely used and important collection of books in marketing and sales currently available worldwide.

As the CIM's official publisher, Butterworth-Heinemann develops, produces and publishes the complete series in association with the CIM. We aim to provide definitive marketing books for students and practitioners that promote excellence in marketing education and practice.

The series titles are written by CIM senior examiners and leading marketing educators for professionals, students and those studying the CIM's Certificate, Advanced Certificate and Postgraduate Diploma courses. Now firmly established, these titles provide practical study support to CIM and other marketing students and to practitioners at all levels.

 The Chartered
Institute of Marketing

Formed in 1911, The Chartered Institute of Marketing is now the largest professional marketing management body in the world with over 60,000 members located worldwide. Its primary objectives are focused on the development of awareness and understanding of marketing throughout UK industry and commerce and in the raising of standards of professionalism in the education, training and practice of this key business discipline.

Books in the series

Forthcoming

Creating Powerful Brands in Consumer, Service and Industrial Markets

Second Edition

Leslie de Chernatony

and

Malcolm McDonald

**Published in association with
The Chartered Institute of Marketing**

OXFORD AUCKLAND BOSTON JOHANNESBURG MELBOURNE NEW DELHI

Butterworth-Heinemann
Linacre House, Jordan Hill, Oxford OX2 8DP
225 Wildwood Avenue, Woburn, MA 01801–2041
A division of Reed Educational and Professional Publishing Ltd

℞ A member of the Reed Elsevier plc group

First published 1992
Reprinted 1993, 1994, 1995, 1996, 1997
Second edition 1998
Reprinted 1998

British Library Cataloguing in Publication Data
De Chernatony, L. (Leslie)
    Creating powerful brands in consumer, service and industrial markets
        – 2nd ed.
    1. Brand name products   2. Product management
    I. Title   II. McDonald, Malcolm, 1938–
    658.8′27

ISBN 0 7506 2240 7

Printed and bound by Biddles Ltd, Guildford and King's Lynn

Contents

Part One   Foundations of Brand Management

Part Two   Brand Management in Different Sectors

Part Three   Winning the Brands Battle

Preface

The first edition of this book was published in 1992 and since then numerous reprints have appeared, paying testimony to the popularity of this text. Positive feedback from students and managers we have taught in lectures and in branding workshops, along with letters from pleased readers, encouraged us to revise the original text. We have developed a more comprehensive text that not only gives a more current perspective on the subject of creating powerful brands, but also takes a broader look at the factors which can either enhance or impede brands' success. This new edition incorporates our continuing research and experience, as well as synthesizing some of the evolving publications on branding which have managerial implications.

The purpose of this book is to clarify the concept of brands and to help plan for building powerful brands, ensuring a better return on investment. Our experience indicates that according to the role of the manager, for example developing advertising or devising new designs, so they see their departments' work as being a key contributor to brand success. We are delighted when we see and hear of such enthusiasm, but are firmly of the opinion that brand success does not result from one area of excellence, but rather is a blending of many company-wide activities. As such this book does not major on a particular functional role but, true to the theme of brand planning, it encompasses many of the diverse activities driving powerful brands.

Since the first edition of this book, the importance of brands in the service and business to business sectors has become more apparent. In view of this we have a new chapter on service brands and have enhanced the material on business to business brands. While the principles of successful branding stem from consumer markets, our research and experience show that these need adapting for these sectors. We do not advocate the need for separate theories for these domains but rather, by understanding the unique characteristics of these sectors, the core principles of consumer branding need fine-tuning. In the service sector we consider it of paramount importance that branding activity be first directed at employees. Only when they understand the vision for the brand, its values, positioning and its desired personality, should branding activity be broadened to consumers and other stakeholders. One of the myths that we encounter in business to business brands is that emotional aspects of branding are not relevant. As we explain in this book, the emotional component of the brand plays a significant role in influencing organizations' choices.

Another area of growing interest to managers is the topic of brand equity and brand evaluation. We have included a new chapter which reviews the concept of brand equity and helps managers assess the health of their brand.

To facilitate understanding of the concepts involved in brand building, we have restructured the contents with the following flow:

Part One   Foundations of Brand Management

The first two chapters address the core characteristics of brands and the factors that influence their evolution.

Chapter 1 sets the scene by considering why it is important to create and sustain powerful brands.

Chapter 2 explains the nature of brands, overviews their evolution, identifies different types of brands and highlights the forces that shape brand strategy.

Part Two   Brand Management in Different Sectors

The next five chapters explore the characteristics of effective brand management for consumer, business to business, service and retailer brands.

Chapter 3 addresses the key question of how consumers choose brands and therefore how managers can influence brand choice.

Chapter 4 concentrates on the psychological and social aspects of consumer brands, exploring their symbolic nature, investigating the importance of values, their expression through brand personality and enactment through relationships.

Chapter 5 focuses on business to business brands, appreciating how they are bought, the importance of value, brands as relationship builders and the role of emotion.

Chapter 6 discusses the importance and characteristics of service brands, addressing issues critical to building them.

Chapter 7 reviews the growing power of retailers with their well-conceived retailer brands blossoming in an era of category management and efficient consumer response. Strategies for growth either as a supplier of retailer brands or as a manufacturer brand are addressed.

Part Three   Winning the Brands Battle

The remaining four chapters address techniques to win the branding battle and evaluate brand success.

Chapter 8 adopts a strategic perspective on positioning, identifying sources of sustainable competitive advantage to beat competitors through building, buying or extending brands.

Chapter 9 explains the critical role of added values, suggesting ways of identifying these and ensuring their relevance in challenging environments.

Chapter 10 considers planning issues that ensure consistent brand values through adopting a holistic perspective on brands.

Chapter 11 explores the concept of brand equity, addressing ways of evaluating the extent to which a powerful brand has been created.

Since the first edition of this book more has emerged to enhance our appreciation of brands and techniques for brand building. This is reflected in the expanded coverage of material, two new chapters, a larger number of references and more advertisements to bring the material to life. To help managers and potential managers (some of whom may well be studying at business school) to capitalize on the material in this book, at the end of each chapter there is a series of questions. These have been devised to help consider the appropriateness of the current brand strategy and to assess the suitability of alternative strategies.

We hope you find the frameworks in this book useful in better understanding the topic of brands and planning for brands. The idea for the book was seeded when one of us was undertaking a PhD concerned with identifying different types of brands in an era of increasing retailer dominance.* Frameworks evolved and were tested through our research, lecturing, consultancy and management development workshops. This book also benefited from discussions with our colleagues, members of the Brands Management Research Unit at the Open University Business School and our colleague Dr. Gil McWilliam at the London Business School.

This book has been written for practitioners and students of brand management. Both groups need to have a good understanding of brand-building techniques which are covered in consumer, service and business to business sectors.

Finally, Leslie de Chernatony would like to thank his family – his wife Carolyn for her support and two growing brands, Gemma and Russell, for their gift of time. All three provided inspiration about relationship building!

Professor Leslie de Chernatony
Professor Malcolm McDonald

---

* Further details of this can be obtained from Professor Leslie de Chernatony, School of Management, Open University Business School, The Open University, Walton Hall, Milton Keynes, MK7 6AA, UK.

Acknowledgements

Every effort has been made to locate the copyright owners of material used and the authors would like to thank the following organizations for granting permission to include material copyrighted to them in the book: Bayer plc; Agfa; AIM the European Brands Association; Apple Computer UK Ltd; Barclays Bank PLC; Glaxo Wellcome; The Jenks Group and a/s blumller; Black Horse Relocation and Primary Contact Ltd; The Boeing Company; Boots the Chemists; Bradford & Bingley Building Society; Britannic Travel Ltd and Upward, Jamie & Brown; Daihatsu (UK) Ltd; De Beers and J. Walter Thompson; Alfred Dunhill Ltd; Tony Muranka (Art Director), Peers Carter (copywriter) and Alan Randall (photographer) for Dyson Appliances Ltd; Elida Faberge; *The Estates Gazette* and Campbell Gordon Consultants; Procter & Gamble, DMB&B and Steve Cavalier (photographer); Farm Energy Centre; Midland Bank PLC; Ford Motor Company Ltd; Green Flag Ltd; Halifax plc and Ken Griffiths (photographer); Hewlett-Packard; IBM UK Ltd and Ogilvy & Mather; Interflora (FTDA) British Unit Ltd and DMB&B; Invergordon Distillers; KLM Royal Dutch Airlines; Kodak Ltd; Land Rover and WCRS Ltd on behalf of Max Forsythe (photographer); Mazda Car (UK) Ltd; NCR; New Zealand Tourism Board, Mustoe Merriman Herring Levy and Ian McKinnell (photographer); Procter & Gamble; Van de Bergh Foods; PPP Healthcare; Price Waterhouse; Raleigh Industries Ltd and Cross Hill Conwill; Primary Contact Ltd on behalf of Redland; Royal Mail; J Sainsbury plc; Seiko UK Ltd; Swissair; Swiss Life Insurance and Pension Company; Taylor Woodrow Group; Tektronix UK Ltd and Mason Zimbler: Umbro International and DMB&B; Vauxhall Motors Ltd; Virgin Direct Personal Financial Services; Waitrose; WD-40 Company; Glaxo Wellcome GmbH & Co. We would like a special acknowledgement to Luisa Helling for her hard editorial work.

Part One

Foundations of Brand Management

Chapter 1

Why it is important to create powerful brands

Summary

This introductory chapter lays the foundations for the remaining chapters of this book. It summarizes the latest thinking and best practice in the domain of marketing and takes a fresh look at the real nature of an organization's assets, such as market share and supplier and customer relationships, all of which are represented by the brand. It also questions traditional thinking and practice in asset accounting and suggests alternative approaches designed to focus attention on the core purpose of this book – how to create powerful brands.

Dispelling misunderstanding about product management

In spite of its somewhat histrionic title, this book is a serious, in-depth attempt by two professional teachers, researchers and practitioners, to focus attention on an aspect of marketing that is frequently misunderstood and consequently neglected – **branding**.

Let us begin the process of orientating our minds towards this important subject by asking ourselves 'what is a product?' or 'what is a service?' The central role that the product plays in business management makes it such an important subject, that mismanagement in this area is unlikely to be compensated for by good management in other areas. Misunderstanding in relation to the nature of *product* management is also the root of whatever subsequent misunderstanding there is about *brand* management.

What is a product?

It should hardly be necessary to explain that a product or a service is a **problem solver**, in the sense that it solves the customer's problems and is also the means by which the organization achieves its own objectives. And since it is what actually changes hands, it is clearly a subject of great importance.

The clue to what constitutes a product can be found in an examination of what it is that customers appear to buy. It is now over thirty years since Theodore Levitt, in what is perhaps the best-known article on marketing ever written ('Marketing Myopia') said that what customers want when they buy $^1/_4$-inch drills is $^1/_4$-inch holes. In other words the drill itself is only a means to an end. The lesson here for the drill manufacturer is that if they really believe their business is the manufacture of drills rather than, say, the manufacture of the means of making holes in materials, they are in grave danger of going out of business as soon as a better means of making holes is invented, such as, say, a pocket laser.

The important point about this somewhat simplistic example is that a company which fails to think of its business in terms of customer benefits rather than in terms of physical products is in danger of losing its competitive position in the market.

We can now begin to see that when customers buy a product, even if they are industrial buyers purchasing a piece of equipment for their company, they are still buying a particular bundle of benefits which they perceive as satisfying their own particular needs and wants.

We can now all begin to appreciate the danger of leaving product decisions entirely to engineers, actuaries, R&D people and the like. If we do, technicians will sometimes assume that the only point in product management is the actual technical performance, or the functional features of the product itself. These ideas are incorporated

Exhibit 1.1   As this advertisement exemplifies, the concept of presenting a product or service as a problem solver is not unique to consumer marketing (reproduced by kind permission of the Farm Energy Centre)

in Figure 1.1 and appear right at the very centre of the circle.

We can go even further than this and depict two outer circles as the 'product surround'. This product surround can account for as much as 80 per cent of the added values and impact of a product or service. Often, these only account for about 20 per cent of costs, whereas the reverse is often true of the inner circle.

The nature of relationships with customers

Figure 1.1 also begins to throw light on the nature of the confusion surrounding the relationships that organizations enjoy with their customers. It is a sad reflection on the state of marketing that in spite of fifty years of marketing education, ignorance still abounds concerning what marketing is. The following are the major areas of confusion, starting with the key point just made:

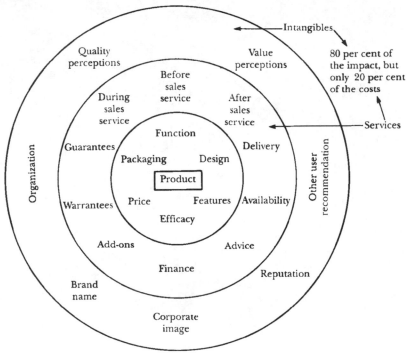

Figure 1.1

1   *Confusion with product management*   The belief that all a company has to do to succeed is to produce a good product still abounds, and neither Concorde, the EMI Scanner, nor the many

thousands of brilliant products that have seen their owners or inventors go bankrupt during the past twenty years will convince such people otherwise.

2   *Confusion with advertising*   This is another popular misconception and the annals of business are replete with examples such as Dunlop, Woolworths and British Airways who, before they got professional management in, won awards with their brilliant advertising campaigns, while failing to deliver the goods. Throwing advertising expenditure at the problem is still a very popular way of tackling deep-rooted marketing problems.

3   *Confusion with customer service*   The 'Have a nice day' syndrome is currently having its heyday in many countries of the world, popularized by Peters and Waterman in *In Search of Excellence*. The banks are amongst those who have spent millions training their staff to be charming to customers while still getting the basic offer fundamentally wrong, although it must be said that some of them have finally begun to realize that the actual product itself must be right. Likewise, in many railway companies around the world, while it helps to be treated nicely, it is actually much more important to get there on time.

4   *Confusion with selling*   Selling is just one aspect of communication with customers, and to say that it is the only thing that matters is to ignore the importance of product management, pricing, distribution and other forms of communication in achieving profitable sales. Selling is just one part of this process, in which the transaction is actually clinched. It is the culmination of the marketing process, and success will only be possible if all the other elements of the marketing mix have been properly managed. Imagine having a horse that didn't have four legs! The more attention that is paid to finding out what customers want, to developing products to satisfy these wants, to pricing at a level consistent with the benefits offered, to gaining distribution, and to communicating effectively with our target market, the more likely we are to be able to exchange contracts through the personal selling process.

The organization's marketing assets

Textbook definitions of marketing have emphasized the satisfaction of identified customer needs as a fundamental article of faith. Various interpretations exist, but the concept of 'putting the customer at the centre of the business' summarizes these viewpoints.

Philosophically, there is little to argue with in this notion. However, it must be recognized that the ability of the business to produce offerings that meet real needs will generally be limited to very specific areas. More particularly, what we find is that an organization's skills and resources are the limiting factor determining its ability to meet market-place needs. The example of a slide rule manufacturer being unable to compete in the age of electronic calculators underlines this point. The strengths and skills of such a company, whatever they may have been, were quite definitely not in the manufacture of electronic calculators, whereas they may well have had a strength in marketing and distribution in specialized markets – thus possibly providing an opportunity to distribute other manufacturers' products aimed at those markets.

marketing should really be seen as the process of achieving the most effective deployment of the firm's assets

What we are in effect saying is that marketing should really be seen as the process of achieving **the most effective deployment of the firm's assets** to achieve overall corporate objectives. By assets in this context, we refer specifically to those assets which might best be described as 'marketing assets'.

What are marketing assets? Typically when we talk about assets, we think first of financial assets, or more precisely those assets that are recognized in the balance sheet of the business. So, fixed assets, such as plant and machinery, and current assets, such as inventory or cash, would be typical of this view of assets.

In fact, the marketing assets of the business are of far greater importance to the long-run health of the business and yet paradoxically rarely appear in the balance sheet. Ultimately, the only assets that have value are those that contribute directly or indirectly to profitable sales, now or in the future. Included in our categorization of marketing assets would be such things as:

- *Market 'franchise'*   Are there certain parts of the market that we can call our own? The loyalty of customers and distributors will be a factor here.
- *Distribution network*   Do we have established channels of distribution which enable us to bring products or services to the market in a cost-effective way?
- *Market share*   The 'experience effect' and economies of scale mean that for many companies there are substantial advantages to being big. For example, costs will be lower and visibility in the market-place will be higher.
- *Supplier relationships*   The ability to have access to raw materials, low-cost components, and so on, can be of substantial advantage. Additionally, close cooperation with suppliers can frequently lead to innovative product developments.
- *Customer relations*   'Close to the customer' has become the motto of the millennium, and many organizations can testify to the

advantage of strong bonds between the company and its customers. This has led to a great interest in what has come to be
known as relationship marketing.

*   *Technology base*   Does the company have any unique skills, proc-
    esses or know-how strengths that can provide a basis for
    product/market exploitation?

It is only through the effective use of these and any other marketing assets that the company can build successful marketing
strategies. There still, of course, remains the crucial task of seeking
market-place opportunities for the exploitation of this asset base;
however, this is an issue outside the scope of this book.

Nevertheless, if we are to be serious about marketing assets,
perhaps managerially we should treat them as we do 'financial' assets. In which case questions such as these arise:

*   How do we value market assets?
*   How do we protect them?
*   How do we grow them?

The question of the valuation of marketing assets is complex
and controversial. Traditionally, the only time that an attempt is made
to put a financial value on these intangible assets is when a company
is bought or sold. It will often be the case that one company, in acquiring another, will pay more than the 'book value' of the acquired
company – as represented, that is, in the balance sheet. The accountants' answer to this is to treat the difference between the purchase
price and the book value as 'goodwill' and then to write it off against
reserves or amortize it through the profit-and-loss account over a
number of years.

The importance of the brand

Perceptive readers will already have observed that, so far, we have
deliberately chosen not to make any reference to brands as assets. It
will also be clear by now that Figure 1.1 depicts not just a physical
product, but a **relationship** with the customer. This relationship is
personified either by the organization's name, or by the brand name
on the product itself. ICI, IBM, BMW, Kodak and Cadbury's are excellent examples of company brand names. Persil, Nescafé, Fosters
and Dulux are excellent examples of product brand names.

First, then, it should be stressed, that when we refer to the term
'brand' in this book, we use it to encompass not only consumer products, but a whole host of offerings, which include people (such as

politicians and pop stars), places (such as Bangkok), ships (such as the *QEII*), companies, industrial products, service products, and so on.

Second, a distinction should be drawn between a 'brand' and a commodity'. Commodity markets typically are characterized by the lack of perceived differentiation by customers between competing offerings. In other words, one product offering in a particular category is much like another. Products like milk or potatoes come to mind or tin and iron ore. Whilst there may be quality differences, the suggestion is that, within a given specification, this bottle of milk is just the same as that bottle of milk.

In situations such as these, one finds that purchase decisions tend to be taken on the basis of price or availability, and not on the basis of the brand or the manufacturer's name. Thus one could argue that the purchase of petrol falls into the commodity category, and whilst the petrol companies do try and promote 'image', they inevitably end up relying either on price or on promotions such as wine glasses and games to try to generate repeat purchase.

There are examples, however, of taking a commodity and making it a brand. Take, for example, Perrier Water: the contents are naturally occurring spring water which, whilst it has certain distinctive characteristics, at the end of the day is still spring water. Yet through packaging and, more particularly, promotion, an international brand has been created with high brand loyalty and consequently it sells for a price well in excess of the costs of the ingredients.

Conversely, one can also find examples of once-strong brands which have been allowed to decay and in effect become commodities. This process is often brought about because the marketing asset base has been allowed to erode – perhaps through price cutting or through a lack of attention to product improvement in the face of competition.

One market where this has happened in the UK is in the fruit-squash drink market. Fifteen or twenty years ago, there were a number of very strong brands – Suncrush, Kia-ora, Jaffa Juice, to name a few. In this, market, the quality of the brand had traditionally been stressed, but a switch in promotional emphasis occurred in the 1960s towards promotional offers of one sort or another. Price cutting became prevalent and resources were switched out of advertising which promoted the values of the brand and into so-called 'below the line' promotional activities. The main effect of this, twenty years later, has been to reduce the bottle of orange squash to the level of a commodity to such an extent that the major brands are now retailers' own label products.

Figure 1.2 depicts the process of decay from brand to commodity as, over time, the distinctive values of the brand become less clear and thus the opportunity to demand a premium price reduces. So, today, we find a bottle of Perrier Water selling at a premium over a bottle of orange squash!

This figure is used again in Chapter 7.

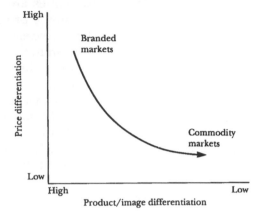

Figure 1.2   *From brand to commodity*

The difference between a brand and a commodity can be summed up in the phrase 'added values'. A brand is more than just the sum of its component parts. It embodies, for the purchaser or user, additional attributes which, whilst they might be considered by some to be 'intangible', are still very real. To illustrate the power of these added values consider the results of a *blind* test (i.e. where the brand identity is concealed) in which Diet Pepsi was compared against Diet Coke by a panel of consumers:

difference between a brand and a commodity can be summed up in the phrase 'added values'

- Prefer Pepsi   51 per cent
- Prefer Coke   44 per cent
- Equal/can't say   5 per cent

When the same two drinks were given to a matched sample in an *open test* (i.e. the true identity of the brands was revealed), the following results were produced:

- Prefer Pepsi   23 per cent
- Prefer Coke   65 per cent
- Equal/can't say   12 per cent

How can this be explained if not in terms of the added values that are aroused in the minds of consumers when they see the familiar Coke logo and pack?

The same phenomenon is also encountered in industrial marketing. In a commodity market such as fertilizers, the initials 'ICI'

printed on a plastic sack have the effect of communicating to the
purchaser a statement about quality and reliability, giving ICI a considerable advantage over lesser-known brands.

Often, these added values are emotional values which customers might find difficult to articulate. These values are given to a
product quite simply through the marketing mix of product, packaging, promotion, price and distribution. All of these elements of the
mix can be used to develop a distinctive **position** in the customers'
mental map of the market. As in all the references to brands thus far,
the concept of 'positioning' is developed in greater detail in the following chapters, but suffice it to say at this juncture that in commodity
markets, competing products, because they are undifferentiated, are
seen by the customer as occupying virtually identical positions and
thus to all intents and purposes are substitutable. The more distinctive a **brand** position, however, the less likelihood that a customer
will accept a substitute.

It is thus the case that the most effective dimensions of competition are the relative added values of competing brands. The 'core'
product is purely the tangible features of the offering – usually easy
to imitate. The added values that augment the product and where
distinctive differences can be created, are to be found in the 'product
surround', summarized again in Figure 1.3.

The larger the 'surround' in relation to the core product, the
more likely it is that the offering will be strongly differentiated from
the competition, and vice versa.

The Coca-Cola example, to which we shall return in the main
body of the text, is one of the best indications of the value of what we
have called the 'product surround'. That it is a major determinant
of commercial success, there can be little doubt. When one company buys another, as in the case of Nestlé and Rowntree, it is
abundantly clear that the purpose of the acquisition is not to buy
the tangible assets which appear on the balance sheet, such as
factories, plant, vehicles and so on, but the brand names owned
by the company to be acquired. This is because it is not factories
which make profits, but relationships with customers, and it is
brand names which secure these relationships.

It might be argued, therefore, that if it is possible to value a
company for sale, then surely it should be possible to do so on an on-
going basis and specifically to recognize the worth of marketing assets
as represented by brands.

The question of asset protection and development is in a sense
what marketing is all about. The 'stewardship' of marketing assets is
a key responsibility which is recognized in many companies by, for
example, the organizational concept of brand management. Here,
an executive is given the responsibility for a brand or brands and

acts as the product 'champion', competing internally for resources and externally for market position. It is but a short step from this organizational concept to a system of 'brand accounting' which would seek to identify the net present value of a brand based upon the prospect of future cash inflows compared with outgoings.

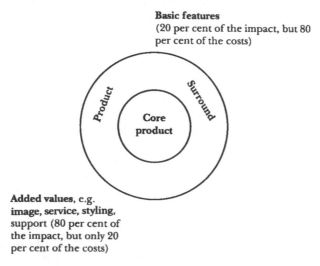

Basic features
(20 per cent of the impact, but 80 per cent of the costs)

Product

Surround

Core product

Added values, e.g. image, service, styling, support (80 per cent of the impact, but only 20 per cent of the costs)

Figure 1.3   *The importance of added values*

One advantage of such an approach is that it forces the manager to acknowledge that money spent on developing the market position of a brand is in fact an investment which is made in order to generate future revenues. There is a strong argument for suggesting that, for internal decision making and on questions of resource allocation, a 'shadow' set of management accounts be used, not the traditional approach whereby marketing costs are treated as expenditure in the period in which they are incurred, but an approach which recognizes such expenditure as investments.

money spent on developing the market position of a brand is in fact an investment to generate future revenues

Buying a major brand via acquisition nowadays often makes more sense to organizations than launching a new brand, with all the risk and uncertainty that this entails. This is just one of the reasons why brand valuation has emerged as a major issue in recent times and why brands are increasingly sought after as assets.

Some of the more spectacular examples of the value of brands as assets can be seen in acquisitions in which colossal premiums were paid above the balance sheet asset value. Philip Morris, for example, bought Kraft for $12.9 bn, four times the value of Kraft's tangible assets. Grand Metropolitan bought Pillsbury for $5.5 bn, a 50 per cent premium on Pillsbury's pre-bid value. RHM, taking its cue from this trend, more than trebled its asset value when it voluntarily valued its own brands and incorporated them on the balance sheet.

Building successful brands

We hope that we have, by now, been able to give some initial signals about the increasing importance of brands in business success. Later in this book, we refer to the PIMS database (Profit Impact of Market Strategies), which, along with other databases, show conclusively that strong, successful brands enable organizations to build stable, long-term demand and enable them to build and hold better margins than either commodity products or unsuccessful brands. (Brands, of course, can be either successful or unsuccessful. Watneys in the UK is a prime example of an unsuccessful brand.)

Successful brand building helps profitability by adding values that entice customers to buy. They provide a firm base for expansion into product improvements, variants, added services, new countries, and so on. They protect organizations against the growing power of intermediaries. And last, but not least, they help transform organizations from being faceless bureaucracies to ones that are attractive to work for and to deal with.

The following chapters of this book contain an in-depth treatment of every aspect relevant to successful brand building. How to create powerful brands is a major challenge facing all organizations today. It is unlikely that this challenge will be met unless a more rigorous approach is taken to the issues surrounding branding.

We urge you to read on!

Book modus operandi

Each of the following chapters covers a number of vital aspects of brand management and concludes with an action checklist. Finally, for the convenience of our readers, we have included a further reading list on the more important aspects covered in each chapter.

Chapter 2

Understanding the branding process

Summary

The purpose of this chapter is to provide an overview of the key issues involved in planning for brand success. It begins by explaining that successful branding is more than merely the use of names, then goes on to discuss the concept of the brand, brand characteristics and the role of brands in relationship marketing. A historical review of the evolution of brands, distributors' brands and generics is presented along with a consideration of ways of categorizing brands. The value of brands to manufacturers, distributors and buyers is addressed along with the importance of brand planning and issues influencing the potential of a brand.

Brand success through integrating marketing resources

When BMW drivers proudly turn the ignition keys for the first time in 'the ultimate driving machine', they are not only benefiting from a highly engineered car with excellent performance, but also taking ownership of a symbol that signifies the core values of exclusivity, performance, quality and technical innovation. Customers of American Express are not just buying Travelers Cheques that are issued promptly and accepted world-wide, or the security of having their lost cards restored quickly. They are also paying to feel they belong to an exclusive club of successful and extraordinary people, leading exciting and adventurous lives. Likewise a managing director outsourcing the IT function of a company chooses Andersen Consulting not just because of the large resources and the expertise offered. He or she is also buying a name that stands for commitment to service excellence, global recognition and sustained credibility.

While these purchasers in the consumer, service and industrial markets have bought solutions to their individual problems, they have also paid a price premium for the added values provided by buying brands. In addition to satisfying their core purchase requirements, they have bought an augmented solution to their problem, for which they perceive sufficient added value to warrant paying a premium over other alternatives that might have satisfied their buying needs.

The added values they sought, however, were not just those provided through the presence of a brand name as a differentiating device, nor through the use of brand names to recall powerful advertising. Instead, they perceived a total entity, the **brand**, which is the result of a coherent marketing approach which uses all elements of the marketing mix. A man does not give a woman a box of branded chocolates because she is hungry. Instead, he selects a brand that communicates something about his relationship with her. This, he hopes, will be recognized through the pack design, her recall of a relevant advertising message, the quality of the contents, her chiding of him for the price he paid and her appreciation of the effort he took to find a retailer specializing in stocking such an exclusive brand. The same goes for a woman buying a man a special box of cigars.

the brand is the result of a coherent marketing approach which uses all elements of the marketing mix

These examples show that thinking of branding as being 'to do with naming products', or 'about getting the right promotion with the name prominently displayed', or 'getting the design right', is too myopic. In the mid-1980s, we came across Scottowels when doing some work in the kitchen towels market. Managers in the company thought that this was a branded kitchen towel, but consumers perceived this as little more than another kitchen towel with a name added – one stage removed from being a commodity. It had a brand name, but because the rest of the marketing mix was neglected, it had to fight for shelf space on the basis of price and was ultimately doomed because of the vicious circle driven by minimum value leading to low price.

There are hundreds of examples of well-known brand names that have failed commercially. There are even some which are reviled by the public. Such unsuccessful brands are examples of a failure to integrate all the elements of marketing in a coherent way.

Thus, branding is a powerful marketing concept that does not just focus on one element of the marketing mix, but represents the result of a carefully conceived array of activities across the whole spectrum of the marketing mix, directed towards making the buyer recognize relevant added values that are unique when compared with competing products and services and which are difficult for competitors to emulate. The purpose of branding is to facilitate the organization's task of getting and maintaining a loyal customer base in a cost-effective manner to achieve the highest possible return on investment. In other words, branding should not be regarded as a tactical tool directed towards one element of the marketing mix, but rather should be seen as the result of strategic thinking, integrating a marketing programme across the complete marketing mix.

Neither is this a concept that should be regarded as more appropriate for consumer markets. Indeed, the concept of branding is increasingly being applied to people and places, such as politicians, pop stars, holiday resorts and the like, whilst it has always been equally relevant to the marketing of products and services. Strategic branding is concerned with evaluating how to achieve the highest return on investment from brands, through analysing, formulating and implementing a strategy that best satisfies users, distributors and brand manufacturers. It is relatively recently that a strategic perspective on branding has emerged, with firms beginning to recognize that they are sitting on valuable assets that need careful attention, as we shall see in the next section.

The concept of the brand

Successful brands, that is those which are the focus of a coherent blending of marketing resources, represent valuable marketing assets. During the 1980s the value of brands was ironically brought to the attention of marketers by the financial community. For example, in 1985 Reckitt & Colman acquired Airwick Industries and put on its balance sheet £127 m as the financial value resulting from the intangible benefits of goodwill, heritage and loyalty conveyed by the newly acquired brand names. While this may have been one of the opening shots to make organizations aware of the financial value of brands, it was Rank Hovis McDougal who really brought the brand debate to life. They announced in 1988 that they had put £678 m on their balance sheet as the valuation of their brand names. In the same year Jacobs Suchard and Nestlé fought for the ownership of Rowntree. At the time of the takeover battle it was estimated that Rowntree's tangible net assets were worth around £300 m, yet Nestlé won control by paying £2.5 bn. This difference of £2.2 bn represented the value that Nestlé saw in the potential earnings of strong brands such as KitKat, Polo, Quality Street and After Eight Mints!

A 1996 survey based on the Interbrand valuation procedure has shown the value brands have acquired today, as can be seen from Table 2.1.

Table 2.1   *The world's most valuable brands (source: Financial World Magazine)*

1996	1995	Brand	Value ($ m)*
1	2	Marlboro	44 614
2	1	Coca-Cola	43 427
3	†	McDonald's	18 920
4	3	IBM	18 491
5	†	Disney	15 358
6	7	Kodak	13 267
7	9	Kellogg's	11 409
8	8	Budweiser	11 026
9	10	Nescafé	10 527
10	11	Intel	10 499

*Value calculated on global sales of products carrying the brand name and the brand's operating income.

† Service brands were not included in the 1995 survey

successful brands are valuable because they guarantee future income streams

Successful brands are valuable because they guarantee future income streams. Companies know that loyal customers will repeatedly buy their brands and are also willing to support them during crises, as shown during the accidents with Johnson & Johnson 'tampered jars'. In those instances the high visibility of the brand together with an effective management of the crisis ensured that sales recovered quickly.

The ultimate assessor of the real value of a brand, however, is not the manufacturer or the distributor, but the buyer or the user. Marketers are able to develop strategies to convey added values to purchasers, but because of what is called the 'perceptual process', the target audience may well focus on only a part of the available information and 'twist' some of the messages to make them congruent with their prior beliefs. For example, should a wallpaper paste manufacturer show an apparently incompetent DIY householder mixing paste in a television commercial in an attempt to communicate the smoothness and ease of application of their brand of wallpaper paste, they run the risk of some consumers interpreting the brand as being more 'suitable for idiots'. This is one example of the perceptual process.

People interpret messages and images through their own perceptions, often with very different results. Exhibit 2.1 uses Escher's deceiving perspective to demonstrate how contrasting views can coexist, each one being real in the eye of the beholder.

It is imperative to recognize that while marketers instigate the branding process (branding as an *input*), it is the buyer or the user

Increasing Shareholder Value depends on seeing the picture clearly

Look at this picture and your eye is deceived into accepting it. Only closer examination reveals that it's an architectural illusion.

Look at ways of increasing your shareholder value with ValueBuilder and all you'll see is the one clear picture you want.

Price Waterhouse developed ValueBuilder as a new and innovative tool to help management enhance shareholder value.

ValueBuilder uses cash flows, not earnings, to value companies and their

investment decisions. It focuses efforts to improve business performance on those actions which will lead to increased shareholder value.

The ValueBuilder approach identifies those actions by benchmarking the key drivers of performance in a business, which together determine its shareholder value and influence its share price. It then prioritises different business opportunities by measuring the effect each will have on shareholder value.

Once the full picture is seen, ValueBuilder brings together all the financial

and business advisory skills within Price Waterhouse, to help formulate and implement practical new value building solutions.

There is no more direct route to achieving today's key corporate requirement – the enhancement of shareholder value.

ValueBuilder
Enhancing Shareholder Value

Price Waterhouse

Southwark Towers 32 London Bridge Street London SE1 9SY Telephone (0171) 939 5999 Facsimile (0171) 403 2283

Exhibit 2.1   *The Price Waterhouse advertisement is a good example of the way people will interpret advertisements in different ways. Where did you start looking on this advertisement and how did you make sense of it? Now ask someone else and appreciate their process of sense-making (reproduced by kind permission of Price Waterhouse)*

who forms a mental vision of the brand (branding as an *output*), which may be different from the intended marketing thrust. While marketers talk about the branding effort they are undertaking, they should never lose sight of the fact that the final form of the brand is the mental evaluation held by the purchasers or users. Branding, then, needs to be appreciated in terms of both the input and the output process. A classic example of this is shown in an Institute of Grocery Distribution study. This research rated the factors which retailers and manufacturers believe linked the success of brands. Table 2.2 lists the criteria retailers use to stock new brands and manufacturers use to produce them. Major mismatches on criteria ratings, such as 'understanding retailer objectives' and 'price' explain one of the reasons for the lack of brand success.

Table 2.2   *Criteria necessary if brands are to succeed (source: Institute of Grocery Distribution 1994)*

Criteria	Retailers (%)	Manufacturers (%)
Understanding retailer objectives	20	1
Product innovation	13	16
Consumer understanding	13	13
Long-term development strategy	11	2
Strong brand image	10	8
Quality	9	–
Category management	6	10
Price	6	13
Brand distinctiveness	2	9
Supply chain linkages	1	10
Open relations	1	9

Drawing on the points discussed so far, we can better clarify the term 'brand' through our definition:

> *A successful brand is an identifiable product, service, person or place, augmented in such a way that the buyer or user perceives relevant, unique added values which match their needs most closely. Furthermore, its success results from being able to sustain these added values in the face of competition.*

Later in this chapter we review the plethora of brand definitions, some of which provide a helpful insight for the practitioner, but none of which fully describes the concept. Our definition above recognizes that brands exist in both product (consumer and industrial) and service domains and even relate to people, for example pop stars, and places, for example, the marketing of cities as tourist attractions (see Plate 2). Brands are also present in non-profit organizations, for example in internationally recognized charities, such as WWF, Greenpeace and Oxfam.

Brands are successful when developed with a clear statement of intent about the product's or service's purpose, the specific group of customers the brand is targeted at and a commitment to equipping the brand with the right types of resources to achieve the stated purpose. For example, Coca-Cola's success is partly attributable to a clear positioning as a refreshing, fun-type drink, targeted at teenagers and backed by a tradition of quality and continual consumer communication. Mercury Minicall, succeeded because it refused to conform to the concept of the pager as a dog collar tying people to the office, but worked to reposition it as a trendy, must-have product that gives people the freedom to communicate on their own terms.

brands are successful when developed with a clear statement of intent

Brands deliver a variety of benefits, which for ease can be classified as satisfying buyers' rational and emotional needs. Successful brands are those which have the correct balance in terms of their ability to satisfy these two needs. For example, cigarette smokers have a variety of rational needs such as seeking the best value, or best taste, or best quality, or a certain aroma or achieving relaxation, etc. The extent to which different brands satisfy particular rational needs will be assessed by the consumer trying different brands, examining the packaging, looking at the shape of the cigarette, considering its price, etc. Besides these rational needs they will also be seeking to satisfy emotional needs, such as prestige, or distinctiveness, or style, or social reassurance, etc. The extent to which different brands satisfy these emotional needs will be evaluated by consumers recalling promotions, or assessing who smokes different brands, or considering what situations different brands are consumed in, etc. To succeed, the marketer must understand the extent to which their brand satisfies rational and emotional needs and then develop marketing programmes accordingly.

Some may question whether the rational dimension dominates industrial branding and therefore whether there is any need to consider emotional aspects at all. Our work has shown that emotion plays an important role in the industrial brand selection process. For example, some managers do not just consider the rational aspects of IT software brands when they intend to install a new payroll system. They also seek emotional reassurance that the correct brand decision might reaffirm their continual career development or that they have not lost credibility amongst colleagues through the wrong brand choice.

Characteristics of brands

a brand as
consisting of four
levels

Our definition of a brand adheres to a model which shows the extent to which a product or service can be augmented to provide added value to increasing levels of sophistication. This model, which is expanded on in Chapter 9, views a brand as consisting of four levels:

- generic
- expected
- augmented
- potential

The **generic** level is the commodity form that meets the buyer's or user's basic needs, for example the car satisfying a transportation need. This is the easiest aspect for competitors to copy and consequently successful brands have added values over and above this at the **expected** level.

Within the **expected** level, the commodity is value engineered to satisfy a specific target's minimum purchase conditions, such as functional capabilities, availability, pricing, etc. As more buyers enter the market and as repeat buying occurs, the brand would evolve through a better matching of resources to meet customers' needs (e.g. enhanced customer service).

With increased experience, buyers and users become more sophisticated, so the brand would need to be **augmented** in more refined ways, with added values satisfying non-functional (e.g. emotional) as well as functional needs. For example, promotions might be directed to the user's peer group to reinforce his or her social standing through ownership of the brand.

With even more experience of the brand, and therefore with a greater tendency to be more critical, it is only creativity that limits the extent to which the brand can mature to the **potential** level. For example, grocery retail buyers once regarded the Nestlé confectionery brands as having reached the zenith of the **augmented** stage. To counter the threat of their brands slipping back to the **expected** brand level, and therefore having to fight on price, Nestlé shifted their brands to the **potential** level by developing software for retailers to manage confectionery shelf space to maximize profitability.

Experienced consumers recognize that competing items are often similar in terms of product formulation and that brand owners are no longer focusing only on rational functional issues, but are addressing the **potential** level of brands.

The evolution of brands is well exemplified by airlines. For example, fifteen years ago airline brands were all competing predominantly at a functional level, striving to meet reliability tar-

If you believe in the importance of creating time to relax, best choose Swissair. The service and comfort in our Business Class are a blessing for body and soul. Time is everything. swissair

Exhibit 2.2 *Swissair clearly differentiates itself by appealing to non-functional brand benefits (reproduced by kind permission of Swissair)*

gets for on-time arrivals. With consumers travelling more by air, and with greater competition, virtually all airlines managed to achieve greater reliability. Today, consumers are being attracted through different branding approaches, such as customer service and emotional appeals that enhance the flyer's psyche. The Swissair brand offers both traditional reliability and modern comfort for 'body and soul', as shown in their advertisement in Exhibit 2.2.

To succeed in the long run, a brand must offer added values over and above the basic product characteristics, if for no other reason than that functional characteristics are so easy for competitors to copy. In the services sector, when all other factors are equal, this could be as simple as a correctly spelt surname on the monthly bank statement or being addressed by name when cashing a cheque at a bank. In the industrial market, it could be conveyed by the astute sales engineer presenting the brand as a no-risk purchase (due to the thoroughness of testing, the credibility of the organization, compliance with industry standards, case histories of other users, etc.). It is most important to realize that the added values must be relevant to the customer and not just to the manufacturer or distributor. Car manufacturers who announced that their brands had the added value of electronic circuits emitting 'computer speak' when seat belts were not worn didn't take long to discover that this so-called benefit was intensely disliked by customers. A garage in a commuter town offering the extra value of a service under the slogan 'We go the extra mile' will win loyal customers by collecting and delivering their car at the station, rather then offering another free duster!

Buyers perceive added value in a brand because they recognize certain clues which give signals about the offer. In industrial markets, for example, buyers evaluate brands on a wide variety of attributes, rather than just on price. As a consequence, price is rarely the most important variable influencing the purchase decision. So it is not unusual for a buyer to remain loyal to a supplier during a period of price rises. However, if the price of a brand rises and one of the signalling clues is weak (say, poor reliability of delivery) compared with the other signalling clues (say, product quality), the buyer may perceive that the brand's value has diminished and will therefore be more likely to consider competitive brands. A further example of the need to provide consistency of signalling clues about brands is that of an advertising agency which produced an advertisement targeted at business people, to portray the added value of in-flight comfort. Depth interviews amongst business people revealed strong feelings about the poor quality of the advertisement and a concomitant rejection of any belief that such a company could deliver in-flight comfort. Sophisticated consumers recognized the high predictive capability of a clue (poor advertising) and rejected the brand's added value.

If brands are to thrive, their marketing support will have been geared towards providing the user with the maximum satisfaction in a particular context. Buyers often use brands as non-verbal clues to communicate with their peer groups. In other words, it is recognized that people do not use brands only for their functional capabilities, but also for their badge or symbolic value. The newly-promoted director takes pride in his choice of a Jaguar, not just

Buyers often use brands as non-verbal clues

because of its sophisticated refinement, but because he is signalling his new role. It has been observed that people take care over their selection of clothes as, according to the situation, their brand of clothes is being used to signal messages of propriety, status or even seduction. Buyers choose brands with which they feel both physical and psychological comfort in specific situations. They are concerned about selecting brands which reinforce their own concept of themselves in specific situations. A very self-conscious young man may well drink a particular brand of lager with his peer group because he believes it will convey an aspect of his lifestyle, whilst at home alone his brand consumption behaviour may well be different, since he is less concerned about the situational context. A further good example is given by Swatch watches, with consumers owning several models and wearing them according to the particular social occasion and peer group. It is worth noting that this phenomenon has been recorded by many researchers. For example, it has been found that for cars and clothing people were more likely to buy brands which they perceived were similar to their own concept of themselves. Where marketers have grounds for believing that their brands are being used by consumers as value-expressive devices, they need to be attuned to the interaction of the marketing mix with the user's environment and provide the appropriate support. In some instances this may involve targeting promotional activity to the user's peer group, to ensure that they recognize the symbolic messages being portrayed by the brand.

Whilst this issue of appreciating the buyer's or user's environment relates to consumer markets, it is also apparent in industrial markets. One researcher found that in a laboratory with a high proportion of well-educated scientists, there was a marked preference for a piece of scientific equipment that had a 'designer label' cabinet, over the same equipment presented in a more utilitarian manner. In a highly rational environment, scientists were partly influenced by a desire to select a brand of equipment which they felt better expressed their own concept of themselves.

Finally, our definition of a brand adopts a strategic perspective, recognizing that unless the added value is unique and sustainable against competitive activity, the life time will be very short. Without such a strategic perspective, then, it is questionable whether it is viable to follow a branding route. Chapter 8 reviews the way that the concept of the value chain can be used to identify where in the value-adding process the firm's brand has a unique advantage over competition and also considers whether any of these strengths can be rapidly copied. For example, in the coffee market Nestlé have a competitive advantage for their brand through consistently sourcing high-grade coffee beans, Porsche's and Swatch's competitive advantage is in excellence of product design, Federal Express in their

Which side are your customers on?
You have a choice.

Everywhere you look, the balance of power is shifting to the consumer.

Banking is no exception.

And to generate loyalty, banks (and all the new non-traditional financial service providers) need to establish a new, more intimate kind of relationship with their customers.

This can be achieved partly through enhanced marketing and branding. Ultimately though, the only guarantee of success is to treat each customer as a 'market of one' by providing products and services which are flexible, individualised and available through the customer's preferred channels.

Of course, consumer-focused products and services require consumer-focused technology and that's where NCR is so strong.

It's always been our philosophy to approach projects from the consumer's perspective and in doing so we've gained a unique and unrivalled understanding of their behaviour. Consequently, nobody is better prepared for the Age Of The Consumer and, as consumers make life harder for banks, we can apply the solutions necessary for banks to make life easier for consumers.

One way in which our expertise will grow is at the NCR Financial Services Knowledge Lab in London. It's a dedicated research facility where, along with our customers and other commercial and academic partners, we will constantly develop new insights into the hearts and minds of financial consumers.

To tilt the balance in your favour, email us at: banking.solutions@unitedkingdom.ncr.com or visit our web site: http://ncr.knowledgelab.com

NCR. Banking Solutions in the Age Of The Consumer.

Exhibit 2.3 *NCR promote the importance of relationship building (reproduced by kind permission of NCR)*

distribution planning and monitoring systems and the Equitable Life Assurance Company in its low-cost sales force. It is our contention that unless brand instigators have a sustainable differential advantage, they should seriously consider the economics of following a manufacturer's brand route and consider becoming a supplier of a distributor's brand. In such situations it is more probable that the firm will follow a more profitable route by becoming a distributor brand supplier (i.e. a supplier of own label products) as discussed in Chapter 7.

Brands as relationship builders

Relationship marketing goes beyond traditional marketing, and focuses more on creating a pool of committed, profitable customers. This is done by identifying a company's individual customers and creating mutually beneficial relationships that go beyond simple transactions. For example, banks recognize that consumers have a broad range of choices and can switch to a new bank at any time. Majoring on this, NCR advertised to bankers that by using their Relationship Marketing Systems brand, they could jointly develop better-tailored products to build more loyal customers (Exhibit 2.3).

Relationship building is neither easy nor straightforward. For example, business travellers on one flight became horrified when seeing, in mid-flight, the pilot and co-pilot locked outside their cockpit using an axe to force open the cockpit door. Adding extra miles on their loyalty cards no doubt was seen by some as a rather insensitive compensation for the experience

Brands can develop different relationships with customers. For example, Hovis plays upon a nostalgic relationship, while Nintendo majors on exciting relationships. A successful brand aims to develop a high-quality relationship, in which customers feel a sense of commitment and belonging, even to the point almost of passion, as with the Manchester United brand, where couples have had part of their wedding ceremonies on the turf. Iberia have been nurturing a relationship with their regular travellers akin to 'this brand plays an important role in my life'. Tracking the behaviour of frequent travellers, they send out flight schedule changes with a direct mailing approach that contributes to building the feeling of being an important consumer.

brands can develop different relationships with customers

Relationship marketing aims to develop long-term loyal customers. The retention can be managed on three levels: through financial incentives, through social/financial bonds and through structural bonds. Financial incentives, such as frequent flyer schemes and the Tesco ClubCard, are very popular and can quickly be copied by competitors. Even Sainsbury capitulated after a long struggle! Social and financial bonds see customers as clients, not numbers. They are quite common among professional services, such as lawyers taking clients to the opera and dentists making brief notes about their clients' social lives, enabling them to take an interest in subsequent dental visits. We became aware of a petrol station manager in Turkey who achieved exceedingly high petrol sales through social bonds. When he filled the tanks of long-distance lorries, he spoke with their owners and promptly recorded key points on his personal computer along with their registration number. Before filling up new arrivals, his rapid database search would show these notes and he was able to greet each customer almost as a long-lost friend. Structural bonds stretch social and financial ones to make clients more productive. For example Federal Express and UPS provide free PCs with logistics software for labelling and tracking. Baxter Healthcare tailor pallets for each hospital to fit individual storage and dispensing needs. Many major retailers are linked through EDI to their suppliers for fast and error-free ordering and invoicing.

Historical evolution of brands

Having clarified the concept of the brand, it is worth appreciating how brands evolved. This historical review shows how different *types* of brands evolved.

There were examples of brands being used in Greek and Roman times. With a high level of illiteracy, shop keepers hung pictures above their shops indicating the types of goods they sold. Symbols were developed to provide an indication of the retailer's speciality and thus the brand logo as a **shorthand device** signalling the brand's capability was born. Use is still made of this aspect of branding, as in the case, for example, of the poised jaguar indicating the power developed by the Jaguar brand.

In the Middle Ages, craftsmen with specialist skills began to stamp their marks on their goods and trademarks. **Distinguishing** between different suppliers became more common. In these early days, branding gradually became a **guarantee** of the source of the product and ultimately its use as a form of **legal protection** against copying grew. Today, trademarks include words (e.g. Duracell and Matchbox), symbols (e.g. the distinctive Shell logo) or a unique pack shape (e.g. the Coca-Cola bottle), which have been registered and which purchasers recognize as being unique to a particular brand. However, as the well-travelled reader is no doubt aware, trademark infringement is a source of concern to owners of well-respected brands such as Rolex.

The next landmark in the evolution of brands was associated with the growth of cattle farming in the New World of North America. Cattle owners wanted to make it clear to other potentially interested parties which animals they owned. By using a red hot iron, with a uniquely shaped end, they left a clear imprint on the skin of each of their animals. This process appears to have been taken by many as the basis for the meaning of the term brand, defined by the *Oxford English Dictionary* as 'to mark indelibly as proof of ownership, as a sign of quality, or for any other purpose'. This view of the purpose of brands as being identifying (**differentiating**) devices has remained with us until today. What is surprising is that in an enlightened era aware of the much broader strategic interpretation of brands, many

view of the purpose of brands as being identifying (differentiating) devices has remained with us until today

of today's leading marketing textbooks still adhere to the brand solely as a differentiating device, for example, 'a name, term, sign, symbol, or design, or a combination of them, which is intended to identify the goods or services of one seller or group of sellers and to differentiate them from those of competitors'. Towards the end of the nineteenth century, such a view was justified, as the next few paragraphs clarify. However, as the opening sections of this chapter have explained, to regard brands as little more than differentiating devices is to run the risk of the rapid demise of the product or service in question.

To appreciate why organizations subscribed to brands as differentiating devices over 100 years ago, and to appreciate why this view held favour until the 1960s, it is necessary to consider the evolving retailing environment, particularly that relating to groceries, where classical brand management developed. In the first half of the nineteenth century, people bought their goods through four channels:

1   retailers;
2   from those who grew and sold their own produce;
3   from markets where farmers displayed produce;
4   from travelling salesmen.

Household groceries were normally produced by small manufacturers supplying a locally confined market. Consequently the quality of similar products varied according to retailer, who in many instances blended several suppliers' produce. With the advent of the Industrial Revolution, several factors influenced the manufacturer–retailer relationship, i.e.:

*   the rapid rise of urban growth, reducing manufacturer–consumer contact;
*   the widening of markets through improved transportation;
*   the increasing number of retail outlets;
*   the wider range of products held by retailers;
*   increasing demand.

A consequence of this was that manufacturers' production increased, but with their increasing separation from consumers, they came to rely more on wholesalers. Likewise, retailers' dependence on wholesalers increased, from whom they expected greater services. Until the end of the nineteenth century, the situation was one of wholesaler dominance. Manufacturers produced according to wholesalers' stipulations, who, in turn, were able to dictate terms and strongly influence the product range of the retailer. As an indication of the importance of wholesalers, it is estimated that by 1900 wholesalers were the main suppliers of the independent retailers, who accounted for about ninety per cent of all retail sales.

During this stage, most manufacturers were:

- selling unbranded goods;
- having to meet wholesalers' demands for low prices;
- spending minimal amounts on advertising;
- selling direct to wholesalers, while having little contact with retailers.

In this situation of competitive tender, the manufacturer's profit depended mostly on sheer production efficiency. It was virtually commodity marketing, with little scope for increasing margins by developing and launching new products.

The growing levels of consumer demand and the increasing rate of technological development were regarded by manufacturers as attractive opportunities for profitable growth through investing in large-scale production facilities. Such action, though, would lead to the production of goods in *anticipation* of, rather than as a *response* to, demand. Not only were manufacturers perturbed by having to adopt the new techniques of planning, but with such large investments they were concerned about their reliance on wholesalers. To protect their investment, patents were registered and brand names affixed by the owners. The power of the wholesalers was also bypassed by advertising brands direct to consumers. The role of advertising in this era was to stabilize demand, ensuring predictable large-scale production protected from the whims of wholesalers. In such a situation, the advertising tended to focus on promoting awareness of reliability and guaranteeing that goods with brand names were of a consistent quality. The third way that manufacturers invested in protecting the growth of their brands was through appointing their own salesmen to deal directly with retailers.

By the second half of the nineteenth century, many major manufacturers had embarked on branding, advertising and using a sales force to reduce the dominance of wholesalers. In fact, by 1900 the balance of power had swung to the manufacturer, with whom it remained until the 1960s. With branding and national marketing, manufacturers strove to increase the consistency and quality of their brands, making them more recognizable through attractive packaging that no longer served the sole purpose of protection. Increased advertising was used to promote the growth of brands and with manufacturers exercising legally backed control over prices, more and more manufacturers turned to marketing branded goods.

This changing of the balance of power from wholesaler to manufacturer by the end of the last century marked another milestone in the evolutionary period of brands. Brand owners were concerned

with using their brands as legal registrations of their unique characteristics. Besides this, they directed their efforts towards consumers
to make them aware that their brand was different in some way from
those of competitors. Furthermore, they wanted their brand names
to encourage belief in a consistent quality level that most were prepared to guarantee. Thus, whilst the **differentiating** aspect of the
concept was initially regarded as the key issue, this soon also encompassed **legal protection** and **functional communication**.

Throughout this century, manufacturers' interest in branding
increased and with more sophisticated buyers and marketers, brands
also acquired an **emotional dimension** that reflected buyers' moods,
personalities and the messages they wished to convey to others.
However, with the greater choice to buyers through the availability
of more competing products, the level of information being directed
at buyers far exceeded their ability to be attentive to the many competing messages. Because of their limited cognitive capabilities,
buyers began to use brand names as **shorthand devices** to recall either their brand experiences or marketing claims and thus saved
themselves the effort of having continuously to seek information.
Chapter 3 provides more information about the role of the brand as
a shorthand device to facilitate buyers' decision processes.

> with more
> sophisticated
> buyers and
> marketers, brands
> also acquired an
> emotional
> dimension that
> reflected buyers'
> moods,
> personalities and
> the messages they
> wished to convey
> to others

The only other major landmark in the growth of branding was
the metamorphosis from manufacturers' brand to distributors' brand
that began to occur around the turn of this century. The advent of
own labels (or more precisely distributor brands) is explained in the
next section, along with the unsuccessful attempt by distributors to
turn the wheel of branding back full circle with generics (products
which have only their function on the label).

Brand evolution: distributors' brands and generics

To appreciate how further tiers of brands evolved, one must again
consider the changing nature of the retailing environment. Around
the 1870s, multiple retailers – those owning ten or more outlets –
emerged, each developing their own range of brands for which they
controlled the production and packaging. These distributor brands
(usually referred to as own labels or private labels) became common
in emergent chains such as Home & Colonial, Lipton and International Stores. The early versions of distributor brands tended to be
basic grocery items. Not only did the chains undertake their own
production, but they also managed the wholesaling function, with
branding being almost an incidental part of the total process.

The reason for the advent of distributor brands was that, due to resale price maintenance, retailers were unable to compete with each other on the price of manufacturers' brands and relied upon service as the main competitive edge to increase store traffic. The multiples circumvented this problem by developing their own distributor brands (own label). The degree of retailer production was limited by the complexity of the items and the significant costs of production facilities. Thus, it became increasingly common for multiple retailers to commission established manufacturers to produce their distributor brands which were packaged to the retailer's specifications. Before World War II, distributor brands accounted for 10–15 per cent of multiples' total sales, but with multiple retailers accounting for only 17 per cent of food sales the overall importance of distributor brands was far exceeded by manufacturer brands. During World War II, distributor brands were withdrawn due to shortages and were not reintroduced until the 1950s.

One of the consequences of the increasing growth of the multiples was the decline of independent retailers (those owning no more than nine shops). As a means of protecting themselves some independent retailers joined together during the 1950s and agreed to place all their purchases through specific wholesalers. The formation of this new category of retailers referred to as symbol/voluntary groups (e.g. Mace and Spar), enabled the store owners to maintain some degree of individual control. With a significant element of their purchasing channelled through a central wholesaler, they were able to achieve more favourable terms from manufacturers. A further consequence of this allegiance was the introduction of a new category of brands, i.e. symbol/voluntary brands, designed to compete against the multiples' brands. These brands carry the symbol/voluntary groups names and are priced cheaper than the equivalent manufacturers' brands. It should also be recognized that the once powerful retailing force of the Co-op, with its not-insignificant farming and processing plants, also has a long history of marketing its Co-op brands (albeit with a variety of brand names). Unfortunately, due to the Co-op's inability to adapt to the changing retailing environment, this sector's importance has fallen. With only a 7 per cent share of the packaged grocery sector in 1995, the overall importance of the Co-op brands has declined.

Whilst distributor brands have their origin in the grocery sector, however, where in 1996 they accounted for approximately 40 per cent of packaged grocery sales, it should not be thought that this is their sole domain. For example, it is estimated that in the late 1980s, over 50 per cent of footwear sales and almost half of all menswear sales were accounted for by distributor brands. In the DIY goods sector, approximately a quarter of sales are from distributor brands and a fifth of furniture and floor covering sales are distributor brands.

In the fierce competition between retailers different options have already been tried, such as loyalty cards, and petrol stations. Since this battle is expected to continue, non-food products (e.g. books, records, clothes and stationery), in-store services and innovative marketing are considered the means to achieve competitive advantage in the next few years.

In the retail banking sector, where the service 'manufacturer' is also the distributor, distributor brands are common.

In the industrial sector, it is less common to see distributor brands, due to the considerable investment in production, the need to understand the technology and the greater reliance upon direct delivery, with less reliance on distributors. Chapter 7 provides more detail about distributor brands.

In the packaged grocery sector, where the first alternative tier to manufacturer brands appeared, innovative marketing in the late 1970s also led to a further alternative – generics. In fact, the term 'generics' may be a misnomer, since it implies a return to the days when retailers sold commodities rather than brands. This trend was originally started by Carrefour in 1976, when they launched fifty 'produits libres' in France, promoted as brand-free products. Some UK grocery retailers noted the initial success of these lines and thought the time was right to follow in the UK. At the time there was growing consumer scepticism about the price premium being paid for branding and with consumers becoming more confident about selecting what in many cases were better quality distributor brands, it was thought that in a harsh economic environment generics would be a popular alternative to manufacturer brands, further increasing distributors' control of their product mix.

The thrust behind generics was that of cutting out any superfluous frill surrounding the product. They were distinguishable by their plain packaging, with the marketing emphasis placed on the content, rather than on the promotional or pack features. On average, generics were priced 40 per cent lower than the brand leader and approximately 20 per cent lower than the equivalent distributor brands. Whilst the quality level varied by retailer, they were nonetheless generally inferior to manufacturers' brands. As Table 2.3 shows, several major grocery retailers launched, and subsequently withdrew, generic ranges.

Table 2.3 *Grocery retailers launching generics*

Retailer	Generic range	Launch	Withdrawn
Argyll	BASICS	October 1981	1987
Carrefour (Gateway)	Brand Free	March 1978	1986
Fine Fare (Gateway)	Yellow Pack	March 1980	1987
International (Gateway)	Plain & Simple	July 1977	1984
Tesco	Value Lines	October 1981	1986

Retailers in the UK who stocked a generic range developed a policy regarding the product, pricing, packaging and merchandising that only too clearly enabled consumers to associate a particular generic range with a specific store. One retailer went as far as branding their generic range (BASICS). But the withdrawal of generics was not surprising, since consumers perceived generics as similar to distributor brands. They were not perceived as a unique tier and they weakened the image, hence the sales, of the distributor brands of those retailers stocking generics. Furthermore, as they were perceived to be similar to distributor brands, more switching occurred with these, rather than with the less profitable manufacturers' brands.

Fierce price wars and the penetration of European hard-core discounters like Aldi and Netto in the grocery market have brought about the relaunch of low-price products. The big retailers have even reintroduced some products as generics, such as Safeway's SuperSaver, Tesco's Blue&White and Sainsbury's Economy.

Chapter 7 considers in more detail the marketing issues associated with generics and the reason for their demise. However, it is worth emphasizing that any organization operating in consumer, services or industrial markets, never has a commodity and is always able to differentiate their offering. Research has shown that marketing a product or service predominantly on the basis of the functional performance of the core product (as was the case with generic groceries), accounts for about 80 per cent of the costs, yet only 20 per cent of the impact. The marketing of generics trims some of the marginal costs away, but leaves the organization having to compete on product dimensions that can be easily copied and which have little impact compared with other attributes (e.g. service, availability, imagery, etc.). Any industrial manufacturers who believe they are marketing a generic product, and therefore have to offer the lowest prices, are deluding themselves. For example, purchasers are not just buying tanker loads of commonly available chemical for their production process. They are also buying a reliable delivery service, a well-administered reordering process, advice from the supplier about the operating characteristics of the chemical, etc. By just considering issues such as these, it is easier to appreciate the fallacy of marketing generics.

any organization never has a commodity and is always able to differentiate their offering

Branding in the 1990s: brand categorization

An advertising perspective

This brief historical review has shown how brands evolved and has also briefly introduced the idea of the different *types* of brands. One of the weaknesses with the current views on branding is that the term is used to encompass a very broad range of issues, encouraging the possibility of confusion.

Two well-known researchers pointed out that the problem with branding is the surprising number of creative directors, planners, account handlers and clients who have a kindergarten knowledge of branding processes and mechanisms. They are rightly critical of those who regard branding merely as a process to ensure that the name on a product or service is highly visible. Based on a consideration of advertisements, they classified brands into nine categories, each representing a role in advertising, varying from simple through to complex branding. For example, at the simple end of the scale there are those brands which operate through straightforward association with the advertising slogan (e.g. the classic 'Sch... you know who'). By contrast, at the most complex end of the spectrum, they identify structural branding, in which for example, objects (scissors, hedge trimmers, etc.) coloured either purple or white are shown in order to ensure a link with Silk Cut cigarettes. Figure 2.1 shows the interpretations of brand types drawn up by these researchers (Langmaid and Gordon 1988). However, whilst their typology is of value to advertisers, its overt advertising bias restricts its value as an aid in evaluating how to employ the other elements of the marketing mix.

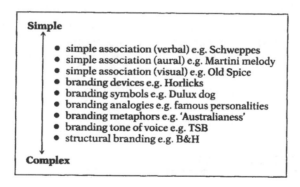

Figure 2.1   *Brand typology (after Langmaid and Gordon 1988)*

An output process

Our research and work with marketing executives have shown that there are other interpretations of the role played by brands, which we will now make explicit, all of which will be addressed in more detail in subsequent chapters. However, a key problem with many of these interpretations is that they place too much emphasis on branding as something that is done *to* consumers, rather than branding as something consumers do things *with*. It is wrong, in other words, to focus on branding as an **input** process. Clearly we need to

branding as something consumers do things with

consider carefully how marketing resources are being used to support brands, but it is crucial to understand the **output** process as
well since, as mentioned earlier, the final evaluation of the brand is
in the buyer's or user's mind. Consumers are not just passive recipi-
ents of marketing activity. They consume marketing activity,
sometimes with a large subconscious appetite, twisting messages to
reinforce prior expectations.

Several highly-regarded branding advisers stress the importance
of looking at brands as perceptions in consumers' minds, a notion
which is comparatively easy to accept and which reinforces the
conclusion about the importance of what consumers take out of the
process rather than what marketers put into it. Whilst it is clear that
marketers design the firm's offer, the ultimate judge about the nature of the brand is the consumer. When buying a new brand,
consumers seek clues about the brand's capabilities. They try to evaluate the brand through a variety of perceptual evaluations, such as its
reliability, or whether it's the sort of brand they feel right with, or
whether it's better than another brand, so that a brand becomes not
the producer's, but the consumer's idea of the product. The result of
good branding is a perception of the values of a product, or service,
interpreted and believed so clearly by the consumer that the brand
adopts a personality. This is so well-recognized that products with
little apparent functional differences are regarded as different purely
because of the brand personality. For example, while many organizations provide charge cards, American Express is 'the one you don't
leave home without'. Parker pens have a personality of their own, as
do Singapore Airlines, Fosters lager, and countless other brands
around the world.

Thus, recognizing the inherent flaw when marketers focus upon
branding as an input process, we have highlighted eight different
types of brands that practitioners employ.

An eight-category typology

1 Brand as a sign of ownership

An early theme, given much prominence in marketing circles, was
the distinction between brands on the basis of whether the brand
was a manufacturers' brand or a distributors' brand ('own label',
'private label'). Branding was seen as being a basis of showing who
instigated the marketing for that particular offering and whether the
primary activity of the instigator was production (manufacturers'
brand) or distribution (distributors' brand). However, this drew a
rather artificial distinction, since nowadays consumers place a far
greater reliance on distributor brands – particularly when brands

such as Benetton and Marks & Spencer are perceived as superior brands in their own right. In fact, some would argue that with the much greater marketing role played by major retailers and their concentrated buying power, the concept of USP (Unique Selling Proposition) should now be interpreted as 'Universal Supermarket Patronage'!

With escalating advertising cost, there is a move to the corporation as a brand, rather than stressing branding at the individual product lines level. This helps form a clear identity and has given impetus to the corporate design industry. There is a danger, however, that consumers do not pick up the values that the corporate brand stands for and how these run through all the product line brands. A further danger is that as a corporation widens its brand portfolio, its core values become diluted.

2 Brand as a differentiating device

The historical review earlier in this chapter indicated that, at the turn of the century, a much stronger emphasis was placed on brands purely as differentiating devices between similar products. This perspective is still frequently seen today in many different markets. Yet with more sophisticated marketing and more experienced consumers, brands succeed not only by conveying differentiation, but also by being associated with added values. For example, the brand Persil not only differentiates it from other washing-powder lines, but is a successful brand since it has been backed by a coherent use of resources that deliver the added value of a high-quality offering with a well-defined image. By contrast the one-man operation, 'Tom's Taxi Service', is based upon branding as a differentiating device, with little thought to communicating added values.

Small firms seem to be particularly prone to the belief that putting a name on their product or service is all that is needed to set them apart from competitors. They erroneously believe that branding is about having a prominent name, more often than not based around the owner's name. Yet there is ample evidence that brands fail if organizations concentrate primarily on developing a symbol or a name as a differentiating device. Chapter 4 gives examples showing the danger of adopting brands solely as differentiating devices. Brands will succeed only if they offer unique benefits, satisfying real consumer needs. Where an organization has reason to believe that their competitors are marketing brands primarily as differentiating devices, there is an opportunity to develop a strategy which gets buyers to associate relevant added values with their brand name and hence gain a competitive advantage.

there's **nothing** different about your products

there's **nothing** different about your company

there's **nothing** different about your people

there's **nothing** different about your pricing

there's **nothing** different about your service

So why should I buy from you?

A tough situation, but one your sales people may face every day. They know their products are different. They know their company has something exceptional to offer. **But how do they convince *him*?** In a sales presentation, research shows that a massive 70% of the impact is from what he sees and only 30% from what he hears. So, arming your sales people with vibrant, colourful, eye catching materials can make the difference between winning and losing - profit and loss.

Tektronix colour printers will help your team deliver high impact reports, proposals that sell, and letters that get the message across clearly. Moving to colour is a simple change you can make today to improve your team's ability to succeed. We can help your people compete more and win more, and we're ready to prove it. For more information call us now on **01628 403600**

Tektronix

Exhibit 2.4   *Tektronix take on board the problem of effective differentiation (reproduced by kind permission of Tektronix UK Ltd and Mason Zimbler)*

Brand distinctiveness allows customers to identify products and services. This occurs not only from the brand itself, i.e. through the packaging, advertising or naming, as shown in Figure 2.2. There are further sources to distinguish the brand. First, consumers perceive the brand in their own way. As explained before, value is in the eye of the beholder and each person can draw very different conclusions.

Secondly, people interacting with the consumers affect their perception of the brand. Especially with consumer goods, consumers focus their attention on certain brands as a result of conversations with peer groups.

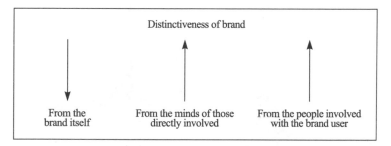

Figure 2.2   *How a brand can be distinctive*

3 Brand as a functional device

Another category of brands is that used by marketers to communicate functional capability. This stemmed from the early days of manufacturers' brands when firms wished to protect their large production investments by using their brands to guarantee consistent quality to consumers.

As consumers began to take for granted the fact that brands represented consistent quality, marketers strove to establish their brands as being associated with specific unique functional benefits by, for example, not just marketing a credit card, but a credit card protection policy.

Functional capabilities should always be focused on consumers, rather than on internal considerations. For instance, providing televisions in waiting rooms to make queues less annoying is less likely to be appreciated than a redesigned system to eliminate queues altogether.

A brief scan of advertisements today shows the different functional attributes marketers are trying to associate with their brand. For example, Dyson, emphasizes the unique features of a carpet cleaner that needs no bag changing; SEAT strives to convey a good value-for-money proposition; Polycell seeks the association of DIY simplicity; and Castrol GTX represents 'high technology' engine protection. Firms adopting the view that they are employing brands as functional communicators have the virtue of being customer driven, but clearly run the risk of an excessive reliance on the functional (rational) element of the consumer choice, as all products and services also have some degree of emotional content in the buying process. For example, a Post Office campaign run in 1990 for a predominantly functional brand advertised the emotional dimension using the slo-

> functional capabilities should always be focused on consumers, rather than on internal considerations

Air and dirt come in here.

The air goes out through
tiny holes in the bag.

The dirt stays in the bag.

But the dirt clogs the holes.

Airflow is reduced, so the
cleaner can't suck properly.

After just one room, suction
could be down by a half.

And as you use the cleaner,
the problem gets worse.

**Bags
kill
suction.
Here's
why.**

dyson

No bag.
No loss of suction.

For more information, please call Dyson on 01666 827200 and quote code 970434

Exhibit 2.5   *Dyson is presented as a functional brand (reproduced by kind
permission of Tony Muranka (Art Director), Peers Carter (copywriter) and Alan
Randall (photographer) for Dyson Appliances Ltd)*

gan 'If you don't want your burning passion to arrive lukewarm,
send it in a Swiftpack.'

4 Brand as a symbolic device

In certain product fields (e.g. perfume and clothing) buyers perceive
significant badge value in the brands, since it enables them to communicate something about themselves (e.g. emotion, status, etc.). In
other words, brands are used as symbolic devices, with marketers
believing that brands are bought and used primarily because of their
ability to help users express something about themselves to their
peer groups, with users taking for granted functional capabilities.

Exhibit 2.6   *The symbolic meaning of diamonds: a sign of eternal love (reproduced by kind permission of De Beers and J. Walter Thompson)*

Where consumers perceive the brand's value to lie more in terms of the non-verbal communication facility (through the logo or name), they spend time and effort choosing brands, almost with the same care as if choosing a friend. It is now accepted that consumers personify brands and when looking at the symbol values of brands, they seek brands which have very clear personalities and select brands that best match their actual or desired self-concept.

For example, in the beer market there are only marginal product differences between brands. Comparative consumer trials of competing beer brands without brand names present showed no significant preferences or differences. Yet, when consumers repeated the test with brand names present, significant brand preferences emerged. On the first comparative trial, consumers focused on functional (rational) aspects of the beers and were unable to notice much difference. On repeating the trials with brand names present, consumers were able to use the brand names to recall distinct brand personalities and the symbolic (emotional) aspect of the brands influenced preference.

Through being members of social groups, people learn the symbolic meaning of brands. As they interpret the actions of their peer group, they then respond, using brands as non-verbal communication devices (e.g. feelings, status). To capitalize on symbolic brands, therefore, marketers must use promotional activity to communicate the brand's personality and signal how consumers can use it in their daily relationships with others. Nonetheless, whilst there are many product fields where this perspective of brands is useful, it must also be realized that consumers rarely consider just the symbolic aspect of brands. Research by the authors of this book across a wide variety of product fields, ranging from chipboard to watches, showed that consumers often evaluated brands in terms of both a symbolic (emotional) and a functional (rational) dimension. Marketers should, therefore, be wary of subscribing to the belief that a brand acts *solely* as a symbolic device.

be wary of subscribing to the belief that a brand acts solely as a symbolic device

A successful example of combining both is given by the Mercedes affinity Visa card, which offers the functional advantages of an internationally accepted credit card with the appeal of showing the user's ownership of a highly prestigious car.

5 Brand as a risk reducer

Many marketers believe that buying should be regarded as a process whereby buyers attempt to reduce the risk of a purchase decision. When a person is faced with competing brands in a new product field, they feel risk. For example, uncertainty about whether the brand will work, whether they will be wasting money, whether their peer group will disagree with their choice, whether they will feel comfortable with the purchase, etc. Successful brand marketing should therefore be concerned with understanding buyers' perceptions of risk, followed by developing and presenting the brand in such a way that buyers feel minimal risk. An example of an industry appreciating perceived risk is the pharmaceutical industry. One company has developed a series of questions which its sales representatives use to evaluate the risk-aversion of doctors. When launching a new drug, the company focuses sales presentations initially on doctors with a low-risk aversion profile.

buyers seek methods of reducing risk

To make buying more acceptable, buyers seek methods of reducing risk by, for example, always buying the same brand, searching for more information, only buying the smallest size, etc. Research

Exhibit 2.7 *Positioning the brand as a risk reducing device (reproduced by kind permission of Bradford and Bingley Building Society)*

has shown that one of the more popular methods employed by buyers to reduce risk is reliance upon reputable brands. Some marketers, particularly those selling to organizations rather than to final consumers, succeed with their brands because they find out what dimensions of risk the buyer is most concerned about and then develop a solution through their brand presentation which emphasizes the brand's capabilities along the risk dimension considered most important by the buyer. This interpretation of branding has the virtue of being output driven. Marketers, however, must not lose sight of the need to segment customers by similar risk perception and achieve sufficient numbers of buyers to make risk reduction branding viable.

6 Brand as a shorthand device

Glancing through advertisements today, one becomes aware of brands whose promotional platform appears to be based on bombarding consumers with considerable quantities of information. To overcome the problem of sifting through large amounts of information, brands are used as shorthand devices by consumers to recall from memory sufficient brand information to make a decision. There is merit in this approach, as people generally have limited memory capabilities. To overcome this, they bundle small bits of information into larger chunks in their memory, and use brand names as handles to recall these larger information chunks. By continuing to increase the size of these few chunks in memory, buyers in consumer, industrial and service sectors can process information more effectively. At the point of purchase, they are able to recall numerous attributes by interrogating their memory.

danger of concentrating too heavily on the quantity, rather than on quality of information

There is, nonetheless, the danger of concentrating too heavily on the quantity, rather than on quality of information directed at purchasers. It also ignores the perceptual process which is used by buyers to twist information until it becomes consistent with their prior beliefs – an error fatally overlooked by the short-lived Strand cigarette brand.

More recently, some brand owners have started to offer only relevant, limited information to maximize the impact of their message. For example, Virgin Direct has been launched as a 'straight-forward and hassle-free' financial service, expecting customers to refer to the well-known brand name and recall a guarantee of quality, capability and innovation.

7 Brand as a legal device

With the appearance of manufacturers' brands at the turn of this century, consumers began to appreciate their value and started to ask for them by name. Producers of inferior goods realized that to survive they would have to change. A minority, however, changed by illegally packaging their inferior products in packs that were virtually identical to the original brand. To protect themselves against counterfeiting, firms turned to trademark registration as a legal protection. Some firms began to regard the prime benefit of brands as being that of legal protection, with the result that a new category of branding appeared. Within this group of brands, marketers direct their efforts towards effective trademark registration along with consumer education programmes about the danger of buying poor grade brand copies. For example, the pack details on Matchbox products boldly state that 'Matchbox is the trademark of the Matchbox group of companies and is the subject of extensive trademark registrations', while Kodak packs all carry the advice 'It's only Kodak film if it says Kodak' (Exhibit 2.8).

trademark registration as a legal protection

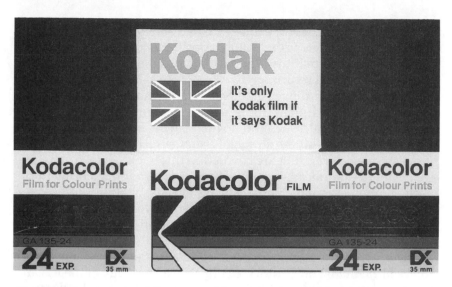

Exhibit 2.8 *A successfully protected brand (reproduced by kind permission of Kodak Ltd)*

The success of retailers' own labels has intensified the need for manufacturers to protect their brands. Consumers can become confused by similar-looking competing brands. A 1997 survey for *Marketing* magazine found that 41 per cent of shoppers believe manufacturers produce retailers' own labels as well as their famous brands if pack designs look alike and that 17 per cent of shoppers, who originally intended to buy premium-brand products, mistakenly bought own label brands instead. In the early 1990s, 412 incidents of lookalike have been reported to the European Brand Association, and over the last few years we have witnessed famous cases of brand warfare: Coca-Cola v. Sainsbury's Classic Cola; Van den Bergh Foods v. Tesco's 'Unbelievable' spread; Kellogg v. Tesco Corn Flakes; United Biscuit v. Asda's Puffin Bar (see Plate 3). The last case is significant since this was the first time a manufacturer took a retailer to court and won the case, with the judge requiring an Asda pack change. This causes a dilemma for manufacturers who have to find a balance between defending their brands against seemingly unfair competition and fighting against their own customers.

Because of their intangible nature, service brands have even greater difficulties coping with counterfeit brands. Financial services have shown a way to circumvent this problem by adapting a particular house style when interacting with consumers.

8 Brand as a strategic device

Finally, more enlightened marketers are adopting the view to which the authors subscribe, that brands should be treated as strategic devices. The assets constituting the brand need to be audited, the forces

brands should be treated as strategic devices

affecting the future of the brand evaluated and, by appreciating how the brand achieved its added value, a positioning for the brand needs to be identified so that the brand can be successfully protected and achieve the desired return on investment. To take full advantage of brands as strategic devices, a considerable amount of marketing analysis and brand planning is required, yet many firms are too embroiled in tactical issues and do not gain the best possible returns from their brands. All the strategic issues associated with capitalizing on strategic branding are covered in this book.

A good example of successful branding through majoring upon a differential advantage and ensuring the sustainability of such an advantage was seen in a colour supplement advertisement by Sharp. Figure 2.3 shows the main points presented in the advertisement. This organization evaluated the forces that could impede their electronic organizer and developed a unique position for their brand that is difficult for competitors to copy. The technology of the IC card gave the brand a competitive edge. In true strategic style, the firm had developed a brand which it had differentiated from its competitors and had used its corporate strengths to satisfy customer needs better than competitors.

The Sharp IQ leads the field in electronic organizers. A compact way to store and retrieve information, it provides you with complete time and information management at the touch of a button.

Of course it has its imitators. Some limited by their capabilities. Others restricted by their memory. Many requiring computer literacy. Most of them vulnerable to obsolescence.

But what keeps the Sharp IQ a breed apart is its IC card technology: a simple system of integrated circuit software cards which give the IQ infinite expandability. All operated quickly and easily through the IQ's keyboard or an integral touch-sensitive pad.

Figure 2.3   *Advertisement for Sharp IQ*

This section has described several different categories of brands and has also highlighted the inherent weaknesses of each type of brand. In Chapter 8 we provide a matrix which enables the marketer to audit what type of brand they have. Based on an appreciation of the brand type, this matrix then enables marketers to consider how resources need to be employed to sustain the brand. The reader may be beginning to wonder, however, why manufacturers undertake the commercial risk of developing manufacturer brands and why distributors extend their activities beyond their area of economic expertize to develop distributor brands.

Brand consumerization spectrum

As Mary Goodyear illustrates (1996), market evolution can be better understood in terms of a continuum of consumerization, which characterizes the degree of dialogue between marketers and consumers. Drawing on this concept, she identifies a chronological schema for categorizing brands, as shown in Figure 2.4. From a commodity market, as a dialogue begins, so the role of the brand progresses to being a reference for quality. Seeking to compete against more intense competitors, marketers begin to understand consumers' emotional needs, enabling the brand to grow into its role of projecting a particular personality (see Plate 4). A closer relationship with consumers, and a highly symbolic language characterize the development of a brand into an icon, such as Levi 501. At the next stage, consumers become so marketing- and advertising-literate that their attitudes change: they purchase consciously and aggressively; they demand the whole *company* to provide customized benefits and individualized communication strategies. In the most developed role, brands become a synonym of the company's *policy* to take larger responsibilities regarding economic values, social commitment, cultural awareness and political issues. Firms can take advantage of this role, as Body Shop did, or be dragged unwillingly into it over environmental problems, as was Shell.

consumerization characterizes the degree of dialogue between marketers and consumers

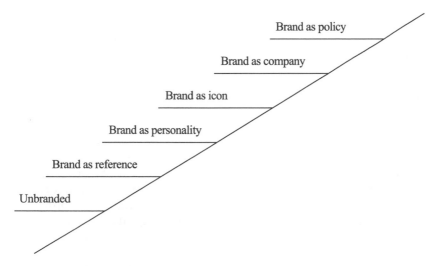

Figure 2.4   *Brand consumerization spectrum (after Goodyear 1996)*

Exhibit 2.9 *Advantage from Bayer plc portrays brand as reference on Goodyear's brand consumerization spectrum (reproduced by kind permission of Bayer plc)*

The value of brands to manufacturers, distributors and consumers

Manufacturers invest effort in branding for a variety of reasons. If the trademark has been effectively registered, the manufacturer has a legally-protected right to an exclusive brand name, enabling it to establish a unique identity, reinforced through its advertising and increasing the opportunity of attracting a large group of repeat purchasers.

brand name, enabling it to establish a unique identity

With the high costs of developing new brands, the emphasis in the 1990s is on existing brand development and line extensions. The most recent examples are Budweiser, a premium-priced beer moving into the jeans market, and retailers such as Sainsbury and Tesco targeting the financial service sector. Virgin provides the best example of a brand being stretched. Already covering cola, retailing, vodka, financial investments and airlines, in 1997 it announced plans to move into the jeans and cosmetics market. Many question whether the Virgin brand risks diluting its value with so many different products under its umbrella. However, its previous successes may disprove such fears. One recent study has assessed the degree of stretchability of brands. It suggests that only few brands, like Marks & Spencer, Virgin and Nike, are capable of successfully leaping into unknown territories. Clearly, good brands keep on building a corporate image and hence reduce the cost of new line additions carrying the family brand name. However, marketers should beware of the dangers of overstretching the brand's core values, as Levi did in the early 1980s with their unsuccessful move from jeans into the suit market.

Brand extension is such a popular choice because it offers an apparently easy and low-risk way of leveraging the brand equity. It is essential, however, to realize that there is a cost to it. First, if a brand loses its credibility in one sector, the whole umbrella range could be affected. Secondly, even successful repetitions of brand

Exhibit 2.10 *Oxfam is a good example of brand as policy with its clearly recognized policy of helping people to help themselves (reproduced by kind permission of Oxfam Publishing)*

extensions may dilute or exhaust the brand value of the core product. Managers should then carefully consider whether it is worth running the risk of tarnishing the brand image and reducing the core brand equity. Only by gathering sufficient information can they decide whether to use brand extension or to develop a unique new brand.

Manufacturers with a history of strong brands are likely to find distributors more receptive to presentations of brand extensions or even of new brands. Those manufacturers with strong brands main-

tain greater control over the balance of power between the manufacturer and distributor and, indeed, some argue that this is one of the
key benefits of strong brands. For example, Kellogg's have been
quoted as saying:

> The only discounts available to our customers are those shown on our
> price list, and all those discounts relate to quantity bought and to prompt
> payment. There is no possibility of special deals.

In view of the pressures facing brand manufacturers from the powerful multiple retailers, such a comment is indeed a brave statement
about a belief in the power of strong manufacturers' brands.

It is also possible for a manufacturer with strong brand names
to market different brands in the same product field which appeal to
different segments. This is seen in the washing detergents and the
soap market, where Unilever and Procter & Gamble market different brands with minimal cannibalization between brands from the
same manufacturer. Furthermore, by developing sufficiently differentiated manufacturer brands that consumers desire, higher prices
can be charged, as consumers pay less attention to price compari-
sons between different products because of brand distinctiveness.
This clearly enhances profitability. Indeed, Table 2.4 shows the profit
impact of powerful brand leaders in the grocery market.

Table 2.4   *Market share and average net margins for UK grocery brands*

Rank	Net margin (%)
1	17.9
2	2.8
3	−0.9
4	−5.9

Retailers see strong manufacturer brands as being important,
since through manufacturers' marketing activity (e.g. advertising,
point of sale material, etc.), a fast turnover of stock results. Also, with
more sophisticated marketers recognizing the importance of long-
term relationships with their customers, many manufacturers and
distributors have cause to recognize that their future success depends
on each other and therefore strong manufacturer brands are seen as
representing profit opportunities both for distributors and manufacturers. Some retailers are interested in stocking strong brands, since
they believe that the positive image of a brand can enhance their
own image. Recent research has provided clear evidence that a favourable image from a manufacturer's brand can further enhance
the image of an already well-regarded store.

Recalling the discussion in the previous section about brand names acting as a means of short-circuiting the search for information, consumers appreciate manufacturers' brands since they make shopping a less time-consuming experience. As already noted, manufacturers' brands are recognized as providing a consistent guide to quality, and consistency. They reduce perceived risk and make consumers more confident and in some product fields (e.g. clothing, cars) they also satisfy strong status needs.

Why, then, do so many manufacturers also supply distributors' brands? First, it is important to understand why distributors are so keen on introducing their own brands. Research has shown that they are particularly keen on distributor brands because they enable them to have more control over their product mix. With a strong distributor brand range, retailers have rationalized their product range to take advantage of the resulting cost savings and many stock a manufacturer's brand leader, their own distributor's brand and possibly a second manufacturer's brand. Trade interviews have also shown that distributor brands offered better margins than the equivalent manufacturer's brand, with estimates indicating the extra profit margin to be about 5 per cent more than the equivalent manufacturer's brand. Some of the reasons why manufacturers become suppliers of distributors' brands are:

distributor brands enable them to have more control

- economies of scale through raw material purchasing, distribution and production;
- any excess capacity can be utilized;
- it can provide a base for expansion;
- substantial sales may accrue with minimal promotional or selling costs;
- it may be the only way of dealing with some important distributors (e.g. Marks & Spencer);
- if an organization does not supply distributor brands, their competitors will, possibly strengthening the competitors' cost structure and trade goodwill.

Consumers benefit from distributors' brands through the lower prices being charged, but it is interesting to note that our own research found that consumers are becoming increasingly confident about distributors' brands and no longer perceive them as 'cheap and nasty' weak alternatives to manufacturers' brands, but rather as realistic alternatives.

The importance of brand planning

As the previous sections of this chapter have shown, brands play a variety of roles and for a number of reasons satisfy many different needs. They are the end result of much effort and by implication represent a considerable investment by the organization. With the recent interest in the balance sheet value of brands, companies are beginning to question whether their financially valuable assets in the form of brands are being effectively used to achieve high returns on investment. To gain the best return from their brands, firms must adopt a broad vision about their brands and not just focus in isolation on tactical issues of design and promotion. Instead, they need to audit the capabilities of their firm, evaluate the external issues influencing their brand (briefly overviewed in the next section) and then develop a brand plan that specifies realistic brand objectives and the strategy to achieve them (covered in more detail in Chapters 8 and 9).

Brand planning is an important but time-consuming activity, which, if undertaken in a thorough manner involving company-wide discussion, will result in a clear vision about how resources can be employed to sustain the brand's differential advantage. Unfortunately, it is only a minority of organizations who undertake thorough brand planning. Without well-structured brand plans there is the danger of what we call brand 'vandalism'. Junior brand managers are given 'training' by making them responsible for specific brands. Their planning horizons tend to be in terms of a couple of years (i.e. the period before they move on) and their focus tends to be on the tactical issues of advertising, pack design and tailor-made brand promotions for the trade. At best this results in 'fire fighting' and a defensive rather than offensive brand plan. The core values of the brand are in danger of being diluted through excessive brand extensions. For example, one of the key core values of the Ribena brand is vitamin C, yet by extending the brand into other fruits (e.g. strawberry) this is weakening the brand's proposition and potentially weakening the brand's strength.

Internally, organizations may be oblivious of the fact that they are hindering brand development. Clearly, by not preparing well-documented strategic brand plans, firms are creating their own obstacles to success. Some of the characteristics that internally hinder any chance of brand success are:

- Brand planning is based on little more than extrapolations from the previous few years.
- When it doesn't look as if the annual budget is going to be reached, quarter 4 sees brand investment being cut (i.e. advertising, market research, etc.).
- The marketing manager is unable to delegate responsibility and is too involved in tactical issues.
- Brand managers see their current positions as good training grounds for no more than two years.

- Strategic thinking consists of a retreat once a year with the advertising agency and sales managers, to a one-day meeting concerned with next year's brand plans.
- A profitability analysis for each major customer is rarely undertaken.
- New product activity consists of different pack sizes and rapidly developing 'me-too' offers.
- The promotions budget is strongly biased towards below-the-line promotional activity, supplemented only occasionally with advertising.
- Marketing documentation is available to the advertising agency on a 'need to know' basis only.

Brand strategy development must involve all levels of marketing management and stands a better chance of success when all the other relevant internal departments and external agencies are actively involved. It must progress on the basis of all parties being kept aware of progress.

British Airways exemplify the notion of brand development as an integrating process, having used this to achieve a greater customer focus. For example, the simple operation of taking a few seats out of an aircraft can be done with confidence, as engineering are consulted about safety implications, finance work out the long-term revenue implication, scheduling explore capacity implications and the cabin crew adjust their in-flight service routines.

brand development as an integrating process, to achieve a greater customer focus

The issues influencing brand potential

When auditing the factors affecting the future of brands, it is useful to consider these in terms of the five forces shown in Figure 2.5. The brand strategist can evaluate the intensity and impact of the following brand-impeding issues.

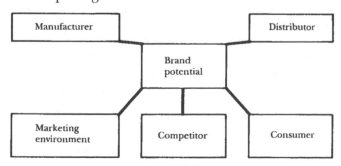

Figure 2.5   *Forces influencing brand potential*

Manufacturers

It is not unusual for an organization to be under-utilizing its brand assets through an inability to recognize what is occurring inside the organization. Have realistic, quantified objectives been set for each of the brands, and have they been widely disseminated? Aims such as 'to be the brand leader' give some indication of the threshold target, but do little in terms of stretching the use of resources to achieve their full potential. Brand leadership may result before the end of the planning horizon, but this may be because of factors that the organization did not incorporate into their marketing audit. But luck also has a habit of working against the player as much as working for the player!

Firms such as 3M and Microsoft have shown how brand and corporate culture are closely interlinked and how they affect each other. Their brand mission focusing on innovation is backed up by a corporate culture encouraging experimentation, banning bureaucracy and publicly recognizing success. Since the culture of an organization strongly influences its brands, mergers and acquisitions can alter brand performance dramatically.

audit how well brand and culture match each other

Marketers should audit how well brand and culture match each other.

Has the organization made full use of its internal auditing to identify what its *distinctive* brand competences are, and to what extent these match the factors that are critical for brand success? For example, Swatch recognized that amongst fashion-conscious watch owners its distinctive competences of design and production could satisfy changing consumer demands for novelty watches.

Is the organization plagued by a continual desire to cut costs, without fully appreciating why it is following this route? Has the market reached the maturity stage, with the organization's brand having to compete against competitors' brands on the basis of matching performance, but at a reduced price? If this is so, *all* aspects of the organization's value chain should be geared towards cost minimization (e.g. eliminating production inefficiencies, avoiding marginal customer accounts, having a narrow product mix, working with long production runs, etc.). Alternatively, is the firm's brand unique in some way that competitors find difficult to emulate and for which the firm can charge a price premium (e.g. unique source of high quality raw materials, innovative production process, unparalleled customer service training, acclaimed advertising, etc.)? Where consumers demand a brand which has clear benefits, the manufacturer should ensure all departments work towards maintaining these benefits and signal this to the market (e.g. by the cleanliness of the lorries, the politeness of the telephonists, the promptness of answering a customer enquiry, etc.). In some instances, particularly in services, the brand planning document can overlook a link in the value chain, resulting in some inherent added value being diminished (e.g. an insurance broker selling reputable quality insurance from a shabby office).

Significant cultural differences within several departments of a company can affect the brand success. The firm should not only audit the process to deliver the branded product or service, but also the staff beliefs, values and attitudes to assess whether the firm's culture is in harmony with the corporate brand identity and whether the firm has the appropriate culture to meet the brand's mission.

Distributors

The brand strategy of the manufacturer cannot be formulated without regard for the distributor. Both parties rely on each other for their success and even in an era of increasing retailer concentration, notwithstanding all the trade press hype, there is still a recognition amongst manufacturers and distributors that long-term brand profitability evolves through mutual support.

Manufacturers need to identify retailers' objectives and align their brands with those retailers whose aims most closely match their own. Furthermore, they should be aware of the strengths and weaknesses of each distributor.

Brand manufacturers who have not fully considered the implications of distributors' longer-term objectives and their strategy to achieve them are deluding themselves about the long-term viability of their own brands.

In the UK, there are numerous instances of growing retailer power, with a few major operators controlling a significant proportion of retail sales (e.g. groceries, DIY, jewellery, footwear). The danger of increasing retailer power is that weaker brand manufacturers acquiesce to demands for bigger discounts, without fully appreciating that the long-term well-being of their brands is being undermined. It is crucial for brand manufacturers to analyse regularly what proportion of their brand sales go through each distributor and then for each individual distributor to assess how important a particular manufacturer's brand is to them. For example, Table 2.5 shows a hypothetical analysis for a confectionery manufacturer.

crucial to analyse regularly what proportion of brand sales go through each distributor

If this hypothetical example were for a Nestlé brand, it is clear that the particular Nestlé brand is more reliant upon Tesco than Tesco is on the particular Nestlé brand. Such an analysis better enables manufacturers to appreciate which retailers are more able to exert pressure on their brand. It indicates that, if the brand manufacturer wants to escape from a position of retailer power, they need to consider ways of growing business for their brands in those sectors other than Tesco at *a faster rate* than is envisaged within this distributor.

Table 2.5   *Power analysis*

Hypothetical Nestlé brand sales to distributors		Hypothetical market share of confectionery brands through Tesco	
Distributor	%	Brand	%
Sainsbury	25	Cadbury	35
Tesco	24	Mars	30
Safeway	19	Nestlé	20
Asda	17	Other	15
Co-op	10		100
Independent	5		
	100		

When working with a distributor, the brand manufacturer should take into account whether the distributor is striving to offer a good value proposition to the consumer (e.g. Kwik Save, Aldi) or a value-added proposition (e.g. high quality names at Harrods). In view of the loss of control once the manufacturer's brand is in the distributor's domain, the brand manufacturer must annually evaluate the degree of synergy through each particular route and be prepared to consider changes.

Does the manufacturer have an offensive distribution strategy, or is it by default that its brands go through certain channels? What are the ideal characteristics for distributors of its brands and how well do the actual distributors used match these criteria? How do distributors plan to use brands to meet their objectives? How do manufacturers' and their competitors' brands help distributors achieve their objectives? Which other forms of support (e.g. discounts, merchandising) are used?

The brand manufacturer must have a clear idea of the importance of specific distributors for each brand and in Chapter 7 a matrix is presented which enables the manufacturer to rank the appropriateness of distributors for each of a manufacturer's brands.

Finally, manufacturers must recognize that when developing new brands, distributors have a finite shelf space, and market research must not solely address consumer issues but must also take into account the reaction of the trade. One company found that a pyramid pack design researched well amongst consumers, but on trying to sell this into the trade it failed – due to what the trade saw as ineffective use of shelf space!

Consumers

To consumers, buying is a process of problem solving. They become aware of a problem (e.g. not yet arranged summer holidays), seek information (e.g. go to travel agent and skim brochures), evaluate the information and then make a decision (e.g. select three possible holidays, then try to book one through the travel agent). The extent of this buying process varies according to purchasers' characteristics, experience and the products being bought. Nonetheless, clearly consumers have to 'work' to make a brand selection. The brand selection and brand 'usage' are not necessarily performed by the same person. Therefore marketers need to identify all individuals and position the brand to appeal to both users and purchasers. In business to business markets several groups are involved in the purchase decision. Marketers need to formulate brand strategy that communicates the benefits of the brand in a way which is relevant to each group. Chapter 3 looks at customer behaviour involved in brand selection in more detail, while Chapter 5 concentrates on business to business markets.

Brands offer consumers a means of minimizing information search and evaluation. Through seeing a brand name which has been supported by continual marketing activity, consumers can use this as a rapid means of interrogating memory and if sufficient relevant information can be recalled, only minimal effort is needed to make a purchase decision. As a consequence of this, brand strategists should question whether they are presenting consumers with a few high quality pieces of information, or whether they are bombarding consumers with large quantities of information and ironically causing confusion. Likewise, in business to business markets, it is important to consider how firms make brand selections. This is covered in Chapter 5.

Not only should strategists look at the stages consumers go through in the process of choosing brands, but they also need to consider the role that brands actually play in this process. For example, a business person going to an important business presentation may **need to consider the role that brands actually play in this process** feel social risk in the type of clothes he or she wears and select a respected brand mainly as a risk-reducer. By contrast, in a different situation, they may decide to wear a Gucci watch, because of a need to use the brand as a device to communicate a message (e.g. success, lifestyle) to their peer group. Likewise, one purchasing manager may buy a particular brand, since experience has taught him or her that delivery is reliable, even though there is a price premium to pay. By contrast, another purchasing manager may be more concerned about rapid career advancement and may choose to order a different brand on the basis that he is or she is rewarded for minimizing unnecessary expenditure on raw materials. Success depends on understanding the way purchasers interact with brands and employing company resources to match these needs.

Competitors

Brands are rarely chosen without being compared against others. Although several brand owners benchmark themselves against competition, it often appears that managers misjudge their key competitors. Rather than collecting useless and misleading data, managers should undertake interviews with current and potential consumers to identify those brands that are considered similar. Once marketers have selected the critical competitors, they need to assess the objectives and strategies of these companies as well as fully understanding their brand positionings and personalities. It is also essential not to be restricted to a retrospective, defensive position, but to gather enough information to anticipate competitive response and be able to continuously update the strategy for brand protection.

Research has shown that return on investment is related to a product's share of the market. In other words, products with a bigger market share yield better returns than those with a smaller market share. Organizations with strong brands fare better in gaining market share than those without strong brands. Thus, firms who are brand leaders will become particularly aggressive if they see their position being eroded by other brands. Furthermore, as larger firms are likely to have a range of brands, backed by large resources, it is always possible for them to use one of their brands as a loss leader to underprice the smaller competitor, and once the smaller brand falls out of the market, the brand leader can then increase prices. Several years ago, Laker took on the major airlines when he launched his Skytrain on the lucrative transatlantic route. The major players recognized the potential danger from this 'no-frills' operation and because they had a wide range of products, they were able to compete at equally low prices, while using their other routes to subsidize this. Without a range of brands Laker was unable to compete and his brand died.

Brand strategists need to have given some thought to anticipating likely competitor response, as Chapter 8 argues in more detail. Filofax appear to have been taken by surprise by competitive activity. When their time organizer became established in the market, they were apparently without any short-term retaliatory plans when faced with an increasing number of 'me-too' competitors.

The marketing environment

Brand strategists need to scan their marketing environment continually to identify future opportunities and threats. Will a shift in the developed countries to a knowledge-based society lead to 'armchair shopping' facilitated by networked personal computers? Will increasing awareness of ecological issues result in the survival of only pure environment-friendly brands? Will the consolidation of three world trade blocks undermine the strength of powerful national brands? To draw an analogy with military thinking, good surveillance helps achieve success.

Conclusions

This chapter has provided an overview of the key issues involved in planning for the future of brands. It has shown that brands succeed when marketers regard them as the end result of a well-integrated marketing process. To view branding as naming, design or advertising, is too myopic and such a perspective will shorten the brand's life expectancy. Branding is about the communication of relevant added values for which buyers are prepared to pay a price premium and which competitors find difficult to emulate. It also provides a way to enhance and lengthen the relationship with customers.

The historical evolution of brands has shown that brands initially served the roles of differentiating between competing items, representing consistency of quality and providing legal protection from copying. With the advent of distributors' brands, more experienced buyers and increasingly sophisticated marketing techniques, eight different types of brands were identified: a sign of ownership of the branding process; a differentiating device; a communicator of functional capability; a device which enables buyers to express something about themselves; a risk-reducing device; a shorthand communication device; a legal device; and a strategic device. To capitalize upon the asset represented by their brand, firms need to recognize where they are on Mary Goodyear's brand consumerization spectrum and adopt strategic brand planning as a way of life. Finally, a model showing the five main factors that influence brand potential was reviewed.

Marketing action checklist

It is recommended that after reading this chapter, marketers undertake the exercises which follow to help clarify the direction of future brand marketing programmes.

1   Either by looking through previous market research reports, or by putting yourself in the position of a buyer, write down the four main reasons, in order of importance, why one of your com-

pany brands is being bought. Then show an advertisement for this brand (or a catalogue page describing it) to one of your buyers and ask them to tell you what are the four key points they took from the message.

If the results from the first and second part of this exercise are the same, your brand is correctly majoring upon relevant buyer choice criteria. However, any discrepancy is indicative of inappropriate brand marketing.

2   Write down the core values of one of your brands and ask the other members of your organization to do the same. Compile a summary of the replies (without participants' names) and circulate the findings, asking for comments about: (a) reasons for such varied replies, and (b) which four core values are the key issues your company is trying to major on. Repeat the exercise until a consensus view has been reached.

3   Having identified your team's views about the core values of your brand, ask your team to write down: (a) what your brand communicates about your company's relationship with the purchaser, and (b) how the different resources supporting the brand are satisfying this relationship objective. Collate the replies from all parties and consider how well your team appreciates your brand propositions.

4   Write down what you understand by the term 'brand' and compare your views with those of your colleagues. Where there are a large number of comments relating to 'differentiation', 'logo', or 'unique design', your firm may not be fully capitalizing its brand asset.

5   After making explicit what the added values are of one of your brands, estimate how long it would take a major organization to buy in resources which would help it copy each of these added values. When considering the results of this exercise, also ask yourself: (a) how relevant to the buyer are the added values that this major competitor would find easiest to emulate, and (b) what added values does the buyer not yet have from any brand and how difficult it is to develop these added values.

6   For each of the added value benefits that your brand represents, write down how each element of the marketing mix is to help achieve it. If there are any instances where different elements of the mix are not operating in the same direction, consider why this is so and identify any changes necessary.

7   For each stage of the life cycle of one of your brands (introduction, growth, maturity, saturation, decline) identify how the added values may have to change to adapt to buyer sophistication.

8   Identify what the clues are that buyers use to evaluate the brand's added values and consider how much emphasis is placed on these clues in your marketing activity.

9   Make explicit the main situations within which one of your brands is: (a) bought and (b) consumed. Evaluate the appropriateness of your current brand strategy for each of these situations.

10   What type of relationship does your brand suggest to your customers (e.g. personal commitment, intimacy, dependence, intimidating superiority)? What strategies have you established to reinforce the bond between the brand and your customers (e.g. financial incentives, social bonds, structural bonds)?

11   If you were to remove the name of your brand from its packaging, is there anything else that would signify the identity of the brand to buyers? How well is this protected against copying?

12   Which of the brand categories outlined in this chapter does each of your company brands reflect (recognize that each of your brands may belong to several of the categories): a sign of ownership; a differentiating device; a functional communicator; a symbolic device; a risk-reducing device; a shorthand information device; a legal device; a strategic device. How are you overcoming the limitations of being in the first seven categories?

13   What strategies have you established to protect your brands from look-alikes? Are you monitoring potential counterfeits? How long does it take for one of your products to be launched? Are you aware of the risk of information leakage during that period?

14   Rank the importance of the different reasons why those people interested in your brand value it. What are you doing to protect the brand on each of these valued attributes?

15   Where on Mary Goodyear's brand consumerization spectrum (Figure 2.4) does your brand fall? Which other brands are at the same level as your brand and what are you doing to move beyond these?

16   Does the marketing department annually prepare a brand plan which audits the forces influencing the brand, has quantified brand objectives and well-considered strategies which are able to satisfy the objectives?

17   Using the audit in the section 'The importance of brand planning', what is your view about whether your firm is helping or hindering brand development?

18   How well positioned is each of your brands in relation to the five forces affecting brand potential? (Outlined in the section 'The importance of brand planning'.)

References and further reading

Allan J. (1981). Why Fine Fare believes in private label. Paper presented at Oyez Seminar: Is the Brand Under Pressure Again. London, Sept. 1981.

Allison R. I. and Uhl K. (1964). Influence of beer brand identification on taste perception. *Journal of Marketing Research*, **1**, (3) 36–9.

Assael H. (1987). *Consumer Behavior and Marketing Action*. Boston: Kent Publishing.

Barwise P., Higson C., Likierman A. and Marsh P. (1989). *Accounting for Brands*. London: London Business School and the Institute of Chartered Accountants.

Buck S. (1997). The continuing grocery revolution. *Journal of Brand Management*, **4**, (4). 227–38.

Copeland M. (1923). Relation of consumers' buying habits to marketing methods. *Harvard Business Review*, **1**, (April), 282–9.

de Chernatony L. (1987). Consumers' perceptions of the competitive tiers in six grocery markets. Unpublished PhD thesis. City University Business School, London.

de Chernatony L. (1988). Products as arrays of cues: how do consumers evaluate company brands? In *Marketing Education Group Proceedings, 1988* (Robinson T. and Clarke-Hill C., eds). Huddersfield: MEG.

de Chernatony L. and McWilliam G. (1990). Appreciating brands as assets through using a two dimensional model. *International Journal of Advertising*, **9**, (2), 111–19.

Doyle P. (1989). Building successful brands: the strategic options. *Journal of Marketing Management*, **5**, (1), 77–95.

Economist Intelligence Unit (1968). Own brand marketing. *Retail Business*, **128**, (Oct.), 12–19.

Euromonitor (1989). *UK Own brands 1989*. London: Euromonitor.

Goodyear M. (1996). Divided by a common language. *Journal of the Market Research Society*. **38**, (2), 110–122.

Gordon W., Corr D. (1990). The space between words. *Journal of the Market Research Society*, **32**, (3), 409–34.

Hawes J. (1982). *Retailing Strategies for Generic Grocery Products*. Ann Arbor: UMI Research Press.

Jacoby J. and Mazursky D. (1984). Linking brand and retailer images – do the potential risks outweigh the potential benefits? *Journal of Retailing*, **60**, (2), 105–22.

Jacoby J., Speller D. and Berning C. (1974). Brand choice behavior as a function of information load: replication and extension. *Journal of Consumer Research*, **1**, (June), 33–42.

Jarrett C. (1981). The cereal market and private label. Paper presented at Oyez Seminar: Is the Brand Under Pressure Again? London, Sept. 1981.

Jefferys J. (1954). *Retail trading in Britain 1850–1950*. Cambridge: Cambridge University Press.

Jones J. P. (1986). *What's in a name?* Lexington: Lexington Books.

King S. (1970). *What is a Brand?* London: J. Walter Thompson.

King S. (1984). *Developing New Brands*. London: J. Walter Thompson.

King S. (1985). Another turning point for brands? *ADMAP*, **21**, (Oct.), 480–4, 519.

Kotler P. (1988). *Marketing management*. Englewood Cliffs: Prentice Hall International.

Lamb D. (1979). The ethos of the brand. *ADMAP*, **15**, (Jan.), 19–24.

Langmaid R. and Gordon W. (1988). 'A great ad – pity they can't remember the brand – true or false'. In *31st MRS Conference Proceedings*. London: MRS, pp.15–46.

Levitt T. (1970). The morality of advertising. *Harvard Business Review*, (July–Aug.), 84–92.

Levitt T. (1980). Marketing success through differentiation of anything. *Harvard Business Review*, (Jan.–Feb.), 83–91.

Marketing (1997). 17% of shoppers take own-label in error. 6 March, p.1

McDonald M. (1995). *Marketing Plans*. Oxford: Butterworth-Heinemann.

Meadows R. (1983). They consume advertising too. *ADMAP*, **19**, (July–Aug.), 408–13.

Murphy J. (1990). Brand valuation – not just an accounting issue. *ADMAP*, **26**, (April), 36–41.

Patti C. and Fisk R. (1982). National advertising, brands and channel control: an historical perspective with contemporary options. *Journal of the Academy of Marketing Science*, **10** (1), 90–108.

Pitcher A. (1985). The role of branding in international advertising. *International Journal of Advertising*, **4** (3), 241–6.

Pitta D. A. and Katsanis L. P. (1995). Understanding brand equity for successful brand extension. *Journal of Consumer Marketing*. **12** (4) 51–64.

Porter M. (1985). *Competitive Advantage*. New York: The Free Press.

Room A. (1987). History of branding. In *Branding: A Key Marketing Tool* (Murphy J., ed.). Basingstoke: Macmillan.

Ross I. (1971). Self concept and brand preference. *Journal of Business*, **44** (1), 38–50.

Schutte T. (1969). The semantics of branding. *Journal of Marketing*, **33** (2) 5–11.

Simmons M. and Meredith B. (1983). Own label profile and purpose. Paper presented at Institute of Grocery Distribution Conference. Radlett: IGD.

Sinclair S. and Seward K. (1988). Effectiveness of branding a commodity product. *Industrial Marketing Management*, **17**, 23–33.

Staveley N. (1987). Advertising, marketing and brands. *ADMAP*, **23**, (Jan.), 31–5.

Thermistocli & Associates (1984). *The Secret of the Own Brand*. London: Thermistocli & Associates.

Watkins T. (1986). *The Economics of the Brand*. London: McGraw Hill.

Part Two

Brand Management in Different Sectors

How consumers choose brands

Summary

The purpose of this chapter is to show how an understanding of consumers' buying processes can help in developing successful brands. It opens by looking at how consumers process information and shows that, depending on the extent to which consumers perceive competing brands to differ and on their involvement in the brand purchase, four buying processes can be identified. It goes on to consider how customers choose brands according to their clusters of needs, thereby resulting in them having brand repertoires in each product category. Through recognizing that different consumers offer different profit opportunities in product categories, the benefits of differential brand marketing are considered. The chapter shows how consumers search for information about brands, explains why this search is limited, goes through the arguments for giving consumers only a few pieces of high quality brand information and illustrates how consumers evaluate brands as arrays of clues, with the brand name emerging as a very high quality clue. The influence of perception on branding is addressed. Building on earlier concepts in the chapter, brand naming issues are reviewed, along with a consideration of the way that brands can be presented as risk-reducing devices.

Brands and the consumer's buying process

There are many theories about the way consumers buy brands and debate still continues about their respective strengths and weaknesses. For example, some argue that brand choice can be explained by what is known as 'the expectancy-value model'. In this model, it is argued that consumers intuitively assign scores to two variables, one being the degree to which they expect a pleasurable outcome, the other being the value they ascribe to a favourable outcome. When faced with competing brands, this model postulates that consumers assign scores to these expectancy-value parameters and, following an informal mental calculation, make a selection based on the highest overall score.

We find this hard to accept, since people have limited mental processing capabilities and many brands, particularly regularly purchased brands, are bought without much rational consideration.

In reality, consumers face a complex world. They are limited both by economic resources and by their ability to seek, store and process brand information. For this reason we are also sceptical of the economist's view of consumer behaviour. This hypothesizes that consumers seek information until the marginal value gained is equal to, or less than, the cost of securing that knowledge. Many researchers have shown that consumers do not acquire perfect information – in fact even when presented with the economist's view of 'perfect' information, they are unable to comprehend it! As an example of this, a Pioneer advertisement with the caption, 'Does the man in the hi-fi shop seem to speak a different language?' was rightly critical of some hi-fi retailers who cause unnecessary consumer confusion by providing incomprehensible information about competing brands.

It is not our aim to become embroiled in a review of the merits of the different consumer behaviour models which could explain the brand selection process. The interested reader can appreciate this by consulting any of the numerous texts on this subject or by consulting the references at the end of the chapter.

Instead, we subscribe to a more well-accepted model of consumer behaviour. This shows the consumer decision process occurring as a result of consumers seeking and evaluating small amounts of information to make a brand purchase. Consumers rely upon a few pieces of selective information with which they feel confident to help them decide how the brand might perform. For example, why does someone flying from London to Amsterdam choose BA rather than KLM? Both airlines offer excellent service, a high degree of reliability and many convenient departure slots. They may then choose BA, when there is so little difference, only because the name is more familiar and it reflects their national pride.

consumer decision process occurring as a result of consumers seeking and evaluating small amounts of information to make a brand purchase

The stages in the buying process, when consumers seek information about brands and the extent of the information search, are influenced by an array of factors such as time pressure, previous experience, advice from friends, and so on. However, two factors are particularly useful in explaining how consumers decide. One is the extent of their involvement in the brand purchase and their perceptions of any differences between competing brands. For example, a housewife may become *very involved* when buying a washing machine, because with her large family it is important that she replaces it quickly. As such, she will show an *active* interest in evaluating different washing machine brands, all of which she can probably evaluate because of her experience. She will be able to evaluate the few brands that broadly appeal and will buy the brand which comes closest to satisfying her needs on one or a number of the key attributes important to her. By contrast, the same housewife is likely to show *limited involvement* when buying a brand of baked beans as they are of little personal importance and evoke little interest in her regular grocery shopping. She may perceive minimal difference between competing brands and, because of the low importance of this purchase, does not wish to waste time considering different brands. As such she is likely to make a rapid decision, based predominantly on previous experience.

With an appreciation of the extent of consumers' *involvement* when in a purchase decision and their perception of the degree of *differentiation* between brands, it is possible to categorize the different decision processes using the matrix shown in Figure 3.1.

	High consumer involvement	Low consumer involvement
Significant perceived brand differences	Extended problem solving	Tendency to limited problem solving
Minor perceived brand differences	Dissonance reduction	Limited problem solving

Figure 3.1   *Typology of consumer decision processes (adapted from Assael 1987)*

The strength of this matrix, as will now be shown, is that it illustrates simply the stages through which the consumer is likely to pass when making different types of brand purchases. Each of the quadrants is now considered in more detail.

Extended problem solving

Extended problem solving occurs when consumers are *involved* in the purchase and where they perceive *significant differences* between

extended problem
solving occurs
when consumers
are involved in the
purchase and
where they
perceive
significant
differences
between
competing
brands

competing brands in the same product field. This type of decision process is likely for high-priced brands which are generally perceived as a risky purchase due to their complexity (e.g. washing machines, cars, hi-fi, home computers) or brands that reflect the buyer's self-image (e.g. clothing, cosmetics, jewellery). It is characterized by consumers *actively* searching for information to evaluate alternative brands. When making a complex purchase decision, consumers pass through the five stages shown in Figure 3.2.

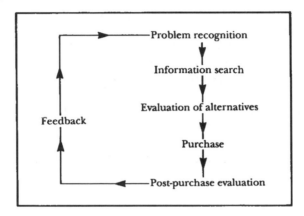

Figure 3.2   *Stages in complex decision making*

The decision process starts when the consumer becomes aware of a problem. For example, a young man may have heard his friend's new hi-fi system and become aware of how inferior his own system sounds. This recognition would trigger a need to resolve the problem and, if he feels particularly strongly, he will embark on a course to replace his system. Depending upon his urgency to act and his situation (e.g. time availability, financial situation, confidence, etc.) he might take action quickly or, more likely, he will become more attentive to information about hi-fi and buy a brand some time later.

The search for information would start first in his own memory and, if he feels confident that he has sufficient information already, he will be able to evaluate the available brands. Often, though, consumers do not feel sufficiently confident to rely on memory alone (particularly for infrequently bought brands), so they will begin to scan the external environment (e.g. visit shops, become attentive to certain advertisements, talk to friends). As they get more information, the highly involved consumer will start to learn how to interpret the information in their evaluation of competing brands.

Even so, consumers do not single-mindedly search for information about one particular purchase. It has been estimated that in any one day people are bombarded by over 1000 different marketing messages – of which they are attentive to less than 2 per cent. Consumers' perceptual processes protect them from information overload and helps them search and interpret new information. The issue of what these perceptual processes are is dealt with later in this chapter. Should something interest them, their attention will be directed to this new source. Even here, however, of the few advertisements that they take notice of, they are likely to ignore the points that do not conform to their prior expectations and interpret some of the other points within their own frame of reference.

Thus, the brand marketer has to overcome, amongst other issues, three main problems when communicating a brand proposition. First, they have to fight through the considerable 'noise' in the market to get their brand message noticed. If they can achieve this, the next challenge is to develop the content of the message in such a way that there is harmony between what the marketer puts into the message and what the consumer takes out of the message. Having overcome these two hurdles, the next challenge is to make the message powerful enough to be able to reinforce the other marketing activities designed to persuade the consumer to buy the brand.

As the consumer in our example mentally processes messages about competing brands, he would evaluate them against those criteria deemed to be most important. Brand beliefs are then formed (e.g. 'the Sony system has a wide range of features, it's well priced', etc.). In turn, these beliefs begin to mould an attitude and if a sufficiently positive attitude evolves, so there is a greater likelihood of a positive intention to buy that brand.

Having decided which hi-fi brand to buy, the consumer would then make the purchase – assuming a distributor can be found for that particular brand and that the brand is in stock. Once the hi-fi is installed at home, the consumer would discover its capabilities and assess how well his expectations were met by the brand. As can be seen from the model shown in Figure 3.2, he would be undertaking post-purchase evaluation. Satisfaction with different aspects of the brand will strengthen positive beliefs and attitudes towards the brand. Were this to be so, the consumer would be proud of his purchase and praise its attributes to his peer group. With a high level of satisfaction, the consumer would look favourably at this company's brands in any future purchase.

Should the consumer be dissatisfied though, he would seek further information after the purchase to provide reassurance that the correct choice was made. For example, he may go back to the hi-fi shop, where the brand was bought, and check that the controls are being used properly and that the speakers are correctly connected. If he finds sufficiently reassuring information confirming a wise brand choice, he will become more satisfied. Without such positive support, he will become disenchanted with the brand and over time will become more dissatisfied. He is likely to talk to others about his experience, not only vowing never to buy that brand again, but also convincing others that the brand should not be bought.

In the event that the consumer is satisfied with the brand purchase and repeats it in a relatively short period of time (e.g. buys a hi-fi for his car), he is unlikely to undergo such a detailed search and evaluation process. Instead, he is likely to follow what has now become a more routine problem solving process. Problem recognition would be followed by memory search which, with prior satisfaction, would reveal clear intentions, leading to a purchase. Brand loyalty would ensue, which would be reinforced by continued satisfaction (should quality be maintained). This process is shown in Figure 3.3.

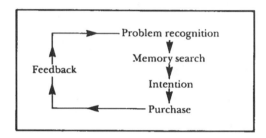

Figure 3.3   *Routine problem-solving behaviour*

When consumers are deeply involved with the brand purchase and when they perceive large differences between brands, they are more likely to seek information actively in order to make a decision about which brand to buy. As such, brand advertising may succeed by presenting relatively detailed information explaining the benefits of the brand, as well as reinforcing its unique differential positioning. It is important for the brand marketer to identify those attributes consumers perceive to be important and focus on communicating them as powerfully as possible. In circumstances such as those just described, as the consumer is likely actively to seek information from several different sources, the brand marketer should use a consistent multimedia promotional approach. Also, it is important to ensure that all retail assistants likely to come in contact with our inquisitive consumer are well versed in the capabilities of the product.

Dissonance reduction

This type of brand buying behaviour is seen when there is a high level of consumer involvement with the purchase, but the consumer perceives only *minor differences* between competing brands. Such consumers may be confused by the lack of clear brand differences. Without any firm beliefs about the advantages of any particular brand, a choice will most probably be made based on other reasons such as, for example, a friend's opinion or advice given by a shop assistant.

Following the purchase, the consumer may feel unsure, particularly if they receive information that seems to conflict with their reasons for buying. The consumer would experience mental discomfort, or what is known as 'post-purchase dissonance', and would attempt to reduce this state of mental uncertainty. This would be done either by ignoring the dissonant information, for example by refusing to discuss it with the person giving conflicting views, or by selectively seeking those messages that confirm prior beliefs.

In this type of brand purchase decision, the consumer makes a choice without firm brand beliefs, then changes his attitude *after* the purchase – often on the basis of experience with the chosen brand. Finally, learning occurs on a selective basis to support the original brand choice by the consumer being attentive to positive information and ignoring negative information. This brand buying process is shown in Figure 3.4.

in this type of brand purchase decision, the consumer makes a choice without firm brand beliefs, then changes his attitude after the purchase

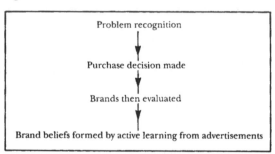

Figure 3.4   *Brand purchasing under dissonance reduction*

Dissonance reduction may be illustrated through the following example. A young business woman is very proud of having just bought her first flat. To reflect her successful life, she wants to furnish the place with modern and stylish comforts. Although she is very busy and financial considerations are hardly crucial, she thinks she should consider carefully which carpet would be the most appropriate for her dining room, in which she hosts many leisure and business parties. So she starts going to different shops, but finds the experience very confusing. She is overwhelmed by the flood of information about carpet attributes she has never heard of before: type of pile, proportion of the wool, whether it is Scotchguarded, etc. Unable to fully evaluate the advantages and disadvantages of the different carpets, she makes a rapid decision based on her perceptions and the reassuring explanations of a particularly helpful salesperson. At her first dinner party after the new carpet has been fitted, one of her guests spills a glass of red wine, which she rapidly cleans up as recommended by the salesperson. The following morning she checks whether there is any stain left. When she sees that the carpet is spotless, she realizes that the Scotchguarding has protected it against this kind of accident. When her guest calls her to apologize for the damage, she is pleased to reassure him that everything is perfectly fine. As a consequence of this experience, she starts reading leaflets to understand the different carpet types. It is only then, with hindsight, that she compliments herself on her wise choice.

When consumers are involved in a brand purchase, but perceive little brand differentiation or lack the ability to judge between competing brands, the advertising should reduce post-purchase dissonance through providing reassurance *after* the purchase. For example, in the wallpaper paste market consumers do not have the ability to evaluate the technical differences between pastes (e.g. adhesion, enabling paper to slip when matching patterns, etc.). However, they are involved in the purchase due to the risk they perceive in ruining the wallpaper decorations. Polycell ran a series of advertisements using the strap line 'You've chosen well' deliberately to reassure consumers after the purchase and to encourage brand loyalty.

Also, close to the point of purchase, as consumers are unsure about which brand to select, promotional material is particularly important in increasing the likelihood of a particular brand being selected. Likewise, any packaging should try to stress a point of difference from competitors and sales staff should be trained to be 'brand reassurers', rather than 'brand pushers'.

Limited problem solving

When consumers do not regard the buying of certain products as important issues, and when they perceive only minor differences between competing brands in these product fields (e.g. packaged groceries, household cleaning materials), then their buying behaviour can be described by the 'limited problem solving process'. The stages that the consumer passes through are shown in Figure 3.5.

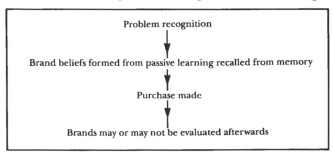

Figure 3.5   *Limited problem solving brand purchase*

Problem recognition is likely to be straightforward. For example, an item in the household may be running low. As the consumer is not particularly interested personally in the purchase they are not motivated actively to seek information from different sources. Whatever information they have will probably have been passively received, say, via a television commercial that the consumer wasn't paying particular attention to.

Alternative evaluation, if any, takes place *after* the purchase. In effect, fully formed beliefs, attitudes and intentions are the *outcomes* of purchase and not the cause. The consumer is likely to regard the cost of information search and evaluation as outweighing the benefits.

Promotions providing information, however, still do have a role to play in low involvement brand purchasing. But whilst they have a positive role, it is different from that in high involvement buying. Consumers passively receive information and process it in such a way that it is stored in their memories without making much of an impact on their existing mental structure. Having stored the message, no behavioural change occurs until the consumer comes across a purchase trigger (e.g. an in-store display of the brand) at the point at which they need to purchase the product in question. After trying the brand, the consumer can then decide how satisfactory it is. If the brand is satisfactory, there will be a kind of belief in their particular brand, albeit a fairly 'weak' one, which will lead to the likelihood of repeat brand buying.

When *regularly* purchasing these kinds of brands, consumers would establish buying strategies that reduce the effort in decision making (i.e. routine problem solving). Following a similar flow chart to that in Figure 3.3, any further purchase decisions about the brand would be based on a memory scan which, if holding details about a satisfactory experience, would result in brand loyalty. Thus, in extended problem solving situations, the consumer considers it important to buy the 'right brand' and it is difficult to induce brand switching. By contrast, in low involvement buying, the 'right brand' is less central to the consumer's lifestyle and brand switching may be more easily achieved through coupons, free trial incentives, etc.

In low involvement purchasing, consumers occasionally show variety-seeking behaviour. There is little involvement with the product and therefore the consumer feels little risk in switching between brands. Over time, consumers feel bored buying the same brand and occasionally seek variety by switching.

Consumers pay minimal attention to advertisements for these kinds of brands. Consequently, the message content should be kept simple and the advertisements should be shown frequently. A single (or low number) of benefits should be presented in a creative manner which associates a few features with the brand. In low involvement brand buying, consumers are seeking acceptable, rather than optimal purchases, i.e. they seek to minimize problems rather than maximize benefits. Consequently, it may be more appropriate to position low involvement brands as functional problem solvers (e.g. a brand of washing up liquid positioned as an effective cleaner of greasy dishes) rather than as less tangible benefit deliverers (e.g. a brand of washing up liquid positioned as smelling fresh).

Trial is an important method by which consumers form favourable attitudes after consumption, so devices such as money-off coupons, in-store trial and free sachets, are particularly effective.

As consumers are not motivated to search out low involvement brands, manufacturers should ensure widespread availability. Any out-of-stock situations would probably result in consumers switching to an alternative brand, rather than visiting another store to find the brand. Once inside a store, little evaluation will be made of competing brands, so locating the brand at eye level, or very close to the check-out counter, is an important facilitator of brand selection. Packaging should be eye-catching and simple.

Tendency to limited problem solving

While the 'limited problem solving' aspect of the matrix describes low involvement purchasing with *minimal* differences between competing brands, we believe that this can also be used to describe low involvement brand purchasing when the consumer perceives *significant* brand differences. It is our view that when a consumer feels minimal involvement, they are unlikely to be sufficiently motivated to undertake an extensive search for information. So even though there may be notable differences between brands, (e.g. the unique dispensing nozzle on Heinz's Tomato Ketchup), because of the consumer's low involvement they are less likely to be concerned about any such differences. Brand trial would take place and, in an almost passive manner, the consumer would develop brand loyalty.

when a consumer feels minimal involvement, they are unlikely to be sufficiently motivated to undertake an extensive search for information

The brand selection process is very similar to that described in 'limited problem solving' and similar marketing issues need to be addressed.

Chapter 2 earlier identified the emphasis marketers place on brands as legal devices. It is now more evident why brand owners feel concern about competitors developing similar looking brands – 'look-alikes'. In packaged groceries, retailers' own labels often employ similar packages and designs to leading brands. Where these look-alikes compete in low involvement categories, consumers are unlikely to invest their time searching for information. Therefore some of the consumers, who superficially glance along the shelves, may pick up a pack because it appears to be the leading brand. An indication of the scale of this error is detailed in Chapter 2 in 'Brand as a legal device'.

This section has shown that, given an appreciation of the degree of involvement consumers have with the brand purchase and their perception of the degree of differentiation between brands, it is possible to identify their buying processes. With an appreciation of the appropriate buying process, the marketer is then able to identify how marketing resources can best be employed. A further benefit of appreciating consumers' buying processes, is that brands can be developed and presented in such a way that consumers perceive them as having added values over and above the basic commodity represented by the brand, as the next section explains.

Consumers' need-states

Brands satisfy different needs. One way of appreciating this is through the three categories of needs identified by Park and his colleagues (1986). Functional brands focus on technical features and mainly solve externally-generated consumption needs, e.g. Microsoft Office solves the need for efficient office communication. Symbolic brands, such as Mercedes or Rolex, stress intangible benefits and fulfil internally-generated needs for self-enhancement, role position, group membership or ego-identification. Experiential brands, e.g. Chanel No. 5, satisfy desires for sensory pleasure, variety and cognitive stimulation.

Wendy Gordon's work (1994), which is well-documented in the references at the end of this chapter, shows that brands are bought to reflect consumers' needs in a particular context and she introduces the term 'need-state' to describe this. Undertaking considerable market research, she has demonstrated that there can be more differences between the same consumer purchasing on two different occasions than between two different consumers choosing a brand on the same occasion. Consumers use brands to meet specific needs at a particular time in a specific situation. Consider, for example, the changing need-states of a housewife buying yoghurts during a week, as shown in Table 3.1. On a Friday, she prepares for an important dinner party. One of the recipes needs 'Real Greek Yoghurt', which in her opinion is proof of being a sophisticated host. To ease her feelings of guilt at the children having to stay upstairs watching television during this dinner party she buys a pack of Mr Men yoghurts. The day after the party she weighs herself and is concerned at her increased weight, as a result of the creamy dessert she has eaten and sees the solution in a diet yoghurt. On Tuesday her weekly shopping brings back the reality of buying within a budget and she chooses the cheaper, own-label yoghurts. Two days later her husband takes the children bowling and she stays at home to watch her favourite television show. Although she is still aware of her diet plans, she wants to indulge herself and chooses a Marks & Spencer brand.

consumers use brands to meet specific needs at a particular time in a specific situation

Table 3. 1   *Need-states and yoghurt brands (after Gordon 1994)*

Need-state	Brand
Sophisticated me	Real Greek Yoghurt
Mummy me	Mr Men
Healthy me	Shape
Budget me	Tesco own label
Indulgent me	Marks & Spencer

This example shows the need to reconsider the concept of brand loyalty. It would be more realistic to consider it in terms of consumers having a repertoire of brands in a particular product field and switching between these brands. Consumers using two brands in a short period of time should not be considered 'disloyal'. Instead this is more an expression of active discernment, choosing brands to meet specific need-states. Most consumers switch between brands.

Differential brand marketing

Gordon's work provides some enlightenment about the reasons why consumers show a greater propensity to use a particular brand yet will also, from time to time, use other brands. Ehrenberg's empirical work (1993) provides considerable insight about consumers' 'loyalty' behaviour, in particular:

- heavy category users have a repertoire of brands;
- big brands are bought within the repertoire more frequently than smaller brands;
- a brand's most loyal consumers are the least valuable, as they buy the category infrequently;
- a brand's best consumers are mostly competitors' consumers who occasionally buy it.

a brand's best consumers are mostly competitors' consumers who occasionally buy it

One of the implications from these findings is that marketers should not regard each consumer in a target segment as being equally attractive and assume that the same brand marketing strategy is equally appropriate across all the target segment. In fact, Hallberg's research (1995) shows the need for different strategies, for the same brand, across the target segment as a result of different buyers having differing degrees of attractiveness. He argues that consumers should be categorized by their 'profit differentials', particularly since 10–15 per cent of buyers in a category produce the majority of a brand's profits. As such, differential brand marketing is needed, whereby the more valuable consumers are the greater the special treatment they deserve.

The way to develop a differential brand marketing strategy is, as Hallberg shows, to segment consumers into four profit opportunity groups, i.e. high, medium, low and no profit segments. To do this requires good market research data, good management information systems showing detailed costs and a database of the brand's consumers, ideally over a number of years. Organizations such as Tesco, Heinz and Buitoni have invested considerable effort in building consumer databases. A case study in the yoghurt category showed that a yoghurt brand was only bought by 48 per cent of households in a year. The 52 per cent of yoghurt-consuming households not buying the brand in that year represent the no profit opportunity group and, particularly if a national television campaign had been used, reflected an unproductive use of resources. The firm knew how many yoghurts each household bought in that year and, arranging households in descending order according to the numbers of yoghurts bought, then divided them into three equally-sized groups, each accounting for 16 per cent of households, as shown in the profit matrix pyramid of Figure 3.6. Analysis then revealed that the high profit segment, the top 16 per cent of households, accounted for 83 per cent of the brand's profits. With analysis such as this showing just how profitable a small group of consumers are, firms can develop much more focused brand strategies. Consumers can be categorized by their profit attractiveness and, particularly since their addresses are known from the firm's database, more productive use can be made of resources through tailoring different strategies to different profit opportunity consumers.

Using this analysis, marketers can benefit from tracking lost

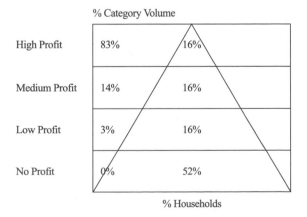

Figure 3.6   *Yoghurt category profit matrix (after Hallberg 1995)*

consumers and, particularly for high profit potential consumers, through understanding their reasons for defecting make appropriate brand changes. Lost consumers can be categorized according to whether they leave the brand due to changing need-states, for example baby growing out of nappies, or through dissatisfaction. Again good market research should help amend the brand's strategies to reduce the defection rate.

Consumers' perceptions of added values

Brands are able to sustain a price premium over their commodity form since consumers perceive relevant added values. For brands with which consumers become personally involved, there may be a complex cluster of added values over and above the brand's basic functional purpose, such as the ability of a clothing brand to signify membership of a particular social group whose distinctiveness is the result of their ability always to be at the forefront of chic fashion. By contrast, for low involvement brands, the added value could be as simple as the friendly smile consistently apparent from a newsagent encouraging the busy commuter buying his daily newspaper to remain a loyal consumer.

The concept of added values is an extremely important aspect of brands, being their *raison d'être*. As there are many different ways in which added values interact with commodity forms in the branding process, we do not have just one chapter dedicated to this. Instead the topic is addressed at appropriate points, in particular Chapter 9. Here we briefly overview some of the aspects of added value and consider its role in relation to consumer behaviour.

The brand's added values are those that are relevant and appreciated by consumers and which are over and above the basic functional role of the product. For example, well-travelled international sales executives may recognize the prime functional benefit of Best Western Hotels as being clean, comfortable establishments to sleep in, but they also appreciate their 'no surprises strategy' as an added value. This hotel group has a policy of consistency of standards throughout the world. For brands with which the consumer feels low involvement, the added values may often be other functional benefits. For example, while the prime benefit sought from a bleach may be its ability to kill germs, Domestos not only meets this requirement but also has the added value of a directional nozzle to ensure that difficult-to-reach corners are reached. The marginal cost from the directional nozzle is an added value contributing to the overall value of the brand, enabling a price premium to be charged. Likewise, while consumers may buy a brand of salt for its taste, they may pay a premium for a particular brand since they appreciate the

Exhibit 3.1 *Promoting Bio-tex's added values of removing localized stains conveniently with the sponge-tipped bottle (reproduced by kind permission of the Jenks Group and a/s blumøller)*

added value of the small hygroscopic capsule inside the container which ensures that the salt always flows freely. A further example of added value can be seen in Nescafé cappuccino. According to a Nescafé executive the cappuccino is more than just another hot beverage: 'it as a reflection of a way of life, where relaxation merges with enjoyment and glamour with convenience'.

For the marketer, the challenge is to appreciate how all of the

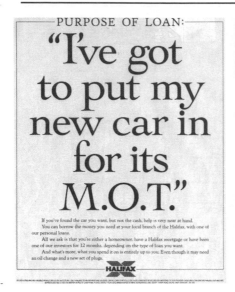

Exhibit 3.2   *The added value consumers perceive from the Halifax loan is the unhindered ability to spend as they wish (reproduced with kind permission of Halifax plc and Ken Griffiths (photographer)*

marketing resources supporting a brand interact to produce the added values which consumers perceive as being unique to a specific brand. The physical (or service) component is combined with symbols and images communicated by advertising, PR, packaging, pricing and distribution to create meanings. These meanings not only differentiate the brand, but also give it added values. Consumers interpret the meaning of the marketing activity behind a brand and project values onto the brand, endowing brands with a personality. Many researchers in the 1960s and 1970s demonstrated the added value of strong brand personalities, showing that consumers tend to choose brands with the same care as they choose friends. By interpreting the personality of brands, consumers felt more comfortable buying particular brands. This can be for a variety of reasons, such as, for example, a feeling of 'being at ease' with the brand (just as we are with an old friend) or the brand coming closest to matching the consumer's actual or aspired self image. For example, whilst there are many credit cards, American Express has evolved such a strong brand personality that many believe 'it's the one you don't leave home without'. Likewise, whilst many firms distribute petrol, Shell is the one 'you can be sure of'.

added value of strong brand personalities, showing that consumers tend to choose brands with the same care as they choose friends

Chapter 4 discusses the added value of brand personality in more depth, but it is worth stressing here that a strong brand personality evolves because of a consumer-focused marketing investment programme. It takes time and resources to build the brand personality and a lack of commitment to brand investment will weaken the brand's personality. For example, competitors in the lager market regard Courage's lack of brand support for Hofmeister as weakening the brand's personality, forcing the brand to concentrate on price offers.

A useful framework to help us understand the diverse types of brand added values was developed by Jones (1986). It consists of four types:

1 *Added values from experience*   With repeated trial, consumers gain confidence in the brand and through its consistent reliability perceive minimal risk. Particularly in grocery shopping, where a consumer is typically faced with over 20 000 lines in a grocery superstore, this added value is particularly appreciated, enabling consumers to complete their shopping rapidly by choosing known names.

2 *Added values from reference group effects*   The way that advertising uses personalities to endorse a brand, is perceived by many target consumers as relating it to a certain lifestyle to which they may well aspire. An example of this is the promotion of perfume using Joan Collins.

3 *Added values from a belief that the brand is effective*   The belief that a brand is effective influences the consumer's views about the actual performance of the brand. For example, for branded pain killers (considered in more detail in Chapter 4), it has been shown that approximately a quarter of the pain relief was attributable to branding. In the suits market, one often hears of men remarking that for a certain event they 'feel' more comfortable with a certain type of suit. Further evidence of this added value is seen when consumers taste brands without their names, then with their names. In Table 3.2 it can be seen that functionally Diet Pepsi is preferred to Diet Coke in blind testing but, through the strong image recalled by the name, the overall preference in the branded product test is for Diet Coke.

Table 3.2   *The impact of branding on taste tests*

	Blind %	Branded %
Prefer Diet Pepsi	51	23
Prefer Diet Coke	44	65
Equal/don't know	5	12
	100	100

4 *Added values from the appearance of the brand*   Consumers form impressions of brands from their packaging and develop brand preferences based on their attraction to the pack design. This is particularly so in the premium biscuit market, where designers use metal tins to enhance the premium positioning of their brand.

Thus, successful brands have consumer-relevant added values which buyers recognize and value sufficiently to pay a price premium. Accepting this, the task for the marketer is to communicate a brand's added values to consumers in such a way that the message penetrates consumers' perceptual defences and is not subject to perceptual distortion. This is not a small problem since, as the next section shows, consumers are attentive to only a small amount of marketing information.

The extent to which consumers search for brand information

The way consumers gain information is shown in Figure 3.7, i.e. first from memory, but if insufficient is held, then from external sources.

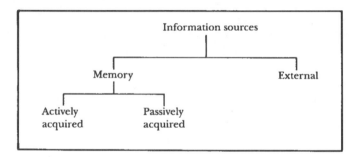

Figure 3.7   *The way consumers get brand information*

Information may be stored in the memory as a result of an earlier active search process, as in the case, for example, of the assessment of a newly-bought brand immediately after purchase. Alternatively, information may be stored in the memory as a result of a passive acquisition process – an advertisement might catch the reader's eye whilst a newspaper was being casually skimmed.

Two relevant factors which influence the degree to which consumers search their memory are the amount of stored information and its suitability for the particular problem. In a study amongst car purchasers, those repeatedly buying the same brand of car over time undertook less external search than those who had built up a similar history in terms of the number of cars bought, but who had switched between brands of cars. Repeatedly buying the same brand of car increased the quantity of *suitable* information in the memory and limited the need for external search.

If there is insufficient information already in a consumer's memory, and if the purchase is thought to warrant it, external search is undertaken. Research into consumer behaviour, however, shows that external search is a relatively limited activity, although there are variations between different groups of consumers. In one of the early studies on consumers' search for information, recent purchasers of sports shirts or major household goods (e.g. TVs, fridges, washing machines, etc.) were asked about their pre-purchase information search. Only 5 per cent of electrical appliance buyers showed evidence of a very active information search process, whilst a third claimed to seek virtually no pre-purchase information. Just under half (47 per cent) of appliance purchasers visited only one store and only 35 per cent considered another attribute in addition to brand name and price. Even less evidence of information search was found amongst purchasers of sports shirts, the conclusion being 'that many purchases were made in a state of ignorance, or at least of indifference'. As was pointed out, however, the apparent lack of deliberation does not indicate irrational decision behaviour. Some purchasers may have found it difficult to evaluate all the features of a product and instead relied upon a limited number of attributes that they felt more comfortable with (see Plate 5).

external search is a relatively limited activity

A further detailed study of consumers buying cars and major household appliances again showed evidence of limited external search. Less than a half of the purchasers interviewed (44 per cent) used no more than one information source, 49 per cent experienced a deliberation time of less than two weeks and 49 per cent visited only one retail outlet when making these major brand purchases. Numerous other instances have been reported of consumers undertaking limited external search for expensive brand purchases in such product fields as financial services, housing, furniture and clothing.

Not surprisingly, for low cost, low risk items (e.g. groceries), external search activity is also restricted. No doubt due to the low level of involvement that these brands engender, far more reliance is placed on memory. For example, when shopping for washing powders, consumers simplify purchasing by considering only one or two brands and by using only three to five brand attributes. Amongst consumers of breakfast cereals, only 2 per cent of the available information was used to make a decision. When using in-store observations of grocery shoppers, 25 per cent made a purchase decision without any time for deliberation and 56 per cent spent less than 8 seconds examining and deciding which brand to buy.

Reasons for limited search for external information

Several reasons exist for this apparently limited external search. Consumers have finite mental capacities, which are protected from information overload by perceptual selectivity. This focuses consumers' attention on those attributes considered important. For example, one study reported that, because of perceptual selectivity, only 35 per cent of magazine readers exposed to a brand advertisement noticed the brand being advertised.

Information is continually bombarding consumers and this information acquisition is a continuous process.

The search for external information represents a cost (the time and effort) and some consumers do not consider the benefits outweigh these costs. This is particularly so for low involvement brands.

In research studies into consumer behaviour, a lot of emphasis has been placed on measuring the *number* of sources consumers use, rather than considering the *quality* of each informational source.

The prevailing circumstances of consumers also have an impact on the level of external search. Consumers may feel time pressure (e.g. newly married couples seeking a home when there is a lack of rented accommodation) or they may not find the information easy to understand (e.g. food labels). The search for information is also affected by the consumer's emotional state. For example, one study, reviewing the way funeral services are marketed, noted that due to their emotional state consumers pay little attention to information during this traumatic period.

Brand information: quality or quantity?

The preceding sections have shown the relatively superficial external search for information which is undertaken in selecting brands. The question marketers need to consider, therefore, is whether increasing levels of information help (or hinder) consumer brand decisions. In one of many studies to assess the decision-making process, consumers were presented with varying levels of information about brands of washing powders and asked to make brand selections. Prior to the experiment they were asked to describe their preferred washing powder brand. The researchers found that accuracy (in the sense that consumers selected the brand in the survey that matched their earlier stated brand preference) was *inversely* related to the number of brands available. Initially, accuracy of brand choice improved as small amounts of brand information were made

available, but a point was reached at which further information reduced brand selection accuracy.

In another study, housewives were given varying levels of information about different brands of rice and pre-prepared dinners
and were asked to choose the brand they liked best. Again, prior to
the experiment, they were asked about their preferred brand. Confirming the earlier survey on washing powders, increasing
information availability from low levels helped decision making but
continuing provision of information reduced purchasing accuracy
and resulted in longer decision periods.

The conclusion is that marketers need to recognize that increasing the quantity of information will not necessarily increase brand
decision effectiveness, even though it may make consumers more
confident (see Plate 6).

increasing the quantity of information will not necessarily increase brand decision effectiveness

It is becoming apparent that consumers follow two broad patterns when searching for information. Some people make a choice
by examining one brand at a time, i.e. for the first brand they select
information on several attributes, then for the second brand they seek
the same attribute information, and so on. This strategy is known as
choice by processing brands.

An alternative strategy is seen when consumers have a particularly important attribute against which they assess all the brands,
followed by the next most important attribute, and so on. This is
known as **choice by processing attributes**.

It has been shown that consumers with limited knowledge of a
product or service tend to process information by attributes, while
more experienced consumers process the information by brands.
Furthermore, choice by processing attributes tends to be the route
followed when there are few alternatives, when differences are easy
to compute and when the task is in general easier.

Clues to evaluate brands

Rather than engaging in a detailed search for information when deciding between competing brands, consumers look for a few clues
that they believe will give an indication of brand performances. For
example, when consumers buy a new car they talk about them as
being 'tinny', or 'solid', based on the sound heard when slamming
the door. Clearly, then, some consumers use the sound as being indicative of the car's likely performance.

There are many examples of consumers using surrogate attributes to evaluate brands, e.g. the sound of a lawn mower engine
as indicative of power; the feel of a bread pack as indicative of the
freshness of bread; the clothing style of banking staff as indicative of
their understanding of financial services; and high prices as being

indicative of good quality. It is now widely recognized that consumers conceive brands as arrays of clues (e.g. price, colour, taste, feel, etc.). Consumers assign information values to the available clues, using only those few clues which have a high information value. A clue's information value is a function of its predictive value (how accurately it predicts the attribute being evaluated) and its confidence value (how confident the consumer is about the predictive value assigned to the clue). This concept of brands as arrays of clues also helps explain why consumers undertake only a limited search for information. If, through experience, consumers recognize a few clues offering high predictive and high confidence values, these will be selected. More often than not, the most sought-after clue, as explained later in this chapter, is the presence of a brand name, which rapidly enables recall from memory of previous experience. However, when the consumer has limited brand experience, the brand name will have low predictive and confidence values and thus more clues will be sought, usually price, followed by other clues. Learning, through brand usage, enables the consumer to adjust predictive and confidence values internally, which stabilize over time.

most sought-after clue is the presence of a brand name

There are numerous studies showing that, when faced with a brand decision, consumers place considerable importance on the presence or absence of brand names. Not only do brand names have a high predictive value, but consumers are also very confident, particularly from experience with this clue. Of all the marketing variables it is the brand name which receives the most attention by consumers and is a key influencer of their perceptions of quality.

Brand names as informational chunks

The previous section has explained that brand names are perceived by consumers as important information clues, which reduce the need to engage in a detailed search for information. An explanation for this can be found by consulting the work of Miller (1956), who carried out research into the way the mind encodes information. If we compare the mind with the way computers work, it can be seen that we can evaluate the quantity of information facing a consumer in terms of the number of 'bits'. All the information on the packaging of a branded grocery item would represent in excess of a hundred bits of information. Researchers have shown that at most the mind can simultaneously process seven bits of information. Clearly, to cope with the information deluge from everyday life, our memories have had to develop methods for processing such large quantities of information.

This is done by a process of aggregating bits of information into larger groups, or 'chunks', which contain more information (Buschke,

1976). A further analogy may be useful. The novice yachtsman learn-ing morse code, initially hears 'dit' and 'dot' as information bits. With experience, they organize these bits of information into chunks (let-ters), then mentally builds these chunks into larger chunks, (words). In a similar manner, when first exposed to a new brand of conven-ience food, the first scanning of the label would reveal an array of wholesome ingredients with few additives. These would be grouped into a chunk interpreted as 'natural ingredients'. Further scanning may show a high price printed on a highly attractive, multicolour label. This would be grouped with the earlier 'natural ingredients' chunk to form a larger chunk, interpreted as 'certainly a high quality offering'. This aggregation of increasingly large chunks would con-tinue until final eye scanning would reveal an unknown brand name but, on seeing that it came from a well-known organization (e.g. Nestlé, Heinz, etc.), the consumer would then aggregate this with the earlier chunks to infer that this was a premium brand – quality contents in a well-presented container, selling at a high price through a reputable retailer, from a respected manufacturer known for ad-vertising quality. Were the consumer not to purchase this new brand of convenience food, but later that day to see an advertisement for the brand, they would be able to recall the brand's attributes rapidly, since the brand name would enable fast accessing of a highly in-formative chunk in the memory.

The task facing the marketer is to facilitate the way consumers process information about brands, such that ever larger chunks can be built in the memory which, when fully formed, can then be rap-idly accessed through associations from brand names. This relates to the category described in Chapter 2 of branding as a shorthand de-vice. Frequent exposure to advertisements containing a few claims about the brand should help the chunking process through either passive or active information acquisition. What is really important, however, is to reinforce attributes with the brand name rather than continually repeating the brand name without at the same time as-sociating the appropriate attributes with it.

facilitate the way consumers process information about brands

The challenge to branding from perception

To overcome the problems of being bombarded by vast quantities of information and having finite mental capacities to process it all, con-sumers not only adopt efficient processing rules (for example, they only use high information value clues when choosing between brands, and aggregate small pieces of information into larger chunks) but they also rely upon their perceptual processes. These help brand decision-making by filtering information (perceptual selectivity) and help them to categorize competing brands (perceptual organization).

Amongst others, Bruner (1957) made a major contribution in helping lay the foundations for a better understanding of the way consumers' perceptual processes operate. He showed that consumers cannot be aware of all the events occurring around them and, with a limited span of attention, they acquire information selectively. With this reduced data set, they then construct a set of mental categories which allows them to sort competing brands more rapidly. By allocating competing brands to specific mental categories, they are then able to interpret and give more meaning to brands. A consequence of this perceptual process is that consumers interpret brands in a different way from that intended by the marketer. The classic example of this was the cigarette brand Strand. Advertisements portrayed a man alone on a London bridge, on a misty evening, smoking Strand. The advertising slogan was 'You're never alone with a Strand'. Sales were poor, since consumers' perceptual processes accepted only a small part of the information given and interpreted it as, 'if you are a loner and nobody wants to know you, console yourself by smoking Strand'.

It is clearly very important that brand marketers appreciate the role of perceptual processes when developing brand communication strategies and the two key aspects of perception are reviewed next.

Perceptual selectivity

Marketers invest considerable money and effort communicating with consumers, yet only a small fraction of the information is accepted and processed by consumers. First of all, their brand communication must overcome the barrier of what is known as **selective exposure**. If a new advertisement is being shown on television, even though the consumer has been attentive to the programme during which the advertisement appears, when the commercial breaks are on the consumer may out of preference choose to engage in some other activity rather than watching the advertisements.

only a small fraction of the information is accepted and processed by consumers

The second barrier is what is known as **selective attention**. The consumer may not feel inclined to do anything else while the television commercials are on during their favourite programme and might watch the advertisements for entertainment, taking an interest in the creative aspects of the commercial. At this stage, selective attention filters information from advertisements, so building support for existing beliefs about a brand ('Oh, it's that Toyota advert. They are good reliable cars. Let's see if they drive the car over very rough ground in this advert') and avoiding contradicting claims ('I didn't realize this firm produces fax machines, besides the PC I bought from them. In view of the problems I had with my PC, I just don't want to know about their products any more').

The third challenge facing a brand is what is known as **selective comprehension**. The consumer would start to interpret the message and would find that some of the information does not fit well with their earlier beliefs and attitudes. They would then 'twist' the message until it became more closely aligned with their views. For example, after a confusing evaluation of different companies' life assurance policies, a young man may mention to his brother that he is seriously thinking of selecting a Scottish Widows policy. When told by his brother that he knew of a different brand that had shown a better return last year, he may discount this fact, arguing to himself that his brother as a software engineer probably knew less about money matters than he did as a sales manager.

With the passage of time, memory becomes hazy about brand claims. Even at this stage, after brand advertising, a further challenge is faced by the brand. Some aspects of brand advertising are **selectively retained** in the memory, normally those claims which support existing beliefs and attitudes.

From the consumer's point of view the purpose of selective perception is to ensure that they have sufficient, relevant information to make a brand purchase decision. This is known as **perceptual vigilance**. Its purpose is also to maintain their prior beliefs and attitudes. This is known as **perceptual defence**. There is considerable evidence to show that information which does not concur with consumers' prior beliefs is distorted and that supportive information is more readily accepted. One of the classic examples of this is a study which recorded *different* descriptions from opposing team supporters who all saw the *same* football match. Many surveys show that selectivity is a positive process, in that consumers actively decide which information clues they will be attentive to and which ones they will reject.

Thus, as a consequence of perceptual selectivity, consumers are unlikely to be attentive to all of the information transmitted by manufacturers or distributors. Furthermore, in instances where consumers are considering two competing brands, the degree of dissimilarity may be very apparent to the marketer but if the difference, say, in price, quality or pack size is below a critical threshold this difference will not register with the consumer. This is an example of what is known as Weber's Law – the size of the least detectable change to the consumer is a function of the initial stimulus they encountered. Thus, to have an impact upon consumers' awareness, a jewellery retailer would have to make a significantly larger reduction on a £2000 watch than on a £100 watch.

Perceptual organization

'Perceptual organization' allows consumers to decide between competing brands on the basis of their similarities within mental categories conceived earlier. Consumers group a large number of competing brands into a few categories, since this reduces the complexity of interpretation. For example, rather than evaluating each marque in the car market, consumers would have mental categories such as the Toyota MR2 as an economic sports car, the Audi A4 as a small family saloon, and so on. By assessing which category the new brand is most similar to, consumers can rapidly group brands and are able to draw inferences without detailed search. If a consumer places a brand such as Safeway's own label washing powder into a category they had previously identified as 'own label', then the brand will achieve its meaning from the class it is assigned to by the consumer. In this case, even if the consumer has little experience of the newly categorized brand, the consumer is able to use this perceptual process to predict certain characteristics of the new brand. For example, the consumer may well reason that stores' own labels are inexpensive, thus this own label should be inexpensive and should also be quite good.

> consumers group a large number of competing brands into a few categories, since this reduces the complexity of interpretation

However, in order to be able to form effective mental categories in which competing brands can be placed and which lead to confidence in predicting brand performance, relevant product experience is necessary. The novice to a new product field has less well-formed brand categories than more experienced users. When new to a product field, the trialist has a view (based upon perceptions) about some attributes indicative of brand performance. This schema of key attributes forms the initial basis for brand categorization, drives their search for information and influences brand selection. With experience, the schema is modified, the search for information is redirected and brand categorization is adjusted, eventually stabilizing over time with increasing brand experience.

An interesting study undertaken amongst beer drinkers is a useful example of how learning moulds brand categorization. Without any labels shown, the beer drinkers were generally unable to identify the brand they drank most often and expressed no significant difference between brands. In this instance, the schema of attributes to categorize brands was based solely on the physical characteristics of the brands (palate, smell and the visual evaluation). When the study was later repeated amongst the same drinkers, but this time with the brands labelled, respondents immediately identified their most often drunk brand and commented about significant taste differences between brands! With the labels shown, respondents placed more emphasis on using the brand names to recall brand images as well as their views about how the brands tasted. As a consequence of consumers using this new schema of attributes to evaluate the brands, a different categorization of the brands resulted.

Whilst it might be thought that the simplest way for consumers to form mental groups is to rely solely on one attribute and to categorize competing brands according to the extent to which they possess this attribute, evidence from various studies shows that this is often not the case. Instead, consumers use several attributes to form brand categories. Furthermore, it appears that they weight the attributes according to the degree of importance of each attribute. Thus, marketers need to find the few key attributes that are used by consumers to formulate different brand categorizations and major upon the relevant attributes to ensure that their brand is perceived in the desired manner.

Gestalt psychologists provide further support for the notion of consumers interpreting brands through 'perceptual organization'. This school of thought argues that people see objects as 'integrated wholes' rather than as a sum of individual parts. The analogy being drawn is that people recognize a tune, rather than listen to an individual collection of notes.

To form a holistic view of a brand, consumers have to fill in gaps of information not shown in the advertisement. This concept, referred to as 'closure', is used by brand advertisers to get consumers more involved with the brand. For example, Kellogg's once advertised on billboards with the last 'g' cut off and it was argued that consumers' desire to round off the advertisement generated more attention. Billboard advertising, showing a fly on a wall with the caption 'The Economist' was also developed to generate more interest through closure. Likewise, not presenting an obvious punch line in a pun when advertising a brand can again generate involvement through closure. This was one of the reasons for the successful 'eau' Perrier advertising (e.g. H_2Eau, Eau la la, Eau Revoir, Eau Pair, etc.). When a brand has built up a respected relationship with consumers, the concept of closure can be successfully employed in brand advertising. For example, Schweppes is such a well-regarded brand that the name didn't have to appear in the early successful 'Schhh... you know who' campaign. The problem with this campaign was that closure initially worked well for the brand but eventually the actor was being promoted more than Schweppes, a problem not dissimilar to that faced by the Bristol & West Building Society campaign using Joan Collins.

Naming brands: individual or company name?

From the previous sections, it should now be clear that consumers seek to reduce the complexity of buying situations by cutting through the vast amount of information to focus on a few key pieces of information. A brand name is, from the consumer's perspective, a very important piece of information and is often the key piece. It is, therefore, essential that an appropriate brand name is chosen which will reinforce the brand's desired positioning by associating it with the relevant attributes that influence buying behaviour.

A brief consideration of some very well-known brand names shows that rather unusual reasons formed the basis for name selection. However, in today's more competitive environment far more care is necessary in naming a brand. For example, the Ford Motor Company was named after its founder; Lloyd's of London because of its location; Mercedes because of a friend's daughter; and Amstrad after conjuring various letters together (Alan M. Sugar Trading plc). Today, however, because of the increasing need to define markets on a global basis, idiosyncratic approaches to naming brands can lead to failure. For example, General Motor's Nova failed in Spain because the name means 'doesn't go', while Roll Royce's plans to wrap a new model in mysterious fog because of the name 'Silver Mist' were fortunately halted when it was noted that 'mist' in German means 'dung', which obviously would have elicited different images. A Beaujolais branded Pisse-Dru faced obvious problems, even though the French vigneron interprets this as a wine to his liking. Even more intriguing is the lager 36/15 from Pecheur et Fischer marketed as La Biere Amoureuse. This brand is brewed with aphrodisiac plants and is named after the telephone number of a dating service advertised on French television!

When examining brand names, it is possible to categorize them broadly along a spectrum, with a company name at one end (e.g. British Telecom, Halifax), right the way through to individual brand names which do not have a link with the manufacturer (e.g. Ariel, Dreft, Daz, Bold and Tide emanating from Procter & Gamble). This is shown in Figure 3.8.

There are varying degrees of company associations with the brand name – there are brand names with strong company endorsement, such as Cadbury's Dairy Milk, Castrol GTX, Sainsbury's Baked Beans, and brand names with weak company endorsement, such as KitKat from Nestlé.

many advantages to be gained from tying the brand name in with the firm's name

There are many advantages to be gained from tying the brand name in with the firm's name. With the goodwill that has been built up over the years from continuous advertising and a commitment to

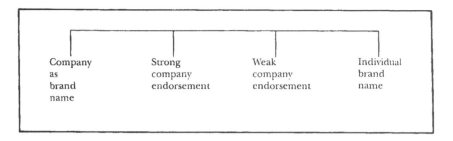

Figure 3.8   *Brand name spectrum*

consistency, new brand additions can gain instant acceptance by being linked with the heritage. Consumers feel more confident trying a brand which draws upon the name of a well-established firm. For example, building upon high awareness and strong associations of the brand with healthy eating and children's tastes, Nestlé's Shreddies was rebranded Original Shreddies and augmented by two brand extensions, Frosted Shreddies and Coco Shreddies. The heavily promoted new brands were able to benefit from similar associations built up over the years by the Shreddies name. In this example, however, the brand name was extended to a sector not dissimilar from that where the original brand's strengths were built. If this is not the case, the company's image could be diluted by following a corporate endorsement naming policy.

In the financial services sector, it is very common to see brands

Exhibit 3.3   *Heinz strongly endorses its brands, whilst Elida Gibbs pursues individual brand names (reproduced by kind permission of Elida Fabergé)*

being strongly tied to the corporation (e.g. American Express, Guardian Royal Exchange's Choices, Abbey National 5 Star Account, etc.). With the Financial Services and Building Societies Act during the 1980s enabling more institutions to sell financial services, branding is quite a new concept in this sector. Consumers and financial advisers have traditionally evaluated policies by considering the parent corporation's historical performances, so company-linked brand names in this sector are common.

Nonetheless, whilst a brand can gain from an umbrella of benefits by being linked with a company name, the specific values of each brand still need to be conveyed. For example, whilst organizations such as Midland Bank have been promoting the benefits associated with their corporate name, there is a danger of not adequately promoting the benefits of the individual brands (e.g. Meridian, Vector, Orchard) leading to the possibility of consumer confusion. Interestingly, when a corporation has developed a particularly novel concept, then the brand is launched without such a strong corporate name tie. Midland's First Direct is a very different approach to banking and the brand was launched very much as a stand-alone brand using the black and white logo to communicate the no-nonsense approach.

There are obvious advantages in all aspects of communication to be gained from economies of scale when an organization ties a brand name in with its corporate name. This advantage is sometimes given an undue importance weighting by firms thinking of extending their brands into new markets. This whole question of brand extension is a complex issue which involves more than just the name and is dealt with in more detail in Chapter 8. However, it is worth mentioning here that in the 1990s more products and services are likely to be marketed under the same corporate-endorsed brand name. Nonetheless, to help the brand fight through the competing noise in the market, it is still essential to know what the brand means to the consumer, how the brand's values compare with competitive brands and how marketing resources are affecting brand values.

There are also very good reasons why in certain circumstances it is advisable to follow the individual brand name route. As the earlier Procter & Gamble example showed, this allows the marketer to develop formulations and positionings to appeal to different segments in different markets. However, the economics of this need to be carefully considered, since firms may, on closer analysis, find that by trying to appeal to different small segments through different brand offerings, they are encountering higher marketing costs resulting in reduced brand profitability.

When striving to have coverage in each segment of the market as, for example, Seiko do with their watches, it is important that individual brand names sufficiently reinforce their different brand positionings. Some firms try to differentiate their brands in the same

in certain circumstances it is advisable to follow the individual brand name route

market through the use of numbers. When this route is followed, however, the numbers should be indicative of relative brand performance – in the home computer market the '2000' model could have approximately double the functional capability of the '1000' model. In some markets, firms do not appear to have capitalized on naming issues. For example, in the telephone answering machine market where it has a notable presence, Panasonic brands four of its models as T1440BE, T1446, T2386DBE and T2445BE. Consumers cannot infer much about relative differences from these brand nomenclatures.

Another advantage of using individual brand names is that if the new line should fail the firm would experience less damage to its image than if the new brand had been tied to the corporation. The following example shows how a failed brand extension damaged the whole company's image. Continental Airlines, inspired by the success of Southwest, decided to enter the low-budget, no-frill cheap flights market using the brand, Continental Lite. However, at the same time it continued to offer a full service under the original Continental brand. The company believed that it was possible to serve both markets and ignored the inevitable trade-offs on cost, service and efficiency. When Continental Lite was ultimately forced to withdraw from the market, consumers became aware of the failure of this venture and, due to the common use of 'Continental', there would have been some adverse perceptions about the parent corporation.

A strategic approach to naming brands

When looking at the way companies select brand names, many appear to follow a process of generating names and then assessing these against pre-determined criteria. For example, with the opportunities presented by the opening of European markets, the following stages of questioning are usual in brand name selection:

* First, in which geographical markets does the firm intend its brand to compete? The wider the geographical coverage the more complex the decision becomes, if for no other reason than the pronounceability of the name. For example, in 1988 Whirlpool, the American white goods manufacturer, acquired 53 per cent of Philips' home appliances business and are obliged by the agreement to phase out the Philips brand name by 1998. A dual brand name policy is currently being run, raising consumers' awareness of Whirlpool across Europe. However, in France Whirlpool is an extremely difficult name to pronounce.
* Secondly, even if the consumer can pronounce a name, the next question would focus on any other meanings or associations

the name might have in different countries. For example, in the USA Fairy Liquid faces the problem of sexual associations in American slang, while Big Macs (from McDonald's) is Canadian slang for big breasts.

- Thirdly, if these issues do not raise problems, the next problem is whether the brand name is available for use on an international basis and whether it can be protected. A major cosmetics house had to reschedule the launch of one of its brands since the legal aspects of the pan-European brand name search revealed that the original name was already being used by a distant competitor in one part of Europe.

Whilst the approach described above has the strength of checking the name against a set of criteria, its weakness is that its tactical orientation doesn't relate the brand name to the wider company objectives that the brand is attempting to satisfy. A better way of developing the brand's name would be to follow the flow chart in Figure 3.9.

Figure 3.9   *Schema to identify most appropriate brand name*

What little has been published about the way firms select brand names shows that few follow a systematic process. The schema developed in Figure 3.9 builds on best current practice.

Let us now consider each of these steps in turn.

Marketing objectives

The marketer needs to be certain about the marketing objectives that the brand must contribute towards. Clearly stated, quantified targets must be available for each segment showing the level of sales expected from each of the product groups comprising the company's portfolio. The marketing objectives will give an indication as to whether emphasis is being placed on gaining sales from existing products to existing customers, or whether new horizons are envisaged

clearly stated, quantified targets must be available for each segment

(e.g. through either product extensions or new customer groups). By having clearly defined marketing objectives, brand managers are then able to consider how each of their brands needs to contribute towards satisfying the overall marketing objectives.

The brand audit

The internal and external forces that influence the brand need to be identified, such as company resources, competitive intensity, supplier power, threats from substitutes, buyer concentration, economic conditions, and so on. This audit should help identify a few of the criteria that the name must satisfy. For example, if the brand audit showed that the firm has a superior battery that consumers valued because of the battery's long life, then one issue the name would have to satisfy would be its reinforcement of the critical success factor 'battery long life'.

Brand objectives

In the brand planning document, clear statements about individual brand objectives should be made, again helping clarify the criteria that the brand name must satisfy. Statements about anticipated levels of sales, through different distributors, to specified customers, will help the marketer to identify criteria for the name to meet. For example, if the primary market for a new brand of rechargeable batteries is 10–14 year old boys who are radio-controlled car racing enthusiasts, and if the secondary market is fathers who help their sons, the primary target's need may be for long inter-charge periods, whilst the secondary market may be more concerned about purchase costs. The primary need for the brand name would be to communicate power delivery, with an undertone about cost.

Other brand objective statements about positioning and brand personality would further clarify some of the criteria that the name must satisfy.

Brand strategy alternatives

The marketer must be clear about what broad strategies are envisaged for the brand in order to satisfy the brand objectives. Issues here would include:

- manufacturer's brand or distributor's brand?
- specialist or niche brand?
- value-added or low-price positioning?

Again, these would clarify issues that the name must satisfy.

Brand name criteria specified

From the previous sections, the marketer should be able to list the criteria that the brand name must satisfy. They might also wish to learn from other companies' experiences what appears to work best with brand names. This issue will be addressed in the next section of this chapter.

Brand name alternatives generated

With a clear brief about the challenges that the new brand name must overcome, the marketer can now work with others to stimulate ideas for possible brand names. It is unlikely that the brand managers would work on this alone. Instead, they would be joined by others from the marketing department, by advertising agency staff, by specialist name-generating agencies where appropriate, and by other company employees. Also at this stage a market research agency may be commissioned to undertake some qualitative research to help generate names. Some of the methods that might be used to generate names would be:

- brainstorming;
- group discussions;
- management inspiration;
- word association;
- in-company competitions amongst employees;
- computer-generated names.

during the name generation stage, any intentions to judge the names must be suppressed

It is important to stress that, during the name generation stage, any intentions to judge the names must be suppressed. If names are evaluated as they are generated, this impedes the mind's creative mode and results in a much lower number of names.

Screen and select the brand name

By scoring each name against the criteria for brand name effectiveness, an objective method for judging each option can be employed. Each name can be scored in terms of how well it matches each of the criteria and, by aggregating each name's score, a value order will result. The more sophisticated marketer can weight each of the criteria in terms of importance, and arrive at a rank order on the basis of the highest aggregated weighted score. Whatever numerical assessment procedure is employed, it should be developed only on the basis of an agreed internal consensus and after discussions with key decision makers. Not only does this enhance commitment to the finally selected brand name, but it also draws on the relevant experience of many executives.

By following this schema, the marketer is able to select a name which should satisfy the company's ambitions for long-term profitable brand growth. This process should also result in a name which is well able not only to defend a sustainable position against competitive forces, but also to communicate added values to consumers effectively. For example, the international courier service 'TNT Overnite' and the pesticide 'Kill'.

Issues associated with effective brand names

When considering criteria for brand name effectiveness, there is much to be gained by drawing on the experience of other marketers as discussed in the literature on branding. Some of the guidelines to be found there include:

- *The brand name should be simple* The aim should be to have short names that are easy to read and understand. Consumers have finite mental capacities and find it easier to encode short words in memory. This is the reason why names with four syllables or more are usually contracted. Listening to consumers talk clarifies the way that long brand names are simplified (e.g. Pepsi rather than Pepsi Cola, Lewis's rather than John Lewis). When consumers get emotionally closer to brands, they are more likely to contract the name, for example, Mercedes becomes Merc.
- *The brand name should be distinctive* Brand names such as Kodak and Adidas create a presence through the distinctive sound of the letters and the novelty of the word. This creates attention and the resulting curiosity motivates potential consumers to be more attentive to brand attributes.
- *The brand name should be meaningful* Names that communicate consumer benefits facilitate consumers' interpretations of brands. For example, Xpelair, Tipp-Ex and Lean Cuisine leave little doubt about the benefits to be gained from these brands. Creativity should be encouraged at the expense of being too correct. A battery branded 'Reliable' would communicate its capability, but would not attract as much attention as the more interesting 'Die Hard'. The brand name should also support the positioning objectives for the brand, e.g. Crown Paints.
- *The brand name should be compatible with the product* The appropriateness of the name Timex with watches is more than apparent, reinforcing the meaningfulness of the brand name. However, marketers should beware of becoming too focused

on specific benefits of the product, especially in a mature market. Orange offered a dramatic and refreshing alternative in a sector where the tradition of brand naming was built on the suffixes 'tel' and 'com', such as Betacom, Vodacom and Cabletel.

- *Emotion helps for certain products*   For those product fields where consumers seek brands primarily because they say something about the purchaser, as for example in the perfume market, emotional names can succeed. Examples here include Poison and Opium.

- *The brand name should be legally protectable*   To help protect the brand against imitators, a search should be undertaken to identify whether the brand name is available and, if so, whether it is capable of being legally registered.

- *Beware of creating new words*   Marketers developing new words for their brand have to anticipate significant promotional budgets to clarify what their invented word means. For example, the successfully invented names of Kodak, Esso and Xerox succeeded because of significant communication resources.

- *Extend any stored-up equity*   When firms audit their portfolio of current and historical brands, they may find there is still considerable goodwill in the market place associated with brands they no longer produce. There may be instances when it is worth extending a historical name to a new line (e.g. Mars to ice cream and milk drink), or even relaunching several historical lines (e.g. Cadbury's Classic Collection of Old Jamaica, Turkish Delight, etc.).

- *Avoid excessive use of initials*   Over time some brand names have been shortened, either as a deliberate policy by the firm, or through consumer terminology (e.g. International Business Machines to IBM, Imperial Chemicals Industries to ICI and British Airways to BA). It takes time for the initials to become associated with brand attributes and firms generally should not launch new brands as arrays of initials. The hypothetical brand North London Tool and Die Company certainly fails the criteria of being short, but at least, unlike the initials NLT&D it does succeed in communicating its capabilities.

- *Develop names that allow flexibility*   The hope of any marketer is for brand success and eventually a widening portfolio of supporting brands to better satisfy the target market. Over time more experienced consumers seek a widening array of benefits so, if possible, the name should allow the brand to adapt to changing market needs. For example, with the recognition of the reliability of Caterpillar Tractors, the company wished to diversify further into the earthmoving equipment market, but the word 'Tractor' blocked diversification. By dropping this word, Caterpillar was better able to diversify.

- *Develop names which are internationally valid*   It is essential to establish during the naming process what geographical coverage the brand will assume. When a name is intended for only one nation or one culture, the cultural associations linked to it are immediately evident. Whenever the brand name spans different languages and cultures, it becomes more difficult to forecast customers' responses. For instance, the Spanish coffee Bonka has different implications in the UK market from those intended in Spain.

Whilst these points should contribute to the way organizations think about the appropriateness of different brand names, we should never lose sight of the fact that it is consumers who buy brands, not the managers who manage them. For this reason it is always wise, when short-listing potential names, to undertake some consumer research and evaluate consumers' responses. For example – are the words harsh sounding? Are there any negative associations with the words? Are the names appropriate for the proposed brand? Do the words 'roll off the tongue' easily? Are the words memorable? – and so on.

Once a decision has been taken about the brand name and the brand has been launched, the firm should audit the name on a regular basis. This will show whether or not the meaning of the brand name has changed over time as a result in changes in the market place. If the environment has changed to such an extent that the firm is missing opportunities by persisting with the original name, then consideration should be given to changing the name. For example, Mars saw economies of scale with a unified pan-European brand name strategy and changed the name Marathon to Snickers in order to capitalize on this.

should audit the name on a regular basis

The brand as a risk reducer

The final issue of relevance to branding to be considered in this chapter is the concept of perceived risk. Earlier parts of this chapter showed that products and services can be conceived as arrays of clues and that the most-consulted clue when making a brand choice is the presence or absence of a brand name. This reliance upon brand name is also confirmed by the considerable volume of consumer behaviour research on the concept of perceived risk. It is clear that, when buying, consumers develop risk-reducing strategies. These are geared to either reducing the uncertainty in a purchase by buying, for example, only advertised brands, or to minimizing the chances of an unpleasant outcome by buying, for example, only previously tried brands. This concept also affects the way organizations buy brands and is also addressed in Chapter 5.

It must be stressed that we are talking only about consumers' **perceptions** of risk, rather than **objective** risk, since consumers react only as they perceive situations. Whilst marketers may believe they have developed a brand that is presented as a risk-free purchase, this may not necessarily be the perception consumers have. Consumers have a threshold level for perceived risk, below which they do not regard it as worthwhile undertaking any risk-reduction action. However, once this threshold level is exceeded, they will seek ways of reducing perceived risk.

We can now start to view brands as being so well formulated, distributed and promoted that they provide consumers with the added value of increased confidence. For example, if the brand is available from a quality retailer, this should signal increased certainty regarding its performance. If there has been a lot of supporting advertising this would also be read as being indicative of a low-risk product. Furthermore, should there also be favourable word-of-mouth endorsement, this too would allay concerns about the brand. Marketers can gain a competitive edge by promoting their brands as low-risk purchases.

By viewing risk as being concerned with the *uncertainty* felt by consumers about the *outcome* of a purchase, it is possible to appreciate how marketers can reduce consumers' risk in brand buying. For example, appropriate strategies to reduce consumers worries about the *consequences* of the brand purchase would include developing highly respected warranties, offering money back guarantees for first time trialists and small pack sizes during the brand's introductory period. To reduce their *uncertainty*, consumers will take a variety of actions, such as seeking out further information, staying with regularly used brands, or buying only well-known brands. Marketers can reduce concerns about uncertainty by providing consumers with relevant, high quality information, by encouraging independent parties such as specialist magazine editors to assess the brand, and by ensuring that opinion leaders are well versed in the brand's potential. For example, by tracking purchasers of a newly launched microwave oven brand, using returned guarantee cards, home economists can call on these innovative trialists and, by giving a personalized demonstration of the new brand's capabilities, ensure that they are fully conversant with the brand's advantages. This can be particularly effective, since early innovators are regarded as a credible information source.

risk as being concerned with the uncertainty felt by consumers about the outcome of a purchase

The favoured routes to reduce risk vary by type of product or service and it is unusual for only one risk-reducing strategy to be followed. It is, however, apparent that brand loyalty and reliance on major brand image are two of the more frequently followed actions.

When consumers evaluate competing brands, not only do they have an overall view about how risky the brand purchase is, but they also form a judgement about *why* the brand is a risky purchase. This is done initially by evaluating which dimensions of perceived risk cause them the most concern. There are several dimensions of risk. For example:

- *financial risk*: the risk of money being lost when buying an unfamiliar brand;
- *performance risk*: the risk of something being wrong with the unfamiliar brand;
- *social risk*: the risk that the unfamiliar brand might not meet the approval of a respected peer group;
- *psychological risk*: the risk that an unfamiliar brand might not fit in well with one's self image;
- *time risk*: the risk of having to waste further time replacing the brand.

If the marketer is able to identify which dimensions of perceived risk are causing concern, they should be able to develop appropriate consumer-orientated risk-reduction strategies. The need for such strategies can be evaluated by examining consumers' perceptions of risk levels and by gauging whether this is below their threshold level. It should be realized, however, that the level of risk varies between people and also by product category. For example, cars, insurance and hi-fi are generally perceived as being high-risk purchases, while toiletries and packaged groceries are low-risk purchases.

Table 3.3 shows the results of a seminal consumer study by Jacoby and Kaplan (1972) indicating how some of the dimensions of perceived risk vary by product field. From these findings, it can be seen that marketers of life insurance policies need to put more emphasis on stressing the relative cost of policies and how well-protected consumers are compared with other competitors' policies. By contrast, the suit marketer should place more emphasis on reference group endorsement of their brand of suit by means, for example, of a photograph of an appropriate person in this suit.

some of the dimensions of perceived risk vary by product field

Table 3.3 *Consumers' views about the dimensions of risk (after Jacoby and Kaplan 1972)*

	Life Insurance	Suit
Financial risk	7.2	6.4
Performance risk	6.7	5.8
Psychological risk	4.9	6.9
Social risk	4.8	7.3
Overall risk	7.0	5.9

1 = very low risk, 10 = very high risk

Conclusions

By adopting an information processing model of consumer behaviour, this chapter has considered how a knowledge of consumers' buying processes can help to develop successful brands. Through an appreciation of the differences consumers perceive between competing brands and their involvement in the brand buying process, we identified different consumer buying processes. According to the type of buying process, so an active or passive approach to brand information acquisition may be followed. If the consumer actively seeks information, it was shown that this would be for only a few key pieces of information regarded as highly indicative of the brand's capabilities.

Consumers choose brands to reflect their needs in a particular context. Market research can help identify, for a particular category, a consumer's differing need-states and thereby aid marketers to blend their brand more closely with a specific need-state. As a consequence, consumers have a repertoire of brands in a specific category and switching behaviour reflects, to some extent, different need-states. Differential marketing builds on the concept of brand repertoires, encouraging marketers to target small groups of highly profitable consumers with special programmes.

When evaluating competing brands, consumers are concerned with appreciating the extent to which the brands have added values over and above the commodity form of the brand. These added values may be as simple as polite service from a bank clerk, through to a complex cluster of lifestyle associations by driving a particular car marque.

One added value often overlooked by marketers is labelling which displays only a few pieces of information, facilitating brand choice. Consumers have finite mental capabilities and seek to process a few, high quality pieces of information as quickly as possible. They often use surrogate clues, such as price, to evaluate brands and place considerable reliance on the presence or absence of brand names.

The problem facing the marketer, however, is that consumers are selective in their search for brand information and they twist some of the information to make it fit their prior beliefs. Brand promotional activity must, therefore, be regularly audited to evaluate the extent to which consumers correctly interpret the message.

To encourage consumer appreciation of the brand's true capabilities, the right type of brand name is needed. In certain circumstances there are strengths in having a brand name tied to the corporation, but in others unique brand names are more appropriate. Brand name selection should not be based on tactical issues, but rather on a more robust, strategic basis which relates the potential name to marketing objectives and other forces influencing the brand.

Finally, marketers should appreciate that consumers perceive risk when buying brands. Through appreciating the extent of perceived risk and the factors causing consumer concern, they can develop strategies geared to reducing this perceived risk.

Marketing action checklist

To help clarify the direction of future brand marketing activity, it is recommended that the following exercises are undertaken.

1   Write down how involved you believe the consumer is when buying a brand in the product field where you have a presence. From the consumer's perspective, evaluate whether competing brands in this product field are strongly or weakly differentiated, stating what the differentiating features are. Then, consulting Figure 3.1, identify the consumer decision process reflecting brand buying behaviour. Ask other colleagues to undertake this exercise individually. If there is a lack of consensus about the level of involvement of consumers, the degree of brand differentiation, or the basis for brand differentiation, your department may be basing its brand communication programme on erroneous assumptions about consumer behaviour. This can be resolved by undertaking qualitative research amongst target consumers to assess dimensions they use to differentiate between brands and the basis for their involvement in the purchase. This should then be followed by a survey to quantify the extent of consumers' involvement and their perceptions of brand differences. On the basis of such market research, the consumer's decision process can be evaluated and by referring to the early parts of this chapter, the appropriateness of the current brand communication strategy can be assessed.
2   When was any market research last undertaken to assess consumers' involvement and their perceptions of brand differences? If this information is more than a year old, consider whether the dynamic nature of your market necessitates a further update.
3   At what stages in the consumer's buying process is any brand information currently being directed? On the basis of the model of the buying process identified in the earlier exercises, when do consumers seek information? Are there any discrepancies?
4   Get your colleagues to write down what stages they believe consumers pass through in the buying process for one of your

brands. Ask someone who does not work in the marketing or sales department (and ideally who is new to the firm) to narrate the stages they went through when buying this particular brand. In an open forum, resolve any differences between what managers' perceptions are and the reality of consumer buying activity.

5   Have you any information about the factors which encourage or discourage consumers to seek more information about your brand (e.g. role of family, previous experience, etc.)? How are you addressing each of these factors in your brand activity?

6   How much do you know about consumers' perceptions of your brands (and, if appropriate, about perceptions of your company)? Are there any differences between the brand communications objectives agreed internally (and specified to your promotions agency) and the way consumers interpret your brands?

7   How do you help consumers evaluate your brand very shortly after it has been purchased for the first time? How well-equipped are retailers to resolve consumers' doubts about the brand?

8   Has any consumer research been undertaken to evaluate the key attributes that consumers use to make a brand selection? What attributes did your last promotional campaign major on? Did these attributes match the findings from the previous research?

9   What are the added values that distinguish your brand from competitors? How relevant are these to consumers? How are *all* elements of the marketing mix being used to achieve these added values? Is there any inconsistency between the elements of the marketing mix?

10   Show several consumers a pack or brochure describing your brand, along with similar material from your competitors. Do not allow them to spend long looking at these examples. Observe how they examine the material. Remove the examples and ask what they recalled and why they recalled this. Discuss the results with your colleagues and consider which aspects of your pack/brochure are critical to the consumer and which parts clutter the central message. What informational clues were consumers using to draw inferences about the capabilities of the product or service? How much marketing attention is being focused on these informational clues?

11   List the brands against which your brand competes. Now categorize these brands into groups that show some form of similarity, starting the basis for brand groupings. Ask colleagues to do this exercise individually and collate the forms. In an open

forum, discuss any differences. Commission a survey to evaluate which brands consumers see as competing in a particular product field, how they would group these brands and what their basis for categorization was. If there is not agreement between consumers' categorization of brands and yours, you may well need to reconsider your brand strategy.

12   What are the strengths and weaknesses of your brand's name? How able is the name to cope with future opportunities and yet overcome any threats? State the criteria that your experience has shown are essential for a brand name to satisfy and critically evaluate your brand name against this.

13   List the aspects of risk that consumers perceive when buying your brand and your competitors' brands. In what order of perceived risk do consumers rank these brands? What actions can you take to reduce consumers' perceptions of risk when buying your brand?

14   How do you ensure that your most profitable customers choose your brand consistently? Have you established special retention programmes tailored to their needs? What tracking is being undertaken to understand why people are defecting from your brand?

15   Consider your marketing budget. Is it spread evenly across all your customers or does it give greater emphasis to the customers that buy the brand more frequently and provide higher levels of profits?

References and further reading

Allison R. I. and Uhl K. P. (1964). Influence of beer brand identification on taste perception. *Journal of Marketing Research*, **1** (3), 36–9.

Assael H. (1987). *Consumer Behavior and Marketing Action*. Boston: Kent Publishing.

Bauer R. A. (1960). Consumer behavior as risk taking. In *Dynamic Marketing for a Changing World. 43rd Conference of the American Marketing Association* (Hancock R. S., ed.). Chicago: American Marketing Association. 389–98.

Beales H., Maziz M., Salop S. and Staelin R. (1981). Consumer search and public policy. *Journal of Consumer Research*, **8** (June), 11–22.

Bennett P. and Mandell R. (1969). Prepurchase information seeking behaviour of new car purchasers: the learning hypothesis. *Journal of Marketing Research*, **6** (4), 430–3.

Bettman J. R. (1979). *An Information Processing Theory of Consumer Choice*. Reading, Massachusetts: Addison Wesley.

Bettman J. R. and Kakkar P. (1977). Effects of information presentation format on consumer information acquisition strategies. *Journal of Consumer Research*, **3** (March), 233–40.

Bettman J. R. and Park C. W. (1980). Effects of prior knowledge and experience and phase of the choice process on consumer decision processes: a protocol analysis. *Journal of Consumer Research*, **7** (Dec), 234–48.

Biehal G. and Chakravarti D. (1982). Information-presentation format and learning goals as determinants of consumers' memory retrieval and choice processes. *Journal of Consumer Research*, **8** (March), 431–41.

Britt S. H., Adams S. C. and Miller A. S. (1972). How many advertising exposures per day? *Journal of Advertising Research*, **12** (Dec), 3–10.

Britt S. H. (1975). How Weber's law can be applied to marketing. *Business Horizons*, **13** (Feb), 21–29.

Bruner J. S. (1957). On perceptual readiness. *Psychological Review*, **64** (2), 123–52.

Bruner J. S. (1958). Social psychology and perception. In 1970 edition of: *Research in Consumer Behavior* (Kollat D.T., Blackwell R. D. and Engel J. F., eds). New York: Holt, Rinehart and Winston.

Bucklin L. P. (1969). Consumer search, role enactment and market efficiency. *Journal of Business*, **42**, 416–38.

Buschke H. (1976). Learning is organised by chunking. *Journal of Verbal Learning and Verbal Behaviour*, **15**, 313–24.

Capon N. and Burke M. (1980). Individual, product class and task-related factors in consumer information processing. *Journal of Consumer Research*, **7** (Dec.), 314–26.

Chisnall P. M. (1985). *Marketing: A Behavioural Analysis*. London: McGraw Hill.

Claxton J. D., Fry J. N. and Portis B. (1974). A taxonomy of prepurchase information gathering patterns. *Journal of Consumer Research*, **1** (Dec.), 35–42.

Cox D. F. (1967). The sorting rule model of the consumer product evaluation process. In *Risk Taking and Information Handling in Consumer Behavior* (Cox D. F., ed.). Boston: Harvard University.

Derbaix C. (1983). Perceived risk and risk relievers: an empirical investigation. *Journal of Economic Psychology*, **3** (March), 19–38.

Ehrenberg A. S. C. (1988). *Repeat Buying: Facts, Theories and Application*. London: Griffin.

Ehrenberg A. S. C. (1993). If you're so strong, why aren't you bigger? *ADMAP*, (Oct.), 13–14.

Ehrenberg A. S. C., Goodhardt, G. J. and Barwise, T. P. (1990). Double jeopardy revisited. *Journal of Marketing*, **54**, 82–91.

Engel J. F. and Blackwell R. D. (1982). *Consumer Behaviour*. Chicago: The Dryden Press.

Gardner D. M. (1971). Is there a generalised price-quality relationship? *Journal of Marketing Research*, **8** (2), 241–3.

Gemunden H. G. (1985). Perceived risk and information search. A systematic meta-analysis of the empirical evidence. *International Journal of Research in Marketing*, **2** (2), 79–100.

Gordon W. (1994). Taking brand repertoires seriously. *Journal of Brand Management*, 2 (1), 25–30.

Haines G. H. (1974). Process models of consumer decision making. In *Buyer/Consumer Information Processing* (Hughes G. D. and Ray M. L., eds). Chapel Hill: University of North Carolina Press.

Hallberg G. (1995). *All Consumers are not Created Equal*. New York: John Wiley & Sons.

Hansen F. (1972). *Consumer Choice Behavior. A Cognitive Theory*. New York: The Free Press.

Hastorf A. H. and Cantril H. (1954). They saw a game: a case history. *Journal of Abnormal and Social Psychology*, **49**, 129–34.

Jacoby J. and Kaplan L. (1972). The components of perceived risk. In *Third Annual Conference, Association for Consumer Research. Proceedings*. (Venkatesan M., ed). University of Chicago. 382–93.

Jacoby J., Chestnut R. W. and Fisher W. A. (1978). A behavioural process approach to information acquisition in nondurable purchasing. *Journal of Marketing Research*, **15** (3), 532–44.

Jacoby J., Speller D. E. and Kohn C. A. (1974). Brand choice behavior as a function of information load. *Journal of Marketing Research*, **11** (1), 63–9.

Jacoby J., Szybillo G. J. and Busato-Schach J. (1977). Information acquisition behavior in brand choice situations. *Journal of Consumer Research*, **3** (March), 209–16.

Jones J. P. (1986) *What's in a name? Advertising and the Concept of Brands*. Lexington: Lexington Books.

Kapferer J.-N. and Laurent G. (1986). Consumer involvement profiles: a new practical approach to consumer involvement. *Journal of Advertising Research*, **25** (6), 48–56.

Katona G. and Mueller E. (1955). A study of purchasing decisions. In *Consumer Behavior. The Dynamics of Consumer Reaction* (Clark L. H., ed.). New York: New York University Press.

Kendall K. W. and Fenwick I. (1979). What do you learn standing in a supermarket aisle? In *Advances in Consumer Research*, Vol. 6 (Wilkie W. L., ed.). Ann Arbor: Association for Consumer Research, 153–60.

Kiel G. C. and Layton R. A. (1981). Dimensions of consumer information seeking behavior. *Journal of Marketing Research*, **18** (2), 233–9.

Krugman H. E. (1975). What makes advertising effective? *Harvard Business Review*, **53** (March–April), 96–103.

Krugman H. E. (1977). Memory without recall, exposure without perception. *Journal of Advertising Research*, **17** (4), 7–12.

Lannon J. and Cooper P. (1983). Humanistic advertising: a holistic cultural perspective. *International Journal of Advertising*, **2**, 195–213.

McNeal J. and Zeren L. (1981). Brand name selection for consumer products. *Michigan State University Business Topics*, **29** (2), 35–9.

Midgley D. F. (1983). Patterns of interpersonal information seeking for the purchase of a symbolic product. *Journal of Marketing Research*, **20** (1), 74–83.

Miller G. A. (1956). The magical number seven, plus or minus two: some limits on our capacity for processing information. *The Psychological Review*, **63** (2), 81–97.

Neisser V. (1976). *Cognition and Reality*. San Francisco: W. H. Freeman and Company.

Newman J.W. (1977). Consumer external search: amounts and determinants. In *Consumer and Industrial Buying Behavior* (Woodside A. G., Sheth J. N. and Bennett P. D., eds.). Amsterdam: North Holland Publishing Company.

Newman J. W. and Staelin R. (1973). Information sources of durable goods. *Journal of Advertising Research*, **13** (2), 19–29.

Olshavsky R. W. and Granbois D. H. (1979). Consumer decision making – fact or fiction? *Journal of Consumer Research*, **6**, (Sept.), 93–100.

Park C., Jaworski B. and MacInnis D. (1986). Strategic brand concept-image management. *Journal of Marketing*, **50** (Oct.), 135–45.

Ray M. L. (1973). Marketing communication and the hierarchy of effects. In *New models for Communication Research* (Clarke P., ed.). Beverley Hills: Sage.

Reed S. K. (1972). Pattern recognition and categorisation. *Cognitive Psychology*, **3** (3), 382–407.

Render B. and O'Connor T. S. (1976). The influence of price, store name and brand name on perception of product quality. *Journal of the Academy of Marketing Science*, **4** (4), 722–30.

Rigaux-Bricmont B. (1981). Influences of brand name and packaging on perceived quality. In *Advances in Consumer Research*. Vol. 9 (Mitchell A., ed.). Chicago: Association for Consumer Research.

Robertson K. (1989). Strategically desirable brand name characteristics. *Journal of Consumer Marketing*, **6** (4), 61–71.

Rock I. (1975). *An Introduction to Perception*. New York: Macmillan.

Roselius T. (1971). Consumer rankings of risk reduction methods. *Journal of Marketing*, **35** (1), 56–61.

Ruffell B. (1996). The genetics of brandnaming. *Journal of Brand Management*, 4 (2), 108–15.

Russo J. E., Staelin R., Nolan C. A., Russell G. J. and Metcalf B. L. (1986). Nutrition information in the supermarket. *Journal of Consumer Research*, **13** (June), 48–70.

Schwartz M. L., Jolson M. A. and Lee R. H. (1986). The marketing of funeral services: past, present and future. *Business Horizons*, (March–April), 40–5.

Shipley D., Hooley G. and Wallace S. (1988). The brand name development process. *International Journal of Advertising*, **7** (3), 253–66.

Venkatesan M. (1973). Cognitive consistency and novelty seeking. In *Consumer Behavior: Theoretical Sources* (Ward S. and Robertson T. S., eds). Englewood Cliffs, N.J.: Prentice Hall.

Which? (1995). Look-alikes. (March), 30–1.

Zajonc R. B. (1968). Cognitive theories in social psychology. In *The Handbook of Social Psychology*. Vol. 1 (Lindzey G. and Aronson E., eds). Reading, Massachusetts: Addison Wesley.

Chapter 4

How consumer brands satisfy social and psychological needs

Summary

The purpose of this chapter is to consider the social and psychological roles played by brands. When consumers buy brands they are not just concerned with their functional capabilities. They are also interested in the brand's personality, which they may consider appropriate for certain situations. They look to brands to enable them to communicate something about themselves and also to understand the people around them better.

The chapter focuses on consumer rather than organizational brands, reflecting the greater emphasis placed on brand personality and symbolism in consumer marketing. This does not necessarily mean they are inappropriate in business to business markets, rather that they are not as frequently employed.

We open this chapter by considering the added values from the images surrounding brands. We then address the symbolic role played by brands, where less emphasis is placed on what brands *do* for consumers and more on what they *mean* for consumers. Different symbolic roles for brands are identified, along with a consideration of the criteria necessary for brands to be effective communication devices. We draw on self-concept theory to explain how consumers seek brands with images that match their own self-image. A model of the way consumers select brands is presented, which shows how consumers choose brands to project images appropriate for different situations. We then examine how personal values influence brand selection and show the importance of brand personification as a means enabling consumers to judge brands easily. Different brand personalities give rise to different types of relationships and we explore these relationships. Finally, we review the way that semiotics, the scientific study of signs, can contribute to brand effectiveness.

Added values beyond functionalism

surrounding the intrinsic physical product with an aura, or personality, gives consumers far greater confidence in using well-known brands

Brands succeed because they represent more than just utilitarian benefits. The physical constituents of the product or service are augmented through creative marketing to give added values that satisfy social and psychological needs. Surrounding the intrinsic physical product with an aura, or personality, gives consumers far greater confidence in using well-known brands. Evidence of this is shown by one study which investigated the role that branding played in drugs sold in retail stores. People suffering from headaches were given an analgesic. Some were given the drug in its well-known branded form, the rest had the same drug in its generic form, lacking any branding. The branded analgesic was more effective than the generic analgesic and it was calculated that just over a quarter of the pain relief was attributed to branding. What had happened was that branding had added an image of serenity around the pharmacological ingredients and, in the consumers' minds, had made the medication more effective than the unbranded tablets.

The images surrounding brands enable consumers to form a mental vision of what and who brands stand for. Specific brands are selected when the images they convey match the needs, values and lifestyles of consumers. For example, at a physical level, drinkers recognize Guinness as a rich, creamy, dark, bitter drink. The advertising has surrounded the stout with a personality which is symbolic of nourishing value and myths of power and energy. The brand represents manliness, mature experience and wit. Consequently, when drinkers are choosing between a glass of draught Guinness or Murphys, they are subconsciously making an assessment of the appropriateness of the personality of these two brands for the situation in which they will consume it, be it amongst colleagues at lunch or amongst friends in the evening.

Brands are an integral part of our society and each day we have endless encounters with brands. Just think of the first hour after waking up and consider how many brands you come across. From seeing the brands used, people are able to understand each other better and help clarify who they are. The young manager going to the office in the morning is proud to wear his Armani suit as he feels it makes a statement about his status, but in the evening with his friends he wants to make a different statement and wears his Levi jeans and Polo casual shirt. Powerful brands make strong image statements and consumers choose them not just because of their quality, but because of the images they project. A study by the advertising agency BBDO found that consumers are more likely to find differences between competing brands where emotional appeals are used, such as for beers, than between those predominately relying on rational appeals. Functional differences between brands are narrowing due to technological advances, but the emotional differences are more sustainable. Having a functional advantage, such as a particular car design, may be a competitive advantage today, but over time it becomes dated. By contrast, when associating a brand with particular values, such as being honest and dependable, these values have a greater chance of lasting as they are more personally meaningful and thus help ensure the longevity of the brand.

Particularly for conspicuously consumed brands, such as those in the beer and car market, firms can succeed by positioning their brands to satisfy consumers' emotional needs. Consumers assess the meanings of different brands and make a purchase decision according to whether the brand will say the right sort of things about them to their peer group and whether the brand reflects back into themselves the right sort of personal feeling. For example, a young man choosing between brands of suits may well consider whether the brands reflect externally that he is a trendsetter and reflect back into himself that he is confident in his distinctiveness. In other words, there is a sort of dialogue between consumers and brands. In the main, consumers do not just base their choice on rational grounds, such as perceptions of functional capabilities, beliefs about value for money or availability. Instead, they recognize that to make sense of the social circles they move in and to add meaning to their own existence, they look at what different brands symbolize. They question how well a particular brand might fit in with their lifestyle, whether it helps them express their personality and whether they like the brand and would feel right using it.

Brands are part of the culture of a society and as the culture changes so they need to be updated. For example, the Oxo brand has been portrayed in television advertisements over the past thirty years by the personality Katie. In the 1960s she epitomised the home-centred housewife devoted solely to the well-being of her family. With the changing role of women in society, the brand has had to move with the times. Today, Katie stands for the busy woman with a full-time job as well as a growing family to take care of. In both of these roles she is shown as a successful person who conveys a no-nonsense, warm, modern personality. Oxo's brand image has been updated to match the lifestyle of the modern consumer and its continuing success is partly due to this.

Brands and symbolism

consumers are increasingly evaluating products in terms of what they mean

A criticism often voiced is that many models of consumer behaviour do not pay sufficient attention to the social meanings people perceive in different products. A lot of emphasis has historically been placed on the functional utility of products, and less consideration given to the way that some people buy products for good feelings, fun and, in the case of art and entertainment, even for fantasies. Today, however, consumer research and marketing activity is changing to reflect the fact that consumers are increasingly evaluating products not just in terms of what they can *do*, but also in terms of what they *mean*. The subject of symbolic interactionism has evolved to explain the type of behaviour whereby consumers show more interest in brands for what they say about them rather than what they do for them. As consumers interact with other members of society, they learn through the responses of other people the symbolic meanings of products and brands. Their buying, giving and consuming of brands facilitates communication between people. For example, blue jeans symbolize informality and youth. Advertising and other types of marketing communication help give symbolic meanings to brands, the classic example of this being the advertising behind Levi jeans.

The symbolic meaning of brands is strongly influenced by the people with whom the consumer interacts (as Plate 7 shows). A new member of a social group may have formed ideas about the symbolic meaning of a brand from advertisements, but if such a person hears contrary views from their friends about the brand, they will be notably influenced by their views. To be part of a social group, the person doesn't just need to adhere to the group's attitudes and beliefs, but also to reflect these attitudes and beliefs through displaying the right sorts of brands.

To facilitate understanding of the symbolic meaning of brands, design and visual representations are important in conveying meanings, especially in the service sector where no tangible product is available. For instance, the visual representation of Merrill Lynch's bull is used to suggest strength and optimism. Visual representations also have the advantage of avoiding the logical examinations to which verbal expressions are subjected and are therefore more

Your car says a lot about you, you great big hunky stud.

Drive a Ferrari? You're sporty and rich. A Rolls-Royce? Successful and dignified. The Daihatsu Hijet MPV? Infallible in the sack. Think about it. Why else would a man need a car that carries a family of six? And in some comfort we might add, with two sunroofs, four reclining seats, five doors (two sliding), a frugal 1 litre engine, even a five-speed gearbox, all for just £9,000 on the road. And that includes a three year or 60,000 mileage warranty. (Probably the only precaution you'll ever take.) For more information call 0800 521 700. **THE SIX SEAT HIJET MPV.**

DAIHATSU

▷ **NO-NONSENSE VEHICLES.**

For more information on the Daihatsu Hijet MPV call free on 0800 521 700, or send this coupon to Daihatsu Information Services, FREEPOST 506, Sandwich, Kent CT13 9BR.

NAME .... ADDRESS .... RT327 MPV

POSTCODE .... TEL .... TICK IF UNDER 18 ☐ CURRENT VEHICLE .... MODEL .... YEAR ....

PRICE CORRECT AT TIME OF GOING TO PRESS INCLUDES VAT, DELIVERY, NUMBER PLATES AND 12 MONTHS ROAD FUND LICENCE. EACH VEHICLE OF THIS MODEL IS A PASSENGER CONVERSION OF A HIJET REGISTERED AS A COMMERCIAL VEHICLE

Exhibit 4.1 *A clear symbolic message is portrayed by the Daihatsu Hijet MPV (reproduced by kind premission of Daihatsu (UK) Ltd)*

likely to be accepted. Customers are less likely to challenge the symbolic freshness of Green Giant's vegetables than the verbal claim stating that canned vegetables are fresh.

Some brands have capitalized on the added value of symbolism, i.e. meanings and values over and above the functional element of the product or service, as in the case, for example, Häagen-Dazs. Symbolism is sought by people in all walks of life to help them better understand their environment. Different marques of cars succeed because they enable drivers to say something about who they are. We may buy different brands of ties, such as Yves Saint Laurent as opposed to Marks & Spencer, not just for their aesthetic design, but to enhance self-esteem.

Consumers perceive brands in very personal ways and attach their own values to them. Elliott's study (1994) of the trainers market shows that even though competing firms were striving to portray unique values for their brands, the symbolic interpretation of each brand varied according to people's age and gender. This challenges the assumption amongst marketers that the brand's symbolic meaning is the same amongst all the target market.

brands are invaluable in helping set the scene

To cope with the numerous social roles we play in life, brands are invaluable in helping set the scene for the people we are with. As such, they help individuals join new groups more easily. New members at a golf club interpret the social information inherent in the brands owned by others and then select the right brand to communicate symbolically the right sort of message about themselves. When playing golf, smart trousers may be seen to be necessary to communicate the social role, but to play with a particular group of people it may be important to have the right *brand* as well. The symbolic meaning of the brand is defined by the group of people using it and varies according to the different social settings.

Brands as symbols can act as efficient communication devices, enabling people to convey messages about themselves and to facilitate expressive gestures. Using the Jaguar Visacard, rather than the standard Visacard, enables the owner to say something about themselves to their friends when paying for a meal in a restaurant. Giving Black Magic chocolates for instance, says something about a sophisticated relationship between two people, while After Eight Mints imply an aspiration for a grand and gracious living style.

Advertising and packaging are also crucial in reinforcing the covert message that is signified by the brand. Charles Revlon of Revlon Inc succeeded because he realized that women were not only seeking the functional aspects of cosmetics, but also the seductive charm promised by the alluring symbols with which his brands have been surrounded. The rich and exotic packaging and the lifestyle advertising supporting perfume brands are crucial in communicating their inherent messages. On a similar basis, Marlboro used the symbol of the rugged cowboy to communicate the idea of the independent, self-confident, masculine image. Consumers of this brand are not only buying it for its physical characteristics, but also as a means of saying something about themselves.

Brands are also used by people as ritual devices to help celebrate a particular occasion. For example, Moët et Chandon champagne is often served to celebrate a wedding, a birthday, or some other special event, even though there are many less expensive champagnes available.

They are also effective devices for understanding other people better. The classic example of this was the slow market acceptance of Nescafé instant coffee in the USA. In interviews, American housewives said they disliked the brand because of its taste. Yet, blind product testing against the then widely-accepted drip ground coffee, showed no problems. To get to the heart of the matter, housewives were asked to describe the sort of person they thought would be using a particular shopping list. Two lists were given to the samples. Half saw the list of groceries including Nescafé instant coffee, and the other half saw the same list, but this time with Maxwell House drip ground coffee rather than Nescafé. The results of these interviews using the different coffee brands led respondents to infer two different personalities. The person who had the Nescafé grocery list was perceived as being lazy, while the drip ground person was often described as a 'good, thrifty housewife'. As a consequence of this research, the advertising for Nescafé was changed. The campaign featured a busy housewife who was able to devote more attention to her family because Nescafé had freed up time for her. This change in advertising helped Nescafé successfully establish their brand of instant coffee.

Brands are also effective devices for expressing something to ourselves symbolically. For example, amongst final year undergraduates there is a ritual mystique associated with choosing the right clothes for job interviews and spending longer on shaving or hair

Exhibit 4.2   PG Tips is positioned in this advertisement in terms of its functional capabilities, while Twinings adds an emotional dimension to its functional capabilities (reproduced by kind permission of Van den Bergh Foods)

grooming than normal. These activities are undertaken not only to conform to the interview situation, but also to give the person a boost to their self-confidence. In these situations, the consumer is looking for brands that will make them 'feel right'. A further example of this is in the specialist tea market, where Twinings advertised their teas using the theme 'Teas to match your mood'. The emphasis of brands

"You can't put too high a price on love. This summer, you don't have to."

Brighten someone's summer by sending them a Summer Pageant Bouquet of roses and carnations. Costing only £14.95, including VAT and local delivery, from any Interflora florist displaying the Summer Pageant banner. Standard relay orders cost just £2.85 extra; although in some cases extra charges may apply. Prices apply almost anywhere in the UK, Channel Islands and Republic of Ireland. Content and colour may also vary, depending on best available locally. Offer ends 30th September 1990. To order, visit or telephone your Interflora florist or, after shop hours, ring the Interflora Flowerline on 0529 304545.   **Interflora**   GUARANTEED TO GET TO HER

Exhibit 4.3 *Interflora's use of Mercury to reinforce the symbolic association between their flowers and swiftly delivered personal messages (reproduced by kind permission of Interflora (FTDA) British Unit Ltd and DMB&B)*

here is to help consumers communicate something to themselves.

So, consumers look to brands in highly conspicuous product fields as symbolic devices to communicate something about themselves or to better understand their peer groups. The symbolic interpretations of some brands are well accepted. For example, Interflora makes use of Mercury in their television and press advertisements to reinforce the symbolic assoication between their flowers and swiftly delivered personal messages. Not only are they building on the mythological associations of Mercury, but they are further reinforcing this by bringing the character to life in their commercials to reinforce associations with Interflora.

Consumers also strive to understand their environment better through decoding the symbolic messages surrounding them. A client working with an architect sees things like certificates on the architect's wall, the tastefully designed office, the quality of the paper on which a report is word-processed, the binding of the report and the list of clients the architect has worked for. All of these are decoded as messages implying a successful practice.

Symbols acquire their meaning in a cultural context, so the culture of the society consuming the brands needs to be appreciated to understand the encoding and decoding process. People learn the inherent meaning of different symbols and through regular contact with each other there is a consistent interpretation of them. To take a brand into a new culture may require subtle changes to ensure that the symbol acquires the right meaning in its new cultural context. For example, Red Cross becomes Red Crescent in the Middle East.

If a brand is to be used as a communication device, it must meet certain criteria. It must be highly visible when being bought or being used. It must be bought by a group of people who have clearly distinguishable characteristics, which in turn facilitates recognition of a particular stereotype. For example, *The Guardian* newspaper reader has been stereotyped as a well-educated person, possibly working in education or local government. In the newspaper market some readers select different brands as value-expressive devices. They provide a statement about who they are, where they are in life and what sort of person they are. Since brands can act as self-expressive devices, users prefer brands which come closest to meeting their own self-image. The concept of self-image is important in consumer branding and is reviewed in the next section.

the culture of the society consuming the brands needs to be appreciated

Self-concept and branding

In consumer research, it is argued that consumers' personalities can be inferred from the brands they use, from their attitudes towards different brands and from the meanings brands have for them. Consumers have a perception of themselves and they make brand decisions on the basis of whether owning or using a particular brand, which has a particular image, is consistent with their own self-image. They consider whether the ownership of certain brands communicates the right sort of image about themselves. Brands are only bought if they enhance the conception that consumers have of themselves, or if they believe the brand's image to be similar to that which they have of themselves. Just as people take care choosing friends who have a similar personality to themselves, so brands, which are symbolic of particular images, are chosen with the same concern. As brands serve as expressive devices, people therefore prefer brands whose image is closest to their own self-image.

This way of looking at personality in terms of a person's self-image can be traced back to Rogers' self-theory. Motivation researchers advanced the idea of the self-concept, which is the way people form perceptions of their own character. By being with different people, they experience different reactions to themselves and through these clues start to form a view about the kind of people they are. A person's self-concept is formed in childhood. From many social interactions, the person becomes aware of their **actual self-concept**, i.e. an idea of who they think they are. However, when they look inward and assess themselves, they may wish to change their actual self-concept to what is referred to as the **ideal self-concept**, i.e. who they think they would like to be. To aspire to the ideal self-concept, the person buys and owns brands which they believe support the desired self-image.

purposes of buying and using particular brands is either to maintain or to enhance the individual's self-image

One of the purposes of buying and using particular brands is either to maintain or to enhance the individual's self-image. By using brands as symbolic devices, people are communicating certain things about themselves. Most importantly, when they buy a particular brand and receive a positive response from their peer group, they feel that their self-image is enhanced and will be likely to buy the brand again. In effect, they are communicating that they wish to be associated with the kind of people they perceive as consuming that particular brand.

There is a considerable amount of research supporting this idea of the self-concept, based on research in product fields such as cars, cleaning products, leisure activities, clothing, retail store loyalty, electrical appliances and home furnishing. Several studies have looked at car buying and have shown that the image car owners have of themselves is congruent with the image of the marque of car they own. Owners of a particular car hold similar self-concepts to those they attributed to other consumers of the same car. Also, if the car purchaser's self-image is dissimilar to the image they perceive of different brands of cars, they will be unlikely to buy one of these brands.

To check whether an appreciation of self-image as an indicator of buying behaviour is as useful for conspicuously consumed brands as it is for privately consumed brands, a study was specially designed to look at car brands (conspicuous consumption) and magazine brands (private consumption). In both of these product fields, people chose brands whose images came closest to matching their own self-concepts. What this study also showed was that for less conspicuously consumed product fields actual, rather than ideal, self-image appeared to be more strongly related to brand choice.

There has been a lot of debate about which type of self-concept (actual or ideal) is more indicative of purchase behaviour. To understand this better, a study was designed which looked at nineteen different product fields ranging from headache remedies, as privately consumed products, through to clothes, as highly conspicuously consumed products. There was a significant correlation between the purchase intention for the actual and ideal self-concept results. This indicated that both are equally good indicators of brand selection.

However, the behaviour of individuals varies according to the situation they are in. The brand of lager bought for drinking alone at home in front of the television is not necessarily the same as that bought when out on a Saturday night with friends in a pub. Situational self-image – the image the person wants others to have of them in a particular situation – is an important indicator of brand choice. According to the situation, the individuals match their self-image to the social expectations of that particular group and select their brands appropriately. The impact of situation on brand choice can be modelled, as shown in Figure 4.1.

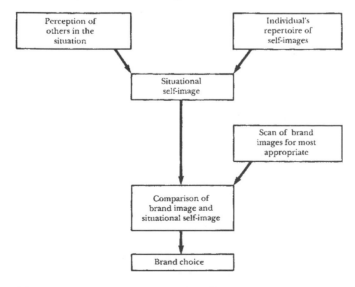

Figure 4.1   *The impact of situation and self-image on brand choice (after Schenk and Holman 1980)*

Consumers anticipate and then evaluate the people they are likely to meet at a particular event, such as those going to an important dinner party. They then draw on their repertoire of self-images to select the most appropriate self-image for the situation ('I can't let my hair down on Saturday night as there are too many of my husband's colleagues there. Better be a lot more reserved, especially as his boss is hosting this party'). If the situation requires products to express the situational self-image, such as a certain type of clothing, the consumer may decide to buy new clothes. When shopping they will consider the images of different clothes and select the brand which comes closest to meeting the situational self-image they wish to project at, for instance, the dinner party.

Finally, it needs to be realized that there is an interaction between the symbolism of the brand being used and the individual's self-concept. Not only does the consumer's self-image influence the brands they select, but the brands have a symbolic value and this in turn influences the consumer's self-image.

Brand values and personality

values are a powerful force influencing the behaviour of people

As people become more integrated into a particular society, they learn about the values of that society and act in ways that conform with these values. Research has shown that *values* are a powerful force influencing the behaviour of people. A helpful understanding of the term values is provided by Rokeach, who defines values as a lasting

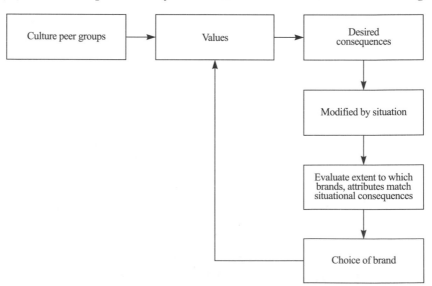

Figure 4.2   *Consumers' values and brand selection (adapted from Gutman 1982)*

belief that a particular type of behaviour, for example being honest or courageous, or state of existence, such as happiness or security, is worth striving for. Identifying the values a consumer adheres to helps in understanding their brand selection and can be used to develop brands. Figure 4.2 helps clarify this.

A young man may work in an organization with a culture that strongly supports the idea of team working and encourages employ-

Exhibit 4.4   Waitrose recognize that some consumers' values result in their being vegetarians and so have developed a wide variety of vegetarian products to satisfy these consumers (reproduced by kind permission of Waitrose)

ees to think less about their own achievements and more about how they have contributed to their team's achievement. By being in daily contact with his colleagues, the young man begins to appreciate the value of being a team player, particularly when his team is set demanding goals which can only be achieved within the tight timescale by working well together. Reinforcement of this team ethos is seen by his team going out for an evening meal together at least once every three weeks. When he is not with his colleagues but with his friends he usually drinks several glasses of his favourite brand of strong lager. However, when going out for dinner with his team from work, he only drinks a brand of low alcohol lager.

In terms of the flow chart in Figure 4.2 his desired consequences, when with his friends, is to have a good time, laughing and narrating funny stories, and on these occasions he drinks a premium lager as it 'gets him into the swing' quickly. By contrast, when with his team at one of their evening dinners he drinks a brand of low alcohol lager since he wants to be alert with his colleagues, to socialize until late in the evening and debate company activities. In essence, he considers the attributes of different brands of lager, thinks about the consequences of these different brands taking into account the situation, and selects a brand which reinforces a particular value. With his work colleagues the important value is being a responsible group member, with his friends it is fun and enjoyment.

For the consumer continually to assess the extent to which each of the competing brands in a particular product field reflects their individual values would make brand selection a lengthy task. An easier approach is for them to personify brands, since by considering brands in more human terms they are then able rapidly to recognize the values portrayed by competing brands. There is a lot of evidence showing that for powerful brands consumers have clear perceptions of the type of people they might be were they to come to life. For example, two brands of credit cards have very similar performance attributes, but where consumers perceive differences it is in their brand personalities. One of these brands might be described as 'Easy to get on with, has a sense of humour, knows lots of people, and is middle class'. By contrast the other brand could be described as 'A little bit dull, harder to find them and quite sophisticated'.

The personality of the brand grows from many sources. One of the main influences on the brand's personality comes from the product or service itself. A brand of washing powder, for example, which cleans using the aggressive nature of enzymes may be perceived to be more masculine than a brand which cleans without the use of enzymes. Another major influence is advertising and the use of celebrities in endorsements. The events sponsored by the brand owners also influence the brand's personality. For example, a genteel persona is associated with bowls sponsorship, as opposed to a gregarious personality associated with sponsoring rock concerts. The challenge for the brand marketer is to manage all points of interaction their brand has with consumers to ensure a holistic brand personality.

The importance of value as an influencer of brand choice behaviour has attracted research interest. A particularly insightful stream of work has resulted from Jagdish Sheth and his colleagues (1991). They argue, as Figure 4.3 indicates, that consumer choice behaviour is influenced by five consumption values.

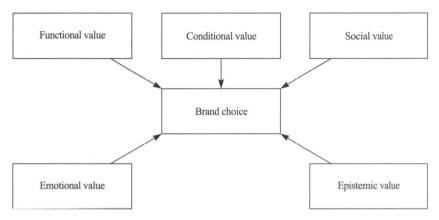

Figure 4.3   *How values affect brand choice (after Sheth et al. 1991)*

These five consumption values are:

*   *Functional value*, reflecting the utility a consumer perceives from a brand's functional capability, for example the perceived engineering excellence of a BMW, or the acceleration of a Porsche (see Plate 8).
*   *Social value* representing the utility a consumer perceives through the brand being associated with a particular social group, such as Jaguar owners being perceived as achievers.
*   *Emotional value* is the utility a consumer perceives from the brand's ability to arouse particular feelings, such as the statement of love when a man gives a woman a gold necklace.
*   *Epistemic value* is the utility a consumer perceives when trying a new brand mainly to satisfy their curiosity, such as switching from their habitual purchase of Kellogg's Corn Flakes on one occasion to a newly launched cereal brand just because they wondered what it might be like.
*   *Conditional value* reflects the perceived utility from a brand in a specific situation. For example, eating ice cream at home may primarily be valued for functional reasons, but having an ice cream in a cinema is regarded as more of a treat and in this situation has a high conditional value.

Exhibit 4.5   *Royal Mail seeks to enhance emotional value (reproduced by kind permission of Royal Mail)*

These values make different contributions in different contexts. When out to impress his new girlfriend, a young man in a restaurant may order a particular wine based on his concerns about maximizing social, emotional and conditional values. By contrast, a few years later he may buy some wines to lay them down for future years, being primarily concerned about functional values. Understanding which values the consumer is particularly concerned about in a specific purchase context enables the brand marketer to give the brand the most appropriate set of values.

Brand personality and relationship building

Appreciating consumers' values provides a basis for developing brand personalities to build stronger relationships, as we next address. When a brand has a well-defined personality, consumers interact with it and develop a relationship, just as people in life do. The nature of a relationship between two people can be inferred by observing their individual attitudes and behaviours. Likewise, as Blackston (1992) argues, the nature of a relationship between consumers and the brand can be determined through the attitudes and behaviours they display towards each other, in particular:

nature of a relationship between consumers and the brand can be determined through the attitudes and behaviours they display towards each other

• how consumers perceive and react to a brand;
• how the brand behaves and reacts to the consumers.

Brand research has traditionally focused on how consumers perceive and react to a brand. By considering both aspects of the interaction, a more appropriate brand strategy can result.

A hypothetical relationship between doctor and patient illustrates how the nature of the relationship can change once both perspectives are taken into account. The patient may perceive the doctor as professional, caring and capable. This would suggest a positive relationship. However, the picture changes when we consider what the patient thinks the doctor thinks of them. The patient's view is that the doctor sees them as a boring hypochondriac. It does not matter whether the doctor really regards the patient as such because the relationship depends on the patient's perception of the doctor's attitude. This private view makes the relationship difficult and unpleasant for the patient, though it may go unnoticed by the doctor. Brand owners may think that consumers have a positive relationship with the brand, but in order to be sure, they also need to ask consumers what they think the brand thinks of them.

The messages conveyed between a brand and its consumers build a two-way communication, in which consumers express their views on the brand and the brand 'responds' by stating a specific attitude towards consumers. As a result, marketers have to deal with two sets of attitudes in consumers' minds: first, they need to understand how consumers perceive the brand as the *object* of their attitudes; secondly, they need to discover the *subjective* brand, with its own set of attitudes. This dual perspective provides a more realistic insight into consumers' perceptions than the single-sided traditional analysis of consumers' views of the brand. Since the second perspective – the brand attitude – can often be the true brand discriminator, marketers need to undertake market research to unearth what consumers think the brand thinks of them.

The following case illustrates how the nature of the relationship can be better understood by including both perspectives. In a market research study about credit cards consumers were asked individually to describe brands and to assess their personalities in order to unearth the dialogue they have with them. Their responses were examined and several brand personality clusters were found. Table 4.1 shows two personalities consumers had identified for a specific credit card.

Table 4.1   *Example of consumer relationships with a credit card brand (after Blackston 1992)*

Personality 1 – Respected person	
Credit card brand as a person	*Credit card brand to consumer*
Dignified	I can help you to be the classy person you really are.
Distinguished	My job is to help you get accepted.
Sophisticated world-traveller	I can open doors for you.

Personality 2 – Intimidating person	
Credit card brand as a person	*Credit card brand to consumer*
Snobbish	Are you ready for me? Can you afford me?
Hard-to-approach celebrity	I am so well-known and established that I can do what I want.
Formal business person	You know what the conditions are. If you don't like them, get a different card.

Amongst those consumers seeing the brand as a respected person, the credit card acknowledged the importance of the card owner and extended its status, authority and power, thereby functioning as a status symbol. The consumers seeing the same brand as being intimidating also attributed it with status and authority, but they felt put down by the brand. Both groups of consumers had the same profiles and the same conventional brand image – but the discriminator was the brand's attitude towards them. Having this information provides a better basis for brand development.

As shown in the previous case, the relationship consumers develop with brands is not simply one of loyalty or lack of loyalty. Brands can also act as relationship partners for consumers, enabling them to resolve personal issues. The nature of these relationships is varied and Fournier (1994) has identified fifteen different types of relationship between consumers and brands:

- *Committed partnership* is a voluntary, long-term relationship, such as when someone becomes an advocate for a brand of hiking boots after years of blister-free walking.
- *Marriage of convenience* i.e. a chance encounter leading to a long-term bond, such as when someone regularly uses a salad dressing after trying it at a friend's party.
- *Arranged marriage* is an imposed long-term partnership, such as when a householder uses only one brand of washing powder because it was the only brand recommended by the manufacturer of their new washing machine.
- *Casual friendship* is one of few expectations and infrequent interactions, such as when an infrequent breakfast eater rotates between cereal brands, without preferring a particular one.
- *Close friendship* relates to bonding through a sense of shared reward, such as when a teenager believes his trainers to be a comrade in his sport activities.
- *Compartmentalized friendship* is a specialized friendship dependent on a particular situation. This would be a man choosing his beer according to the group of people he is drinking with.
- *Kinship* is an involuntary union, such as when a cook feels obliged to use the same kind of flour that mother used.
- *Rebound relationship* is about a wish to replace a prior partner, for example a woman switches air freshener to avoid any sensory association with the house she used to share with her ex-husband.
- *Childhood friendship* is about the brand evoking childhood memories, such as when a man chooses a brand of orange juice because he recalls drinking it in his childhood.
- *Courtship* is a testing period before commitment, such as when a woman experiments with two perfumes before committing herself to one.
- *Dependency* relates to obsessive attraction, as may be the case of a man upset when his favorite beer is out of stock.
- *Fling* is about short-term engagement, such as when a woman tries another perfume for one evening, though she feels guilty about neglecting her traditional brand.

Become A Hilton HHonors Member
And We'll Give You Something In Return.

A World Of Free Travel. From 1 February 1997, enrol
in Hilton HHonors® Worldwide and you can earn Hilton HHonors points when you stay at more
than 400 Hiltons in 50 countries worldwide. HHonors points can be exchanged for stays at HHonors
hotels all over the world. It's simple. Once you're a member you'll receive your personal HHonors
account number. Just give us that account number when you make your reservations and we'll
automatically keep track of your points. You can also save points with one of 19 major airlines' loyalty
programmes at the same time as you save Hilton HHonors points. You can even exchange your
HHonors points for airline flights. Drop by any Hilton to pick up an HHonors enrolment form or
call your nearest HHonors Customer Service Centre at 0345 466677 in the UK, at 44-990 466677
across Europe or at 972-788-0878 in the Americas. Or visit us online at http://www.hilton.com.

HHonors points can also be earned and redeemed at Conrad International and Vista hotels. Membership, earnings and redemption of points is subject to HHonors Terms and Conditions and excludes taxes. Airline mileage earnings subject to rate restrictions. ©1997 Hilton HHonors Worldwide.

HILTON
HHONORS
WORLDWIDE

Exhibit 4.6   *The business traveller who stays away from home in hotels may
well have a casual friendship relationship and the Hilton loyalty scheme is
trying to change this type of relationship, possibly to one of close friendship*

- *Adverserial relationship* reflects bad feelings as seen by consumers refusing to buy a brand of computer they 'hate'.
- *Enslavement* is an involuntary forced relationship, such as when a pensioner is unhappy with the local bank branch but has no

alternatives in the small town.
- *Secret affair* is a private risky relationship, such as when someone indulges in their favourite food, hiding it from their partner.

For a good brand relationship, the following attributes are necessary:

- *Love* and *passion*   Consumers must feel affection for the brand and want to have it at all costs.
- *Self-concept connection*   The brand must give consumers a sense of belonging or make them feel younger.
- *Interdependence*   The brand must become part of the consumer's everyday life.
- *Commitment*   Consumers need to be faithful to the brand through good and bad times, as in the case of Coke and Persil.
- *Intimacy*   Consumers should be very familiar with the brand and understand it well.
- *Partner quality*   Consumers seek those traits in the brand, such as trustworthiness, which they would in a friend.
- *Nostalgic attachment*   The brand should evoke pleasant memories because the consumer, or somebody close to them, used it in the past.

By focusing on these attributes, managers can identify strengths and weaknesses in the relationship between consumers and the brand.

The contribution of semiotics to branding

People make inferences about others from the brands they own, since some brands act as cultural signs. Semiotics, the scientific study of signs, is a qualitative market research technique that is widely used in France and is beginning to gain popularity elsewhere. It helps clarify how consumers learn meanings associated with products and brands. If marketers are able to identify the rules of meaning that consumers have devised to encode and decode symbolic communication, they can make better use of advertising, design and packaging. For example, gold has been enshrined in our culture as a symbol of wealth and authority and can convey meanings of luxury, love, importance, warmth and eternity. But to use this as the prime colour on a box for a cheap, mass produced plastic moulded toy car runs the risk of it being interpreted as vulgar.

Some researchers postulate that brands act as communicative sign devices at four levels. At the most basic level, the brand acts as

semiotics helps clarify how consumers learn meanings associated with products and brands

a utilitarian sign. For example, a particular brand of washing machine may convey the meaning of reliability, effectiveness and economic performance. At the second level, a brand acts as a commercial sign conveying its value. For example, Porsche and Skoda signify the extremes in value perceptions. At the third level, the brand acts as a socio-cultural sign, associating consumers with particular groups of people. For example, having certain brands 'to keep up with the Joneses', or wearing a particular tie to signify membership of an exclusive club. At the fourth level, the brand can be decoded as a mythical sign. For example, Napoleon Brandy, Cutty Sark Whisky and the Prudential Corporation, all build on mythical associations.

Semiotics provides a better understanding of the cultural relationship between brands and consumers. Checking the communications briefs for brand advertising against the way consumers interpret the messages can result in the more effective use of brand resources. For example, British Airways wished to increase the number of female executives using its airline. They developed an advertising campaign, targeted at women business travellers, which spoke about the ergonomics of seats. Semiotics Solutions, a UK research consultancy specializing in semiotics, undertook research to evaluate the new campaign. They found that it was not sufficiently sensitive to the fact that women are not as tall as men, and the copy was rejected by women business travellers who felt that 'talking about 6 $^1/_2$ foot women was an insult'.

Semiotics can help in the design of brands, as was the case with a hypermarket in the Mammouth chain. Using group discussions, the different values consumers ascribed to hypermarkets were identified and designs developed to match these. Patterns of similarity were sought in terms of the way consumers associated different values with hypermarkets and four segments were tentatively identified from the qualitative research:

- *convenience values*, characterized by 'Find the product quickly, always enough in stock, always on the same shelf';
- *critical values*, characterized by 'My husband isn't interested in frills and friendliness. He's only bothered about his wallet. He looks at the quality of the products, and at the prices';
- *utopian values*, expressed by comments such as 'I like being somewhere on a human scale, and not somewhere vast and overwhelming';
- *diversionary values*, such as 'I get the basic stuff out of the way first, and then I give myself a little treat, such as browsing in the book department'.

In the group discussions, consumers spoke about spatial issues, and it was inferred that:

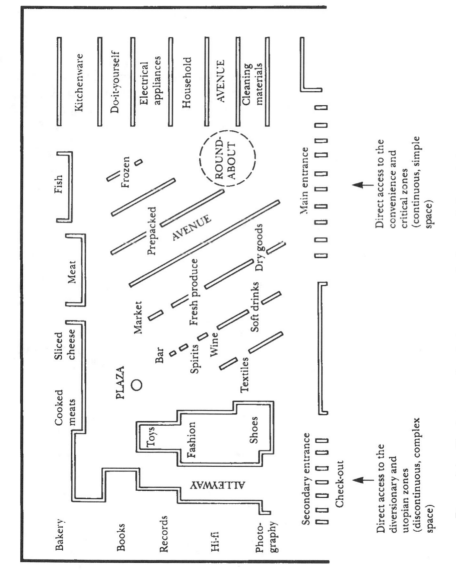

Figure 4.4 The hypermarket design proposed after semiotic analysis

- convenience values were associated with interchanges and avenues;
- critical values were associated with roundabouts and orientation maps;
- utopian values related to markets and public gardens;
- diversionary values encompassed covered arcades and flea markets.

Further analysis revealed that consumers expressing convenience and critical values wanted simple, continuous space. By contrast, consumers with utopian and diversionary values preferred complex, discontinuous space. Then, by considering customers in these two broad categories, the semiotic analysis led to the suggested design shown in Figure 4.4. It was anticipated that as they gained more experience shopping in the hypermarket, the two consumer groups would use separate entrances. As such, a different store design was conceived for each entrance. Most consumers would seek all four values of the hypermarket, but would be particularly drawn to the section that reflected their values. Decisions about where to locate the produce were aided by the group discussions. After the store accepted them, the designs had to be adjusted to cope with operational issues, such as ease of rapidly replenishing shelves, lighting, safety regulations, etc. However, overall, Mammouth found this approach helpful in conceiving a new design for their hypermarket.

Another good example of how semiotic analysis can help brand development is provided by Gordon and Valentine (1996) examining consumer behaviour in retail outlets. The different forms of retail outlets, such as supermarkets, corner stores, garages and off-licences, not only represent different retailing operations but also convey different messages to customers. These messages can be lined on a continuum from the planned purchase to the impulse buy, as shown in Figure 4.5. The brand's position along the continuum will depend on the triggers present in each outlet.

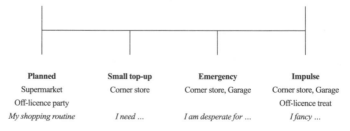

Figure 4.5   *The retail outlet continuum (from Gordon and Valentine 1996)*

Supermarkets, represent planned shopping and communicate a message of efficient domestic management and functionality. During their routine visits to a supermarket consumers enjoy the familiar orderliness that the same layout and product displays offer. Although this is a typical location for planned purchases impulse buying can also occur, provided promotions give people the feeling that it is right to break the codes of efficiency they are following.

Because of the strong message of order conveyed by supermarkets, consumers often attach a sense of 'disorder' to shopping in **corner stores** and experience these visits almost with a sense of guilt and confusion. They are suspicious of the limited choice and expensive price range common in corner stores and welcome the reassurance offered by familiar brands. Corner stores present opportunities for secondary or niche brands which people usually choose on impulse, due in part to their feelings of not needing to be an orderly shopper.

In **garages**, two types of purchase can occur: the planned purchase of petrol, and the emergency/impulse buy of other products. Customers travelling on business seek rest and treats from the stress or fatigue of the journey, whereas customers travelling on pleasure want to indulge themselves and underline the sense of fun and holiday. The opportunity for brands in petrol stations is to match the needs of these two groups.

Off-licences are the preferred location for buying alcohol as in this type of retail outlet with its calm atmosphere and the depth and breadth of range, consumers feel it is legitimate to purchase their favourite drinks without other shoppers' disapproval. Here customers receive advice and are encouraged to experiment with a broad range of wines, spirits and beers. Their visit can be planned and they can respond to an impulse of experimentation or indulgence.

The previous description of retail outlets shows that they are not only distribution channels but they also communicate specific messages to consumers. Likewise, within a store, single categories convey their particular messages to consumers in the way brands are displayed. For example, are they positioned on the shelf with almost military precision, or are they almost randomly placed on the shelf? Also, does the category sit comfortably between other categories?

Brands are chosen as a result of habit, of an impulse or of a well-thought-through choice. The challenge for brand owners is to exploit the features of each retail outlet so that the automatic purchase is reinforced and the trial buy from impulse or from browsing is encouraged. To increase the likelihood of consumers purchasing their brands, marketers need to consider:

- **Specific category areas** *within the store* dedicated solely to the category, enabling it to communicate in its own language and conveying a strong message of added value. For example, it is common to see bakeries in stores, transmitting their own signals, which are distinctly different from other categories separated from this section.

- **Active packaging** allowing brands to have a dialogue with consumers through their design and format. These elements evoke sensory associations.
- If the **relationship between packaging and advertising** is strong, consumers are reminded of the advertising message when they see the brand. For example, Gordon and Valentine found consumers looking at Weetabix packs and instantly talking about the advertising. This not only reinforces the brand's positioning, but also acts as a further competitive barrier.

Semiotics, as Alexander (1996) showed, can be a helpful tool to identify, evaluate and exploit the cultural myth which exists at the heart of most successful brands. A myth is a sacred, heroic story of doubtful authenticity. In marketing terms, myths are associated with very powerful brands, such as Nike, Body Shop and Virgin.

Myths provide a logical framework to overcome contradictions in society and successful brands capitalize on this. The myth of the 'Persil Mum' reconciles two opposites: the distance of a detached factory producing the detergent and the closeness of a loving member of the family taking care of the family needs. From this contradiction the Persil myth is about 'caring detachment'.

As Alexander argues, the stronger the oppositions, the stronger the myth and the stronger the brand positioning. The starting point for semioticians helping marketers position brands is to identify the attributes of the brand and at the same time to specify their opposites. They then take pairs of these oppositions and examine the resulting myth diagrams. For example, an attribute of a ready-prepared meal is real food and thus one opposition could be real food/junk food. Another attribute is home made and the opposition would be home made/commercially made. The myth diagram is then constructed from these two oppositions as shown in Figure 4.6.

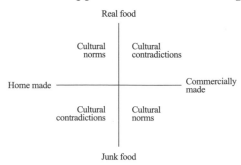

Figure 4.6 *The myth diagram for ready-prepared meals (after Alexander 1996)*

The opportunity for the myth explaining the brand positioning is in the two cultural contradiction boxes, i.e. commercially made real food and home made junk food. Often only one of these quadrants is viable – not many would contemplate home made junk food! Marks & Spencer focused on the opportunity presented by the cultural contradiction of commercially made real food and became the legendary myth of the store selling high quality ready-prepared meals.

In essence, in this approach to identifying brand positionings semioticians keep on taking pairs of oppositions, construct myth diagrams and then explore possibilities for brand positionings.

Conclusions

This chapter has shown how brands perform a social and psychological role beyond that provided by their physical features. Consumers rely on brands to help them understand and communicate with different groups of people. The fact that consumers report greater pain relief after using a branded, rather than a generic version of the same analgesic, provides evidence of added values from brand images. Creative marketing has successfully positioned brands as effective problem solvers, with personalities that contribute to greater effectiveness.

Brands have the added values of symbolism – meanings and values over and above their physical constituents. Consumers look to brands not only for what they can do, but also to help say something about themselves to their peer groups. Rolex watches are not worn just for their functional excellence, but also to say something about who the owner is. To ensure that brands are effective symbolic devices, it is crucial for marketers to communicate their capabilities to users, and their peer groups, through advertising, public relations, packaging, merchandising, etc.

The symbolic aspect of brands makes them all the more attractive to consumers since they:

- enable consumers to convey messages about themselves and understand others better;
- help set social scenes and enable people to mix with each other more easily;
- act as ritual devices to celebrate specific occasions;
- provide a basis for a better understanding of the way people act;
- help consumers say something to themselves.

In effect, consumers are encoding messages to others by buying and using particular brands and are hoping that their target audience decodes the message the right way. Unfortunately, this is not always the case. For example, two friends meeting after several years may decide to go for a drink. One may order a Britvic Orange Juice, encoded to communicate their concern about not drinking when having to drive. The second person may decode this as: 'time has dulled their sociability'.

When consumers buy brands, they are making decisions about how well specific brands maintain or enhance an image they have of themselves. Just as consumers have distinct personalities, so do brands. Consumers take as much care choosing highly conspicuous brands as they do choosing their friends, since they like to be surrounded by like-minded personalities. Brands whose images match consumers' actual or ideal self-images are likely to be bought. When friends or colleagues admire someone's newly-bought brand, that person feels pleased that the brand reinforces their self-image and will continue to use the brand. The situation in which consumers find themselves will dictate, to some extent, the type of image that they wish to project. Through anticipating, and subsequently evaluating, the people they will meet at a particular event, consumers then seek brands to reflect the situational self-image that they wish to display.

brands whose values reflect those of target consumers stand a greater likelihood of being bought

Individuals' values are a powerful determinant of their brand choice behaviour. Much has been published showing that brands whose values reflect those of target consumers stand a greater likelihood of being bought. To make these value assessments, consumers interpret brands in humanistic terms, and through the metaphor of the brand as a person are rapidly able to judge brands. Marketers are able to influence the personality of the brand through many routes, such as functional characteristics, packaging, advertising and sponsorship.

According to the type of personality clothing the brand, so there is a particular relationship between consumers and brands. Instead of just considering this from the perspective of the consumer, valuable insights about promotion strategies result from considering how brands perceive and react to consumers. A typology of relationships between brands and consumers has been reviewed and, by considering the criteria necessary for an effective relationship, the strengths and weaknesses of the consumer–brand relationship can be assessed.

Semiotics, the scientific study of signs, can help brand development by assessing the cultural signs portrayed by different brands. For example, our culture brands the 07.00 train running ten minutes late as the late 07.00, carrying critical associations of inefficiency. However, in lesser developed economies, the train would be branded as the 07.10, portraying the triumph of mass transportation running against many odds in an under-resourced environment. Semiotics analyses brands' communication capabilities at four different levels

– utilitarian, commercial, socio-cultural and mythical. It can provide guidance about merchandising and displays. Brand advertising and design can benefit from checking communication briefs against the ways that consumers have interpreted the marketing activity as part of the social system. Furthermore, semiotics is a helpful tool analysing the cultural myth at the heart of a brand to help develop a more powerful positioning.

Marketing action checklist

To help clarify the direction of future marketing activity, it is recommended that the following exercises are undertaken:

1   When did you last evaluate the added value of the image surrounding your key brands? If this has not been done within the past 12 months, it may well be advisable to assess this.

   One way of doing this is to identify the main competitor to one of your brands. Recruit a representative sample of consumers to try your brand and also that of your nearest competitor, seeking their comments about which brand they most preferred and why. This is a 'branded product test'. With another matched sample of consumers, repeat the product test but, this time, remove any branding and use identifying codes when presenting the brands. This is referred to as a 'blind product test'. Again, ask consumers which one of the two brands they most preferred, with their reasons. Calculate the proportions who prefer each of the two brands on the branded and the blind product test. Comparing the preference scores when the brands are assessed blind and then branded gives an indication of the value consumers ascribe to functional and emotional aspects of the brand.

2   Do you know what image surrounds your brand? If little is known about this, it would be wise to conduct some qualitative depth interviews with consumers. Ideally, this should be done by a skilled qualitative market researcher, preferably with a background in psychology, sociology or anthropology. Some of the ways of gauging the image associated with a brand are to ask consumers the following types of questions:
'If **brand** came to life, what sort of person would it be?'
'If **brand** were a person, and they died what would be written on their epitaph?'
'If **brand** were to be a car, what sort of car would they be?'
'Tell me the first thing that comes to mind when I say **brand**'
'What would a friend of yours most like about **brand,** and what would they most dislike about **brand?**'

They could also be asked to role-play the way your brand solves a problem and then repeat this for a competitor's brand.

Once you have identified the image dimensions of your brand, it would then be useful to see how strongly your brand is associated with each of these statements, comparing this against competitors' brands. This could be done using a questionnaire which asked respondents to use a five-point agreement–disagreement scale to state how well they felt each of the statements described each of the brands. By administering this to a representative sample of consumers, the image profiles of your brand, and those of your competitors, can be assessed.

3   When did you last evaluate whether the characters portraying your brands are appropriate for today's consumers? If you feel your brands compete in a fashion-driven market, it would be advisable to undertake qualitative market research to assess the suitability of the people in your brand advertising.

4   To what extent do your key brands satisfy the following symbolic roles? Do they:
    • enable people to convey messages about themselves?
    • enable people to join new groups more easily?
    • help celebrate special events?
    • aid people to understand the actions of their peer group?
    • allow consumers to say something about themselves to themselves?
    Having undertaken this symbolic brand audit, evaluate how well your marketing activity helps support these symbolic roles.

5   If on exporting your brands you found a hostile consumer response, did you subsequently conduct qualitative market research to assess why your brands failed? Was any work undertaken to assess whether the symbols surrounding your brands meant something different overseas from that in the UK? For example, putting your hand to your ear in the UK indicates that the person is talking too quietly, but in Italy is taken as an insulting gesture.

6   How well matched is your brand's image with the self-image of your target consumers? One way of assessing this is by comparing the image profile of your brand against the self-image profile of your target market. If you have no data on this, question 2 in this section explains how to measure the image of your brand quantitatively. The same battery of attributes should also be administered to a representative sample of your consumers, asking them to use a five-point scale to assess how much they agree or disagree with each of the statements describing them-

selves. Compare the average brand image scores against the average self-image scores to assess how well your consumers' self-image matches that of your brand. Highlight the attributes showing the largest differences – these indicate areas where your brand does not meet consumers' expectations and should be investigated further.

7   How much is your brand the subject of situational influences? Do you know what supporting roles your brand plays when consumers use it in different situations? Does your marketing activity promote the appropriateness of your brand for particular situations?

8   If you are unsure about the values consumers perceive to be represented by your brand, consider undertaking the following exercise. Recruit a consumer and make it clear that you want to talk with them for about an hour. Show them your brand, ask them which other brands they would use besides your brand, then present them with all the brands they have mentioned. Explore the characteristics they believe your brand has. Having recorded these as they spoke, show the consumer the list of characteristics and ask them which one is the most important to them. For example, for a brand of crisps they may have said it has a very strong taste. On a separate sheet of paper record this characteristic, then ask them why this is important to them. They may have replied with the first consequence, 'I eat less when it tastes so strong'. Record this, then again ask, 'and why is that important to you?' They might now give the second consequence 'I don't get so fat'. Record this consequence and continue with this probing and recording until finally you arrive at the value associated with the base attribute. In our example it might be self-esteem. This is the first attribute–consequences–value ladder (similar to Figure 4.2). Return to the list of characteristics and ask the consumer which is the second most important characteristic. On a separate sheet of paper record this, then repeat the questioning until you have arrived at the second value, i.e. you need to explore the second ladder. Repeat this process until you feel you have sufficient understanding of this consumer's perceptions of your brand's values.

In this qualitative approach, we would encourage you to consider interviewing around ten consumers. This starts to give you a better appreciation of your target market's views. Due to the time and the expertise needed for these interviews, you may find it better to recruit a market research agency for this.

9   In Figure 4.3, five types of brand values were identified. Use this framework to assess the extent to which your brand draws

on each of these values. How does this profile of value importance vary between your light, moderate and heavy brand users?
How is your brand strategy reflecting the importance of these
values between these user groups?

10   Evaluate the information you have on consumers' perceptions
      of your brand. Does it also give an indication of how they think
      the brand thinks of them? How do you know that your con-
      sumers do not feel threatened, humiliated or otherwise
      negatively affected by the brand? What type of relationship have
      they developed with the brand? How can you enhance the rela-
      tionship in the long-term?

11   Using Fournier's typology of relationships described in the sec-
      tion on 'Brand personality and relationship building', audit your
      consumer market research data for one of your brands and as-
      sess what type of relationship describes the consumer–brand
      bonding. Is this relationship congruent with the desired brand
      personality? If not, assess what changes are needed better to
      harmonize your brand strategy.

12   Take one of your recent brand advertisements and evaluate, with
      your colleagues, what the brand is communicating as a utilitar-
      ian sign, as a commercial sign, as a socio-cultural sign and as a
      mythical sign. Are these messages consistent at all four levels?
      Were the interpretations consistent across your team?

      Repeat the exercise with consumers and compare the find-
      ings between yourselves and the consumers. Any dissonant
      findings should be considered in more detail and corrective ac-
      tion taken.

13   If you feel that there may be a need to improve the position of
      one of your brands, consider the following exercise. With your
      marketing team, prepare a list of the attributes of your brand.
      Brainstorm these attributes to identify their opposites. Randomly
      choose two pairs of opposites and plot them on a diagram. Us-
      ing the analogy of Figure 4.6, identify the possible positionings
      that could characterize cultural contradictions. Evaluate each
      of these to assess new ideas for the brand's positioning.

References and further reading

Alexander M. (1996). The myth at the heart of the brand. In The big brand challenge.
    Esomar Seminar, Berlin Oct. 1996. Esomar Publication Series, Vol. 203.
Belk R., Bahn K. and Mayer R. (1982). Developmental recognition of consumption sym-
    bolism. *Journal of Consumer Research,* **9** (June), 4–17.
Biel A. (1991). The brandscape: converting brand image into equity. *ADMAP* **26** (10) 41–6.
Birdwell A. (1968). A study of the influence of image congruence on consumer choice.
    Journal of Business, **41** (Jan.), 76–88.

Blackston M. (1992). A brand with an attitude: a suitable case for treatment. *Journal of Marketing Research Society*, **31** (3), 231–41.

Branthwaite A. and Cooper P. (1981). Analgesic effects of branding in treatment of headaches. *British Medical Journal*, **16** (May), 282, 1576–8.

Broadbent K. and Cooper P. (1987). Research is good for you. *Marketing Intelligence and Planning*. **5** (1), 3–9.

Chisnall P. (1985). *Marketing: A Behavioural Analysis*. London: McGraw Hill.

Combs A. and Snygg D. (1959). *Individual Behavior: A Perceptual Approach To Behavior*. New York: Harper & Bros.

Dolich I. (1969). Congruence relationships between self images and product brands. *Journal of Marketing Research*, **6** (Feb), 80–4.

Elliott R. (1994). Exploring the symbolic meaning of brands. *British Journal of Management*, **5** Special Issue (June), 13–19.

Floch J. (1988). The contribution of structural semiotics for the design of a hypermarket. *International Journal of Research in Marketing*, **4** (3), 233–52.

Fournier S. (1994). A Consumer-brand Relationship for Strategic Brand Management. Doctoral dissertation at the University of Florida.

Gordon W. and Langmaid R. (1988). *Qualitative Market Research. A Practitioners' and Buyers' Guide*. Aldershot: Gower.

Gordon W. and Valentine V. (1996). Buying the brand at point of choice. *Journal of Brand Management*, **4** (1), 35–44.

Grubb E. and Hupp G. (1968). Perception of self, generalized stereotypes and brand selection. *Journal of Marketing Research*, **5** (Feb.), 58–63.

Gutman J. (1982). A means-end chain model based on consumer categorisation processes. *Journal of Research*, **46** (Spring), 60–72.

Heigh H. L. and Gabel T. G. (1992). Symbolic interactionism: its effects on consumer behavior and implications for marketing strategy. *Journal of Services Marketing*, **6** (3), 5–16.

Hirschman E. and Holbrook M. (1982). Hedonic consumption: emerging concepts, methods and propositions. *Journal of Marketing*, **46** (Summer), 92–101.

Landon E. (1974). Self concept, ideal self concept and consumer purchase intentions. *Journal of Consumer Research*, **1** (Sept.), 44–51.

Lannon J. and Cooper P. (1983). Humanistic advertising: a holistic cultural perspective. *International Journal of Advertising*, **2**, 195–213.

Levitt T. (1970). The morality of advertising. *Harvard Business Review* (July–Aug), 84–92.

Munson J. and Spivey W. (1981). Product and brand user stereotypes among social classes. In *Advances in Consumer Research* (Munroe K., ed.) Vol. 8, 696–701. Ann Arbor: Association for Consumer Research.

North W. (1988). The language of commodities: groundwork for a semiotics of consumer goods. *International Journal of Research in Marketing*, **4** (3), 173–86.

Restall C. and Gordon W. (1993). Brands – the missing link: understanding the emotional relationship. *Marketing and Research Today*, **21** (2), 59–67.

Ross I. (1971). Self-concept and brand preference. *Journal of Business*, **44** (1), 38–50.

Rokeach M. (1968). The role of values in public opinion research. *Public Opinion Quaterly*, **32** (Winter), 554.

Schenk C. and Holman R. (1980). A sociological approach to brand choice: the concept of situational self image. In *Advances in Consumer Research*, (Olson J., ed.) Vol. 7, 610–15. Ann Arbor: Association for Consumer Research.

Sheth J., Newman B. and Gross B. (1991). Why we buy what we buy: a theory of consumption values. *Journal of Business Research*, **22** (2), 159–70.

Sirgy M. (1982). Self-concept in consumer behavior: a critical review. *Journal of Consumer Research*, **9** (Dec.), 287–300.

Solomon M. (1983). The role of products as social stimuli: a symbolic interactionism perspective. *Journal of Consumer Research*, **10** (Dec.), 319–29.

Wilkie W. (1986). *Consumer Behavior*. New York: J. Wiley.

Chapter 5

Business to business branding

Summary

The aim of this chapter is to consider the issues associated with the way organizations buy brands. We open by making the point that brands play as important a role in business to business as they do in consumer markets. The unique characteristics of organizational marketing are considered, along with brand implications. We identify the people likely to be involved in organizational brand purchasing and discuss their roles. The stages involved in brand purchasing are presented, with a consideration of the effort put in by the buyers. The importance of value in industrial brands is reviewed, focusing on the tangible and intangible components of four aspects of brand performance. The contribution of relationship marketing to industrial branding is considered, including the criteria used to assess the appropriateness of potential partners, factors associated with successful relationships and how these vary over the duration of the relationship. The rational and emotional factors affecting brand choice are reviewed. The traditional way that marketers present brand information is compared with buyers' views of the most useful sources. Finally, we address the important role played by corporate identity programmes and the corporate images perceived by buyers.

Brands and organizational marketing

The difference between consumer and business to business marketing

A distinction is frequently drawn between consumer and organizational (or business to business) marketing. Consumer marketing is

principally concerned with matching the resources of the selling organization with the needs of consumers. It focuses heavily on those
people at the end of the value chain who purchase brands to satisfy
either their own personal needs, or those of their families or friends.
By contrast, organizational marketing is concerned with the provision of products and services to *organizations*. They are not the final
consumers of the products and services. For example, Eastern Electricity is actively involved in organizational marketing by buying
electricity from suppliers. They add value by distributing this in the
most effective and efficient manner to other organizations (e.g. farmers, car producers, etc.), who use the energy to produce products
and services which are ultimately bought by consumers.

Emotional issues in business to business brands

While there are differences between consumer and organizational
marketing, brands are just as important in both areas. Successful
business to business branding is not a cold, stark form of branding
which clinically targets companies. Rather it seeks to interest well-
targeted business people, who are very time-constrained, with vibrant
propositions that are beneficial to them and their firm and which
encourage particular types of relationships. As budgets for business
to business campaigns are often smaller than those for consumer
campaigns, marketers need to be more involved in the client's strategy to understand how best their brand can help each client. It could
even be argued that business to business branding is more interesting than consumer branding, since one can only refresh consumers
with Coca-Cola, but IBM computers can change people's lives.

> **successful business
> to business
> branding is not a
> cold, stark form of
> branding**

Some argue that organizational buying is far more rational than
consumer buying, yet emotional factors still play an important role.
This can be appreciated by an advertisement by Primary Contact for
Redland Roof tiles (Plate 9). While the functional benefits of this brand
are described, the campaign shows a country house with the evoca-
tive copy 'I fell in love with Rosemary's looks'. The brand of tiles
don't just keep the house dry, they also add to the home's look and
character. The importance of emotional factors can be further appreciated by comparing advertisements from two European providers
of financial services, Commerzbank and Swiss Life, as shown in Exhibit 5.1. Whereas the former presents a rational perspective on the
brand's benefit (through the vast amount of information), the latter
adopts a stronger emotional appeal, reassuring managers who feel
lost looking for banking assistance about international employee
benefit plans.

Despite the importance of emotional factors, industrial brands
are often characterized at the level of 'brand as reference' on
Goodyear's consumerization spectrum, discussed earlier in Chapter

VIEWPOINT

Commerzbank's focus on German
and European economic issues   4/97

The lure of monetary union for German banks

The most hotly debated questions regarding monetary union – whether it will begin on time in 1999 and which countries will be involved from the outset – tend to obscure a rather paradoxical aspect. According to the European Commission, monetary union will primarily benefit Europe's citizens as consumers and employees. Yet in many countries, not only in Germany, these are the very people who have serious reservations about this far-reaching project. On the other hand, groups that by and large stand to lose, namely certain sectors and above all banks, are often advocates of monetary union.

UNDOUBTEDLY, perspectives differ from country to country. German exporters, for instance, and companies facing import competition would certainly benefit if they no longer had to cope with major currency misalignments within Europe, as in early 1995, for instance. Conversely, suppliers and unions in the former soft-currency countries will have to adjust to a new situation once the safety valve of devaluation is finally closed.

FOR BANKS the situation is different; the extent to which they are affected varies less from country to country. One important aspect of Emu, however, is that German banks will lose the major advantage conferred by the D-mark's international prominence. In the medium to long term, the euro can certainly play a far greater international role than the D-mark does today – provided, of course, that the promised stability can be delivered. But the number of banks wanting a share of this cake will increase disproportionately.

IN ADDITION, even ignoring conversion costs, which will be higher in banking than in most other sectors, Emu will mean that certain areas of the banks' business will disappear, while competition and pressure on margins will increase further, leading to concentration and job-shedding. Naturally, many of the changes would have come about without monetary union, but they would have been less severe and slower to emerge. Emu will add a new dimension of the notion of "banks under stress" (OECD) even more appropriate.

CLAIMS BY POLITICIANS that Emu will have a neutral impact on competition are completely unfounded. The overwhelmingly pro-Emu German banking industry is a good example. The savings and cooperative banks, which currently have large market shares, will find it particularly difficult to cope with the new situation, as it will require them to develop wide-ranging skills in euro wholesale business.

IN VIEW OF their size, degree of specialization and international orientation, the private-sector banks will be at a distinct advantage. All the same, it is doubtful whether as a group they will be winners, due not least to the great potential attractiveness of the euro market for strong foreign rivals from the U.S., Britain and Switzerland.

THE GERMAN government could quite easily acknowledge the banks' pro-Emu stance by forcefully paving the way for Frankfurt to become the Continent's main financial centre, setting the benchmark for government bonds and handling the bulk of euro-derivatives business. This would provide the German banking community with a more rational basis for supporting Emu, while still leaving ample challenges in the new century.

For more information about Commerzbank's broad scope of research capabilities and financial services, just contact the bank's head office in Frankfurt. Fax +49 69 13 62-98 05 http://www.commerzbank.com

Total assets of Europe's 50 largest banks
by country, 1995

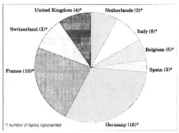

COMMERZBANK
German know-how in global finance

Exhibit 5.1   *Commerzbank promotes a rational appeal while Swiss Life incorporates an emotional appeal (reproduced by kind permission of Swiss Life Insurance and Pension Company)*

2. An examination of industrial advertisements shows that they often focus on the functional capabilities of the brand, to guarantee its quality. An example of this is the advertisement in Exhibit 5.2 for the Agfa Arcus II scanner.

Brands permeate all areas of organizational marketing (e.g. Prozac in pharmaceuticals, Hewlett Packard Laserjet in printers, Pyrotenax in fire-resistant cables, Novex in polyethylene). They succeed because purchasers and users value the commitment of suppliers behind their brands. Purchasers are proud to be associated with suc-

WHEN THE TOUGH GET GOING.

Looking for clear directions for your international employee benefit plans? Swiss Life is the way to go for coordinated global programs and real financial savings. As the world's leading international network of life insurers, we're never far from where you need us. And every Swiss Life Network Partner is a local leader, with the expertise, flexibility and service capabilities to meet your most challenging insurance and benefit requirements. It's a sign of the times that more and more top multinationals follow the Swiss Life route. Call us in Zurich on +411/284 3797, or contact your local Network Partner. It can be tough out there. But with Swiss Life, you're never on your own.

 ZwitserLeven (Swiss Life)
Apollolaan 153
1077 AS Amsterdam / The Netherlands
Telephone: +3120 / 573 5735
Telefax: +3120 / 573 5334

Danica Danica
Parallelvej 17
2800 Lyngby / Denmark
Telephone: +4545 / 23 23 23
Telefax: +4545 / 23 20 20

 Société suisse (Swiss Life)
41, rue de Châteaudun
75304 Paris Cédex 09 / France
Telephone: +331 / 40 82 37 14
Telefax: +331 / 40 82 37 95

IMPÉRIO Império
Rua Garrett, 62
1200 Lisboa / Portugal
Telephone: +3511 / 340 3320
Telefax: +3511 / 346 3927

THE RIGHT DECISION

Exhibit 5.1 *continued*

cessful brands. For example, in the computer industry many firms are proud to promote the fact that their PCs are based on Intel microprocessors.

In Chapter 2 we defined a successful brand as:

An identifiable product, service, person or place, augmented in such a way that the buyer or user perceives relevant, unique added values which match their needs most closely. Furthermore, its success results from being able to sustain these added values in the face of competition.

This definition is appropriate for both consumer and organizational

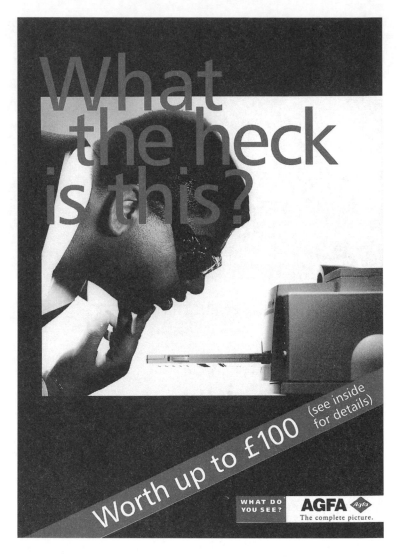

Exhibit 5.2   *Agfa scanners focus on functional capabilities (reproduced by kind permission of Agfa)*

marketing since in both sectors marketers are striving to make buyers aware of their added values.

Company or produce/services brand name?

It is more common to see organizational brand names bearing the name of the company. This enables a wide range of products from the same company to benefit from its corporate identity (see Plate 10). As a consequence of this naming policy, many buyers see a brand's added values resulting from two factors. First, the added values from dealing with a particular firm and, second, the benefits from the specific product or service. As such it is not uncommon in organizational marketing for buyers to talk about suppliers as brands (e.g. SKF, IBM, ICI). In such situations the supplier has succeeded in augmenting their product with the added value of the firm's corporate identity. Consequently, the brand selection process for these buyers will be one of company selection first and then, at a later stage in the evaluation process, consideration of each company's brands. By contrast, where other firms have concentrated less on corporate brand endorsement and more on individual product branding, buyers will be less interested in the firm as a brand. For example in the anti-ulcer drug market Zantac, from Glaxo, and Tagamet, from SmithKlein Beecham Pharmaceutical, compete against each other without excessively relying on the added values of their corporate origins.

Are brands important in business to business marketing?

Organizational marketers who think that brands have no role to play are ignoring a powerful tool. More often than not, in a rather blinkered sense, they perceive brands to be little more than 'commodity items with a name stuck on', or they attach to them a very strong emphasis on functional capabilities with minimal presentation of any type of brand value. As several case histories show, this is naive and is an ineffective use of resources. An American study, published late in the 1980s, reported that established producers of wood and plywood panels were facing increasing competition from new entrants. Producers felt that the best way to counter this challenge was to brand their products. In this case all they did was to develop names for their lines, with the prime objective of differentiating themselves from competitors. Several months after the adoption of this so-called branding strategy, interviews were conducted with timber merchants. They were asked what criteria they used when deciding between wood suppliers. In the majority of cases, the first consideration was price. The buyers clearly regarded the competing products as commodities and not brands. If they had perceived any changes, they would have recognized the competing items as being differentiated because of their added values, for which price premiums could be charged. A further irony of this study was that the timber merchants were highly critical of the consumer confusion caused by these 'branding strategies'. The producers had used names that were only appropriate for distributors. They had ignored the fact that consumers could not relate the brand names to the performance capabilities of the different types of wood panels.

organizational marketers who think that brands have no role to play are ignoring a powerful tool

Brands and the value chain

To succeed, brands in organizational markets must take into account the needs of everyone in the value chain. In the man-made fibres market, suppliers thought that it was more important to stress brand names without carefully relating the name to the uses of the fibres. As a consequence, in a market rich with competing brand names (e.g. Dacron, Terylene, Acrilan, Celon), but poor in brand explanation, users were confused about the capabilities of different fabrics. A more effective strategy would have been to identify the different customers and influencers in the value chain (e.g. the weavers, knitters, designers, manufacturers, distributors). Promotional strategies suitable for each group should have then been developed, unified by a corporate theme, to clarify the unique capabilities of the different fibre brands.

Our concern in this chapter is to show how an appreciation of the differences between organizational and consumer marketing can help in developing successful brands. Some of the key differences are addressed in the next section.

The unique characteristics of organizational marketing

More people involved

In consumer marketing brands tend to be bought by individuals, while many people are involved in organizational purchasing. The business to business brand marketer is faced with the challenge of not only identifying which managers are involved in the purchasing decision, but also what brand attributes are of particular concern to each of them. The various benefits of the brand, therefore, need to be communicated to all involved, stressing the relevant attributes to particular individuals. For example, the brand's reliable delivery may need to be stressed to the production manager, its low level of impurities to the quality control manager, its low life cycle costs to the accountant, and so on.

Lower prices and costs involved

Consumers are generally faced with relatively inexpensive brands which, therefore, they do not spend much time evaluating. By contrast, organizational purchasing involves large financial commitments. To reduce the risk of an inappropriate purchase decision, organizations involve several managers from different departments to help in the evaluation process. For example, when

IBM was looking for a firm to manufacture transistor–transistor logic chips, it had a team consisting of engineers, accountants and a purchasing manager. After an assessment of all potential suppliers, only five were able to match IBM's requirements. Engineers then visited each firm and eliminated one of the potential suppliers because of worries about quality capabilities. Price and delivery quotations subsequently ruled out two other firms. Commissioned prototypes were then asked for so that they could choose between the final two firms. This detailed evaluation took several weeks to complete. During this time, a considerable amount of technical and financial information was sought and assessed.

More time involved

It is not unusual to observe consumers making a brand choice with only a short deliberation time. By contrast, organizational buying generally involves much longer deliberation periods. Salespeople in organizational marketing are more frequently regarded as technical advisers compared with salespeople in consumer marketing. They often expect to have several meetings with potential purchasers before the firm feels sufficiently confident to make a purchase decision. The implication of this is that the effectiveness of brand support needs to be assessed over a much longer period of time than in consumer marketing.

More loyalty involved

Whilst consumers are generally loyal to particular brands, from time to time they like to experiment with new brands. In organizational marketing, however, it is much more common for purchasers to seek long-term buying relationships with particular suppliers. They have invested a considerable amount of work in the selection process and have learnt the idiosyncrasies of working with their suppliers. To experiment by trying out new supplier's brands has implications throughout the whole organization (e.g. delivery, quality control, production, invoice processing, etc.) and is not lightly entertained.

Segmentation is important

Just as certain groups are prone to buy certain types of brands in consumer markets, so clearly identifiable segments are also apparent in organizational purchasing. The characteristics of these segments, however, differ from those seen in consumer markets. For example, marketers of computer software brands (e.g. SPSS, BMDP, SAS) find it beneficial to segment potential purchasers according to their computing experience. Compared with more experienced users, novices appreciate a service that includes on-site programme loading facilities and training workshops to learn how to use the software.

Buyers are more rational

Organizational buying is generally more rational than consumer buying, even though emotional considerations still influence the final decision. They may not be a particularly dominant force, but they can still be part of the brand selection criteria. For example, some buyers like to be treated as very important people by sales repre-

Exhibit 5.3   *KLM recognize that there is an emotional side to the highly rational executive when presenting their brand (reproduced by kind permission of KLM Royal Dutch Airlines)*

sentatives and others question whether they can 'get on with the people in that firm'. If these 'less rational' issues are not satisfied, the competitor may succeed.

Greater risks are involved

Chapter 3 showed that perceived risk helps us to understand better why consumers select certain brands. Likewise, an understanding of perceived risk is useful in organizational buying. Buyers perceive risk when buying a new brand for the first time and look for ways of reducing it. One way is to involve more people in the evaluation process. One pharmaceutical company took heed of perceived risk in its marketing strategy. Its sales representatives had an estimate of the extent to which each GP is risk-averse. When launching a new drug they directed their calls initially towards those GPs with a high threshold for risk. Once these GPs have prescribed it and are satisfied with the results from the new drug, they are then encouraged to talk about the new drug with their colleagues. This is facilitated by the company hosting meetings at which, for example, there may be a lecture by a hospital consultant on a novel surgical technique.

It is important that marketers do not overlook the risk dimension in career advancement. Some buyers may be particularly ambitious to gain rapid promotion and are keen to show what improvements they have achieved for the firm. If approached by a new supplier, with a particularly attractive brand proposition, they are likely to be receptive to change. By contrast, the purchasing manager who has gradually achieved promotion may be more cautious and therefore less receptive to a new brand proposition.

In conclusion, there are differences between consumer and organizational markets. These differences, however, are subtle. Consequently, marketers do not need to get to grips with a whole new series of branding tools. Rather they have to appreciate how to fine-tune the techniques widely practised in consumer marketing. One topic that warrants particular attention is the number of people involved in the organizational brand buying process.

Who buys brands?

Brand buying in organizations typically involves several people. A buying centre, sometimes also called a decision-making unit, is a group of people from different departments who are involved in the evaluation and selection of a particular brand. When buying a particular brand of capital equipment, for example, it is likely that representatives from engineering, purchasing, finance, manufacturing, marketing and site services will be involved. It is not unusual,

a decision-making unit, is a group of people from different departments who are involved in the selection and evaluation of a particular brand

What some relocating employees go through is painful.

Companies who try to relocate people themselves can often run into trouble.

By underestimating the emotional turmoil, they risk creating unhappy, resentful employees and losing valuable productivity; moreover, the whole exercise can send budgets distinctly into the red.

Work with Black Horse Relocation, on the other hand, and you'll see that the advantages of expert help clearly outweigh the costs. Indeed, our unique expense management service can save you time and money.

As part of Lloyds TSB, we've all the resources to buy employees' homes, so they can move with the least hassle.

Equally, we invest time and effort to understand what you want from relocation and to ensure that every concern is met, every detail covered.

In fact, it's because we're so proactive that we are the UK's leading relocation company.

To find out more, call us free on 0800 371047, or e-mail us at solutions@bhrs.co.uk.

It could be the best move you'll ever make.

Black Horse Relocation Services Limited,
Black Horse House, 59-60 Thames Street, Windsor, Berkshire SL4 1TX. Fax: 01753 854940.

 Black Horse Relocation

Exhibit 5.4 *Both the Black Horse Relocation advertisements raise different aspects of risk in employee relocation, then show how choosing this brand is a risk reducer (reproduced by kind permission of Black Horse Relocation and Primary Contact Ltd)*

particularly when larger firms buy expensive and complex brands, to see as many as twenty people involved in the buying centre. This typically occurs when the organization has little experience of a new brand, or when they perceive a high degree of risk in purchasing a complex and expensive item. One of the reasons for such a wide range of skills and functional backgrounds, is the greater sense of confidence amongst the decision makers.

International relocation.
For some, the feeling of isolation is total.

An assignment abroad is a positive challenge for most employees. Yet it can also resemble being cast adrift when family and friends are hundreds of miles away.

Black Horse, though, has ways to make the most exotic destination quickly feel like home.

In fact, whether you're relocating people from London to Lisbon, or from Southampton to Singapore, you can depend on us.

That's because we operate across 75 countries through a centrally-managed network that offers the same degree of care and attention to detail which has helped build our reputation in the UK.

This includes giving employees a personal Relocation Adviser who handles everything before departure.

Once abroad, a local consultant supports employees and their family, helping to familiarise them with the area, find a home and settle into their new life.

For further details, call us free on 0800 371047, or e-mail us at solutions@bhrs.co.uk. You'll see how we ensure international relocation is a rewarding experience.

Black Horse Relocation Services Limited,
Black Horse House, 59-60 Thames Street, Windsor, Berkshire SL4 1TX. Fax: 01753 854940.

Exhibit 5.4 *continued*

Where the user has a continual need for specific items, such as, rubber seals for car doors, the buying will typically be left to the purchasing manager. Even here, however, the user is likely to produce and update the specification for the purchasing manager.

In situations where the user has expert knowledge of a particular area and is not involved in major financial expenditures, they alone will make the brand decision. An example of this is the market research manager deciding which consultant to employ for a specific project.

The matrix in Figure 5.1 is a useful guide when anticipating who is likely to be involved in the organizational brand purchase decision. This can be predicted from the commercial risk facing the organization and its perception of the degree of product/service complexity. When, for example, the firm feels there is a considerable financial commitment, both in the initial purchase cost and in running and maintenance costs, in buying a brand that is difficult to assess functionally because it involves unfamiliar features the organization will feel at its most vulnerable. In such a situation there is likely to be at least one person from each of the interested departments. After they have evaluated alternative brands, it is probable that recommendations will then be channelled to more senior levels for final consideration.

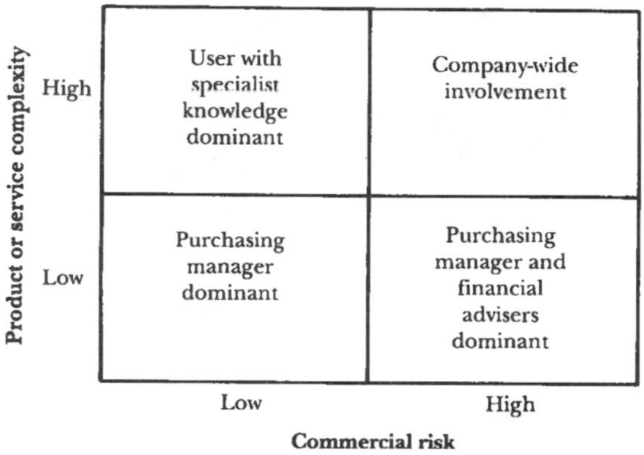

Figure 5.1   *Predicting who will be involved in brand purchasing*

As the matrix indicates, the purchasing manager rarely makes brand purchase decisions alone. In general buying centres, rather than individuals, become involved in brand selection when:

*   the size of the purchasing firm becomes larger;
*   the firm has little experience of buying or using the brand;
*   there is weak loyalty towards a supplier;
*   the brand is regarded as being an important part of the production process;
*   the financial size of the order increases;
*   individuals perceive risk of any kind in buying the brand.

membership of the buying centre changes as more information becomes available

Membership of the buying centre changes as more information becomes available. For example, if in the early stages of the evaluation process it was learnt that one of the competing brands could be either bought or leased, then the team would be supplemented by a financial adviser able to evaluate these options.

Brand marketers need to put themselves in the organization's position and consider which departments will be most affected by their brand. If the brand offers a significant opportunity for the organization to cut production costs, but after-sales service will deteriorate for a few months, it is likely that production, marketing, customer service and finance will be involved in the buying decision. The relative importance of any member in the buying centre varies according to the type of product being bought. For example, plant managers and engineers are more influential than purchasing managers when buying technically sophisticated capital equipment. Plant managers are the most active information seekers in buying centres and members of the buying centre often refer to them rather than going to external sources for information.

Having identified the members of the buying centre, the brand marketer needs to monitor it to identify any shifts in terms of who the key deciders are. X-ray film used to be sold to hospitals on the basis that the deciders in the buying centre were the radiologists and the technicians. However, with the government's review and changes to the NHS, this led to a greater involvement of administrators in the buying process. It has been argued that brands in the medical X-ray film market succeeded because marketers recognized the changing composition of the buying centres and altered their presentations to reflect the increasing importance of administrators.

Anticipating the role of buying centre members

Often, recommendations about brand purchases are referred to senior management or directors, because the evaluating team have a limit on how much they can spend. Yet even after this highly rational process, the decision may be overruled for an emotional reason. We learnt about one organization who employed an IT consultant to work with its managers in evaluating and recommending which computer to buy. A recommendation was made to the board about two possible brands. The decision was overruled in favour of the more expensive and less technically sophisticated option. The chairman thanked the team for its work, but felt that it was safer to stay with a well-known brand, even though he had very little knowledge of IT. If the brand marketers had had more insight into the roles played by the purchasing team, this outcome may have favoured their brand.

One of the most widely-employed ways of understanding the different roles of members of the buying centre is based on the five categories: users; influencers; deciders; buyers; and gatekeepers.

Users

Users are those people in the firm who will be using the brand. These people usually start the buying process and write the requirement specifications. Problems are sometimes created for the marketer when there are two or more groups of users, with conflicting objectives. For example, a chemist in a laboratory may want a particular brand of spectrometer because of its high resolution capabilities, but the R&D manager, who would make less frequent use of the spectrometer, is concerned about the lack of space to house the equipment. The shrewd marketer needs to identify who the primary and secondary users are and find the right balance in appealing to each group.

Influencers

often consultants are employed to write brand specifications or to help evaluate the competing brands

Influencers are sometimes difficult to identify as they can either exert influence directly, by defining brand criteria requirements, or indirectly, through informally providing information. For example, a manager evaluating particular brands of oscilloscopes would seek information from potential suppliers, but in a chance corridor meeting may learn the views of a colleague in a different department. Influencers are not just those people inside the organization, but can include external consultants. Often consultants are employed to write brand specifications or to help evaluate the competing brands. They may also include individuals working in competing firms who, because of their perceived expertise, are approached through the informal networking system.

Deciders

Deciders have the power to make the final decision about which brand should be bought. Ironically, it is sometimes difficult to identify these people. For example, the user may have written the specification requirement in such a way that only one brand can be bought. Or, in the final debate, conducted in a closed session, the managing director may make the decision but leave the purchasing manager to place the order. Thus, the purchasing manager may appear to be the decider, when in fact it is the managing director.

Buyers

Buyers are those with the formal authority for arranging the purchase. While the purchasing manager may appear very forceful in negotiations, often the objectives are specified by others in the organization. For relatively routine, low-cost purchases, the purchasing manager will proceed without recourse to company-wide discussion.

It should be appreciated that purchasing managers are keen on main-taining and improving their status within the firm. To do this, they employ several tactics. For example, some are deliberately rule-ori-ented. Regardless of who approaches them, they insist on working by the book and take no actions until in receipt of formal notifica-tion, even though verbal decisions were reached earlier. Such an approach causes frustration amongst all those who need to work with purchasing. Another tactic seen is that of favouring a few colleagues. Just for these few individuals, purchasing managers project an aura of friendship and willingness to help, expecting in return favours to be done for them.

Gatekeepers

Gatekeepers are individuals who control the flow of information into the buying centre. They may be the managing director's secretary, opening the daily post and deciding which circulars should be seen. Or the purchasing manager, insisting to the receptionist that any salespeople seeking new business with the firm should always be directed to the purchasing department. Gatekeepers tend to exert their influence at the early stage of the buying process when the full range of competing brands needs to be identified.

It must be appreciated that the same person can perform several of these roles. The challenge facing the brand marketer is to identify who is playing which role and when any one member of the buying centre becomes more influential. Evidence suggests that the purchas-ing department becomes more influential when:

- commercial considerations, e.g. delivery, terms of payment, are seen to be more important than technical considerations;
- the item is routinely bought;
- the purchasing department is highly regarded within the firm because of their specialized knowledge of suppliers;
- the technology underpinning the brand has not changed for some time, neither have the evaluation criteria.

When members of the buying centre meet, individuals from different departments with different motivations are bought together. Group dynamics may cause tension and covert attempts are made by some members to gain a more influential position. In a large buy-ing centre, people sense that those who have expert knowledge are more powerful influencers. Surveys have shown that these individu-als are also powerful when the firm does not feel it is under pressure to arrive at a rapid brand decision.

Armed with a better understanding of who is likely to be involved in the buying centre and of the roles these individuals are likely to play, brand marketers should be better able to decide how to position their brand to appeal to the different participants. They should also be able to anticipate where the influencing power lies and thus, where more effort should be directed. By also appreciating the stages of the buying process, they should be able to assess when more effort needs to be put behind their brand, an issue which is considered next.

The organizational buying process

An eight-step process

Robinson developed a model that charts the organizational buying process as an eight-stage process

In common with the way we model consumer buying behaviour as a process, starting with problem recognition and progressing through to post-purchase evaluation, so the same logic satisfactorily describes organizational buying. Robinson and his team of researchers (1967) developed a model that charts the organizational buying process as an eight-stage process, shown in Figure 5.2.

The process starts when the firm becomes aware of a problem. For example, their product is outdated, an opportunity for a new line has been identified, a piece of capital equipment has broken, and so on. Someone within the organization recognizes this problem and starts to involve others. They would consider how their particular problem should be solved. A detailed specification would be drawn up at the third stage and, following internal discussions, this would be redrafted until it reflected a consensus view. If marketers know who will draw up the specification, they can target their brand's commercial and technical promotion. At the fourth stage, the organization searches for potential suppliers and qualifies these. The criteria for qualification are considered later in this chapter. Some of the possible suppliers will be eliminated at this stage.

```
1  Anticipation/recognition of a problem
2  Determine what item is necessary
3  Describe characteristics and quantity of item needed
4  Search and qualification of potential suppliers
5  Acquisition of proposals
6  Proposals evaluation and supplier selection
7  Selection of order routine
8  Performance feedback and evaluation
```

Figure 5.2   *The organizational buying process (after Robinson et al. 1967)*

The screened suppliers would then be invited to submit their brand proposals. This normally entails a series of meetings to ensure that the supplier fully understands the company's needs. Each of the proposals are analysed against the agreed evaluation criteria and a brand purchase decision made. The purchasing manager is then given the authority to place the order and undertake any negotiations about terms and deliveries. Finally, once the brand has been used, an internal review takes place and assesses how well the brand and the supplier are performing against the evaluation criteria. This would usually only be done formally if the brand proved unsatisfactory. However, it is likely that there would be an informal review, where individuals would talk amongst themselves about the brand's capabilities.

While this eight-phase model describes the buying stages passed through, the amount of time and effort devoted to any one phase depends on the type of purchase. Robinson and his team identified three types of purchases: **new task**; **modified rebuy**; and **straight rebuy**. These three types of purchases give some indication about the amount of effort undertaken by the buying centre.

New task

In the new task purchase, the organization has no previous experience of buying the product or service. In this situation, the purchasing firm will put in a lot of work and will seek a considerable amount of information about different brands. Marketers have to work hard explaining how their brand can solve the purchaser's problem. The buying centre feel that there is a lot of risk in this purchase and the marketers should present their brands as a low-risk option, describing how other firms have successfully benefited from using the brand.

Modified rebuy

In the modified rebuy situation, the firm has experience of buying brands in the product field but feels it is time to consider whether significantly better brands are available. An example of this would be the office services manager becoming aware of the benefits of fax machines with laser printers, rather than with thermal printers. The organization knows that there will be a lot of work involved in finding a new brand, as well as in adapting its internal processes to absorb the change. It feels, however, that the benefits from change warrant the review.

For the firm currently supplying the organization, news of a re-evaluation of alternative suppliers should alert them to the dangers of complacency. A thorough and rapid review should be instigated to assess:

news of a re-evaluation of alternative suppliers should alert them to the dangers of complacency

- how the supplier is currently working with the purchaser (e.g.

Has there been a change in personnel causing friction? Have deliveries been on time? Are there any problems with quality?);
- what market changes are occurring?;
- what competitive brands are available and how these compare against their brand.

A meeting should be convened with the purchasing firm to identify their revised needs fully and a programme of change instigated. One lesson that can be learnt from this is that organizations often seek relationships with suppliers based on an expectation that they will always be trying to improve their brands in order to give their customers an even better deal. We are aware of an industrial advertising agency which holds regular seminars for its clients about new issues in marketing. These seminars are valued by its clients, who feel that not only do they have a good advertising agency but they are also being kept up to date and are able to become more effective.

Straight rebuy

The straight rebuy situation involves repeat purchasing of previously bought brands. In such cases, the purchasing process is relatively fast and simple. It is handled on a routine basis, increasingly using electronic reordering. The purchasing organization has a lot of relevant experience about the brand and, apart from the reordering mechanics, little other effort is expended. In some industries (e.g. packaging), it is not unusual for the purchaser to split the order between two suppliers. If problems occur with one supplier, the purchaser immediately increases the order with the second supplier. It is clearly in the interest of the 'in' supplier not only to ensure customer satisfaction with their brand, but also to make the reordering procedure as easy as possible.

Once the customer starts to order the brand routinely, it may well prove profitable for the marketer to develop and pay for the customer to have a computerized reordering system. Otherwise, the 'in' supplier may face the problem of technological developments in purchasing making it easier for buyers to change brands. For example, AT&T Istel developed a computer system, Formtrac, facilitating the purchasing of business stationery. Business customers enter their requirements in a computer network and promptly receive a list of potential suppliers. The user can then send an electronic invitation for quotations to specified suppliers through the system and subsequently place an electronic order. The Internet is now making this more common.

The importance of the different departments in the firm varies according to the type of purchase. One study (Naumann *et al.* 1984) looked at the top two influential departments in firms buying small components. In Table 5.1 we see how the source of influence varied through the buying process according to the firm's buying experience. In the **new buy** situation, engineering emerged as the most influential department throughout most stages of the buying process, surpassed only in the final brand selection stage by purchasing. In the **modified rebuy** situation, purchasing took the initiative in suggesting the need to reconsider alternative suppliers, with engineering being the dominant party when preparing the revised specification. From this stage onwards, purchasing played the leading role, supported by engineering. In the **straight rebuy** situation, production alerted the firm about the need to buy component parts, from which point onwards purchasing was the dominant department.

Table 5.1   *Most influential departments (after Naumann et al. 1984)*

	Purchase situation		
Purchase stage	New buy	Modified rebuy	Straight rebuy
Need identification	Engineering Purchasing	Purchasing Production	Production Purchasing
Prepare specification	Engineering Purchasing	Engineering Purchasing	Purchasing Engineering
Evaluate proposals	Engineering Purchasing	Purchasing Engineering	Purchasing Engineering
Brand selection	Purchasing Engineering	Purchasing Engineering	Purchasing Engineering

Brand values in industrial branding

Although many competing industrial brands have similar physical specifications and performance capabilities, in each market only one of these brands achieves and maintains the dominant market position. One of the reasons for this is that the brand leader has been well differentiated and customers perceive greater value, anticipating the leading brand to be superior in some way. Mudambi and her colleagues (1997) developed a framework which helps us better understand the nature of brand value in industrial marketing. They argue that brand value is a function of the expected price and the expected performance of four components. These components are the product itself, the distribution of the brand, the services support-

brand value is a function of the expected price and the expected performance of four components

ing the brand and the company itself. Each of these four performance elements has a tangible component (e.g. the physical quality of
the product) and an intangible component (e.g. the reputation of the
company). When seeking to differentiate an industrial brand through
its value to customers, this framework, displayed in Figure 5.3, therefore helps managers to assess how each of the four performance
elements is adding value on both the tangible and intangible components.

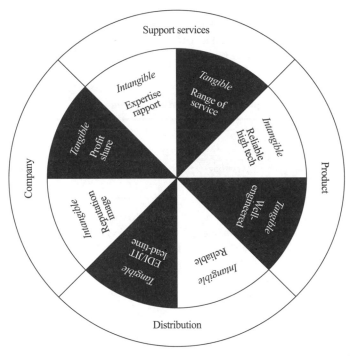

Figure 5.3   *The pinwheel of industrial brand value (after Mudambi et al.
1997)*

Product performance is the core of the brand's value. In the
case of a computer the tangible product performance characteristics
include its processing speed and the size of its memory. A model
may be preferred due to the intangible component of perceived reliability. **Distribution performance** includes ease of ordering,
availability and speed of delivery. Office stationery retailers assess
their suppliers through tangible measures, such as lead-times and
range of products available. However, the final choice will also be
influenced by intangible factors, such as the willingness and ability
to respond rapidly to an unusually large and urgent order. **Support
services performance** involves issues such as technical support, training and financial support. Many car manufacturers assess suppliers
on the tangible basis of whether they are able to provide technical

support during the research and design stages. Some of these suppliers may be chosen because, on the intangible dimension, they also tailor their communication systems to meet the manufacturer's request. **Company performance** covers all aspects of the company. There is an underlying assumption that industrial customers prefer to deal with companies that are reliable and successful. The tangible evaluation of a management consultancy could include its size, geographical coverage and financial stability. In the final decision, intangible aspects will also be considered, such as its reputation and perceived experience in different industries.

This framework was tested in the UK precision bearings market, where interviews were undertaken with manufacturers, distributors and purchasers. The results indicated that although price is rated overall as the most important criteria, it is considered less important at the early screening stage. Price plays a less dominant role during the purchase of original equipment, as opposed to that of replacement parts. The research highlighted the importance of intangible product and company attributes in adding value, as shown in Table 5.2. This research demonstrated that intangible factors are important in rational and systematic decision making. These factors can provide a key source of differentiation, especially when it is difficult to continue to compete on product quality or price. There is a limit to how much brands can be improved through enhancing their physical performance. Once this limit is exceeded, the brand becomes criticized as being over-engineered.

Table 5.2 *Summary of perceived sources of value in precision bearings (after Mudambi et al. 1997)*

Product	Distribution	Support	Company
Tangible	*Tangible*	*Tangible*	*Tangible*
Precision	Stated availability	Design advice	Financial stability
Load Bearing	Stated lead-times	Product testing	Years of experience
Dimensions	EDI and JIT	Site support	Global coverage
Intangible	*Intangible*	*Intangible*	*Intangible*
Innovation	Ease of ordering	Understands our	World class
Fit for purpose	Reliable delivery	needs/business	Technical leadership
Well-engineered	Emergency response	Troubleshooting	Global perspective

Brands as relationship builders

A weakness of the Robinson model is that it does not address sufficiently well the relationships between buyers and sellers. In the 1980s our understanding of organizational brand buying was increased by an international project undertaken by the IMP Group which subsequently led to a lot of research into relationship marketing. They found that both buyers and sellers were seeking close, long-term relationships. Many of their interviews with different industrialists showed a desire for stability. The broad implications for brand marketers are that they should look at brand marketing, not just in terms of marketing resource management, but also in terms of employing the right interpersonal skills and managing relationships through the most appropriate negotiating style.

Buyers were reticent about switching between competing brands because:

- they did not want to keep on spending more time in finding and evaluating alternative brands;
- they were worried about technical problems in adapting their production processes for a new brand;
- they might have had internal production problems which could be easier to resolve by involving a loyal supplier.

Many purchasers were of the opinion that they had a very good working relationship with their suppliers. As such, any brand alternative had to be extremely good to warrant any thought about change.

The IMP Group showed that the relationship between the brand marketer and the purchasing organization was influenced by four factors: the interaction process; the organizations involved; the atmosphere affecting and affected by the interaction; and the environment within which the interaction took place.

The interaction process

In the interaction process, a series of 'episodes' take place between an order being placed and delivered. For example, the brand exchange, information exchange, financial exchange and social exchange. Over a period of time, these exchange episodes lead to institutionalized expectations about the respective roles of buyer and seller. For example, there are unwritten rules about which party will hold stock. Many case histories showed that stable relationships were characterized by frequent social and information exchanges.

Organizations

By looking at the characteristics of the two organizations, there is some indication of the likely relationship. Technical issues are often important indicators of the likely buyer–seller relationship. Ultimately the interaction process is concerned with matching the production technology of the seller to the application technology of the buyer. Where the two organizations are at different stages of technological development, then their working relationship will be different from that where two firms have a similar level of technical expertise. Likewise, where the two firms are of a different size, or have little experience of working together, or have individuals with differing backgrounds, then the relationship between buyer and seller will take a lot of work to ensure harmony.

Atmosphere

The relationship between the two firms is affected by the overall atmosphere, which itself can be characterized by several factors. For example, the firms' mutual expectations, the overall closeness or distance of the relationship, whether there is a sense of conflict or cooperation and whether the dominant firm is trying to use its power over the weaker partner. Where there is an atmosphere of overall closeness, cost advantages can be gained through a variety of sources, such as more efficient negotiation and administration, joint work on redesigning existing brands and more effective distribution. By contrast, some atmospheres may be characterized by a power–dependence relationship. For example, to ensure brand deliveries are scheduled primarily for the convenience of the powerful purchaser, the purchaser will take advantage of the supplier's dependence on his firm.

Environmental issues

The wider environmental issues such as social systems, channel structure and market dynamism have an effect on the interaction relationship. The buyer and seller have to appreciate the type of social system they are working in. For example, the brand supplier has to be aware of any nationalistic buying preferences they are facing. The relationship will also be affected by the type of channel used – an electronic components' producer may sell to an actuator producer who in turn sells a range of actuators to another firm working on aircraft systems. The relationship between any two firms in this extended channel will be influenced by the relationships between other members of the channel. Highly dynamic markets, characterized by frequent new brand launches, make suppliers and purchasers aware of the need for a large number of relationships which are not as intense as may be the case with much more stable markets.

By taking account of these four influencing factors, brand marketers can better appreciate the basis for their relationships with purchasing organizations. They should make all of the brand team aware of the institutionalized activities that each purchaser takes for granted and protect these from being cut in recessionary periods. Making changes to institutionalized activities without thorough negotiation is likely to sour the working relationship.

The IMP research shows that the same brand support teams cannot work as effectively with every customer. The relationship of trust and mutual respect will be nurtured when people are selected because their backgrounds and personalities are ideal for sustaining a long-term working relationship with certain customers. This research makes the point that both rational and emotional factors influence brand selection, an issue that we consider in more detail.

managers have little time to continually explore alternative long-term relationships with new partners

Managers have little time to continually explore alternative long-term relationships with new partners. The pressure to achieve higher quality standards, implement JIT and reduce the time taken to launch new brands has led them to work more closely with a lower number of partners. Wilson (1995) has developed a useful matrix to reflect which potential candidates could become effective relationship partners, as shown in Figure 5.4.

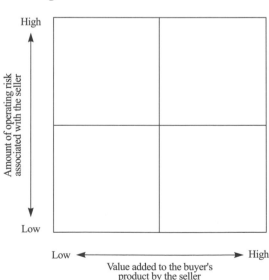

Figure 5.4   *Classifying potential partners (after Wilson 1995)*

Those firms who represent a low operating risk as a partner and who show high value added to the buyer's business are ideal relationship partners. Relationships between buyers and sellers have always existed, but today's increasing competition, pressure to reduce costs and the need for profitable alliances have transformed these relationships into key strategic tools which improve a company's performance.

Wilson has expanded on the four factors of the IMP research and identified variables that can predict the success of a relationship between buyer and seller. These are:

- *commitment*: the desire and the effort of both parties to continue the relationship;
- *trust*: the belief that each partner will act in the best interest of the other;
- *cooperation*: complementary actions taken to achieve mutually beneficial outcomes – if the outcomes are beneficial to only one partner, this bodes badly for the future relationship;
- *mutual goals*: the degree to which partners share goals;
- *interdependence and power*: the degree of power balance between partners, which determines the degree of dependence of one partner on the other;
- *performance satisfaction*: the degree to which firms can meet or exceed the expectations of the partner;
- *structural bonds*: systems, such as shared technology, interlinking the two companies so closely that it becomes difficult to end the relationship;
- *comparison level of the alternatives*: the number of choices a company has among available high-quality outcomes. The fewer high-quality partners a company has, the more dependent the company will be on the current ones;
- *adaptation*: the degree of modifications one company undergoes to accommodate the needs of the partner;
- *non-retrievable investments*: the amount of resources a company commits specifically to that relationship;
- *shared technology*: the degree to which one partner uses the technology contributed by the other partner to the relationship;
- *social bonds*: the degree of personal relationship that develops between the firms.

These factors measure the degree of dependence between the two parties in a relationship and help anticipate the likelihood of the relationship continuing. Their importance varies according to the stage of the relationship. For example, trust has more importance in the early stages than later on. There are five stages in the relationship:

- *search and selection* of an appropriate partner;
- *definition of the purpose* of each partner, so that a satisfactory balance of power can be developed;
- *setting boundaries,* which consider where each partner's organization ends and the hybrid exists and when they can make legitimate claims on each other;
- *creating value,* which consider the processes which will add greatest value to each partner and the best way to share the value;
- *maintaining the relationship,* when both parties strive for the long-term survival of their bond. At this stage most of the factors become latent.

Figure 5.5 shows when the different relationship factors (including the new factor of *reputation*) become more important over the five stages of the evolving relationship.

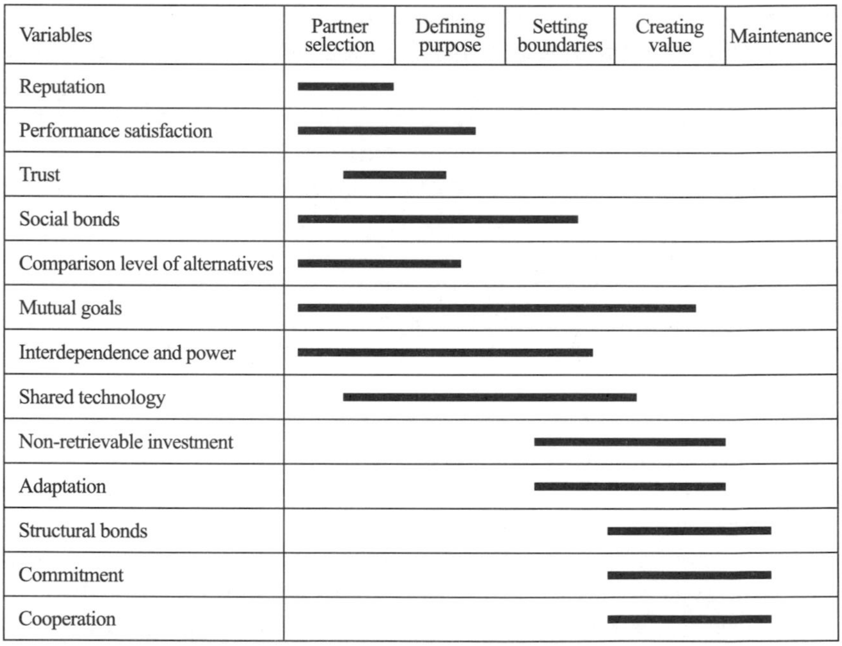

Variables	Partner selection	Defining purpose	Setting boundaries	Creating value	Maintenance
Reputation	▬				
Performance satisfaction	▬▬				
Trust	▬				
Social bonds	▬▬▬				
Comparison level of alternatives	▬▬				
Mutual goals	▬▬▬▬▬				
Interdependence and power	▬▬▬▬				
Shared technology	▬▬▬▬				
Non-retrievable investment			▬▬▬		
Adaptation			▬▬▬		
Structural bonds				▬▬▬	
Commitment				▬▬▬	
Cooperation				▬▬▬	

Figure 5.5 *The changing nature of business relationships (after Wilson 1995)*

character and content of a buyer–seller relationship evolves over time

Wilson's framework indicates that the character and content of a buyer–seller relationship evolves over time, though these changes are not necessarily sequential or as clearly defined in practice. Each stage is an opportunity for both partners to assess the relationship and decide whether to maintain, broaden or curtail it.

One of the key drivers for developing relationships is the chance to create more value. However, assessing whether extra value has resulted from the relationship can be difficult and a dogmatic calculation of individual benefits may damage the relationship. Nevertheless, the relationship exists in order to add value or reduce costs to the parties engaged. Therefore, some attempt needs to be made to agree upon a reasonable system to determine the degree of value created by each party and their share of the profits. This will necessitate an 'open-book' policy, where both parties provide full details about how they have helped to enhance value.

There clearly are costs involved in developing a relationship and these should be identified, then balanced against the extra value that the relationship might bring. Some of the extra costs include the effort to coordinate the activities of both parties, the time necessary for each party to learn about the other organization, and the work to blend both production, selling and administration systems.

Factors influencing brand selection

When choosing between competing brands a thorough evaluation, particularly for brands new to the firm, takes place, often with an agreed list of attributes. This reflects the views of all members of the buying centre. But a more covert assessment also takes place. This is based on social ('Can I get on with this rep?') and psychological ('Will I be respected if I'm seen to be buying from that firm?') considerations. Let us now examine some of these rational and emotional issues.

Rational brand evaluation criteria

In business to business marketing, considerably more emphasis is placed on the use of resources which appeal to buyers' rational, rather than emotional considerations. For instance, a survey amongst firms marketing high technology brands showed that considerable importance was placed on having state-of-the-art technology, employing effective salespeople, backing the brand with a strong service capability, being price competitive and offering a complete product range. Much less importance was placed on engendering a favourable attitude between the buyer and the sales representative.

It is not possible to generalize about the kinds of functional components of a brand that might appeal to buyers since this depends on several factors, some of which include:

- the different requirements of members of the buying centre;
- the type of industry buying the brand;

• the type of product being bought.

It is unlikely that all members of the **buying centre** will be equally interested in the same attributes. People work in different departments, with different backgrounds and different expectations of the brand. In fact, the brand marketer may well face a situation where different members have opposing views about relevant brand criteria. A chief chemist may be particularly concerned about the purity of a brand of solvent, while the purchasing manager's sole concern is keeping costs down. In a study considering the marketing of solar air conditioning systems, it was shown just how diverse the evaluation criteria were amongst members of the buying centre. Plant managers were more attentive to operating costs, whilst general managers were more concerned about the modernity of the brand and its potential for energy saving.

If the same brand is being sold to **different industries**, it is unlikely that they will be using the same evaluation criteria. In a study comparing the evaluation criteria used by manufacturing companies and hospitals, it was found that while there were some similarities, there were also major differences – both manufacturers and hospitals regarded reliability and efficiency as being very important issues, but hospitals saw after-sales service as a key factor, whilst the manufacturers rated the technical capabilities of the brand as very important.

The greater the similarity between purchasing industries, the greater the likelihood of similar evaluation criteria being used. When comparing the use of twenty brand evaluation criteria between electric power generating industries and electronic manufacturers, there were only four criteria not considered to be of the same importance (repair service, production facilities, bidding compliance and training aids).

The **type of product** also influences brand evaluation criteria. One particularly informative study was able to classify industrial products into four categories and showed that similar attributes were considered according to the category. Specifically, the four most important considerations for each category were:

1   for frequently ordered products that pose no problems in use: reliable delivery; price; flexibility; and reputation;
2   for products requiring training for use: technical service; ease of use; training offered; and reliability of delivery;
3   for products where there is uncertainty about whether the product will perform satisfactorily in a new application: reliability of delivery; flexibility; technical service; and information about product reliability;
4   for products where there is considerable debate amongst the

buying centre, price; reputation; information on product reliability; and reliability of delivery.

There is an erroneous belief amongst some business to business marketers that brands succeed if they offer an attractively low price to purchasers. This is not so. A team of researchers examined the buying records of large manufacturing companies. They focused on 112 purchases of capital equipment. From this database they found that, on average, three competing brands were evaluated before a purchase decision was made and, in 41 per cent of the purchases, the

an erroneous belief amongst some business to business marketers that brands succeed if they offer an attractively low price

Exhibit 5.5   *Mercedes Trucks directly counter the incorrect way of evaluating a truck just on its purchase price (reproduced by kind permission of Mercedes-Benz (UK) Ltd)*

BEAT THE MONEY CRUNCH#1

Nabisco doesn't tie up your money in warehouse costs.

Money's never been more expensive. So you can't afford to tie yours up in warehouse inventory of crackers and cookies. With Nabisco you won't.
• Nabisco delivers crackers and cookies direct to your stores - You save on transportation costs.
• Nabisco carries the inventory - You cut warehousing costs.
• No overstocking - Deliveries are adjusted to individual store movement.
• Nabisco products usually sell through before payment is due.

Here are other ways Nabisco helps you beat the money crunch:
• **Fast turnover** - An average of 25 times a year-up to double the average of other cookies and crackers.
• **High monthly return** - Almost 39% return on investment based on a 24% gross margin and 2.08 turns per month.
• **Maximum ROI** - Nabisco provides two studies to help you maximize profits on your entire cookie and cracker investment. A computerized ROI study plus a Space Management Study.

For more information on how Nabisco can help you, ask for Nabisco Biscuit Division Sales Representative for profit making details for your stores. Free of charge or obligation.

NABISCO; INC.
BISCUIT DIVISION
NABISCO. We're even more appetizing during the money crunch.

Exhibit 5.6   *Nabisco promotes the low cost of stocking its brands by explaining how ancillary costs are reduced*

successful brand was *not* the lowest priced bidder. The buyers paid a price premium for:

- interchangeability of parts;
- short delivery time;
- working with prestigious suppliers;
- full range of spare parts rapidly available;
- lower operating costs;
- lower installation costs;
- higher quality materials.

Only when competing brands are perceived as being very similar does price become important. A study investigated buyers' perceptions of different brands of electrical devices (oscilloscopes, switches, resistors, etc.). When buyers perceived *little* brand differentiation, the three main choice criteria were price, specifications and delivery. By contrast, when buyers perceived *significant* differences between competing brands, price was not one of the ten criteria considered. A similar finding resulted in another study amongst buyers purchasing undifferentiated brands of industrial cleaners, lubricants and abrasives. Price was viewed as being one of the key choice criteria when choosing between mainly undifferentiated brands.

Even when price is a dominant choice criterion, different aspects of price are considered by the buyers. The purchase price of the brand may appear to be high, but when taking into account longer term economies resulting from the brand, such as lower defect rates in production, the buyer may well look at the purchase in terms of the long-term savings and quality improvements. Buyers also consider the brand's life cycle costs – the total costs likely over the lifetime of the brand. Mercedes-Benz trucks were once advertised using the slogan 'Are you buying a truck or an iceberg?', underneath which was an iceberg depicting the fact that over the vehicle's life the buying price represented 15 per cent of the cost and the running costs 85 per cent. Another example was a press advertisement from Fujitsu ICL for their ErgoPro range of networked PCs. The caption 'Penny wise, pound foolish?' highlighted the fact that buyers do not face just the cost of buying a PC, but also the long-term costs of ownership.

Going with too low a price makes the buyer wonder what has been cut. We are aware of one consultant who lost a project because his price was too low compared with the other bidder. The client could not understand how the consultant could do a sufficiently thorough piece of work at such a low price. It transpired that as he worked alone he had much smaller overheads and was content to operate at lower margins than the more expensive firms, yet his low price lost him the contract. Thus, in common with consumer brand marketing, there exists a feeling of 'you get what you pay for'.

There are other reasons why pitching the brand at a low price may not be wise. Some buyers are evaluated on their ability to negotiate discounts and pricing low allows little leeway for negotiations. There are also some buyers who seek the satisfaction of always being able to negotiate a better price.

In conclusion, functional issues are important components of organizational brands which appeal to the rational side of the buyer. But buyers are not solely concerned with quantitative measures to assess technical and commercial performance. The next section explores some of these non-rational criteria.

Emotional brand evaluation criteria

The individuals involved in the brand selection process enjoy the challenge of finding the best solution to the firm's problems. They are also motivated by more personal issues such as job security, a desire to be well-regarded by colleagues inside and outside the firm, the need for friendship, ego enhancement, aspirations of career advancement, loyalties based on their beliefs and attitudes and a whole host of other social and psychological considerations. In a study we undertook for a tin packaging manufacturer, we became very aware of these emotional brand selection issues. Our brief was to find out why purchasers only awarded small contracts to this firm. In a depth interview, one purchaser told us that he used to place large orders, but felt that the quality standards were too variable and only used this supplier for small runs. When asked why he still bothered to use them, he spoke about the good social relations he had built with the firm's managing director. He viewed our client

> as an old friend, whose company you value because of the years you've been together. But as you get older, you develop particular idiosyncrasies, which as a good friend you just accept and try to still enjoy their company.

He clearly valued his friendship with the managing director and, at a lower level of commitment, was still prepared to buy tin packaging, albeit for jobs where tin quality was not a critical issue.

The way buyers make decisions influenced by rational (objective) issues and emotional (subjective) factors can best be summarized in Figure 5.6.

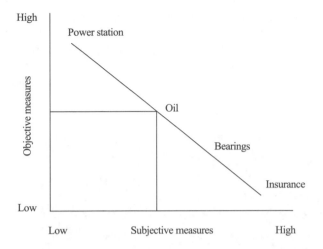

Figure 5.6   *The impact of objective and subjective issues on decisions*

It is obvious that a power station with significant capital costs, runnings costs and environmental impact, will be purchased primarily on objective/functional grounds. However, there is often little to choose between competing products and services such as lubricants, ball bearings, insurance and the like. In such cases, it is personal relationships and the perceived quality of the supplying company that make the difference. In these situations subjective measures become more important.

Buyers, as emotional individuals, take account of how the brand will affect them socially and psychologically. Having a brand delivered late not only affects production schedules, but also causes personal anguish. Late delivery is interpreted by some buyers as 'you're not that important to us'. It is a broken agreement, which is read as an attitude of complacency, and hurts their pride. They feel that the supplier is not serious about their business and start to wonder whether they can trust someone who shows such disinterest.

Buyers like to deal with prestigious suppliers as they feel this increases their status within the firm. They are proud to tell their colleagues that they are using particular suppliers as they believe they gain more credibility and authority, particularly when the supplier's corporate identity has clearly communicated associations of excellence.

The size of a supplier is not considered just in terms of production capabilities, but also as indicative of the type of relationship. Larger suppliers are sometimes viewed as impersonal, unapproachable, self-centred, bureaucratic firms, who are unlikely to be flexible. By contrast, smaller firms are perceived as warmer, friendlier, more attentive and more flexible in responding to the supplier's problems.

One purchasing manager was part of a team deciding whether

buyers, as emotional individuals, take account of how the brand will affect them socially and psychologically

to buy glass or tin packaging for a new grocery brand. In spite of the fact that technical data was obtained and evaluated, he recommended tin because he personally found glass aesthetically unappealing. To get around this personal dislike, the glass packaging manufacturer appealed to his emotional instincts by leaving a small glass statue on his desk. He hoped that the sight of this expensive statue on his desk would change the purchasing manager's attitude. In this case, func-

The new HP LaserJet 6L.
The personal printer that does
everything for you.

Like any respectable butler the HP LaserJet 6L wouldn't dream of keeping you waiting. It operates at a servile 6 pages per minute in any PC environment you care to choose. It also works best alongside its fellow servants, the Hewlett-Packard range of custom designed supplies. And with the 6L in charge, picking the paper up may be about the only thing left for you to do. For more information call HP on 0990 474747.

 HEWLETT®
PACKARD

HP PRINTERS. PAPER THAT WORKS FOR YOU.

Exhibit 5.7   *Hewlett-Packard is a respected, prestigious brand which users feel proud to be associated with (reproduced by kind permission of Hewlett-Packard)*

tional issues were less important to the buyer than emotional considerations.

This is but one of many examples showing the importance of positioning organizational brands to satisfy the emotional needs of buyers. For example, a surgical instrument manufacturer succeeded when they spoke about their brands not in cold, medical terms, but using instead the terms surgeons would use – 'smooth and elegant'.

Exhibit 5.8   *Allen & Hanburys present Beconase b.d. to GPs in a manner which not only satisfies their rational considerations but which also emotionally communicates the satisfaction of their patients (reproduced by kind permission of Glaxo Wellcome)*

In this case the manufacturer won through blending a technical approach to the communication with a more personal tone.

Understanding the psychological concerns of organizational buyers can give the brand an edge if other competitors are focusing solely on functional issues. In another study to understand why firms continued to purchase computers from the same organization we became aware of the importance of psychology. A buyer was ap-

Exhibit 5.9   *The Philips Pocket Memo appeals to managers' emotional desire to succeed in their careers*

proached by another supplier whose computer virtually matched the performance and cost characteristics of the incumbent. A few days later the buyer broke his leg and rang the incumbent computer firm to reject their invitation to a Grand Prix because of his accident. He was impressed by the way they sent a luxurious car to chauffeur him, and provided special facilities in their hospitality room at the race. This feeling of 'being special' helped maintain his loyalty.

As was pointed out earlier in this chapter, managers perceive risk when buying brands. By understanding managers' concerns about brand buying, marketers should then be able to devise ways of presenting their brand as a risk reducer. One study (Hawes and Barnhouse 1987) investigated purchasers' perceptions of personal risk when choosing between competing brands in a modified rebuy situation. Their concerns, after feeling personal remorse due to purchasing incompetence, were that relations with the internal user would be strained, the status of the purchasing department would decrease and there would be a less favourable annual career performance review, with less chance of promotion. Further details are shown in Figure 5.3.

Table 5.3   *Rankings of perceived personal risk in a modified rebuy (after Hawes and Barnhouse 1987)*

Perceived personal risk	Ranking of buyers' concerns
You will feel personally incompetent	1
Your relations with the company user will be strained	2
The status of the purchasing department will fall	3
Your performance review will be less favourable	4
You will have less chance of promotion	5
Your annual rise will be smaller	6
You will lose status among your peers	7
You will lose your job	8
Your popularity will fall	9

In order of importance, these buyers felt that the most effective way of reducing personal risk was to visit the supplier's plant and then to ask some of the supplier's customers about their opinion of the supplier. The rankings of the preferred ways of reducing personal risk are shown in Table 5.4 and indicate the emphasis marketers should place on these factors when trying to allay concerns about their brand.

Table 5.4   *Rankings of preferred ways to reduce personal risk (after Hawes and Barnhouse 1987)*

Perceived risk reduction	Buyers' preference ranking
Visit the supplier's plant	1
Talk with the supplier's customers	2
Multi-source the product	3
Insert penalty clauses in the contract	4
Ask colleagues' opinions	5
Only buy from firms used before	6
Seek senior managers' opinions	7
Only use well-known suppliers	8

As organizational buyers' perceptions of risk increases, they are more likely to consult informal, personal sources of information. Henthorne and his colleagues (1993) examined how organizational buyers' perception of risk is influenced by talking to people inside and outside their firm. A conclusion from their study is that suppliers should identify those sources who reduce buyers' perceptions of perceived risk, then consider whether they can be used to minimize other buyers' concerns in different firms. Specifically, marketers could provide names of satisfied customers and independent experts who can attest to the quality of the purchase. They found that the credibility of external advisers is often higher than that of internal staff.

Brand marketers can develop strategies that position their brand as an effective risk reducer. The Caterpillar Corporation is but one of many firms who benefited from understanding buyers' perceived risk. They were faced with the problem of firms producing inferior quality spare parts for after-sales service. These looked similar to the genuine Caterpillar part, but sold at a considerably lower price. Their lifetime was less than the genuine part and premature failing while in use could cause considerable engine damage. To counter this threat, Caterpillar developed a series of leaflets for its customers showing dice next to Caterpillar equipment. The headlines were 'Don't gamble with it', 'Don't play games with it', 'Don't risk it'. Each brochure showed photographs of the damage caused by using pirate parts. These successfully communicated the functional excellence of the brand, as well as resolving the buyer's personal risk about using only genuine parts.

Providing organizational buyers with brand information

In business to business brand marketing, buyers undertake a thorough evaluation of competing brands. Due to the more complex and expensive nature of brands, they rely much more on personalized messages. As such, more emphasis is placed on using sales representatives to present brand information. Their task, particularly when approaching new firms, is that much easier when the brand is recognized as emanating from a well-respected organization. Corporate advertising, reinforcing a clear corporate identity, can pave the way for a more effective sales presentation. The sales representatives don't have to spend long reassuring the buyer about the company, and can devote more time to explaining the brand's benefits.

Due to the more complex and expensive nature of brands, they rely much more on personalized messages

This promotional push, using advertising to give reassurance to customers and to enable salespeople to focus on brand capabilities, is seen in many industrial sectors. A survey (Traynor and Traynor 1989) amongst high technology firms, detailed in Table 5.5, showed that suppliers felt it was most important to promote their brands using the salesforce, advertising in trade magazines and displaying at trade shows. In fact, the average high technology firm spent 9 per cent of its annual revenue on the sales force, 3 per cent on advertising and 2 per cent on trade shows.

Table 5.5 *Sellers' importance ranking of promotional methods (after Traynor and Traynor 1989)*

Promotional method	Sellers' importance ranking
Sales representatives	1
Advertising in trade magazines	2
Trade shows	3
Technical seminars	4
Sales promotion materials	5
Direct mail advertising	6
Packaging	7
Newspapers/TV/radio advertising	8

We need to be careful, however, not to place too much emphasis on figures that talk about the importance that brand manufacturers place on different types of promotions. It emphasizes branding as an **input**, rather than an **output** process. It is more relevant to appreciate, from the buyer's perspective, how useful they believe different sources to be.

A study (Dempsey 1978) amongst purchasers of capital equipment and component materials found that buyers rated their purchasing records as the most useful source of information. This was followed by visits from salespeople and then discussions with their colleagues in other departments. Marketers who have a **range** of brands, may find it easier to widen their business with their existing customers since they can reassure themselves about their track record from their purchasing records. These results also indicate that brand marketers should build a favourable relationship with other departments in the firm, to give the purchaser a greater sense of confidence when they talk with other colleagues. The fourth most useful way of finding out about the brand was by visiting the supplier's factory and glancing through the relevant brochures. The results, in Table 5.6, show that trade advertisements are not seen as being that useful, mainly because the buyers consider these as being too general.

Table 5.6   *Buyers' ranking of information sources (after Dempsey 1978)*

Information source	Buyers' importance ranking
Consult purchasing records	1
Visit from sales person	2
Talk with other colleagues	3
Visit vendor's factory	4
Brochures	5
Look through purchasing directories	6
Credit and financial reports	7
Phone calls from sales person	8
Talk to external purchasing manager	9
Articles in trade press	10
Trade advertisements	11
Trade shows	12

The key points that the organizational brand marketer should not lose sight of are that buyers and their colleagues in the buying circle may well:

(a)   perceive the contents of the brand message differently from the marketer
      and;
(b)   perceive the content of the brand message differently between themselves.

As Chapter 3 discussed, people have finite mental capabilities and, to protect themselves from excessive amounts of information,

Exhibit 5.10   *Due to perceptual processes, the target audience's skim reading of this advertisement may not have registered that it is promoting Valentine Wood Business Park (reproduced by kind permission of* The Estates Gazette *and Campbell Gordon Consultants)*

their perceptual process filters much out. An example of this is shown in the advertisement in Exhibit 5.11 for Zantac in Germany (where it is known as Zantic). Glaxo wanted to communicate the anti-ulcer capabilities of this drug to GPs in Germany and took a one-page advertisement in a respected medical journal. At the bottom of the advertisement there is a detailed explanation of the brand's pharma-

FRAME 2
THE ZANTIC AD TESTED IN THE *ÄRZTE ZEITUNG*

Exhibit 5.11   *Due to legal requirements medical advertisers have to give considerable information about prescriptions when advertising their brands. Providing such a large quantity of information to busy GPs results in many skimming the points (reproduced by kind permission of Glaxo Wellcome GmbH & Co)*

cology. Subsequent research showed that none of the doctors read the detailed explanation about the drug. Most read the caption, skimmed over the brand name, but took little further notice of the advertisement.

Loctite is a good example of an organization that took steps to avoid the problem of different perceptions amongst members of the buying centre. It was concerned about the way different types of engineer in the buying firm interpreted their trade advertisements for its range of industrial adhesives. They conducted some market research and found that design engineers felt strong pressure on themselves to be 'right' and not make a bad decision. They were risk avoiders who liked to see diagrams, charts and graphs in brand advertisements, with explanations of how the brand worked. By contrast, plant engineers saw themselves as fixers, who kept things running by being creative in solving problems. They felt more comfortable with advertisements showing photographs of products rather than graphs. With this understanding of the different needs of members of the buying centre, Loctite then developed trade advertisements to appeal to specific types of engineers. A consequence of this was a greater similarity of perception amongst engineers about Loctite's industrial adhesives and this in turn led to greater sales success.

The company as a brand

In any purchase, organizational buyers are primarily concerned with the company's overall brand identity, rather than with the specific product they want to buy, and will remember their image of the company longer than any product information. An industrial buyer always questions a potential supplier's credibility, particularly whether they really are a specialist in their field. However, as we have discussed, as business decisions are taken by people, about people, there are also emotional factors involved and the supplier needs to ensure they have a well-conceived identity underpinned by a respected personality.

The purpose of corporate branding is to:

* make the company name known, distinct and credible in the mind of potential buyers;
* facilitate the building of relationships with buyers and suppliers;
* portray the benefits it offers to the buyer;
* embody the value system of the corporation.

To present themselves in the most favourable way, firms develop a **corporate identity** programme, ensuring that all forms of external communication are coordinated and presented in the same way. The problem is that corporate identity is akin to 'branding as an input process', as discussed in chapter 2. Owing to the problems created by the buyer's perceptual process, the resulting perception of the firm, its **corporate image**, may well be different from what was intended.

Corporate identity is a valuable asset which, if efficiently managed, can contribute to brand success. As such, any firm needs to manage its corporate identity programme in such a way that all members of a particular buying centre perceive a similar corporate image, encouraging a feeling of trust and confidence in the supplier. Each member of the buying centre could have a different line of contact with a particular supplier. Without a cohesive approach to managing the corporate identity, each member of the buying centre may perceive a different corporate image – a result which bodes badly for the brand. Buyers are impressed by the consistency with which the firm presents itself. Their increased confidence places the brand in a more favourable light.

A good example of a cohesive approach to managing corporate identity is the change in British Airway's corporate identity in 1997. Senior management had identified a need to change the BA brand strategy from being an airline to becoming a world travel expert and ultimately the undisputed leader in world travel. Market research had identified that perceptions of BA echoed dated Thatcherite values. The new values that BA wished to portray are being adaptable, culturally diverse and innovative. Working with Newell & Sorrell a new corporate identity was developed to reflect the new brand strategy and the new values. This resulted in 50 'world images' as designs for the aircraft tails. Prior to its launch, all 57 000 staff were briefed about BA's plans and its new corporate identity. Only when all staff were aware of the change did the launch take place.

Any corporate identity programme is supported by a myriad of resources. For example, the firm's name, its structure, employees, offices, letter-headed paper, promotional activity, core values, culture, logo, promotional work and even the way the telephone is answered. It is wrong to think that corporate identity equates to the logo – this is but the tip of the iceberg. Many people were amazed late in the 1980s to see ICI spending large sums of money on what amounted to only a slight change in their logo. In reality, the logo change was but a small part of the corporate identity. ICI had undergone a major review to question why their performance was not better. They had carefully evaluated their strategy and were signalling a move to more added-value products. Internally and externally they were communicating that the good things about ICI were remaining and that the 'World Class ICI' had changed to take advantage of the new environment.

To maximise the assets of the company as a brand, more enlightened firms expect their employees to act as 'ambassadors' for the firm. Most employees come in contact with other firms and they must be able to present a personality of knowledgeable helpfulness. The personnel director should no longer be concerned just with an *internal* focus on strategic human resource management, but should also take an *external* orientation looking, for example, at recruitment in terms of the individual's abilities to 'sell' for the firm. Training programmes need to be devised that give employees the skills to talk knowledgeably with all external contacts. They need to take 'ownership' of problems and structure their department around customers' needs.

There are many advantages from adopting a well-thought-through corporate identity programme. The first advantage is coping with shorter brand life cycles. The dynamic nature of markets and the continual pressure on performance improvement is resulting in shorter brand life cycles. To succeed, the brands must be adaptable. Uncompromising, staid brands blur the firm's image. Courtauld's corporate identity change reflected the corporation's desire to communicate modernity and the logical interlinkage between its divisions. Buyers associated Courtaulds as being in the textile market, and mentally pictured them as trading in a hostile, declining sector. Yet the reality is that Courtaulds has evolved six strong businesses, all of which have very clear strategic intents. To help communicate this externally, as well as making employees aware of their relations with other divisions, Courtaulds developed a new corporate identity in 1989.

A second advantage of corporate identity is that it sustains a real point of differentiation. It is more often the case that functional advantages are soon surpassed by technology leapfrogs. This is particularly so in financial services, where it is only a matter of days before new 'look-alikes' follow the innovator. Where, however, the point of difference is based on an emotional, rather than a functional discriminator, buyers normally perceive extra value and competitors take longer to copy this. For example, the buyer may constantly receive fast responses from a technical representative who takes an active interest in their business and, on the odd occasion when the rep is unobtainable, receives a similar level of service. The emotional benefits from customer service are valued by buyers, who are unaware of the fact that this is one of the core values that the supplier has worked hard to instil internally (e.g. communication systems and training). This aspect of corporate identity is not just apparent from the promotional campaign, but from the way that *all* points of contact with the customer are geared to delivering customer service.

A third advantage is that in the current environment, where media inflation exceeds retail price increases, it can be a cost-effective means of communicating the broad values to which the company

corporate identity sustains a real point of differentiation

subscribes. The presence of the letters ICI with the individual brands instantly enables the buyer to form an image about what the brand might be like.

We do not believe, however, that the promotions budget should just be directed towards corporate communication. Instead, a process has to be developed whereby corporate advertising helps communicate the corporate identity, allowing each brand to benefit from the corporate goodwill, yet not stifling the individual brand's personalities.

Corporate identity can be a powerful tool helping business to business marketers to promote their brands. However, its power is limited by the extent to which all of the component parts are co-ordinated and whether they reinforce each other. The supplier needs to identify the different ways in which it comes into contact with all members of the buying centre, e.g. brochures, staff, delivery vehicles, stationery, etc. For each of these elements, it then needs to assess whether a unifying device (e.g. logo) should be displayed and whether each of the elements supports the corporate identity objectives. The corporate identity objective of communicating concern for quality may be well-supported by impressive brochures, smartly presented and knowledgeable sales staff – but will fail when dirty lorries deliver the products, with impatient lorry drivers thrusting badly prepared invoices at the goods inward clerk.

It should now be very apparent that the logo is not the sole basis for such programmes, although it is a useful device to communicate corporate objectives. Particularly when the firm is responding to a changed environment, it can be a very visible way of communicating change to all interested publics. An example of this is Allied Irish Banks. Over the years its growth had taken it into international markets, with a widening range of financial services. Yet it was still perceived as being Irish, it did not have a cohesive identity in the capital markets and its logo, a roundel with three spokes, was confused with Mercedes-Benz. As part of a strategic push to become more customer-orientated, the mission statement changed from being:

> *The premier Irish Financial Services Organization, capable of competing worldwide by consistently delivering high quality service on a competitive basis to our customers in Ireland and throughout the world.*

to:

> *Value and service are at the heart of our business. We aim to provide real value to every one of our customers and to deliver the highest standards of service in banking and financial services.*

Consistent with this new mission, all aspects of the bank's activities were audited and changed where necessary. An ark was chosen as the new logo, since it was thought this communicated the bank's heritage, security and the many groups that it serves.

Conclusions

This chapter has shown that branding plays as important a role in business to business marketing as it does in consumer marketing. The organizational buyer has the encouragement to assess rationally competing brands, yet emotional considerations also influence brand buying. Not only do buyers seek performance reassurance, but they are also influenced by emotional aspects such as the prestige associated with specific brands.

Aspects of organizational marketing are different from consumer marketing and these issues need considering when developing organizational brands. For example, several people from different departments are likely to be involved in the brand selection decision, each having different brand expectations. By appreciating the needs of the different individuals, presentations can be tailored to different groups.

Non-routine purchasing in organizations typically involves about five people, but increases for more complex purchases. One way of anticipating which departments are likely to be involved in the brand purchase is through a consideration of the organization's view about the commercial risk and technical complexity of the brand. High technology brands from a well-respected supplier will attract considerable interest from technical specialists, but only a small amount of interest from company accountants.

Further insight to the challenges facing the brand can be gained by identifying which members of the buying centre will be the users, influencers, deciders, buyers and gatekeepers. Brand marketers must work to ensure that brand information is not blocked by gatekeepers. Brand presentations then should not just be directed at the needs of the decider, but also at the needs of key influencers, such as architects influencing the choice of office heating systems.

An eight-stage model of the buying process enables marketers to anticipate the way organizations go about deciding which brand to select. The amount of work undertaken by members of the buying centre will vary according to how much previous experience they have of buying the particular product. With little experience, they seek a considerable amount of information and undertake a detailed review of alternative brands. As they gain more experience, so they demand less data from suppliers and eventually they place considerable value on the ease of rapid reordering. Just as consumers are keen on buying the best value brands, so are industrialists. Their concern is the trade-off between performance and price. One way to enhance a brand's value is to increase its performance, while holding price constant. Four aspects of performance present opportunities for increasing value – the product itself, supporting systems, distribution and the company's reputation. By looking at the tangible and intangible aspects of these four performance characteristics there is greater scope for better matching the value of the brand with buyers' needs.

The IMP Group have shown that many buyers seek a long-term relationship with their suppliers, due in no small part to the joint benefits to be gained from the supplier continually improving their portfolio of brands. Partnerships are more likely to occur when a new supplier can show that they can add more value and there are few risks working with them. Twelve factors were reviewed that influence the success of a relationship and the importance of each of these varies according to the stage of the relationship's development.

To facilitate the buying centre's evaluation of both rational and emotional aspects of the brand, personal visits by sales representatives are of considerable value. However, buyers also place a lot of importance on the supplier's track record with the firm, as well as discussing matters with colleagues and visiting the supplier's factories. The brand purchase decision is more confidently made when the buyer favourably associates the supplier's brand with a well-respected corporate image.

Marketing action checklist

To help clarify the direction of future brand marketing activity, it is recommended that the following exercises are undertaken:

1   Write down the criteria that you believe your customers use to evaluate your brands. If you only have rational reasons listed, discuss this with your colleagues and identify the emotional issues that your customers take into account. Does your marketing programme take account of your customers' rational and emotional needs?

2   For one of the contracts that your firm is trying to win, work out with the rest of the team the composition of the buying centre. Do you know who is playing the roles of user, influencer, decider, buyer and gatekeeper? How are you tailoring your brand presentation to appeal to the different members of the buying centre? Have you made sure that *all* members of the buying centre have relevant brand information?

3   For a contract that you recently lost, work with your colleagues to identify who was in the buying centre and the roles they played. With hindsight, were you correctly targeting and tailoring your brand presentation?

4   For a new contract that you are bidding for, assess whether the buying centre's experience makes the purchase a new task, modified rebuy or straight rebuy. With this assumption made explicit, use Figure 5.2 to map out the stages that the buying centre is likely to pass through, and estimate where it will devote most effort. For each of these stages identify the action you need to take to help the buyers.

5   What actions are you taking to ensure that your customers can place repeat orders? Have you investigated developing a computerised reordering process for each of your customers?

6   When did you last audit the way that all members of your organization interact with your major customers? For each major account, do you know whether:
   •   there have been any organizational changes?
   •   there is any personal friction between your staff and the buying centre?
   •   deliveries are always on time, with the correct product mix?
   •   the buyers are satisfied with the consistency of quality?
   •   there are market changes occurring that will result in the buyer changing his brand purchasing?

7   What are you doing with your major customers to make them feel that you are always trying to improve your brands and help their business grow?

8   For a contract that you are currently bidding for, prepare a table comparing your brand against the other competing brands showing
   •   purchase price;
   •   installation costs;
   •   operating costs;
   •   regular maintenance costs;
   •   depreciation costs.
   If any of this information puts your brand in a favourable perspective, how could you incorporate this into your brand presentation?

9   Choose a brand which is under pressure from competition. By looking at the four performance factors of the product, supporting services, distribution and your company, consider what tangible and intangible value you are providing. By repeating this exercise for your competitor's brand identify, on a relative

basis, where you are offering more or less value. Through considering how your customer uses your brand, follow through this analysis to identify how more value could be delivered.

10   For each of your partners with whom you believe you have established a relationship, use the two-dimensional matrix in Figure 5.4, to plot where they lie in terms of the amount of value they add to your brand and the operating risk of being associated with them. Why are you dealing with partners who do not fall in the high value added–low risk quadrant?

11   Using the factors shown in Figure 5.5 which are associated with successful relationships, audit each of your partners to assess the well-being of each relationship. For those relationships where over half these factors receive low scores, identify the value these partners are adding to your brand and whether the cost of maintaining the relationship warrants this.

12   For a new contract that you are bidding for, consider how confident the buying centre is about your brand. Have you identified previous customers and independent experts that could attest to the quality of your brand and thereby enable you to present your brand as a low-risk purchase?

13   When was a market research study last undertaken to assess buyers' views of your brands and those of your competitors? If this was longer ago than two years, it may be worthwhile commissioning a new study. This should identify buyers' evaluation criteria and their assessment of competing brands. It should also investigate those aspects of risk that buyers perceive when buying your brand and their preferred ways of reducing risk.

14   Do you know which sources buyers most value when seeking information about competing brands? If not, interviews should be undertaken with key buyers and your promotional strategy adjusted accordingly.

15   What are your corporate identity objectives? How well do these match the corporate image buyers have of your firm? What actions are you taking to reduce any differences between your objectives and buyers' perceptions?

16   When did you last evaluate the appropriateness of your corporate identity? How much has the market changed since this was last done? Is your corporate identity programme able to adapt to market changes or is it now necessary to undertake a major review?

References and further reading

Anderson J. (1995). Relationships in business markets: exchange episodes, value creation, and their empirical assessment. *Journal of the Academy of Marketing Science*, **23**(4), 346–50.

Berkowitz M. (1986). New product adoption by the buying organization: who are the real influencers? *Industrial Marketing Management*, **15**, 33–43.

Blois K. (1996). Relationship marketing in organizational markets: when is it appropriate? *Journal of Marketing Management*, **12**, 161–73.

Chisnall P. (1985). *Strategic Industrial Marketing*. Englewood Cliffs: Prentice Hall.

Choffray J. and Lilien G. (1978). Assessing response to industrial marketing strategy. *Journal of Marketing*, **42** (April), 20–31.

Dempsey W. (1978). Vendor selection and the buying process. *Industrial Marketing Management*, **7**, 257–67.

Dichter E. (1973). Industrial buying is based on same 'only human' emotional factors that motivate consumer market's housewife. *Industrial Marketing* (Feb.), 14–18.

Diefenbach J. (1987). The corporate identity as the brand. In *Branding: A Key Marketing Tool* (Murphy J., ed.). Basingstoke: Macmillan.

Hakannson H. (ed.) (1982). *International Marketing And Purchasing Of Industrial Goods*. Chichester: J. Wiley.

Hawes J. and Barnhouse S. (1987). How purchasing agents handle personal risk. *Industrial Marketing Management*. **16**, 287–93.

Henthorne T., LaTour M. and Williams A. (1993). How organizational buyers reduce risk. *Industrial Marketing Management*, **22**, pp 41–8.

Hill R. and Hillier T. (1986). *Organisational Buying Behaviour*. Basingstoke: Macmillan.

Hutt M. and Speh T. (1985). *Industrial Marketing Management*. Chicago: The Dryden Press.

Ind N. (1990). *The Corporate Image*. London: Kogan Page.

Kelly J. and Coaker J. (1976). The importance of price as a choice criterion for industrial purchasing decision. *Industrial Marketing Management*, **5**, 281–93.

King S. (1991). Brand-building in the 1990s. *Journal of Marketing Management*, **7** (1), 3–13.

Kiser G. and Rao C. (1977). Important vendor factors in industrial and hospital organizations: a comparison. *Industrial Marketing Management*, **6**, 289–96.

Kohli A. (1989). Determinants of influence in organizational buying: a contingency approach. *Journal of Marketing*, **53**, (July), 50–65.

Lehmann D. and O'Shaughnessy J. (1974). Difference in attribute importance for different industrial products. *Journal of Marketing*, **38** (April), 36–42.

Mattson M. (1988). How to determine the composition and influence of a buying centre. *Industrial Marketing Management*, **17**, 205–14.

McQuinston D. (1989). Novelty, complexity and importance as casual determinants of industrial buyer behavior. *Journal of Marketing*, **53** (April), 66–79.

Mudambi S., Doyle P. and Wong V. (1997). An exploration of branding in industrial markets. *Industrial Marketing Management*, **26** (5) 433–46.

Naumann E., Lincoln D. and McWilliam R. (1984). The purchase of components: functional areas of influence. *Industrial Marketing Management*, **13**, 113–22.

Parket I. (1972). The effects of product perception on industrial buying behavior. *Industrial Marketing Management*, **3**, 339–45.

Patton W., Puto C. and King R. (1986). Which buying decisions are made by individuals and not by groups? *Industrial Marketing Management*, **15**, 129–38.

Pearson S. (1996). *Building Brands Directly*. London: Macmillan.

Robinson P., Faris C. and Wind Y. (1967). *Industrial Buying and Creative Marketing*. Boston: Allyn and Bacon.

Saunders J. and Watt F. (1979). Do brand names differentiate identical industrial products? *Industrial Marketing Management*, **8**, 114–23.

Sheth J. (1973). A model of industrial buyer behavior. *Journal of Marketing*, **37**, (Oct), 50–6.

Shoaf F. (1959). Here's proof – the industrial buyer is human. *Industrial Marketing*, **43** (May), 126–28.

Sinclair S. and Seward K. (1988). Effectiveness of branding a commodity product. *Industrial Marketing Management*, **17**, 23–33.

Stewart K. (1990). Corporate identity: strategic or cosmetic? In *Marketing Educators Conference Proceedings* (Pendlebury A. and Watkins T., eds). Oxford: MEG.

Traynor K. and Traynor S. (1989). Marketing approaches used by high tech firms. *Industrial Marketing Management*, **18**, 281–7.

Webster F. and Wind Y. (1972). *Organizational Buying Behavior*. Englewood Cliffs: Prentice Hall.

Wilson D. (1995). An integrated model of buyer–seller relationships. *Journal of the Academy of Marketing Science*. **23** (4), 335–45.

Woolfson K. (1990). British Telecom plans a name with a new ring. *The European* (Oct. 5–7).

Chapter 6

Service brands

Summary

The purpose of this chapter is to examine the issues associated with the creation and development of powerful service brands. It opens by considering the increasing importance of the services sector. By analysing the successes and failures of brands in the financial services sector, the chapter goes on to illustrate the major challenges associated with service branding. We outline the differences between goods and service branding and how the fast-moving consumer goods (FMCG) approach to branding services needs to be adjusted. Particular emphasis is placed on the intangible nature of services and how problems linked to intangible offerings can be overcome. The chapter ends by considering the roles of employees and customers in the delivery of the service brands and how these roles can be strategically designed to strengthen service brands.

The importance of services

The services sector has become a dominant force in the economy of many Western countries and has created a wealth of new jobs: in the UK two-thirds of the workforce are now employed in service companies, in the USA three-quarters. The services sector has not only spurred economic growth; it has also challenged the traditional approach of doing business by creating revolutionary service solutions. Innovative entrepreneurs have set new standards of service quality in markets where their competitors failed to please today's demanding customers. In the airline industry, for example, EasyJet has questioned the assumption that all travellers are prepared to pay for a meal and drinks during their flights. The company has identified a segment of price-sensitive travellers torn between the punctuality of business airlines and the low prices of charter flights. It has then offered these travellers a welcome compromise of punctual no-frills flights at lower prices. In the banking sector, companies such as First Direct have responded to the reluctance of many banking consumers to visit their local retail branch and queue. After discovering that

the services sector has challenged the traditional approach of doing business by creating revolutionary service solutions

*Survey undertaken by NOP Market Research among 1,000 randomly selected bank customers. Interviews were conducted by telephone between 20 Nov 1996 and 12 Dec 1996. Enquirers must be aged 18 or over. In order to safeguard our customers, certain transactions may require written confirmation. First Direct reserves the right to decline to open an account for you. First Direct credit facilities are subject to status. For written details of our services write to First Direct, Freepost, Leeds LS98 2RF. First Direct is a division of Midland Bank plc. Calls may be monitored and/or recorded. LLOYDS Cheque Account details are based on the Classic Account. The costs comprise fees of £8 per month. BARCLAYS Cheque Account details are based on the Barclays Bank Account. The costs comprise fees of £5 per month. NAT WEST Cheque Account details are based on the Current Plus Account. The costs comprise fees of £5 per month. All fees may vary in the future. First Direct variable interest rate for overdrafts up to £250 is 12.6% EAR. All information based on authorised overdrafts of 5 days or more per month and correct at 11 March 1997.
Member HSBC ⬡ Group

first direct

Free from charges

Banking with First Direct is free because we do not charge Cheque Account customers for everyday banking transactions, even if you're overdrawn. And all our customers automatically receive an overdraft up to £250 – also free of any fees. So compared to other high street bank accounts you're better off with First Direct from day one. We're a member of the HSBC Group which is one of the largest banking and financial services organisations in the world, and in the course of a year you'll find we offer more cost effective current account banking. And the service we provide means you benefit in many other ways too.

By telephone, 24 hours a day

We provide the ultimate in convenience. You can bank with us at any time, 365 days (and nights) of the year, from wherever there's a telephone, in your home, office or car. And all UK calls are charged at local rates.

Personal and professional service

Every call is answered by our Banking Representatives. They have all they need at their fingertips to deal with your day-to-day banking needs. And when you require more specialised assistance, such as a loan, they can instantly refer you to someone who can help.

Getting cash is easy

Every Cheque Account customer receives the First Direct Card. This allows you to withdraw up to £500 a day from over 11,500 cash machines around the UK, including those of Midland. It also guarantees cheques for £100 and includes the Switch payment facility.

So is paying bills

Our service includes a free bill payment service. Simply call, tell us who to pay, how much and when, and we do it. This means you can arrange to pay your bills at the most convenient time without the need to keep having to remember to organise it.

A full banking service with more benefits

As well as our Cheque Account we offer saving, borrowing, travel and insurance services cost effectively by telephone. Take saving; our rates are always competitive, we offer transfers to and from your Cheque Account. So your money is always working hard without the need for you to do the same.

We work hard to maintain the service

The best people to demonstrate the quality of a banking service are its customers – 87%* of ours have recommended us to their friends and colleagues in the last 12 months.

Opening an account is easy too

We also appreciate how daunting changing bank accounts can be. So we make it easy. Easy to open a First Direct account, then easy to arrange for your salary to be paid in and easy for all your standing orders and direct debits to be transferred to your account. And it's easy (and free) to find out more right now. Call us on **0800 24 24 24** or complete the coupon.

Why pay to bank when First Direct is free?

Annual current account charges
(annual fees for use of £250 overdraft)

Lloyds Classic	£96.00
NatWest Current Plus	£60.00
Barclays Bank Account	£60.00
First Direct Cheque Account	£0.00

If you're paying more are you with the right bank?

☎ **0800 24 24 24**

Call free or complete the coupon and post to:
First Direct, FREEPOST, Leeds LS98 2RF

Mr/Mrs/Miss/Ms or Title

Surname

Forename(s)

UK Address

Postcode

Telephone No

BL056

Exhibit 6.1 *By understanding consumers' views about banking, First Direct developed their services to cater for those who prefer a different approach (reproduced by kind permission of Midland Bank plc)*

Exhibit 6.2 *Technological developments have allowed other banks to offer the home banking service pioneered by First Direct (reproduced by kind permission of Barclays Bank plc)*

Escort Azura
1.3 5dr/1.4 3dr
- Driver's airbag
- Safeguard engine immobiliser
- Stereo radio/cassette

£9,595
on the road*

Escort Silhouette
1.4 3dr
- Power assisted steering
- Sunroof • Metallic paint
- Stereo radio/cassette
- Body coloured bumpers
- Also available as 5dr and Estate[1]

£10,995
on the road*

Escort Flight
1.6 3dr
- Power assisted steering
- Electric front windows
- Sunroof • Metallic paint
- Central double locking
- Passenger airbag
- Also available as 4dr, 5dr and Estate

£11,995
on the road*

Escort Chicane
1.6 3dr
- Power assisted steering
- Electric front windows
- Tailgate spoiler • Alloy wheels
- Sunroof • Metallic paint
- Also available as 5dr and Estate[1]

£11,995
on the road*

0% APR finance**
Free insurance†

Visit your Ford dealer this summer and you'll find four very special edition Escorts.
They all offer you more for less; more features, more style, more value.
Plus you'll also be able to take advantage of "One Price"[1] and choose from 4 door,
5 door or estate models (where available), all for one simple price.[1]
So, you'll discover it's never been easier to drive away the car that perfectly meets your individual requirements.

 as the nation's favourite

For more details and a '21 Offers' brochure call 0345 21 11 21

Exhibit 6.3   *Through Ford Credit Europe, Ford have become a notable player in the financial services market (reproduced by kind permission of Ford Motor Company Ltd)*

most customers would rather complete all bank transactions by telephone, First Direct created a bank without branches that still offers all standard banking services, 24 hours a day, 365 days a year. First Direct's rapidly growing consumer base and the large number of financial institutions copying their strategy illustrate the revolution they have initiated in the banking system.

The success of service organizations such as First Direct and EasyJet has been stimulated by dramatic global trends which created opportunities to gain sustainable competitive advantage. **Computerization and technical innovation**, especially in telecommunications, enabled companies to establish service brands by radically innovating the way they do business with consumers. Being the first bank to use modern call-centre technology allowed First Direct to become the leading 'direct' banking brand. To profit from these opportunities, organizations need to invest in educating consumers how to use the new technologies and in communicating the brand benefits.

The **deregulation** of many industries and the **privatization of public corporations** have also been important factors in the UK and other European countries, and more recently in some Asian and Latin American nations. The deregulation of the airline and utility industries allowed new brands like EasyJet to enter the market and force established companies to cut costs and refocus on their consumers. The impact of privatization on service quality is well illustrated by the BT brand, which has been transformed from a sluggish monolith to a world-class performer.

The changes in the services sector have also caused many manufacturing companies to create **service profit-centres** which operate independently from their parent companies. For example, General Electric and Ford have become important players in the financial services industry through the development of their credit financing and leasing divisions. Furthermore, as physical goods alone are no longer sufficient to gain competitive advantage, many companies focus on providing consumers with high levels of service. In the computer industry, for example, the service support provided by IBM is an integral part of the brand strength.

Finally, the use of franchising agreements and the world-wide trend to remove trade barriers have allowed many service businesses to profit from increased **globalization** of their operations. Service providers such as airlines, hotel chains and car rental firms are able to deliver their services internationally through distribution systems owned by local investors. Companies which decide to 'go global' however, should beware of possible cultural differences. These differences pose a greater threat to services than to goods, since service brands depend strongly on the people providing the brand and it is very difficult to standardize staff–customer interactions across cul-

the
"it's great being a global company, pity about the global travel bill"
solution

Ever noticed how a supposedly simple business trip can quickly turn into a crippling spendfest? With a simple solution from IBM, you can actually shrink your communication and administrative costs even at a time when growth is your primary concern.

The bigger you get, the smarter you have to be.

When you do business globally, all those planes, hotels, conference calls and couriers add up faster than a Tokyo taximeter. But for a lot of the everyday stuff, you could easily replace setting-up-a-meeting in Indonesia with setting-up-a-meeting on the Internet. Or on your company's own intranet, a private secure network. Based on Lotus Notes and Lotus Domino, it lets you share documents, expertise or opinions anywhere in the world as easily as sharing them in the same room. Even a full-blown presentation, in real time, with selected clients and colleagues alike.

Less globetrotting, more profit.

With IBM, you can take advantage of new tools that facilitate a constant flow of information, sharing of ideas and better, faster decisions. Can you imagine how much more effective, and cost-effective, your company could be? Why not visit us on www.ibminfo.com/nc/uk8 or call us on 0800 675 675 (quoting RTB1) for details. We'd be happy to accompany you on your journey to greater profitability.

Solutions for a small planet

tures. Neglecting cultural issues can have disastrous consequences even for strong and popular brands, as Disney learnt from the EuroDisney experience when it tried to use service principles popular in America. For example, by not originally allowing alcohol on site, when in France wine is a standard part of a meal.

The challenge of services branding

The increased competition in services markets has made many companies realize that a strong service brand is an essential part of their competitive advantage. Unfortunately, the understanding of service branding has not kept pace with the growth of the services sector. Service-based brands are characterized by multiple interactions as consumers frequently have to talk with several people in a service firm. One has only to consider the traveller at an airport and the numerous interactions they have with different people as they pass from checking in to security to passport control to ticket checking prior to boarding the airplane and then the cabin crew. Each interaction gives a message about the brand of the airline. Due to the different people having contact with the traveller, so the chance for conflicting messages about the service brand increases, unless managers have worked with staff to ensure a consistent style of behaviour. The early thoughts of many service marketers to the new challenges from service brands was based on the assumption that the principles of goods branding would apply equally to service branding. They soon discovered, however, that the specific nature of services requires more tailoring to suit different consumers and that goods branding principles cannot be directly transferred to services without any adaptation. We do not believe that a new theory should be developed for service branding. Rather, the existing goods branding theories should be finetuned and adapted to the service environment.

existing goods branding theories should be fine-tuned and adapted to the service environment

According to the traditional view of goods branding, a brand is a set of differentiated perceptions. The brand strength depends on the extent to which these perceptions are consistent, positive and shared by all consumers. To improve the brand strength, managers need to shape consumers' perceptions so that the target audience will think of the brand in positive terms. It is in the execution of service branding that more thought is required. Alas, many service suppliers have not sufficiently considered this.

In the financial and insurance sectors, for example, very few brands have managed to create a strong set of positive associations in people's minds. Many consumers have problems differentiating between competing brands in the banking or insurance sectors. The fact that the financial services industry spends about £1 bn a year on advertising highlights the difficulties of building a service brand.

However, the airline industry has demonstrated that it is possible to achieve a clear differentiation of service brands. If travellers were asked to assess Virgin, Lufthansa or Singapore Airlines in terms of important characteristics such as punctuality, in-flight entertainment and attentive cabin staff, consumers are very likely to give answers without much hesitation.

The challenges marketers face when establishing service brands can be illustrated by the recent history of the British insurance sector. To the average consumer daunted by the complexity of competing types of insurance, it appeared that little effort went into simplifying the purchase decision and a lot of emphasis was placed on pushy salespeople. Marketing efforts failed to overcome consumers' lack of interest in insurance brands, which translated into a low degree of perceived brand differentiation. Many insurance companies appointed advertising agencies with traditional FMCG backgrounds, which followed the FMCG approach of building name awareness, rather than communicating brand benefits. Little was done to develop relevant brand distinction. Furthermore, advertising was mainly targeted at insurance brokers, rather than consumers, who regarded the 'brands' as commodities. The intermediaries were in a very strong position and could easily delete brands from their portfolios.

The deregulation of the UK financial services market in 1986 and subsequent legislation increased the degree of competition in the insurance sector, allowing other players such as banks to enter the market. These changes significantly decreased the importance of insurance brokers, as the responsibility for choosing insurance brands shifted more towards consumers. However, many insurance companies have yet to better adapt their communication strategies to the varying needs of their consumers.

Factors such as deregulation and increased competition, which led to the changes in the insurance industry, also affected other financial services sectors. Banks face the same challenges as the grocery market did twenty years ago. Banking is perceived by many as a commodity service. Yet there are opportunities through better satisfying consumers' ever-increasing demand for much improved quality, enhanced service and greater convenience. Banks and building societies can learn much from the likes of Tesco and Sainsbury about how to transform a commodity into a strong brand as may well occur now that these grocery retailers have moved into the financial services sector.

Financial services companies along with all service providers need to realize that brands are even more important for services than for goods since consumers have no tangible attributes to assess the brand. It is harder to communicate the values of services brands. An effective route to convey the values of a service brand is through 'the way the company does things', therefore the company's culture acts

Today my Dad got life

A gentle reminder to insure yours

Let's face it, you would give your life for your kids. More than likely, you are already giving them a fair chunk of your income. For many of us they are the biggest investment we make.

Now the boffins have put a figure on the cost of bringing up a child – £100,000.* You might not begrudge them a penny but what would happen if you're not around to pick up the tab? How will you ensure your child's future if you or your partner are not there to look after them?

Well, you could do nothing. But before you turn the page, consider this. Think of the parents of five families that you know, including yourselves. The chances are, one of you will be dead before you're sixty**. So the odds are in your favour . . . but is it worth the risk? Especially as it could cost from just £6 a month to insure your life?

If you'd rather not leave your child's future to fate, call Virgin Direct on 0345 95 95 95. You could be covered in less than 10 minutes if you pick up the phone right now.

If you're clear about what you want...

We have two types of protection. Our family capital protector pays out a tax-free cash sum on your death, while our family income protector would make sure your family receives a regular tax-free income.

Tell us which you want and how much cover you need until your children 'fly the nest'. For example, for your first child this could be a cash sum of £100,000. We can usually give you a guaranteed price in less than ten minutes.

We'll send you an information pack with all the forms already filled in for you. And if we've given you a firm price, you'll also get two weeks free cover. So you'll have time to think it over or shop around to try and find better value.

If you decide you like what we have to offer, just sign the forms and return them to us. Life couldn't be simpler.

If you would like help in deciding what's right for you...

When you call, ask for an appointment to be made with one of our authorised advisers.

We will send you an information pack explaining Virgin Direct's approach to giving financial advice. Our adviser will then call you at the agreed time. He will be able to explain your options and will recommend a solution which fits your own personal circumstances.

This will usually take between 30 and 40 minutes if you want to discuss everything. If you only want to discuss life insurance, it will usually be quicker.

Our adviser will then send you an information pack with his recommendations and all the forms already filled out for you.

To insure your life, all you need to do is check, sign and return the forms to us.

❝ At Virgin Direct we offer straightforward, good value for money products and no gobbledygook. Plus the outstanding level of service you associate with Virgin. ❞ *Richard Branson*

0345 95 95 95

Open seven days a week from 8am to 10pm

* Source: Asda's 'What price a child?', May '96
** Source: Munich Re. 1 in 10 thirty year olds will die before they reach sixty.

Exhibit 6.5   *Virgin Direct challenge the competiting brands of insurance by deliberately making their insurance easy to understand (reproduced by kind permission of Virgin Direct Personal Financial Services)*

Exhibit 6.6   *American Express is a good example of a service brand where staff are customer-focused and, through providing exemplary service, are a critical contributor to successful brand building*

Plate 1 *The advertisement from Hewlett-Packard is a good example of how they have taken a product with a set of functional capabilities and, by drawing on human associations, have developed a brand (Chapter 1) (reproduced by kind permission of Hewlett-Packard)*

It prints, it copies and it scans. Doesn't it deserve it?

The HP OfficeJet Pro 1150C.
From $599 (inc. VAT).

It does it All-in-One and it does it all in colour. If your office is hectic, don't you deserve it?

For more information about the range of
HP All-in-One products and supplies, phone 0990 474747 or visit us at http://www.hp.com/go/all-in-one

**HEWLETT®
PACKARD**

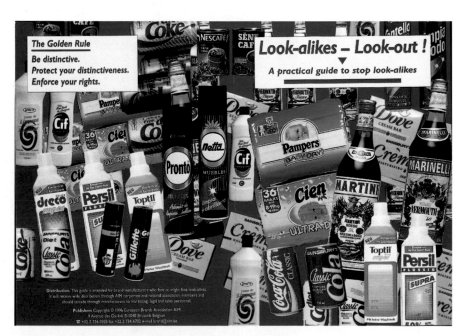

The Golden Rule
Be distinctive.
Protect your distinctiveness.
Enforce your rights.

Look-alikes – Look-out !
A practical guide to stop look-alikes

Distribution. This guide is intended for brand manufacturers who face or might face look-alikes.
It will receive wide distribution through AIM corporate and regional association members and
should cascade through manufacturers to marketing, legal and sales personnel.

Publishers Copyright © 1996 European Brands Association AIM
9 Avenue des Gaulois B-1040 Brussels Belgium

Plate 3 *The European Brands Association highlights the problems of look-alikes to brand manufacturers (Chapter 2)*

Plate 2 The tourist authorities of Portugal and New Zealand are very aware of the distinctive benefits of their brands, which are portrayed in these two contrasting advertisements (Chapter 2) (reproduced by kind permission of New Zealand Tourism Board, Mustoe Merriman Herring Levy and Ian McKinnell (photographer)

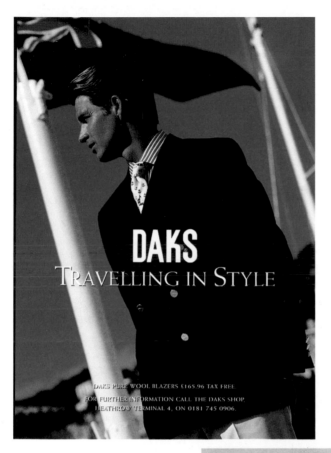

Plate 4 *Daks is at the brand as personality stage of Goodyear's brand consumerization spectrum (Chapter 2)*

Plate 5 *By using a blurred picture of a bee attracted to pollen, then a clearer picture, Optrex is a powerful shorthand brand presenting a few pieces of high quality information, rather than a large quantity of information and the visual rapidly communicates the brand benefit (Chapter 3)*

Plate 6 *The creative approach used to convey the softness of clothing washed with Non-Biological Fairy Pure is a good example of communicating a small amount of high quality information – using the analogy of prickly and cuddly animals (Chapter 3) (reproduced by kind permission of Proctor & Gamble, DMB&B and Steve Cavalier (phototographer))*

Plate 8 *The functional value of the Astra 1.6i is its good petrol consumption performance, allowing longer between refuelling (Chapter 4) (reproduced by kind permission of Vauxhall Motors Ltd)*

Plate 7   Umbro's advertising majors upon the fact that supporters of a particular football team display their affiliations through portraying the brand identity colours of the 'brand' they so proudly follow (Chapter 4) (reproduced by kind permission of Umbro International and DMB&B)

Plate 9 *The three Redland Roof Tiles' advertisements show how successful brands succeed in business to business marketing by blending rational and emotional appeals (Chapter 5) (reproduced by kind permission of Primary Contact Ltd on behalf of Redland)*

"A week of back-to-back meetings. Could I reward myself this weekend without exceeding my credit limit?"

YES.

At Diners Club, we don't confine you by presetting a spending limit. Rather, you can relax and enjoy the flexibility that you have earned. So when two clients turn into eight for dinner, or you simply want to extend your trip to include some playtime, you can count on us. Diners Club says "yes" in more than 175 countries around the world. So don't take chances. Take Diners Club.

DINERS CLUB THE RIGHT ANSWER IN ANY LANGUAGE.

Plate 11   Diners Club has worked to get itself recognized as a key travel and expenses card (Chapter 11) (reproduced by kind permission of Diners Club International)

Plate 10   Taylor Woodrow, with their portfolio of building services, capitalize upon the benefits of corporate branding (Chapter 5) (reproduced by kind permission of Taylor Woodrow Group)

MET RO POLI TAN

Taylor Woodrow have an international reputation for developing some of Central London's most exclusive residential projects – schemes of exceptional quality in some of the capital's finest locations

For further information or our catalogue from stunning locations please contact Taylor Woodrow Capital Developments Limited

The London Sales Office
80 Blandford Street
London W1 6UA
T +44 (0) 171 638 2558
F +44 (0) 171 487 8194

TAYLOR WOODROW

Plate 12   *British Airways was a pioneer in loyalty cards and is still regarded as one of the leading firms using their loyalty cards to build relationships with their travellers (Chapter 11)*

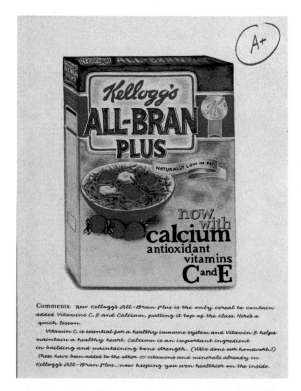

Plate 13   *With a well-protected name, Kellogg's All-Bran Plus scores well on protection (Chapter 11)*

as a key communicator of values. This means that a brand personality cannot just be communicated by a press or television advertisement, but it also depends very much on everyone in the company, from the CEO to anyone who has contact with consumers, since staff are an integral part of service brands. It is therefore important to train staff to ensure a greater likelihood of consistent delivery of the service brand. Brand building needs to be undertaken by everyone in the firm and involves a profound analysis of every aspect of the interaction between consumers and the company.

Just as the consumer doesn't want Persil washing powder, but clean clothes, so the brands of financial institutions should reflect the fact that consumers purchase them not as an end in themselves, but rather as a means to achieve other goals. After all, customers do not want a Halifax or Abbey National mortgage, but they do want to buy a house in an area that suits them best.

The lack of powerful brands in the financial services sector is indicative of new challenges and the need for a new mindset when developing services brands. A service brand has to be based on a clear competitive position, which in turn has to be derived from the corporate strategy. This requires a holistic approach involving everyone in the company. Only when the brand's positioning and benefits have been communicated to staff who understand it and have been trained and are therefore capable and confident in delivering the brand's promise should these be communicated to consumers.

> a service brand has to be based on a clear competitive position derived from the corporate strategy

Furthermore, to successfully develop and maintain service brands marketers should take heed of Conrad Free's contention (1996) that an effective brand strategy must reflect a true competitive advantage, encompassing factors such as:

- *High-quality top management* – The commitment of high calibre management is fundamental to guarantee excellent service brand delivery.
- *Vision* – All employees need to understand and be committed to the brand vision. Long-term rather than short-term plans are required to ensure the development of meaningful relationships with consumers.
- *Results driven* – The vision should be translated into clearly defined goals for all staff.
- *Competitiveness* – The company should benchmark its performance against best practice, both inside and outside the sector.
- *Use of technology* – Effective exploitation of new technologies is a fundamental source of sustainable competitive advantage.
- *Consumer focus* – The consumer needs to be regarded as central to everything the organization does.

If we don't reach you within an hour, we'll give you £10.*

The AA and RAC won't.

WHEN YOUR CAR LETS YOU DOWN, Green Flag won't. On average, we rescue our members in just 35 minutes.**

And if we're not with you in less than one hour, you can claim £10 back. Plus, we offer a choice of 5 levels of cover. What's more, our 6000 skilled mechanics will repair most problems at the roadside.

To find out more, contact us right now.

CHOOSE FROM 5 LEVELS OF COVER†
- Recovery Only £29.50
- Roadside Assistance £38.00
- Comprehensive £69.00
- Comprehensive Gold £93.00
- Total Protection £145.00

*Upon receipt of claim £10 cheque will be issued. **Verified from customer satisfaction questionnaires. †Prices quoted are for continuous payment methods only. Cars registered before 31/7/87 are subject to an additional fee of £15.

Green Flag
Motoring Assistance
WE LEAVE EVERYONE STANDING BUT YOU

call free today on
0800 001 340
http://www.greenflag.co.uk
quote ref. no. A3604 and your credit/debit card
number or complete the coupon.

POST TODAY – NO STAMP NEEDED
GREEN FLAG, Freepost, Leeds, West Yorkshire LS99 4GF.
Please send me further information about GREEN FLAG.
Name (Mr/Mrs/Miss/Ms)
Address
Post code   Home tel

A3604

Exhibit 6.7 *Green Flag has developed a clear competitive position and their holistic approach, developing an effective recovery service through a customer-focused system, exemplifies their commitment to delivering the brand's promise (reproduced by kind permission of Green Flag Ltd)*

Moving beyond the fast-moving consumer goods model

The previous section has highlighted various difficulties associated with service branding and in particular the danger of applying the traditional fast-moving consumer goods model without adapting it to the characteristics of the services sector. The following two cases illustrated how the goods branding concept can be adjusted for the development of successful service brands.

Brookes (1996) is but one amongst many who argue that goods brands and service brands can be developed through broadly similar process, i.e.:

- setting clear brand objectives;
- defining a clear positioning;
- selecting appropriate values.

He provides an interesting case study using the Liverpool Victoria Friendly Society (LVFS) to bring out service branding principles. LVFS was founded in 1843, has over a million premium-paying members and manages funds of about £3 bn but had to improve its poor sales, faced with an ageing customer base. LVFS decided to rebrand and reposition itself from being the number 46 insurance company to the number one friendly society. It focused on three objectives: developing a well-recognized identity; having a strong positioning; and providing a clear message to existing and new members.

The company examined its competitive environment and decided to focus on its traditional market of financially unsophisticated, ordinary people. This group were all the more attractive as many retail banks were moving away from this market to win over high net worth individuals. As a next step, LVFS analysed the existing relationships among the company's head office, the agents and its consumers to identify the most appropriate values for the brand. It emerged that head office generally had poor communications with the other parties, whereas the relationships between consumers and agents were good. Further analysis showed that the more emotive values associated with consumers choosing LVFS included:

- home service in familiar surroundings;
- family tradition over many generations;
- close contact between agents and consumers;
- profile similarity between consumers and employees;

- serving consumers according to their needs in the language they understand.

These values formed the basis of a clear brand identity and were translated into a brand that reflected the new positioning of the friendly society.

The development of the new brand was followed by thorough training of all staff to ensure their commitment to and their understanding the brand's benefits. A booklet explaining the brand's values was distributed to staff and consumers. The entire LVFS's literature was rewritten to reflect the newly launched brand. Sponsorship of a national snooker event as well as of local charities guaranteed in-depth advertising coverage to communicate the brand's values to consumers. The brand benefits were effectively conveyed and improvements included: sales increased by up to 70 per cent; consumers' propensity to consider LVFS doubled in the target regions; brand awareness rose by 10 per cent; and staff morale improved remarkably.

The new LVFS brand was developed through a modified FMCG branding approach: the modification was limited to the fact that the brand values were derived not from goods or from the perceptions of goods, but from an analysis of the complete interaction between consumers and the service organization.

the modification was limited to the fact that the brand values were derived not from goods or from the perceptions of goods, but from an analysis of the complete interaction between consumers and the service organization

Levy (1996) provides a further example of how successful service brands can be developed by adapting the FMCG model. This focuses on the changes undertaken by NatWest to develop a new niche brand, NatWest Small Business Adviser. Increased competition in the financial services sector made NatWest marketers more aware of the complexity and blurred demarcations of their services. Their analysis showed the need to adopt the FMCG model, taking into account services differences such as:

- *Product definition* – Financial services are not as well-defined as FMCG brands. A current account is not a single physical entity, but consists of a collection of several elements, from the cheque book to the conversation with the cashier.
- *Brand differentiation* – FMCG marketers strive to differentiate their brands by communicating a competitive edge and by avoiding launching 'me-too' products. Marketers in financial services, however, focus on building long-term relationships with their consumers through having a broad product range to satisfy all their needs. Since the maintenance of existing relationships lies at the core of their strategy, emulating competitors' products to fill a gap in the firm's portfolio is more often considered than would be in the goods sector.

- *Consumer motivation* – While in FMCG markets consumer loyalty is hard to win and retain, consumers in the financial sector are reluctant to switch between companies because they perceive the differences as negligible and not worth the possible disruptions.
- *Measurement of brand strength* – Measuring awareness levels and propensity to repurchase provides a reasonable assessment of brand strength in the FMCG domain. With financial brands, the concept of repeat purchase is less meaningful, as it needs to be measured over years. Likewise, brand loyalty is hardly relevant, as inertia prevents consumers from switching. Thus marketers of financial services draw more on qualitative data about the interactions with existing customers.
- *Product benefits* – Although product features can help attract consumers, they are not the obvious brand discriminator. Furthermore, in financial brands, extra features can confuse an already reluctant consumer about the benefits of the brand and provide them with an excuse to reject it.

NatWest took all these factors into account to ensure the successful launch and establishment of the new brand, NatWest Small Business Adviser. In the early 1980s NatWest identified the 'small business' market as a highly attractive target for a new financial niche brand. An increasing number of entrepreneurs were setting up their own businesses, all having similar needs and attitudes during the initial stage. Because of this group's typically low involvement in financial products, the critical task was to find the key factors which would help distinguish the new brand. Three areas were chosen: the current account; lending; and service. These three areas were analysed through qualitative research and it emerged that customers perceived lending and the current account as integral parts of every bank's business and as such were unlikely to provide an element of distinctiveness. On the other hand, NatWest's advice services were regarded as an essential support during the starting-up phase of small businesses. Further qualitative research focused on concrete aspects of the interaction between customers and the bank, such as the type of questions customers were likely to ask and the level of security they were prepared to accept. It revealed, for example, that entrepreneurs felt threatened by initial contracts with senior managers and preferred to deal with someone competent but less authoritative. From this market research, attributes were used to build the Small Business Adviser brand and to target a well-defined audience. NatWest successfully launched the new brand and used it for cross-selling other products.

The distinctive nature of services

To build strong brands in the services sector, a better understanding of the differences between goods and services can help brand managers to fine-tune branding principles. The following factors encompass the main differences between goods and services and help highlight the implications for service brands.

Nature of the product

A good can be described as 'an object', whereas a service is a performance. Marketing a performance is different from marketing a physical object. When consumers rent a car, for instance, whilst they are interested in a specific model they are strongly influenced by other factors such as the rental firm's office hours, the reservation system and the kind of people serving them. Although the service performance often involves tangible elements, such as the car and insurance documents, much of it is intangible in nature and its performance comes to life through the actions of service personnel.

service brand implications are that all employees must deliver the service in a way which is consistent with the brand promise

The service brand implications are that all employees must deliver the service in a way which is consistent with the brand promise. Some organizations, such as McDonalds and Disney, have highly-regarded staff training centres and sophisticated systems to ensure consistent service delivery. Other companies such as American Express or Marriott Hotels, while investing in training staff, also pay attention to empowering their employees to deal with unexpected situations. This is reflected in their recruitment policy, seeking staff who fit with their service culture and who are capable of taking the initiative to resolve varied and challenging problems.

Intangibility

Services cannot be felt, tasted, touched or seen in the same way as goods; however, there are always some tangible components which help consumers evaluate services. On a flight, for example, the total service experience is an amalgam of many disparate components, such as the experience at the airport, the nature of the service on board and the in-flight entertainment. There are clearly many tangible elements during the flight but this is hardly comparable with buying a television or a suit, where the total product can be seen, examined and evaluated.

Barclays have a question for anyone thinking about saving. Why are you bothering? No really,

why are you doing it? A new car? That dream holiday? School

fees for the nippers? Or because your Dad once said a penny

saved is a penny earned? Don't worry if you don't have an answer.

Nor do a large number of our customers. (And they've trusted us with

nearly £20 billion of their money, which is a very large number indeed.)

There's no law that says you have to know what you're saving for before

you start saving. A love of money is fine as far as we're concerned.

Which is why our **One Year Fixed Rate TESSA** appeals to so many of you. (Well

it can't be the name.) It's a devilishly clever yet fiendishly simple scheme that

works like this: to start with, you need £3,000, either from a maturing TESSA

or a new investment. Over five years, you can invest up to a total of £9,000.

Now here's the clever bit: for one year, the interest is fixed at a solid 6.50% p.a. After that, a variable rate

applies. So at the end of five years, you've either made a nice little profit, or an even bigger nice little

profit. And it's all utterly, completely, joyously tax-free. You can see why some people get addicted to

these schemes. So never mind that you don't want a new car, never go on holiday, haven't any kids and

your Dad was a spendthrift. Do it for the money. Give us a call, absolutely

free, on **0800 400 100** for more details of our full range of savings plans. **BARCLAYS**

Limited issue only. *Subject to the annual deposit limits set by the government. Tax-free refers to personal income tax under current legislation.   AJ2
Barclays Bank PLC. Reg. No. 1026167. Registered in England. Reg. Office: 54 Lombard Street, London EC3P 3AH. Barclays Bank PLC is a member of the Banking Ombudsman Scheme (UK branches only).

Exhibit 6.8 *Barclays try to take the risk out of consumers' choice decisions by talking about the £20 bn other savers have deposited, thus using size to help them infer reliability (reproduced by kind permission of Barclays Bank plc)*

Since the nature of a service in inherently abstract, the development of a brand image should enhance the reality of the offering through the representation of tangible clues. Consumers are reassured about service quality through tangible elements. For instance, they may infer the quality of a legal firm through knowledge of its size, its track record and its location. Companies using distinctive logos and physical facilities to build a strong corporate identity are helping consumers appreciate the characteristics of their service brand. For example, the red running telephone of Direct Line is a clear symbol of the company's readiness to respond quickly to customer calls. Federal Express has managed to create in consumers' minds a definite image of the company's reliability through the promise 'Positively overnight'.

Greater difficulty evaluating services

By drawing on the classification schemes developed by economists, it becomes apparent why consumers have difficulty evaluating the quality of services. As shown in Figure 6.1, there are those offerings which are high in 'search qualities', i.e. attributes consumers can identify and assess before making a decision. These include price, size, shape, colour, smell and feel. Physical goods are typically high in search qualities. A second category of offerings are those which are characterized by 'experience qualities' since the differentiating attributes can best be evaluated while being used – for example, having

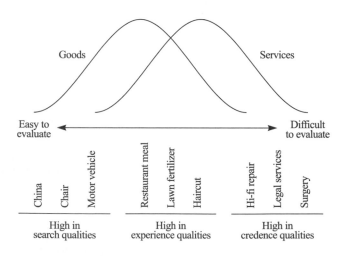

Figure 6.1   *The evaluation spectrum of products and services* (after Zeithaml and Bitner 1996)

a meal in a restaurant or having a holiday using a particular tour operator. The third category, typifying numerous services, covers those offerings high in 'credence qualities' where consumers have insufficient knowledge to fully evaluate these services, even after being consumed. For example, many people would find it difficult to fully assess the quality of major surgery.

Organizations need to assess the position of their services on the evaluation spectrum when designing effective communication strategies to help consumers evaluate service brands. The difficulties consumers have evaluating services forces them to rely on any available clues and processes. Thus, while the lawyer may be extremely qualified, the abrupt secretary may strongly influence the potential client's perceptions. The more difficult it is to evaluate a service, the greater the perceived risk associated with it and therefore the more important the need to use the brand as a risk-reducing device.

difficulties consumers have evaluating services forces them to rely on any available clues and processes

For service brands which are high in search qualities, a popular strategy involves encouraging consumers to recommend the brand to other customers through promotions such as 'Introduce a friend and you will receive a present'. Word-of-mouth acts as a credible source of information. For service brands high in experience qualities, demonstrations of the service help people make judgements. For example, some travel companies offering ocean cruises invite potential consumers to social evenings where there are video presentations of their cruises. Service brands high in credence qualities present the need to communicate more creatively the brand's qualities. For example, many customers rarely check their mortgage rates and tend to forget that it is the mortgage which enables them to enjoy living in their own house. In this situation it may be more appropriate for marketers to communicate once a year that their house has appreciated in value and that they are achieving this increased prosperity through a mortgage with a well-managed firm. Likewise the publication of an easy to understand annual statement about the performance of a PEP can be an easy way to bond policy holders, particularly when they are not bombarded with vast amounts of facts which are difficult to understand. Brands which are high in credence values should convey a strong message of trust, almost along the lines of 'Don't even think about whether it will be good – of course it will. Just trust us. Now relax and enjoy the service.'

Heterogeneity

Since services are predominantly performed by people, it is more difficult to ensure that the same standard of service will be delivered by two different people in the same firm. Staff, who represent the service in the eyes of consumers, may not only deliver the service differently between each other, but the service may differ from day to day. For example, a member of the cabin staff on a long haul-flight may provide different service levels between the outward and return flights because of the extent to which they have adjusted to the various time zones. The perceptions of the service quality may also vary because consumers differ in their individual demands, expectations and their own assessment criteria.

Many organizations try to standardize staff performance through careful planning, control and almost automation. While they achieve a high degree of homogeneity in service delivery, they increase the risk of being inflexible and their staff may react poorly to unforeseen problems. Some organizations regard heterogeneity as an opportunity for strengthening their brand by customizing their service to better serve the needs of individual consumers through greater empowerment. If organizations follow the latter approach of empowering their staff, they need to shape their employee relations and their internal communication channels to motivate and retain these customer-focused employees.

Consistency of quality

the implication for service brands is that staff training needs particular attention

Whether goods meet quality standards can be checked before they leave the supplier, whereas the quality control of services needs to be assessed when consumers come in contact with staff and this is more problematic to check. The implication for service brands is that staff training needs particular attention, as every member of staff plays a major role in ensuring the quality of the service. Regular training 'refreshers' are useful in ensuring that staff are continually providing a high service. Furthermore, organizations need to place more emphasis on closer collaboration between staff so they can learn from each other's experiences and build on best practice.

Involvement of consumers

Consumers are often actively involved in creating the service, either by undertaking a lot of the service themselves, as in a launderette, or by cooperating with the staff, as in a hair salon. Consequently, it is important that consumers are made aware of the roles they are expected to undertake as they can affect the service delivery. For example, consumers at Prêt-à-Manger are expected to get their own sandwiches and pay at the service counter, whereas in a Little Chef restaurant they need to take a seat and wait to be served. Consumers need to be informed about changes in the nature of a service, which affect the role they play in the service delivery process. British Airways introduced a new service with the E-ticket where a traveller having only hand baggage checks in at one of the self-service machines at the airport and, using their Executive Club Card, gets their boarding pass and ticket. BA were aware of the need for customers to 'learn the system'. Prior to its launch, holders of the Executive Club Card received a brochure with clear instructions about how to use the new service.

Simultaneous production and consumption

While goods are generally produced then sold and finally consumed, most services are sold first, then simultaneously produced and consumed. The consumer is present while the service is being produced and needs to participate in the production process. This presents an opportunity to influence customers' perception of the service during its delivery since, through close contact, staff can better sense consumers' views and either amend their approach, or suggest to consumers how their own actions can improve the outcome. For example, a waiter at a buffet breakfast in a hotel seeing a look of dissatisfaction when the toaster burns the toast, stops to show the guest how to adjust the toaster.

Consumer-to-consumer contact

Services can be characterized by the degree to which consumers come in contact with other consumers – for example, minimal contact in legal services yet high consumer-consumer contacts in the economy section of a flight. In service brands, consumers' appreciation and enjoyment may be adversely affected not only by the poor performance of the service provider, but also by their contact with other consumers. For instance, a couple going out to an expensive restaurant celebrating their wedding anniversary may appreciate the polite and formal style of the waiter but be appalled by the loud remarks of a group nearby who have had too much wine. Brands which are designed to appeal to different consumer segments need systems to ensure they are kept separated. For example, curtains separate business travellers from tourists in the economy class of most airlines. Furthermore, consumers within some segments may wish to reduce their contact with other consumers. Airlines respond to this by having wider seats and bigger gaps between passengers for business class travellers.

Perishability

Unlike goods, a service brand cannot be stored. An hour of an accountant's time which is not used cannot be reclaimed and used later. This perishability highlights the importance of synchronizing supply and demand. An unused seat on an aircraft shows no profit to the airline when the aircraft takes off. Likewise, sudden increases in the numbers of consumers, such as people arriving at a restaurant at the end of a cinema performance, are difficult to satisfy because there is no 'inventory' available for back-up. Service organizations need strategies to cope with fluctuating demand or to smooth demand to match capacity more closely. Failure to address this problem not only leads to increased costs and lost revenues, but also to weakened brands. Long queues at checkouts can ruin the brand image of a supermarket chain, unless ways are found either to reduce waiting times or to entice consumers to shop at off-peak periods.

many services are bought long before they are experienced

Associated with the fact that services cannot be stored is the issue that many services are bought long before they are experienced, as with pensions. Thus, many service brands face a double challenge: first, they need to develop an image and a reputation to attract consumers; secondly, they must then retain these consumers, as competitors try to attract them away, even thought they have yet to experience the actual service.

Criticality of time

For most services, consumers are prepared to wait only for a limited time before receiving the service. Since organizations cannot always ensure no waiting time, they need to find the best compromise to satisfy consumers.

When queues do occur, companies should first analyse the operational processes and possibly redesign them to remove any inefficiencies. If the queues are inevitable, long waiting times can be alleviated through a reservation system, for example in dentists. A pleasant and efficient receptionist can help shift demand to off-peak times. Another strategy is to differentiate between consumers according to their importance or the urgency of their requests. As a last resort, consumers' tolerance of queues can be increased by making the waiting time enjoyable, or at least more tolerable, through such actions as:

5.40pm

book your

business travel

5.44pm

have the airline ticket

in your hand

Business travel is demanding enough without the hassle of waiting for tickets to be delivered or queuing at airport ticket desks. That's why we've introduced innovative technology to smooth the way for you and your colleagues.

An automated ticket and boarding pass printer in your office can deliver travel documents into your hands **almost instantly,** in a state-of-the-art format. And at airports using this technology, you won't need to check-in - you can go straight to the departure gate.

As Britain's leading independent business travel management company, we do more than anyone to **speed your journey.**

For a better solution and a creative approach to business travel, **don't waste a minute.** Phone Lynne Briggs on **0181 336 4004.**   BL 2

BRITANNIC
business travel management

always a better solution

Exhibit 6.9   *Britannic Business Travel Management recognize the criticality of time to the businss traveller and use technology to bypass the problems of queuing at airport ticket desks (reproduced by kind permission of Britannic Travel Ltd and Upward, Jamie & Brown)*

- *Entertaining consumers* – Company switchboards often play music when they put callers on hold. Some theme parks have videos to occupy guests as they wait their turn on a ride.
- *Starting the process* – Reading a menu in a restaurant or filling out medical forms at the doctor's surgery are perceived as activities which are part of the service and not waiting time.
- *Reassuring consumers* that they are waiting for the right service, for instance signposts in an airport which point out which flights are being checked in by the specific lane.
- *Informing consumers* when they will be served or at least reassuring them that they have not been forgotten. For example, when someone is 'on hold' in a telephone queue, stopping the music every 30 seconds to play a message apologizing for the delay and explaining that the staff are busy but that they are aware the caller is waiting.
- *Explaining* the reasons for the delay, for example through automatically updated arrival-screens in airports and railway stations.
- *Establishing a first-come first-served rule* – The allocation of waiting numbers to consumers helps avoid jostling. Nevertheless, consumers are prepared to accept apparent inequality in exceptional cases, such as hospital emergencies.

Branding to make tangible the intangible

One of the most problematic aspects associated with service brands is that consumers have to deal with intangible offerings. In an attempt to overcome this problem, marketers put a lot of emphasis on the company as a brand, especially in sectors such as financial services, since this is one way of making the service more tangible. Research in the financial services sector has shown that consumers know little about specific products, often they do not want to know more and they are content to assume that the best-known companies have the best financial products. This further compounds the problem of service branding! A study by Boyd *et al.* (1994) showed that the most important criterion for customers selecting a bank is reputation, and the next most important the interest on savings accounts.

services brands need to be made tangible to provide consumers with well-defined reference points

Because of their intangible nature, service brands run the risk of being perceived as commodities. To overcome this problem, strong brands with a clear set of values which result in positive perceptions amongst consumers are essential. However, these common and consistent perceptions amongst consumers are difficult to establish for intangible offerings. Services brands need to be made tangible to provide consumers with well-defined reference points.

An effective way to make brands tangible is to use as many physical elements as possible that can be associated with the brand, such as staff uniforms, office décor, and the type of music played to customers waiting on the telephone. A service brand can project its values through physical symbols and representations, as Virgin airlines has so successfully done with its vibrant red colour reflecting the dynamic, challenging position being adopted. The first points of contact with a service organization, such as car parking, design of building and appearance of the reception area, all interact to give consumers clues about what the service brand will be like. Other ways that brands communicate with consumers are through tangible elements such as stationery, the way employees dress and brochures. One major retailer had a full-length mirror that all its staff passed as they left the canteen to go into the store. Above the mirror was a sign saying, 'This is what the customer sees', to draw their attention to the importance of thinking about the tangible cues consumers are presented with as representative of the brand.

Package design plays an important role for branded goods, and in service brands this likewise represents an opportunity for more effective differentiation. McDonald's boxes for childrens' meals, for instance, have been shaped as toy houses to reflect the playful element associated with the experience of a lunch in the fast-food chain. The tangible elements surrounding the brand can also serve to facilitate the service performance: the setting within which the service is delivered may either enhance or inhibit the efficient flow of activities. The yellow and blue stripes in IKEA stores, for example, not only allude to the Scandinavian tradition of the company but also guide consumers through the different sections. The design of the surroundings also plays a socialization function, informing consumers about their expected behaviour, the roles expected of staff and the extent to which interactions are encouraged between them. Club Med dining facilities are structured so that customers can easily meet and get to know each other. Finally, the design of the physical facilities may be used to *differentiate* the service brand from its competition. The polished steel interiors of Prêt-à-Manger restaurants allow consumers to distinguish them clearly from other sandwich bars bistros.

The tangible elements of a service brand encourage and discourage particular types of consumer behaviour. For example, a 7-Eleven store played classical symphonies as background music to retain their 'wealthier' customers while driving away teenagers who tended to browse the shelves rather than spend any money. Different aromas can elicit emotional responses and thereby influence consumer behaviour – some food retailers pump the fragrance of freshly baked bread into their stores, evoking a more relaxed, homely feeling.

The previous examples have shown different ways in which service organizations can make their brands more tangible. The approach adopted when 'tangibalizing' the service brand must be consistent with the service and should not promise more than the service will actually deliver. BA and Forte ensure that the perceptions of their consumers are affected in a consistent manner by taking a holistic approach to presenting their brands: they use the same music from their television advertising while customers are put on hold on the phone. The elegant uniforms worn by sales assistants at Marks & Spencer clearly communicate the brand message of fashion and excellence, and the staff dress at Woolworths is representative of good value-for-money core brand values. If the physical evidence of the brand is unplanned, inconsistent or incompatible with the message of the added values the brand aims to convey, consumers will perceive a gap and reject the brand. The following questions can help marketers to assess the extent to which they are capitalizing on tangible cues to support their brand strategy:

- Do all the elements of the physical evidence convey a consistent message?
- Do the physical evidence and the conveyed message appeal to the target market?
- Does the physical evidence appeal to employees and motivate them to develop the brand?
- Are there additional opportunities to provide physical evidence for the service?
- What are the roles of the surrounding elements of the service? How does each tangible element contribute to the development of the brand?

Consistent service brands through staff

Even though the service organization may have developed a well-conceived positioning for their brand and devised a good communication programme, the brand can still flounder because of insufficient attention to the role the staff play in producing and delivering the service. In particular, the following factors can compromise the success of the brand:

- ineffective recruitment;
- conflict in the duties staff are required to perform;
- poor fit between staff and technology.

Furthermore, as the quality and process of every service performance can vary and often requires the involvement of several employees, empowering employees and building a culture based on teamwork is likely to enhance consumer satisfaction.

Staff embody the service brand in the consumer's eyes. In many cases the service staff are the only point of contact for the consumer and by thoroughly training staff and ensuring their commitment to the brand, its chance of succeeding are greater. The success of the Disney brand results from the firm's insistence that employees recognize they are always 'on stage' whenever in public, encouraging them to think of themselves as actors who have learnt their roles and are contributing to the performance and the enjoyment of visitors.

staff embody the organization in the customer's eyes

The staff of a service organization can posititively enhance the perception consumers have of the service quality through their:

- *Reliability* – For example, Lufthansa pilots strive to ensure that their brand has an outstanding track-record of punctuality.
- *Responsiveness* – A member of cabin staff may be sympathetic to the family who have been split up on their flight and take the initiative to enable them to sit together.
- *Assurance* – While the plane is kept waiting before taking off, the pilot informs travellers of the reason, the expected length of delay and that all is being done to minimalize the delay.
- *Empathy* – Cabin staff may show empathy by comforting a crying child who is flying for the first time.
- *Appearance* – The uniform worn by the Alitalia crew is perceived as particularly elegant and fashionable as some travellers recognize that it is designed by Armani.

Failing to take heed of these factors can have a negative impact on the perceived quality of the service.

Empirical analysis has shown that not only are the actions of employees fundamental to a high-quality delivery of the service, but also that the morale of staff influence consumer satisfaction with a service brand. A study about a British bank revealed that the branches with the lowest staff turnover and absenteeism were also those with the highest levels of profitability and customer retention. A good example of the link between satisfied staff and satisfied consumers is shown by Southwest Airlines. In 1995, the employees of this airline paid $60 000 for an advertisement in *USA Today* to thank Herb Kelleher, their CEO, for the success of the company.

To ensure staff are willing and able to deliver high-quality services, organizations should motivate their staff and encourage customer-orientation culture by considering the following:

- *Recruit the right people* – Successful companies such as Hewlett Packard or Microsoft are regarded as preferred employers. The brands of the major consultancy firms are built on their policy of hiring only the best people. Some firms explore the values of potential staff to assess whether these are similar to the values of their firm.
- *Train staff to deliver service quality* – The consistency of the McDonald brand is ensured by the formal education employees undergo at the famous 'Hamburger University'. To enhance their brands, companies such as Federal Express invest heavily in the training of their employees. Nordstrom, the American retail store, is a good example of a brand built on staff empowerment: the only rule staff are taught at Nordstrom is 'use your judgement'. Furthermore, staff need to regard each other as internal customers within the service process, enhancing the quality of the brand through teamwork and cooperation.
- *Provide support systems* – Appropriate technology and equipment are essential to support staff in delivering quality service. For example, bank clerks need to have easy and fast access to up-to-date customer records if they are to deliver accurate and prompt customer service.
- *Retain the best people* – Although many organizations are aware of the importance of recruiting the best people, there are instances where firms do not put as much effort into retaining them as they could do. A high staff turnover usually translates into low consumer satisfaction and poor service quality. In order to retain their employees, organizations need to involve them in the company's decision-making process and devote as much attention to them as to their customers. Moreover, they should reward employees for good service delivery through financial and non-financial measures, such as McDonald's scheme 'The employee of the month'.

By addressing some of these issues a company can establish a more customer-focused service culture, which is a prerequisite for delivering consistently high-quality services and for building successful service brands. A customer-centred focus should pervade the whole organization so that the commitment to customers becomes second nature for all employees. The development of a genuine service culture is neither easy nor quick, but companies that have overcome this challenge have been duly rewarded. The development of a service culture at SAS, for example, contributed to turning the loss-making business into a successful brand.

Service brands with the optimum consumer participation

While the previous section has shown how service organizations can enhance their brands by building on the role employees play during the service delivery, this section focuses on how consumers contribute to the development of the service brand. The way consumers evaluate a service brand depends largely on the extent to which they participate in the delivery of the service. If a yachting enthusiast did not get on too well with an instructor at Club Med, this interaction would affect their view of the brand. When subsequently hiring a dinghy at the end of the course and having difficulties rigging the sail, he may complain to his friends about ageing equipment. Yet the real reason for his problems is that he did not pay proper attention to his instructor.

way consumers evaluate a service brand depends largely on the extent to which they participate in the delivery of the service

If the service performance requires a high degree of consumer involvement, it is vitally important that consumers understand their roles, and are willing and able to perform their roles, otherwise their inevitable frustration will weaken the brand. Large, easy to read signs and displays at the entrance of IKEA stores inform consumers how they are supposed to take measurements, select pieces of furniture and collect them.

The level of consumer participation varies across services. In service sectors such as airlines and fast-food restaurants, the level of consumer participation is low, as all that is required is the consumer's physical presence and the employees of the organization perform the whole service. In sectors such as banking and insurance, consumers participate moderately and provide an input to the service creation through providing information about their physical possessions. When consumers are highly involved in the service, for example participating WeightWatchers, they need to be fully committed and actively participate.

Consumers can be regarded as productive resources and even as partial employees of the service organization, because they provide effort, time and other input for the performance of the service. They are also contributors to the quality and value of the service thereby influencing their assessments about the service brand. Consumers who believe they have played their part well in contributing to the service tend to be more satisfied. The IKEA brand is built on the principle that consumers are willing to be involved in 'creating' the service, not just in consuming it. Since actively-involved consumers feel the responsibility is theirs when the service turns out to be unsatisfactory, they are particularly pleased when the service provider attempts to redress the problem.

To involve consumers in the service-delivery process, organizations can implement different strategies which are based on the following three factors:

- defining the role of consumers;
- recruiting, educating and rewarding consumers;
- managing the consumer mix;

The organization needs to determine the level of customer participation by defining the consumer's 'job'. Some strong brands such as Federal Express and DHL are built on low consumer involvement, as consumers rarely see the service provider's facilities and have only very brief phone contact with its employees. In these cases, as consumers are minimally involved in the service delivery process and their role is extremely limited, strong service brands can be developed through standardized offerings and precisely defined procedures. On the other hand, for service organizations like business school and health clubs, there are higher levels of consumer participation and more tailored offerings can be developed.

Effective consumer participation may require that consumers go through a process similar to a new company employee – a process of recruitment, education and reward. In telephone banking, consumers are first recruited, and then they receive formal training and information about the service. Only then will they be rewarded with easier access to financial services. Brands such as First Direct have been successful because they have effectively communicated the benefits consumers can gain from their participation. Service brands can be strengthened through an effective management of the mix of consumers who simultaneously experience the service. All major airlines, for example, are aware of the need to separate different segments.

effective customer
participation may
require that the
customers go
through a process
of recruitment,
education and
reward

Conclusions

The growing importance of the services sector has made firms aware that the creation and development of service brands represents a source of sustainable competitive advantage. Despite similarities between the principles of branding for goods and services, the specific nature of services requires tailored approaches. The case studies of the insurance and financial services sectors have illustrated some of the challenges marketers face when establishing service brands. The Liverpool Victoria Friendly Society and the NatWest Small Business Adviser brands are examples of how strong service brands can be developed by adjusting the traditional FMCG branding model to the service sector.

We have argued for a fine-tuning of the existing branding theories, as opposed to the creation of a whole new theory, and examined the distinctive differences between goods and services to help managers fine-tune the brand development process. Since every service is based on a series of performances, service brands run the risk of being perceived as commodities. To overcome this problem, service brand need to be made tangible to provide consumers with a favourable set of perceptions. An effective way to do this is to use the physical components associated with the service. These representations, which need to be compatible with the added-value message the brand aims to convey, can be used to inform staff and consumers about their expected roles and to differentiate the service brand.

Consumer's appreciation of service brands depends on a variety of factors such as the role played by the staff; the role consumers play and the interaction between consumers. All employees, as they embody the organization in consumers' eyes, can influence perceptions of the service brand. Marketers therefore need to carefully consider their recruitment processes, the role staff are expected to play and their technical support to ensure they are able and motivated to deliver high-quality services.

Consumers can contribute to the development of a service brand. Though their level of participation may vary, it can be a fundamental aspect of building service brands. Organizations can determine the level of consumer participation by defining their role, by recruiting, educating and rewarding them and by managing the consumer mix.

Marketing action checklist

To better help determine brand marketing activities, it is recommended that the following exercises are undertaken:

1   For each of your service brands, list the tangible elements that are used to convey a consistent message of the brand's added value.
    • How clearly do these elements communicate the brand benefits to customers?
    • What other functions, for example, socializing or facilitating, do they have?
    With your marketing team, identify opportunities to use these elements to differentiate your brand from competitors.
2   From the list of tangible elements in the previous exercise, assess whether these elements encourage only the target consumer segment to purchase the service and whether they discourage other segments. Is this discouragement intended because the other segments are incompatible with the primary target segment? Does the target segment need this 'protection' from other segments?
3   If you are planning to launch a new service;
    • How well does it fit with your existing products and consumer base?
    • Will the existing consumers relate to the new brand?
    • Will they be confused by contrasting messages?
    • Does the new brand need a product-specific name or could it build on the current corporate identity?
4   For any of your service brands, how easy it is for consumers to evaluate the quality of the service delivery? Where do they gather information about brand benefits and whether these will satisfy their needs? Do consumers perceive a high risk associated with purchasing the service? What strategies, could be used to minimize this perceived risk?
5   Are the benefits of your brands delivered consistently by all employees? What are you doing to ensure consistency between your staff members and over time? What would be the implications for your brands if your company decided to take a more empowerment-orientated approach?
6   Are your consumers informed about the role they are expected to play during the service delivery? Does your brand require a low, medium or high degree of consumer involvement? What guidelines do consumers receive prior to or during the delivery

of the service to be aware of their expected behaviour?

7   As the service offered by your brand cannot be stored, what strategies have been implemented to smooth fluctuating demand and supply? When waiting time cannot be avoided, how can consumers still be satisfied?

8   Examine the role of your staff during the production and delivery of the service brand, according to factors such as:
   - reliability;
   - responsiveness;
   - assurance;
   - empathy and appearance.

   Do these factors offer further opportunities to enhance consumer perceptions of your brand?

9   The long-term success of the service brand depends on the ability and motivation of your staff.
   - Is the recruitment process geared to provide the organization with employees who share the corporate vision and the message the brand aims to convey?
   - Does your organization provide regular training for employees to ensure a consistent delivery of the service over time?
   - What technical support do employees receive to deliver the brand benefits?
   - How does your company strive to retain good employees?

10   What role do consumers play in the delivery of your service brand? Do they receive sufficient information to understand this role and perform it effectively? How can you enhance their participation to make brand stronger?

References and further reading

Boyd, W.L. *et al.* (1994) Customer preferences for financial services: an analysis. *International Journal of Bank Marketing*. 12(1), 9–15.

Brookes, J. (1996) Awaking the 'sleeping dinosaur': a case study of the Liverpool Victoria Friendly Society Ltd. *The Journal of Brand Management*. 3(5), 306–12.

Camp, L. (1996) Latest thinking on the optimisation of brand use in financial services marketing. The Journal of Brand Management. 3(4), 241–7.

De Chernatony, L. and Dall'Olmo Riley, F. (1996) Experts' views about defining service brands and the principles of service branding. Paper presented at 9th UK Services Marketing Workshop, University of Sterling.

Denby-Jones, S. (1995) Retail banking: Mind the gap. *The Banker*. Vol. 145/828, 66–7.

Free, C. (1996) Building a financial brand you can bank on. *The Journal of Brand Management*. 4(1), 29–34.

Levy, M. (1996) Current accounts and baked beans: Translating FMCG marketing principles to the financial sector. *The Journal of Brand Management*. 4(2), 95–9.

Lovelock, C.H. (1996) Service markets (Upper Saddle River: Practice Hall International)

Onkvisit, S. and Shaw, J.J. (1989) Service Marketing: Image, Branding and Competition. *Business Horizons*. Jan.–Feb., 13–18.

Shostack, G.L. (1977) Breaking free from product marketing. *Journal of Marketing*. 41 (4), 73–80.

Watters, R, and Wright, D. (1994) Why has branding failed in the UK insurance industry? In *ESOMAR Seminar: Banking and Insurance*, 137–51 (Amsterdam: ESOMAR).

Zeithaml, V.A. and Bitner, M.J. (1996) *Services marketing*. (New York: McGraw-Hill).

Chapter 7

Retailer issues in branding

Summary

The purpose of this chapter is to look at the way branding is influenced by retailers. It opens by reviewing the changing nature of own labels, and examines the resources retailers are using to back their quality positioning. It discusses the launch of generics and clarifies why this secondary own label tier failed. The shift in the balance of power from manufacturers to retailers is documented and the response of weak and strong brand manufacturers is compared. Brand manufacturer strategies appropriate for convenience and non-convenience retailer types are reviewed. The expansion of retailers across Europe is considered and the problems of finding pan-European positionings discussed. The issues manufacturers should consider before working on own labels are reviewed along with the criteria retailers use to assess potential own label suppliers. The brand strength–distributor attractiveness matrix is presented as a device to prioritize the effort behind different brands being sold through specific major accounts. Some of the strategies manufacturers can implement to develop and defend strong brands, despite the increasing power of retailers, are reviewed. Finally, category management and ECR are considered.

Brands as a sign of ownership

Retailers' interest in own labels stemmed originally from being able to circumvent resale price maintenance (RPM) and offer a lower priced range of goods to compete against manufacturers' brands. Up until 1964, when RPM was abolished, retailers' pricing policy had to follow manufacturers' stipulations about selling prices. By commissioning manufacturers to produce and pack products to their own specification, retailers were able to sell their own labels more cheaply than manufacturers' brands.

The era of own labels being positioned primarily as a cheap

alternative to manufacturers' brands lasted from the turn of this century up until the mid-1970s. One of the ways retailers achieved a price advantage was to accept quality levels lower than those normally associated with manufacturers' brands. Consumers were content to accept this, since they were trading off quality frills against price savings.

During the 1960s, multiple retailers began to take advantage of the economies of scale that could be achieved by owning even more stores. Particularly in the grocery retailing sector, a few companies emerged, such as Sainsbury and Tesco, who controlled an increasingly large number of stores. Multiple retailers – those owning ten or more outlets – became more powerful. For example, in 1961 only 27 per cent of grocery products were sold through multiple retailers. By 1975 this had risen to 49 per cent and in 1995 multiple retailers accounted for 82 per cent of grocery sales.

Ironically, in their quest for growth multiples saw that further profit opportunities could be achieved by reducing the number of stores, but with each remaining store being of a much larger size. The advent of superstore retailing, where stores in excess of 25 000 square feet became increasingly common, enabled retailers, in particular multiples, to capitalize further on the opportunities presented through economies of scale. In 1980 there were 239 grocery superstores – by 1996 this had grown to 1015.

As multiple retailers became more professional in managing their stores, so they began to realize the value of own labels in reinforcing their positioning. Up until the 1970s own labels were generally used to help communicate a store's low-price proposition. However, multiple retailers shifted away from competing against each other just on price and instead began to emphasize quality and service. This became increasingly apparent as more superstores were opened with much wider product ranges. With a change in retailer positioning came a change in own label emphasis. Retailers became more concerned with the quality of their own labels, which were no longer 'cheap and cheerful' alternatives to quality brands. Instead, higher quality standards were stipulated in own label briefs. Advertising strategies were also prepared, aimed at refreshing own labels' personalities and giving them a quality element.

With new, well-conceived identities for stores and own labels, consumers began to recognize and appreciate the distinctive qualities and personalities of own labels. This can be seen from the following quotes from a consumer research study. To assess brand personalities, respondents were asked to describe the sort of person each of the own labels would be if they came alive. As is apparent from the quotes, these own labels have very strong brand personalities

as multiple retailers became more professional in managing their stores, so they began to realize the value of own labels in reinforcing their positioning

I'm classy. I'm confident, I'm smart enough to put on the dinner table. I ape no one and I broadcast a simple message:'I'm a classic'.

Waitrose Tartar Sauce

You feel comfortable with me. I don't have to be flash because you trust me. I'm Sainsbury's and this is a packet of stuffing mix. Enough said.

Sainsburys Sage and Onion Stuffing Mix

In 1961, when multiple grocery retailers accounted for 27 per cent of packaged grocery sales, own labels were generally 20 per cent cheaper than manufacturers' brands, but were of a *poorer* quality level. By 1995, with multiple retailers controlling 82 per cent of packaged grocery sales, own labels are of an *equivalent*, if not *better* quality level than manufacturers' brands, yet still offer a price advantage. Grocery multiple retailers are increasingly setting high standards for the quality of own labels. Some are only prepared to launch a new own label if it at least matches, and preferably exceeds, the brand leader in consumer product testing.

This change in own labels and manufacturer brands, particularly in packaged groceries, is shown in Figure 7.1. Some manufacturers, feeling the squeeze of retailer expansion, cut back on their quality standards. For example, one study was critical of the way that some ice cream manufacturers had increased air content in their brands to cut costs in meeting the demands of retailers. Also, more manufacturers began to compete on price, while in some instances retailers increased the prices of their own labels. In fact, in some product fields, such as fresh fruit juice, many own labels have a similar price to manufacturers' brands.

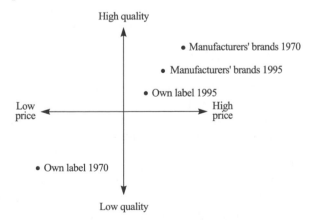

Figure 7.1   *The changing nature of brands and own labels*

Own labels are becoming increasingly popular. According to Taylor Nelson AGB Superpanel data, own labels accounted for 23 per cent of grocery sales in 1977, yet by 1995 they had grown to 39 per cent. Consumers have become much more confident in using own labels and are now proud to display them. In one study, for example, we came across a consumer who used to fill a branded bottle of whisky with a retailer's own label whisky and pour this when less-discerning visitors asked for whisky. With this consumer's increased respect for own labels, however, the retailer's own label whisky is now on display when friends are entertained.

The backing behind own label

Retailers in many sectors are committed to growing their own labels. This is more apparent in Europe than in the USA due to the greater experience of European retailers, resulting in average pre-tax profits of 7 per cent in European grocery stores, compared with 2 per cent in American stores. Retailers are using **promotional activity** to communicate their high quality levels and to reinforce their 'brand' personalities. In 1995 Sainsbury was the twelfth biggest advertiser, spending £41.4 m just promoting the umbrella Sainsbury name, compared with the biggest advertiser, Procter & Gamble, spending £157 m across its many different brands of detergents and health and beauty products.

the commitment behind good value own label is apparent

The commitment behind good value own label is apparent, both in the tight **product specifications** given to manufacturers and in the considerable effort invested in identifying and evaluating potential own label producers. Some retailers have significant R&D departments which undertake preliminary product development research prior to briefing potential producers. For example, at Marks & Spencer there are over 200 people working in its food R&D laboratories.

In terms of striving for higher quality standards and communicating these to consumers, Safeway launched its 'Refund & Replace' promotion in 1991. To communicate their backing of higher quality levels for own labels, they erected posters in their stores stating that if their consumers are not completely satisfied with their own label, they would be offered a refund and replacement. Midway through 1993 Sainsbury launched a stringent quality control programme for its 2500 own label suppliers worldwide, going as far as stipulating staff training. It enhanced the quality of its own labels and in 1997 ran a campaign, 'Better quality, same price', to communicate to customers that quality had risen while prices have remained stable.

Retailers are responsive to changing consumer needs and have **innovative own label** programmes which rapidly take advantage of

Exhibit 7.1   *Waitrose is continually aiming to enhance the quality of its grocery range with new fine foods (reproduced by kind permission of Waitrose)*

market opportunities. The fact that they are in direct contact with the consumer no doubt gives them a slight advantage over manufacturers in identifying new trends. A good example of innovative own label development was Tesco's launch of chlorine-free own label paper products. They became aware of increasing consumer interest in environmentally-friendly, 'green' products. A major market research programme was undertaken which identified different consumer groups, such as:

• 'Bright Greens' who are very concerned about the damage be-

ing done to the environment and who actively campaign for green products;
- 'Light Greens' who, as mothers of young children, are aware of the damage being done to the environment and are worried about whether food is safe for their children;
- 'Hints of Green' are well-off people, probably with two cars, aware of environmental issues but not quite sure about what role they should play in environmental protection;
- 'Turquoise' are rural people keen on preserving their way of life and who like the countryside the way it is.

The study showed that 67 per cent of people were prepared to pay more for having environmentally-friendly products. With all these findings, they started to work on launching their own range of green products under the banner 'Tesco cares'. To compete against Ark Washing Powder, for example, they had their own phosphate-free product.

While developing their new 'green' range, a *World in Action* television documentary was broadcast. This showed that bleaching paper with chlorine to make it white can leave small traces of the deadly dioxin chemical. Peaudouce nappies were featured showing how they had to be withdrawn and relaunched with a safer creamy-coloured nappy, bleached with peroxide. Shortly after this programme, Tesco received lots of letters from worried consumers, asking if chlorine bleaching was being used. They quickly sensed the market's awareness of the issue and cut short a market research programme, launching instead their own brand of non-chlorine bleached toilet paper. To find a pulp mill that didn't use chlorine bleaching, Tesco technologists visited numerous mills throughout Europe, eventually awarding the contract to a firm in Sweden.

Retailers have stringent standards about own label **pack designs**, insisting that they not only communicate the characteristics of the individual line but also reinforce their store's image. In the 1970s, when retailers fought on a low-price proposition, their own label packaging was functional and stark. Graphics did little more than identify the name of the store and convey an impression of low cost. Today, retailers recognize the 'silent persuader' value of own label packaging. For example, the basic bottle containing beer now has a gold label on it and a design that implies the retailer is a specialist in the beer sector. The pack satisfies the functional requirements of being easy to carry and enables the beer to be easily poured, while at the same time promoting its message of quality.

Quite clearly, retailers are using well-tried branding techniques to develop quality propositions for their own labels. They have devised well-conceived personalities for their own label ranges that support the image of their stores. They are using innovative advertising campaigns that memorably reinforce their positioning. In fact, in 1997 at the annual Marketing Society award, Tesco won five out of ten category awards and was voted by 3000 marketers as one of the country's most potent marketing forces. In view of the way that retailers are developing their 'brands', we believe it is misleading to call them own labels. A more appropriate term is 'retailers' brands'.

The arrival and demise of generics

As was briefly discussed in Chapter 2, some retailers in the 1970s and 1980s experimented with a second tier in own labels – generics. Thinking that consumers were sceptical of the frills associated with some brands and that they would be more receptive to an even lower price proposition, particularly in a worsening economic climate, generic ranges were launched in grocery and DIY sectors. Generics are products distinguishable by their basic and plain packaging. Primary emphasis is given to the contents, rather than to any distinguishing retail chain name.

Carrefour in France pioneered this route in 1976 with its Produits Libres, and was quickly followed by Promede's Produits Blancs, Paridoc's Produits Familiaux and Euromarche's Produits Orange. In Germany, Carrefour, Deutsche Supermarkt and the Co-op encountered problems of poor quality perceptions, due to the low prices. In Switzerland, where there is a significant own label presence and consumers are primarily concerned about quality, generics had little success.

In the UK, as Table 2.3 showed, several retailers experimented with generics. Some were very committed to the concept, such as Fine Fare. Others, notably Tesco, were less certain, particularly as this conflicted with their move to shift their store's positioning upmarket.

The problem was that a cheaper range was being introduced with a quality level inferior to that of own labels. Consumers had previously been experiencing improvements in quality and service and were confused by the return of the 'pile it high, sell it cheap' era. Furthermore, what had happened was that retailers had not launched a unique, stand-alone range. Instead, they had created a secondary own label range, perceived by consumers as an alternative to the current own label range.

retailers had not launched a unique, stand-alone range

The true generic concept had not been implemented. By definition, generics have no promotional backing nor any distinctive labeling. Yet their launch was heralded by a considerable promotional spend. For example, during 1977 Carrefour spent FF10 m promoting generics, compared with Euromarche's FF6 m. A not insignificant effort was devoted to pack designs which, while less sophisticated than conventional own labels, still clearly linked each range with a specific store. In particular, Tesco's stark white packs with blue print resulted in a range which was very prominent on the shelves and which was quickly recognized and associated with Tesco.

As consumers began to think of generics as an extension of own labels, so they switched from the higher margin own labels to the lower margin generics. This was contrary to retailers' hopes that generics would take sales from manufacturers' brands. Retailers saw generics weakening their overall profitability and tarnishing the quality image that they were striving for. They had misjudged consumers' needs. Low prices are no longer the prime reason driving choice. Instead consumers, as experienced buyers, are seeking value for money – rather than low prices – along with a cluster of added values.

During the mid-1990s generics or, more correctly, budget own labels, reappeared in stores such as Sainsbury, Tesco and Safeway. To some extent this may have been a response to the move of aggressive marketers of discount stores, such as Kwik Save, Aldi, Netto and Lidl.

The increasingly powerful retailer

The past thirty-five years have seen a swing in the balance of power from manufacturer to retailer. The early 1960s saw a boom in retailing, due to such issues as relaxation of building controls, the success of self-service, and more professional management who identified smaller retailers ripe for acquisition. The abolition of resale price maintenance in 1964 gave a further boost to retailers, who were freed from the pricing stipulations of brand suppliers. As evidence of concentrated retailer power, Taylor Nelson AGB Superpanel/TCA data shows that in 1975 the top four multiple retailers accounted for 22 per cent of grocery sales, yet by 1995 they accounted for 61 per cent.

Retailers became more efficient through centralized buying and centralized warehousing. They shut their smaller stores and opened a smaller number of stores, all of much larger selling areas. Between 1971 and 1979, for example, the number of multiple grocers' stores fell by approximately 5000 outlets, yet this sector's selling area increased from 21.9 to 27.6 m square feet. Part of their increased profitability was passed on to consumers in the form of cheaper prices, further enhancing their attractiveness to consumers. By 1995, multiple grocery retailers accounted for 82 per cent of grocery sales.

The reasons for the increasing concentration of multiple retailers can be appreciated from Figure 7.2. As certain groups became larger, many manufacturers found it difficult not to pass on more favourable volume discounts. They rationalized these above-average discounts on the basis that they justified very large orders. Retailers used some of these discounts to fund their own label programmes and to present their range as being better value than those of independent or cooperative retailers. More consumers were attracted by this proposition, contributing to the profitability of multiples. Ever aware of the future, the multiples invested in better stores and further increased their share, forcing out less profitable smaller retailers.

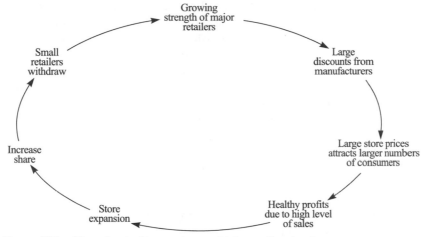

Figure 7.2   *The wheel of increasing multiple retailer dominance*

Manufacturers were aware of this shift in power to the retailers but, surprisingly, took little action. Their response lacked any long-term strategic thinking. They failed to appreciate how retailers were becoming more innovative, more consumer driven, more concerned about developing strong images for their stores and increasingly committed to growing their own labels. Instead of communicating their brands' added values to consumers, they cut back on brand advertising in favour of buying shelf space.

This shift in the balance of power resulted in retailers no longer being passive pipelines for branded goods. Instead, they became highly involved coordinators of marketing activity. As one retailer said:

> *We now see ourselves as the customer's manufacturing agent, rather than the manufacturer's selling agent.*

failed to appreciate how retailers were becoming more innovative, more consumer driven, more concerned about developing strong images for their stores and increasingly committed to growing their own labels

The responses of weak and strong manufacturers

Weaker brand manufacturers, particularly those lacking a long-term planning horizon, were unable to find a convincing argument to counter retailers' demands for extra discounts. They were worried about being de-listed and saw no other alternative but to agree to disproportionately large discounts. Many erroneously viewed this as part of their promotional budget and failed to appreciate the implication of biasing their promotion budget to the trade at the expense of consumers. Retailers' investment in own labels brought them up to the standard of manufacturers' brands. For example, a Lockwood's subsidiary supplying own labels invested in new equipment, which cut down the soaking and blanching of baked beans from the traditional 20 hours to less than an hour, before most of its major competitors. With increasing investment in own labels and less support behind manufacturers' brands, consumers began to perceive less differences between brands and own labels, and choice began to be influenced more by availability, price and point of sale displays. As retailers had more control over these influencing factors, weaker brands lost market share and their profitability fell.

Weak manufacturers' brands were not generating sufficient returns to fund either maintenance programmes or investments in new products. At the next negotiating round with retailers, it was made

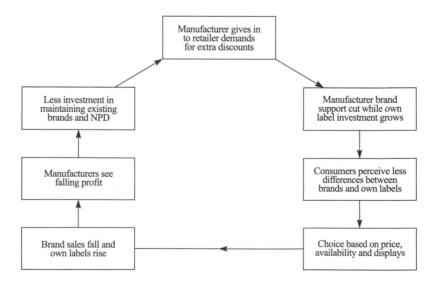

Figure 7.3   The weakening manufacturer's brand

clear that their sales were deteriorating and again they were forced to buy shelf space through even larger discounts. In the vicious circle shown in Figure 7.3, they were soon on the spiral of rapid decline.

From the vicious circle of deteriorating brand position, it can be appreciated that own labels are particularly strong in markets where:

- there is excess manufacturing capacity;
- products are perceived as commodities: inexpensive and low-risk purchases;
- products can be easily compared by consumers;
- low levels of manufacturer investment are common and the production processes employ low technology;
- there are high price gaps in the market and retailers have the resources to invest in high-quality own label development;
- variability in quality is low and distribution is well-developed;
- the credibility of a branded product is low because of frequent and deep price promotions as opposed to the increasing credibility of own labels;
- branded products are offered in few varieties and with rare innovations, enabling the own label producer to offer a clear alternative.

Examples of markets in 1995, where own label shares were particularly high and where these characteristics were evident, include fresh poultry (78 per cent own label), cream (74 per cent own label), kitchen towels and clothes (64 per cent own label) and pre-cooked sliced meat (60 per cent own label).

By contrast, strong brand manufacturers such as Unilever, Heinz and Nestlé, realized that the future of strong brands lies in a commitment to maintaining unique added values and communicating these to consumers. They 'bit the bullet', realizing that to succeed they would have to support the trade, but not at the expense of the consumer. Instead, they invested both in production facilities for their current brands and in new brand development work. With strong manufacturers communicating their brands' values to consumers, these were recognized and choice in these product fields became more strongly influenced by quality and perceptions of brand personality. Retailers recognized these manufacturers' commitment behind their brands and wanted to stock them. Distribution increased through the right sorts of retailers, enabling brand sales and profits to grow. Healthy returns enabled further brand investment and, as Figure 7.4 shows, strong brands thrived.

future of strong brands lies in a commitment to maintaining unique added values and communicating these to consumers

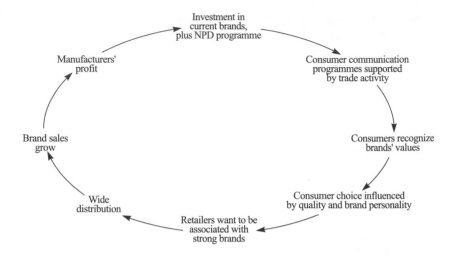

Figure 7.4   *Strong brand's response*

The confectionery market in the UK is a good example of a sector where strong manufacturers' brands dominate. The major players Mars, Nestlé and Cadbury are continually launching new brands and heavily advertising their presence. Interestingly, the power of multiple retailers is also dissipated by virtue of a significant proportion of sales going through confectioners, tobacconists and newsagents, along with vending machines and garage forecourts. The same circumstances apply to Coca-Cola and Pepsi-Cola, who are less dependent on the multiple retailers.

Convenience versus non-convenience outlets

In the broadest terms, retail outlets can be classified as being convenience or non-convenience outlets, for which two different types of brand strategies are appropriate. Convenience outlets have a geographical coverage, making it easy for consumers to access them. The goods sold are not speciality items and consumers generally feel confident making brand selections. Consumers do not need detailed pack information to make a choice between alternatives. In convenience outlets, retailers strive for volume efficiencies. They typically include retailers of grocery and home improvement products.

In convenience outlets, manufacturers' brands will thrive only if they are strongly differentiated. This necessitates having added values that consumers appreciate, a strong promotional commitment and packaging that rapidly communicates the brands' added values. Displaying a lot of information on the packaging may well be ineffective, since consumers want to make fast brand selections with minimal search effort. Brand manufacturers need to ensure that they gain listings in retailers with the broadest coverage, ensuring minimal travel difficulties for consumers.

In non-convenience outlets, such as jewellers and electrical retailers, consumers will be more likely to seek more information and may well be prepared to spend time visiting a few retailers. To thrive in these outlets, manufacturers need to ensure that clear information is available at point of purchase. In particular, retailers' staff need to be fully aware of the brand's capabilities, since consumers often seek their advice. Unless sales assistants display a positive attitude about the brand and correctly explain its capabilities, they will not help it sell.

Retailers' own label expansion across Europe

With the removal of trade barriers opening access to 325 m European Community consumers, more retailers and manufacturers are moving into Europe. Consumers from different cultural backgrounds are experiencing new retail groups. These are either retailers who have joined an alliance, such as Argyll, Ahold and Casino, forming the European Retail Alliance, or foreign stores who have maintained their independence while crossing borders, such as Tengelmann.

The advantages for retailers forming a European alliance are many. It allows the sharing of marketing research, management information and experience amongst members. It facilitates the coordination of marketing, product development, distribution, logistics and information technology. It also offers significant economies through sourcing low-cost suppliers and negotiating very large orders at favourable terms.

With pricing structures in the grocery trade being related to volume discounts, manufacturers are becoming increasingly worried about pan-European alliances. For example, when Ahold approached a computer manufacturer for a specially designed till, they were in a weak position asking for only 500 units. However, with their alliance partners, they were in a much stronger position, with an order for 55 000 tills. A further concern of manufacturers is that alliance members will discuss how much they are paying for the same manufacturer's products, when different factories across Europe are being used. The indications are that retailers are going to become even more powerful in Europe.

Some retailers, such as Aldi, have decided not to participate in

European alliances. Their reasons include believing that they already have strong buying power, they are satisfied operating in their current markets and they do not want to have their expansion plans subjected to debate by other retailers.

However, while a more open Europe may offer opportunities for own label expansion, it also creates problems. There does not yet appear to be a consensus view about how to position and name own labels. A true Euro-own label, if ever successfully developed, has to overcome the problem of finding a positioning that would appeal to consumers in cities as diverse as Leeds, Lisbon, Lausanne and La Rochelle. With strong cultural differences existing across Europe, it is unlikely that a homogeneous Euro-consumer will evolve. However, with satellite television and the greater mobility of people, it is likely that a convergence of tastes and opinions will occur. This may well be accelerated by retailers' pan-European expansion.

> with strong cultural differences existing across Europe, it is unlikely that a homogeneous Euro-consumer will evolve

Different retailers have followed diverse approaches to developing pan-European own labels. The Belgian GIB group, a member of the Euro-group alliance, has cooperated with its members to develop own labels with names that make them appear to be manufacturers' brands. For example, Le Bon Petit Diable biscuits and Star-Cat petfoods. While these can be carried across Europe, they lack the support of the retailers' names and are likely to be ignored by risk-averse consumers, who have never come across such names and are unable to recall any advertising.

By contrast, Asko Deutsche Kaufhaus attempted to introduce a Euro-own label. They developed their own label range under the umbrella brand name of the fictitious character, Isabelle O'Lacy. This is internationally protected and was conceived to blend across different European cultures. This strategy assumes that the own label's personality will appeal to consumers from different countries. This is a brave assumption – if nothing else one has only to think of consumers' difficulties in pronouncing the name!

Whether to become an own label supplier

Increasingly, manufacturers are faced with the decision about whether or not to accept invitations from retailers to produce an own label version of their brand. The short-term attraction of extra sales needs to be weighed against long-term issues – not least of which is creating their own competitor. Firms like Kellogg's and Coca-Cola are not prepared to produce an own label. They believe they have very successful brands whose formulation others find difficult to emulate. They argue that they have such strong brand assets that they have little to gain in the long-term from own label production. Mars is a particularly good example of this. Their experience of producing the world famous Mars Bar is such that no other company can emulate the quality of their brand at a cheaper, or similar price. In fact, one manufacturer's trials for a retailer indicated that a poor quality own label could only be produced with a price 50 per cent higher than the current Mars Bar!

One of the issues that needs considering is the economics of being a brand manufacturer versus an own label supplier. The firm needs to identify whether the pay back in the long term from branding exceeds that from following an own label route. The analysis needs to identify all the activities involved in converting raw materials into final products and costs put against these. The first series of costs are those based on supplying an own label. The premium that the firm must pay for undertaking the extra work involved in branding then needs to be identified. Finally, the extra margin, if any, attributable to marketing a brand, rather than an own label, needs to be gauged. Providing the economics are sensible and any differential advantage can be sustained, and as consumers recognize the quality difference over own labels, it would be wise to remain a brand manufacturer.

Production levels need to be evaluated. If there is 10 per cent excess capacity in the factory, and it is estimated that own label production will take 20 per cent of normal production, the manufacturer is faced with the problem of deciding which lines to limit.

If the brand's differential advantage is difficult to sustain – for example, patents expire in a year's time – own label may be an attractive option. Before progressing down an own label route, however, the manufacturer needs to consider whether there is a lot of goodwill inherent in the brand's name which, in the short-term, others may find difficult to overcome. If so, it is worth trading on this brand asset, rather than rushing into own label production.

It is necessary to question whether there is a commitment internally to investing in the future of brands. If a new director has recently been appointed, will they sway the board's views away from continually supporting brands? If the firm has recently been the subject of a takeover, will the new owners show the same concern about investment? To adopt a half-hearted approach may result in a secondary brand, which at best can look forward to a short life span as retailers employ systems such as Direct Product Profitability (DPP) to rationalize their range. As Figure 7.5 indicates, in its early days a successful brand has well-differentiated benefits which consumers appreciate and for which they are prepared to pay a price premium. Without investment, the point of difference will fade as more 'me-toos' appear, reducing the price premium once charged. As the brand slides deeper into the commodity domain, it is common for manufacturers to place more reliance on price cutting, further damaging the brand. In reality, this is just another representation of the process described in Figure 7.3.

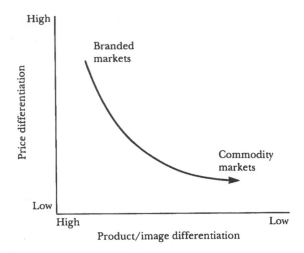

Figure 7.5   *Sliding down the commodity curve*

Some firms argue that if they do not supply own labels, their competitors will. This argument of 'blocking' competition was used by ICI with Wickes DIY group. To limit the sales of Crown paints, ICI persuaded Wickes to let them supply their own label. This forced Crown out, enabling ICI to supply both an own label and also their Dulux range.

In some firms there is a motivational issue involved in deciding whether to supply own label. Some managers think that they will have less contact with their advertising agencies or that they will have to change their style of always looking for the best to one of finding the cheapest. They worry that if they subsequently stop supplying own label, the retailer will reveal their point of difference to one of their competitors. While previously they may have enjoyed negotiating from a position of strength, they may feel that they are becoming very dependent on the own label orders of a few, very large retailers.

Small manufacturers who underestimate sales potential may be particularly attracted by own label contracts. Taking a less than optimistic view of the future, they may short-sightedly see own label as their insurance. It would be far better if these firms evaluated the strength of their consumer franchise and assessed the potential for growing in a niche, selling their brand only through carefully selected retailers.

When managers argue for own labels because this helps build a closer working relationship with retailers, there are signs that they are not making the most of their current brands. There is no excuse for not maintaining regular contact with retailers through the existing portfolio of brands. This can be done through invitations to the manufacturer's sales conferences, to hospitality events, to hear about new product developments, etc. If anything, there is an argument that broadening the portfolio with own labels may well dilute the quality of discussions with retailers, since more lines need discussing at each meeting.

Retailers are unlikely to be equally interested in selling manufacturers' brands and their own labels, as some managers incorrectly argue. They view some lines as being particularly good for reinforcing their store image, or to generate store traffic or to boost profits. They place a different emphasis on different parts of their range and may well give the own labels better shelf positioning, at the expense of the original brands.

In some cases, own label can provide a basis for growth, particularly through expansionary retailers. However, against this must be weighed weak retailers who are ineffective in countering the encroachment of other retailers. They survive by adopting a policy of 'management by line of least resistance', giving prominence to those lines that sell best and putting little effort into slower moving lines. Producing own labels for these retailers is unlikely to lead to increasing profitability.

It can be misguided to take the view that own labels can be used to cover overheads. The marketer needs to question why overheads are becoming significant and take action to resolve this problem. Launching an own label range for this reason may well be a short-term solution to a problem which will reappear. Retailers are likely to negotiate very low prices, probably giving the manufacturer a poorer rate of return for own labels than might otherwise be expected from brands.

misguided to take the view that own labels can be used to cover overheads

How retailers select own label suppliers

With increasing demands for higher quality own labels, retailers are becoming more selective when choosing potential own label suppliers. Some of the considerations taken into account when assessing potential suppliers are:

- Can they produce the quality standards consistently?
- Are they financially sound?
- Do they have adequate capacity to meet the current targets and sufficient spare capacity to cope with increasingly successful own labels?
- Do they have the transport infrastructure to ensure reliable delivery?
- Is the production machinery up to date and well maintained?
- Do they have good labour relations?

- Will they be committed to the retailer?
- Do they have the flexibility to respond to short-term market fluctuations?
- Will they be able to hold adequate stock?
- Do they have a good marketing department that the retailer feels they can work with?
- Will the supplier maintain good communications with the retailer, regularly informing them of any relevant issues?
- Will the supplier agree to the retailer's payment terms?
- Would the retailer be happy to be associated with the supplier?

Prioritizing brand investment through different retailers

Even though retailer power is increasing manufacturers, particularly those with strong brands, need to adopt an offensive rather than a defensive strategy when deciding where brand investment is needed. Ideally, manufacturers with strong brands always want to sell their brands through particularly attractive retailers. For some manufacturers, a retailer may be extremely attractive because of the high volume being sold, the retailer's image may be ideal for the brand and the retailer may well have a policy of strongly supporting the brand through good in-store positioning and rarely being out of stock. Such retailers need identifying and nurturing.

It is rare, however, for a firm to have a portfolio of brands that are all very strong. Likewise, it is rare for all possible retailers to be classified as highly attractive retailers. To prioritize brand activity through different retailers, we have found a simple two-dimensional matrix to be particularly helpful. This is shown in Figure 7.6.

Using the dimensions of brand strength and retailer attractiveness, it is possible to rank the order in which resources should be allocated.

using the dimensions of brand strength and retailer attractiveness, it is possible to rank the order in which resources should be allocated

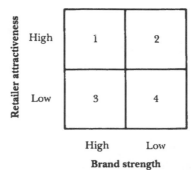

Figure 7.6   *Brand strength–retailer attractiveness matrix*

The first dimension of the matrix, **brand strength**, needs to be defined. A manufacturer's brand is a strong one if it scores well on the factors critical for brand success. Brands thrive because their manufacturers have identified precisely what benefits consumers are seeking and have geared their firms to producing brands which meet these critical success factors. The critical success factors vary from market to market. For example, in the greetings card market one of the more important critical success factors is a very varied range, whilst in the colour film market trueness of colour and wide availability are important issues. To appreciate fully the strength of their brands in a particular market, the brand's team need to go through their consumer research data and extract the critical success factors. Normally, the list of critical success factors will be between five and seven attributes. In the hypothetical example shown in Table 7.1, five factors were identified as being crucial for brand success.

Some of the factors are more important than others, and the brand team could put a weighting against each of the factors to indicate their relative importance. In the example in Table 7.1, the brand team knew from market research that the camera's ability to produce lifelike photographs was the most important issue, followed by ease of use. In a meeting, they came to the consensus view that a weighting of 0.35 should be assigned to 'produces lifelike photographs' and a weighting of 0.25 for 'easy to use'. The weighting factors should total 1.00.

Table 7.1 *Calculating the strength of camera brand A*

Critical success factors	Scoring criteria			Weighting (W)	Brand A score (S)	$S \times W$
	10–7	6–4	3–1			
Life like						
photographs	High	Med.	Low	0.35	10	3.50
Easy to use	High	Med.	Low	0.25	5	1.25
Light to carry	High	Med.	Low	0.20	5	1.00
Makes consumer feel						
like professional	High	Med.	Low	0.15	1	0.15
Camera bodies						
come in a range						
of colours	High	Med.	Low	0.05	5	0.25
Total				1.00		6.15

A scoring criteria needs to be applied next. In our example, it was felt that brands should be rated as either 'high', 'medium' or 'low' on each of the critical success factors. Furthermore, the brand's team wanted to keep the exercise simple, so if a 'high' score was felt to be appropriate for a brand that met a particular attribute, it would be given a numerical score of between 10 and 7. A medium score would be 6 to 4 and a low score 3 to 1.

The first camera brand – brand A – was evaluated on the brand strength dimension. For the most important attribute of being able to produce lifelike photographs, it was thought to be very good at meeting this and was therefore given a score of 10. Its weighted score on this dimension is 10×0.35, i.e. 3.50. On the next most important attribute, 'easy to use', it was felt to be only quite easy to use and because of this it was scored '5'. Its weighted score on this attribute is 5×0.25, i.e. 1.25. In a similar manner, the brand was assessed on the other three attributes. The five weighted scores for the brand were then aggregated and a total weighted score of 6.15 calculated. This brand strength score of 6.15 indicates a somewhat mediocre brand, since a score of 10 represents a very strong brand and 1 a very weak brand.

The brand strength scores need to be calculated in a similar manner for each of the other camera brands in the firm's portfolio which compete in this market.

The second dimension of the matrix, **retailer attractiveness**, then needs defining and applying to each current and potential camera retailer. The management team need to agree which are the five or seven factors that characterize the attractiveness of retailers. For example, Table 7.2 shows the five key attributes this team used to assess the attractiveness of camera retailers. Some of the attributes are more important than others and a weighting needs to be assigned to each to reflect their importance. In the example in Table 7.2, the high volume of camera sales was thought to be particularly important and this factor was given a weighting of 0.40. As before, the weightings need to add up to 1.00.

Table 7.2 *Calculating the attractiveness of retailer Z*

Attractiveness factors	Scoring criteria			Weighting (W)	Distributor score (S)	S×W
	10–7	6–4	3–1			
High volume of camera sales	High	Med.	Low	0.40	1	0.40
Quality image	High	Med.	Low	0.30	5	1.50
Strong supporter of our firm's brands	High	Med.	Low	0.15	1	0.15
Knowledgeable sales staff	High	Med.	Low	0.10	5	0.50
Wide geographical coverage	High	Med.	Low	0.05	5	0.25
Total				1.00		2.80

Using a similar scoring system to that previously described, each retailer then needs to be assessed on each attribute. For example, the team felt that retailer Z does not have a particularly high annual camera sales level. As such a score of 1 was given and a weighted score of 1 × 0.40, i.e. 0.40, assigned. On the next most important attribute, 'having a quality image amongst consumers', this retailer was felt to have a medium image. It was, therefore, given a score of 5 and its weighted score calculated as 5 × 0.3. In this way, retailer Z was assessed on each of the five attractiveness factors and by aggregating each of the weighted factor scores it received an overall attractiveness score of 2.80. This low score indicates that retailer Z is not a particularly attractive retailer through which to distribute these brands.

Having calculated the scores for the strength of each brand and the attractiveness of each retailer through which the brand is sold, these can be plotted on the matrix shown in Figure 7.6.

Using this matrix, managers can prioritize their use of resources, in the order shown on the matrix. Resources should first be considered for strong brands being sold through highly attractive retailers. This is the ideal situation, with the brand and retailer perfectly matched. In the (probably unlikely) event of these retailers demanding better terms, the brand manufacturer is in an excellent position to counter such demands by clarifying the value of the brand.

resources should first be considered for strong brands being sold through highly attractive retailers

From the manufacturer's perspective, after allocating resources to support those brands in quadrant 1, resources then need to be planned for brands which are not particularly strong, but which go through highly attractive retailers (quadrant 2). This represents an opportunity to the manufacturer, since the change needed is one which is under their control and, once completed, the strengthened brand can capitalize on the synergistic effects from trading with highly attractive retailers. The danger brands face in quadrant 2 is that retailers also regularly review their product mix and these brands would be regarded as under-performing. Corrective action for these brands can rapidly be diagnosed from the way that the brand scored on the different factors constituting the brand strength dimension.

After allocating resources for these two quadrants, attention should next be directed towards those brands in quadrant 3 – strong brands going through relatively unattractive retailers. The manufacturer needs to evaluate the strengths and weaknesses of these retailers, using the scores on the various factors of the retailer attractiveness dimension. They should also consider whether there are any other reasons which have not been captured indicating why strong brands are going through less attractive retailers (e.g. retailer will only stock a brand from quadrant 2 if brands in quadrant 3 are part of the total package, etc.). Once fully aware of the situation, the manufacturer then needs to decide whether to invest effort in improving the retailer (own team of merchandisers sent in on a more regular basis, etc.), or whether to cut brand support through that retailer (reduce the frequency of delivery, insist on larger drop sizes, etc.).

Finally, after having supported brand activity in these three quadrants, the brand manufacturer needs to consider brands in quadrant 4 – weak brands being sold through unattractive retailers. The manufacturer should question why it is marketing brands with low brand strength scores which are available through unattractive retailers. In such situations, the most viable route may be divestment. By contrast, where mediocre brands are going through mediocre retailers, the manufacturer should consider whether investment would lead to a more equitable future.

Winning with brands rather than own labels

Since the early 1990s, own labels have become a stronger force and look likely to pose a serious threat to brands because of their improved quality, the development of premium own labels and their expansion into new product categories such as clothing and beauty products. Despite this discouraging trend, brands remain strong and healthy and are likely to remain so in the future. This is due to three reasons. First, the very nature of the purchase process favours manufacturers' brands, as consumers need the quality assurance and the choice simplification they offer. Secondly, manufacturers' brands have built a solid foundation through years of investments in advertising and consistent quality. Retailers need the traffic-building power of these brands and cannot afford to rely solely on their own brands. Finally, retailers may overstretch their names by moving into too many categories resulting in customers doubting their quality across the entire product range.

Brand manufacturers should carefully weight the strengths and weaknesses of becoming an own label producer. They usually enter into own labels production to fill occasional excess capacity, to increase production in categories where the brand is weak or to lower overall manufacturing and distribution costs. Although these may appear valid reasons at the time, in the long run companies run the risk of cannibalizing their own branded products.

a more precise evaluation, based on a full cost, shows that in many cases production of own labels is less profitable

Analysis of the financial viability of own label production is usually undertaken on an incremental marginal cost basis. This exaggerates the benefits of selling own labels by neglecting the fixed overheads associated with excess capacity. A more precise evaluation, based on a full cost, shows that in many cases production of own labels is less profitable, particularly when compared with branded counterparts.

Some companies move into own label production for fear that a competitor might do so. It is sometimes argued that dual production enables them to influence the category, the shelf-space allocation, the price gaps and the promotion timings. It also allows them to learn more about consumers, thus improving their ability to protect their brands. In reality, however, few companies have used own label production as a strategy to achieve competitive advantage. In the majority of cases, own label production appears to increase a company's dependence on a few large retailers, forcing it to disclose its cost structure and share its latest innovations with them.

From these considerations, companies should be more cautious about producing own labels. If they already manufacture own labels, they should evaluate whether this decision is still beneficial. They should undertake an own label audit and calculate the own label profitability on both a full cost and a marginal cost basis. They also need to evaluate the impact own label has had on the market share of their brands. This will enable them to consider whether it would be wise to withdraw from own label production.

Coca-Cola is a good example of a company that successfully responded to the own label threat by changing its strategy. In the mid-1990s, Coca-Cola's biggest threat in the UK was not posed by Pepsi-Cola, but by the new entrant, Cott. Cott supplies Sainsbury's Classic Cola, Virgin Cola, Woolworth's Genuine American Cola and Safeway Select, all premium own label versions of the famous Coca-Cola.

Coca-Cola undertook a detailed analysis of premium own labels and their impact on retailers. They firstly discovered that the own label cost was greater than the traditional less-quality-for-less-money drinks which retailers used to offer, because of higher ingredient and packaging costs. Secondly, retailers were forced to compete on price if they wanted to increase the volume of premium own labels against branded versions. Thirdly, the promotion of own labels and the large allocation of shelf space to own labels at the expense of brands depressed the overall size and value of the soft-drink category. According to Coca-Cola's analysis, the reasons for these effects were that many consumers already knew what they liked and tended to shop in those stores that offered their favourite drink brands. Moreover, more shelf space for own label meant less space for famous and well-marketed brands, which was often translated into lost profits for retailers.

Coca-Cola's original strategy was built on the three As: availability; acceptability; and affordability. The company achieved success because everywhere in the world consumers could get a Coca-Cola, liked the drink on the first tasting and were able to afford a can regardless of the local economic conditions. However, competition from own labels has forced Coca-Cola to redirect its strategy focusing on the three Ps: presence; pervasive penetration; and price related to value. Coca-Cola claims that this strategic shift is the main reason behind its 40 per cent increase in its American stock market value during 1996. The Coca-Cola success story shows that despite the threat of premium own labels, brand owners can successfully maintain their position and strengthen their brands.

Quelch and Harding (1996) suggest further strategies brand owners can use to defend themselves against own labels. To reinforce their brands' positionings, companies need to invest consistently in product improvements. They should beware of introducing brands positioned to compete between their traditional brands and the own label equivalent. Few companies have been successful in doing this. One of them, Philip Morris, has used brands such as L&M and Chesterfield to defend Marlboro. More often, however, these 'middle' brands prove unprofitable and end up competing with the company's traditional brands.

By building trade relationships with retailers, brand owners may be able to demonstrate that own labels are usually less profitable than expected because of additional promotion, warehousing and distribution costs. They may also find that consumers of branded products spend more in a store compared to purchasers of own labels.

Manufacturers need to monitor the price gap between their own brands and own labels and to adjust prices continually to maximize their brand's profitability.

performance should not be measured by market share and volume, but by using category profit pools

Brand producers would be wise to invest in separate management of each product category and strive for greater efficiency in promotions and merchandising. Performance should not be measured by market share and volume, but by using category profit pools, in which the profit is calculated as a percentage of the total profit generated by all companies competing in the category. Historically this measure has shown own labels scoring weakly due to low volume and low profit and highlights the danger of becoming an own label producer.

Finally, manufacturers of branded products should take the own label challenge seriously and be prepared to invest or even redirect their strategy, as Coca-Cola successfully did.

Encouragingly, Tesco announced in 1997 that they would stop copy-catting manufacturers' brands and invited suppliers to work more closely with them. However, Tesco's new strategy of abandoning 'me-too' products and developing their own differentiated marketing platform poses threats to brand owners. Brand manufacturers are being asked to collaborate in joint marketing programmes, sharing their expertise on pricing, range and promotions, rather than simply offering their brands for distribution. Secondly, they face increasing pressure to offer bespoke packages and line extensions which better fit Tesco's marketing strategies. Finally, as other retailers are likely to follow Tesco's example, brand owners will have to handle more complex relationships with more partners and support the needs of each retailer while striving to maintain their overall brand strength.

Understanding the balance of power

The last section showed some of the challenges brand manufacturers face due to increasing retailer power. To be able to cope with stronger retailers, manufacturers need to understand their bases for power. The following framework by French and Raven (1959) explains how one party can exert power over another and helps to identify the most powerful party.

Power is the ability of one party to control the actions of another and can be conceived in terms of the continuum in Figure 7.7.

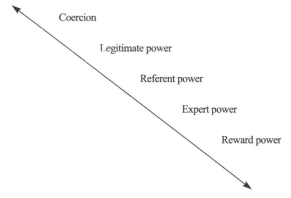

Figure 7.7 *The continuum of power (adapted from French and Raven 1959)*

The **coercive basis for power** is the expectation of one party that the second will be able to punish them if they fail to fulfil the other's wishes. For example, a retailer may de-list a supplier who does not agree to their demands, or a brand manufacturer may refuse to supply a retailer who sells their premium brand at a substantial discount. The magnitude of the power base depends on the effect that carrying out the threat can produce. Thus in markets where products are undifferentiated, or where retailers carry broad product ranges, or where a few retailers account for a large proportion of sales, most suppliers are too small to pose a credible threat.

One party may exert **legitimate power** when the other accepts its legitimate right to influence them. In franchising, for example, a franchisee agrees to run the business according to the standards specified by the franchisor.

Referent power occurs when members of the distribution channel are willing to defer to a highly-regarded channel member. For example, the strict controls required by Marks & Spencer ensure their suppliers gain an excellent reputation for quality in their own circle and thus enable these suppliers to win further business.

Expert power exists when a retailer recognizes that a supplier has a certain expertise, for example in sales training or in stock-control, and they are likely to defer to the manufacturer and follow their requests if this expertise leads to better and more effective decisions.

A manufacturer can exert **reward power** when a retailer expects financial reward by deferring to them – a discount for an increase in the display area, for example.

Another helpful way of appreciating where the power lies in manufacturer–retailer relations is provided by Davies (1993). His model, shown in Figure 7.8, illustrates the balance of power between suppliers and retailers and highlights possible strategies either party might implement to respond to possible threats. The logarithmic scales on both axes indicate that power becomes an issue once either party accounts for about 10 per cent of the other's business.

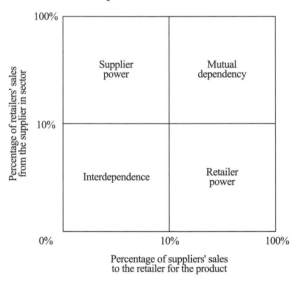

Figure 7.8   *Sources of dependency (after Davies 1993)*

A car dealer with a Ford franchise would be an example of **supplier power**, as the manufacturer can maintain exclusive control over the dealership. The dealer is wholly dependent on Ford, while Ford with its numerous dealers sees only a small proportion of sales going through each dealer. By contrast, Marks & Spencer's dictation of standards to most of its suppliers is an example of **retailer power**. A large proportion of each supplier's sales come from Marks & Spencer, who have a considerable number of suppliers. The close relationship in the 1980s between MFI and Hygena represents a clear case of **mutual dependency**, in which a retailer distributes most of the manufacturer's produce and the manufacturer accounts for most of the retailer's turnover. Finally, most retailers and manufacturers fall in the bottom left quadrant as they operate at arm's length, in a relationship of **interdependence**.

Although the degree of power is a function of the level of concentration in the sector, the actual extent to which power is exerted depends on individual firms. For example, as we discussed earlier, the grocery sector is marked by high retailer power but in the case of strong brands such as Coca-Cola and Heinz, power still remains in the suppliers' hands. However, a brand is only a source of power for the manufacturer when consumers leave the store that does not stock it, refusing to accept any of the alternative brands. To ensure that the retailer needs the manufacturer the brand needs to guarantee and communicate quality and innovation.

a brand is only a source of power for the manufacturer when consumers leave the store that does not stock it

In the absence of either a dominant retailer or supplier, the relationship between the two may evolve as a strategic alliance with clearly-defined roles and goals. The retailer sells and provides sales data and forecasts, the manufacturer supplies promptly and both are responsible for brand promotions. During the relationship conflicts may arise even though responsibilities and objectives have been set. Companies which have developed a clear trade marketing strategy based on both long-term and short-term planning, are more likely to resolve conflicts than those relying entirely on negotiating skills.

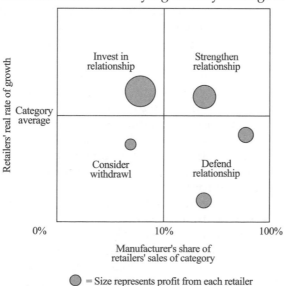

Figure 7.9   *Possible strategies on how to serve different retailers (after Davies 1993)*

A further way for manufacturers to decide upon their retailer strategy is to consider the use of the matrix in Figure 7.9. Different retailers will be growing at rates above or below the average for the category sector. Those growing faster than the average category growth are the more attractive retailers. Where the manufacturer has a high share of the retailer's sales of the category, particularly where the retailer is growing fast, this represents a very attractive business partnership. By considering where each of the manufacturer's retailers lies on this matrix, along with some indication of the brand's profit through each of these retailers, strategies are shown for each of the quadrants.

Category management

The previous section considered the implications of an uneven balance of power between retailers and manufacturers and suggested appropriate strategies. However, the issue of whether retailers or manufacturers have more power is less relevant nowadays, as we are moving from adversarial to cooperative relationships.

Retailers and manufacturers recognize that they are more likely to achieve long-term success if they collaborate. One way in which manufacturers can support retailers is to recognize that retailers do not sell individual brands, such as Pantene, Salon Selectives, Wella, L'Oreal, but rather categories, such as shampoos. Manufacturers should also be aware that retailers do not think only about brand leaders per se, indifferent to manufacturers trying to increase the sales of their brands at the expense of all the others. Retailers are more interested in gaining the collaboration of manufacturers to increase overall sales and profits of the category. In the USA, companies such as Procter & Gamble and Coca-Cola began to promote this type of relationship to cope with the concentration of retailer power and changes in consumer purchasing behaviour. They placed greater emphasis on collaborating with retailers and developing marketing programmes that grow retailers' total category sales. Since then, more manufacturers have sought to build their brands by working in collaboration with retailers to grow the total category, following a category management route.

category management involves the control of each category as an independent business and the customization of the product categories on a store-by-store basis

Category management is a process in which both retailers and manufacturers manage product categories as business units. For retailers who are faced with the challenge of ever increasing numbers of new brands and increasing consumer sophistication, category management involves the control of each category as an independent business and the customization of the product categories on a store-by-store basis to satisfy local customer needs and maximize profitability. For manufacturers managing families of brands and competing for limited shelf space, category management offers the opportunity to increase sales and build the brand share by helping retailers to identify the best category mix for a given store or area. Harlow (1995) defines category management from the perspective of the manufacturer and regards it as

> *the joint strategic planning with retailers to build total category sales and profit for mutual benefits.*

Table 7.3 provides more insight into this definition by comparing the traditional relationship between retailers and suppliers with the category management relationship.

Table 7.3   *Appreciating the essence of category management (after Harlow 1995)*

Traditional approach	Category management approach	
Adversarial	*Joint*	Cooperative
12-month fiscal horizon	*Strategic*	Long-term perspective (3–5 years)
Pushing supplier's agenda	*Planning with retailers*	Retailer committed to the strategy by being involved in its development
Promoting supplier's brand	*Total category*	Focus on total category rather than individual brands
Increase offtake of own products	*Sales and profit*	Increasing total consumer offtake
Concern is only for supplier's benefits	*For mutual benefits*	The retailer benefits and the supplier must also be able to derive benefits through increased sales of their products

To thrive suppliers need to exploit the increased category consumption they have helped to generate. The suppliers who gain from this are the category leaders and in each category only one manufacturer takes this position. To be a successful category leader, a manufacturer must provide consumer marketing expertise, a high level of innovation and effective information technology. They should also understand and strive to meet the service needs of the retailers and, through a good appreciation of each retailer's objectives and strategies, grow the relationships by supporting the retailers' activities.

Traditionally manufacturers put the emphasis predominantly on their brands. Category management has shifted this focus. The brand still plays a fundamental role, but it is no longer the focal point: instead, managers consider how the brand fits with the category and how the manufacturer could be better structured to deliver better brand benefits. The company needs to be structured so that the emphasis is placed on the long-term building of the brand through innovations within its category. Traditional structures have chopped firms up into different skills, very much akin to triangles with boards of directors at the apex and functional departments beneath them. Category management helped companies to recognize that business processes are critical and that these run across the functional silos. By restructuring to concentrate on business processes, firms are better able to capitalize on category management opportunities. For example, at Elida Gibbs, the Marketing Director is responsible for the processes of brand development. Day-to-day questions from retailers about such issues as price changes and short-term promotions are dealt with by the Customer Development Director. Innovation Managers take responsibility for developing completely new propositions for each brand. One of the results of category management is that retailers are better able to identify weaker brands and, for the poorer performing suppliers, this puts more pressure on them to improve.

Category management is regarded as a very helpful strategic tool to improve customer satisfaction and profitability. In particular, manufacturers see it as a route to strengthening their brands to become category leaders. Retailers see it as enhancing their expertise in pricing and promotion, better satisfying consumers and improving efficiency and profitability. Its implementation requires a major cultural change for manufacturers as they allow categories to take precedence over brands, and for retailers the category has precedence over the traditional department. Companies have restructured their organizations into more adaptable structures and invested in better communication systems. Greater collaboration builds more trust and achieves better performance.

Using information in category management

one of the dangers is being drowned by a sea of data

Retailers and manufacturers achieve most from category management when they work together sharing information and areas of expertise. One of the dangers is being drowned by a sea of data and thus they need to identify efficient ways to share market research data about aspects such as merchandising, shopper studies and scanning. Better software gives retailers instant and more user-friendly access to information on issues such as space allocation, consumer trends and promotion tracking. Retailers are gaining more knowledge of the category and market situation through their loyalty cards. To adopt category management successfully, retailers and manufacturers need to create high-quality databases to link consumer and retail data. They need adaptable organizational structures, training in the evolving techniques of category management and the full involvement of suppliers' and retailers' senior management.

Category managers have a rich set of data at their disposal, but to use this efficiently they need a coherent and flexible framework. The model in Figure 7.10 was developed by Nielsen (1993) to help managers achieve better category profits.

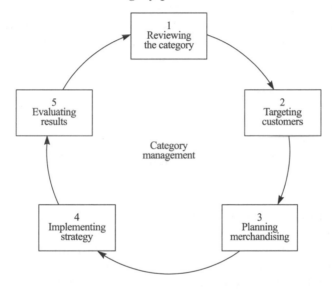

Figure 7.10   *The process of category management (after Nielsen 1993)*

The following case provides an illustration as to how categories can be managed. By tracking their database a retailer became aware of the poor performance of their health and beauty sales, in particular shampoos. They collaborated with one of their leading suppliers to address this problem. They jointly **reviewed the category** and discovered that the manufacturer's leading brand was under-performing in the retailer's stores because of less competitive prices, infrequent promotions and the manufacturer having too narrow a range of shampoo brands. The two companies examined the consumer panel data and the geo-demographic databases. These helped identify the most appealing shampoo range for the retailer's consumers. The analysis revealed that the consumer profiles varied significantly depending on the location of the stores. Three distinct consumer segments with different purchasing needs were identified: 'upscale affluent', 'middle-class families' and 'inner city'. To improve sales it was decided that each location needed to **target their consumers** by providing a product range appropriate for that specific group of shoppers.

The retailer and the manufacturer then worked to optimize the product range, the pricing and the promotion. This **merchandise planning** involved adding new brands as well as de-listing some of the manufacturer's weaker brands.

Both companies worked on the **implementation of the strategy** and developed detailed price plans, promotion schedules and shelf allocation fixtures. Sales information and consumer databases were used to track the effectiveness of the strategy and to assess the response of key target groups to promotions. These **results were evaluated** and they demonstrated the success of the new relationship: the retailer's overall sales and profits increased and the manufacturer's leading brand achieved a larger market share.

Category management should be regarded as a continuous programme for continual improvement. Analysis of the results should prompt regular reviews of the category so that retailers and manufacturers can jointly work out the best strategies and ensure long-term success.

Efficient consumer response

After adopting the principles of category management, many retailers and manufacturers started to consider how they could further enhance the benefits of working closely together and examined tasks that they had historically undertaken individually. They identified new opportunities to integrate their resources and activities, and the era of 'efficient consumer response' (ECR) evolved. Beside the core issue of category management, the key elements of ECR are: new product development; consumer and trade promotions; store assortment; and product replenishment. Their integration, as shown in Figure 7.11, is the challenge managers are addressing to achieve better performance and higher consumer satisfaction.

At the core of ECR lies category management. In the early days
at the core of ECR lies category management categories were developed through managers' assumptions as to the most appropriate brand groupings. Increasingly categories are being defined that better reflect consumers' usage and purchasing behaviour, by placing more emphasis on consumers' values. Thus ECR is at the heart of the interactions between manufacturers, retailers and consumers, as shown in Figure 7.12.

The evolution of ECR

Like category management, ECR was developed in the USA. In the mid-1990s, Wal-Mart and Procter & Gamble reassessed their relationship and recognized that their individual attempts to maximize

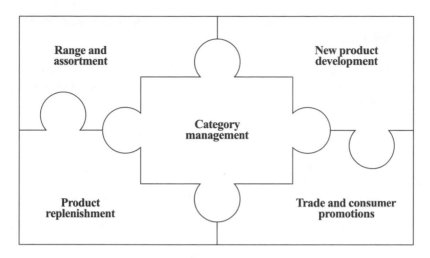

Figure 7.11   *The key elements of ECR*

their gains were at the expense of the other party. For example, Procter & Gamble often used money-off coupons that generated sudden increases in demand, which necessitated Wal-Mart having to increase stock and manage short bursts of shelf dynamics. On their side, Wal-Mart changed its buying patterns, preferring to purchase very large quantities of P&G brands only when on special trade discount promotions. In turn this caused Procter & Gamble significant production and logistics problems. They recognized that these promotions confused consumers and were detrimental to Wal-Mart and P&G. They therefore decided to switch to a policy of every day low pricing, which delivered value to consumers and reduced promotion, production and storage costs. The implementation of ECR allowed them to improve consumer satisfaction by delivering more desirable brands at lower prices and with higher quality. It also improved business effectiveness by eliminating non-value added activities and saving costs. In brief, for manufacturers, retailers and consumers the value of ECR could be summarized as follows:

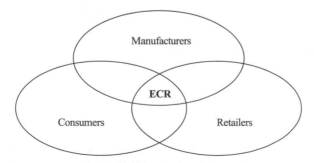

Figure 7.12   *The relationships in ECR*

ECR is a supply chain strategy to satisfy customers with a better range, faster and at a lower cost.

These two companies were soon followed by others, who recognized that ECR is not just about improving logistics: it completely challenges the way companies do business. It is not so much about a new set of techniques, but rather a new way of bringing previous techniques together in a coherent and coordinated way. Companies have to learn to re-evaluate the way they do business. They need to collaborate to design promotions, product ranges and new products, which often requires a change in the company's culture.

Amongst other benefits, the implementation of ECR can help:

- companies achieve competitive advantage by adding value jointly;
- companies gain large savings through higher margins, faster growth and lower stocks;
- consumers benefit from a product range better tailored to their preferences.

Moreover, when companies closely collaborate to implement this programme of continuous improvement, costs are not reallocated but removed. The increased integration of activities between manufacturers and retailers leads to further benefits, especially during the process of brand development including:

- activity-based cost accounting enable manufacturers to show retailers the true costs of meeting their needs;
- EDI improves stock holding;
- continuous replenishment programmes enable manufacturers to replenish brands on the basis of actual store demand.

How firms implement ECR

To understand why companies have adopted ECR and how it is implemented, it is useful to examine the following principles of ECR:

1   consumer/shopper focused;
2   total category consideration;
3   data based;
4   multifunctional/total system perspective;
5   collaborative/trust based.

Procter & Gamble used these principles to reassess their business processes and the way they support their relationships with retailers. First, they realized they understood the *consumer at home* but were less sure about them as *shoppers* in store. They knew when their brands were used and how satisfied consumers were with them, but were less confident about who bought them in the stores, why they bought them or how they felt during the purchase. In order to better understand shoppers, they gathered data on their purchasing behaviour and their response to promotions. In the laundry category, for instance, it emerged that promotions attracted consumers who were neither loyal nor who were likely to increase their spending. This meant that the company was spending money but did not encourage loyalty or market growth. Furthermore, they discovered that most consumers were not interested in promotions and would have preferred constant low prices to special offers, for which they knew they had to pay in some other way. This newly-gained knowledge of consumers as shoppers allowed the company to take better decisions about the whole category, covering, for example promotions, range, replenishment and new brands.

This holistic approach on the whole **category** instead of only on single brands, required a shift in the focus of Procter & Gamble. Their analysis revealed significant differences about the impact of promotions in different categories. Investigating audit data provided by Taylor Nelson AGB showed that promotions are not necessarily the best way to grow their market share and their impact varies by category. Previously they had been analysing the impact of promotions on individual brands. Looking at the impact of promotions on whole categories gave insight about the varying effects of promotions and led to ideas about different ways of rewarding loyalty.

Suppliers and retailers already have a vast amount of data on their markets, consumers and shoppers. However, to maximize category development and profit, they need to share it more between each other. The mutual benefits to be gained are enormous. By implementing ECR with their key customers, for example, Procter & Gamble reduced inventory by one-third and increased the volume of one category by a fifth.

Sharing with partners a wide amount of data is not sufficient if the company itself is unable to work *multifunctionally* in their strategy development. At Procter & Gamble a multifunctional team was set up to look at the range of brands being supplied. This team asked different departments to identify the fundamental factors for the most efficient product range. Building on these findings, they discovered that in the laundry category 40 per cent of the existing stock-keeping units could be eliminated and yet 95 per cent of consumer needs could still be met.

Finally, it is essential that all these principles are followed by both the manufacturer and the retailer in a relationship based on **collaboration** and **trust** if they want to meet their customer needs and mutually achieve long-term success. Companies are still reluctant to share information and trust their partners.

How firms measure the success of ECR

Manufacturers and retailers are keen to assess the contribution their partners, or potential partners, are making to enhancing ECR. With the aid of the ECR scorecard, companies can measure the strengths and weaknesses of their current and potential partners. The ECR scorecard, which has been developed by the Institute of Grocery Distribution, is shown in Figure 7.13.

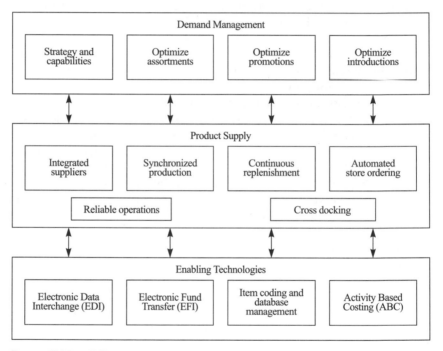

Figure 7.13   *ECR scorecard (after IGD 1997)*

The ECR scorecard allows marketers to challenge every activity a company undertakes within the supply chain by asking whether this activity delivers value to the end consumers. With such a radical, and some might say ruthless, assessment of each activity, marketers can determine their real contributions. For example, they may wonder whether the benefits derived from a line extension compensate for the extra costs and increased operational complexity this introduced.

Some companies have already adopted the ECR logic to distinguish between strong and weak brands and seriously to question brand proliferation. As a result, the range of brands within their portfolio had decreased. In these companies the focus has shifted from 'consumer loyalty to brands' to 'shopper loyalty to both store and brands'. This change brings a new perspective to the core concept of consumer satisfaction, because extra brands do not necessarily generate extra sales. For example in the confectionery category, the top ten brands in the UK market account for £900 m sales and the following forty brands for £1100 m sales. Are these extra brands enhancing the choice experience, or just confusing consumers?

Conclusions

An own label metamorphosis has occurred. They are now high quality retailer brands, backed by significant corporate promotional campaigns reinforcing clear personalities. Retailers are increasingly attentive to changing environmental circumstances, launching innovative own labels to capitalize on new consumer trends. Pricing policies position own labels as good value lines, rather than cheap alternatives to manufacturers' brands. In view of these developments, we feel the term 'own label' is no longer appropriate. For too many managers this term is synonymous with a poor quality, cheap alternative to manufacturers' brands. Today, with retailers likely to play an even more dominant marketing role, we believe it would be better to use the term 'retailers' brands'. This recognizes that the full repertoire of branding techniques are being employed by retailers, who are just as sophisticated in their strategic marketing, as 'blue chip' brand manufacturers. Their rapid acceptance of information technology is but one example of their sophistication, enabling them to gain a further competitive edge.

There may well be scope for retailers to develop alternative types of own labels, such as 'lifestyle own labels', targeted at different consumer groups frequenting specific retailers. An essential ingredient for their success in such cases must be consumer-relevant added values – not just lower prices. As the generics experience has shown, it is only a minority of consumers who are prepared to trade off added values for low prices. Experienced consumers are no longer primarily motivated by low prices.

Experienced consumers are no longer primarily motivated by low prices

Retailer dominance is likely to be a feature common to more markets in the new millennium. More professional retail management will be better served by information technology, enabling them to make more rapid adjustments to their portfolio of brands, as new opportunities evolve. Manufacturers will succeed with their brands if they recognize the basis of their consumer franchise and continue to invest in this – rather than diverting their marketing budgets to buying shelf space.

As barriers to trading across Europe fall, more retailers are likely to expand their operations into new geographical areas. This will be either through forming retail alliances, or by maintaining their independence and growing organically across Europe. The problem that retailers are having to face is how to position their own labels so that they appeal to a significant proportion of consumers from different cultural backgrounds, with minimal fine-tuning for each country. For those retailers who have entered into alliances, this problem is confounded by the need to make the Euro-own label equally appropriate for each of their members' stores.

Manufacturers can adopt a more proactive approach to brand marketing in a retailer-dominated environment. They can assess the strengths and weaknesses of being an own label supplier by considering issues such as the economics of branding, the strength of their consumer franchise and the more effective use of production facilities. They can evaluate how well-equipped they are to meet the needs of own label contracts. Furthermore, they can use the brand strength–retailer attractiveness matrix to prioritize brand investment programmes through different retailers.

Despite the increasing strength of own labels, brands have managed to remain strong due to their ability to offer consumers quality assurance and choice simplification. The example of Coca-Cola has shown that, despite the threat of premium own labels, brand owners can successfully maintain their position and strengthen their brands. Own label production should not regarded as a short-term solution for excess capacity and brand owners should consider implementing some of the strategies reviewed earlier to protect themselves against own labels.

The relationship between retailers and manufacturers is often characterized by an uneven balance of power. Both parties need to understand the degree to which they depend on each other so that they can identify appropriate strategies to optimize the relationship. In the absence of a clear leader, a suitable strategy is to regard the relationship as a strategic alliance and clearly define roles and goals.

In the new era, manufacturers and retailers can improve both consumer satisfaction and profitability by adopting a 'category management' approach, which involves managing product categories as business units and developing marketing programmes for the total category. The experience of many retailers and manufacturers has shown that by collaborating and exchanging information, both parties gain.

Further integration between retailers and manufacturers can be achieved through ECR. This strategy enables companies to improve consumer satisfaction by delivering good value brands and improves business effectiveness by eliminating non-value added activities. For its successful implementation, companies need to gather and store data on consumer purchasing behaviour for the whole category. They also need to ensure that each firm understands and is fully committed to ECR as a multifunctional approach. Additionally, there needs to be a relationship of trust and collaboration.

The ECR scorecard helps assess the strengths and weaknesses of a potential partner as well as examining the real value to consumers of supply chain activity. This scorecard is no doubt likely to make firms more cautious about widening their brand portfolios.

Marketing action checklist

It is recommended that, after reading this chapter, marketers undertake the following exercises to test and refine their brand strategies.

1   On a two-dimensional map for a specific market, with the axes representing price and quality, plot the position of your brand(s), your other branded competitors' brands and the own labels from the main retailers. Repeat the exercise, but do so thinking back ten years. As a management team, consider why any changes have occurred and assess which factors have had a particularly strong impact on your brand.

2   Ten years ago, how did the leading retailers in your product field manage to sell their own labels more cheaply than popular brands? Today, how are these own labels achieving their price advantage? What are the implications of this for your brands?

3   In the market where your brands compete, what propositions do each of the major retailers' own labels offer? Thinking back ten years, how have these propositions changed, if at all? What are the implications of these changes for your brands?

4   For any one of your markets where your brands compete against own labels, what are the differences between the leading retailer's own labels and your brand(s)? Where the retailer's own label has an advantage over your brand(s), evaluate how this advantage has been achieved and consider how you could better your brand on this attribute, if consumers would value such a change. Where your brand(s) has an advantage over the leading retailer's own labels, consider what is required to sustain this.

5   What proportion of your brand sales in a particular market go through multiple retailers? How does this compare against the situation five, ten, and fifteen years ago? What factors are giving rise to multiple retailer dominance? Will these factors continue to aid the growth of their power? How do you plan to

compete in a market dominated by increasingly powerful retailers?

6   What personalities do consumers associate with your brands and the own labels against which they compete? How clear are these personalities? Has your brand's personality become less distinctive over time, while retailers' own label personalities have become sharper? Do the personalities of the leading retailers' own labels mirror their stores' brand personalities? If there is any difference between the personality of a retailer's store and its own labels, evaluate why such a difference has occurred and what the implications are for your brands.

7   Are your brands sold through convenience or non-convenience outlets? Does your promotional strategy take into account the need for simple on-pack information through convenience outlets and the need to educate sales assistants in non-convenience outlets?

8   If you are currently involved in exporting, what will be the implications for your brands of the emergence of more European retailer alliances? What plans do you have to cope with increasing retailer dominance across Europe?

9   Should you be debating whether to supply an own label version of one of your current brands, focus your decision by scoring the advantages against the issues:
    •   others finding it difficult to emulate your brand;
    •   whether there is a lot of goodwill tied up in the brand name;
    •   the economic implications of own labels and brands;
    •   whether patents are soon to expire;
    •   the production implications in terms of existing capacity;
    •   whether there will be continuing internal support for brand investment;
    •   what internal morale will be like if own label contracts are accepted;
    •   whether own label production will help block competitors;
    •   the accuracy of sales forecasts for brands and own labels.

10 Should you wish to work on own label contracts, assess whether you will be in a strong or a weak negotiating position when pitching for this business by applying the audit questions in the section 'How retailers select own label suppliers'.

11 Evaluate the appropriateness of your priorities for brand support through different major accounts by using the brand strength–retailer attractiveness matrix.

12 Is your company currently manufacturing own labels or considering this option for the future? What analysis have you undertaken to assess the level of profitability resulting from own

label production? What will be the long-term consequences of your own label production for your brands? Are you running the risk of cannibalizing them? What competitive advantage will you gain from the label production? If the answer to this last question is none, you should carefully consider whether the problem of excess capacity could be solved in another way.

13 (For a manufacturer) Are your brands threatened by own labels? As defensive strategies to cope with these threats:
 • Are you investing consistently in product improvements?
 • Do you have any plans to introduce new brands between your own traditional brands and own labels?
 • What type of trade relationship are you building with retailers?
 • Do you monitor the price gap between your brands and own labels?
 • Do you measure performance by using category profit pools?

14 Consider the relationship you have with your trade partner using the matrix shown in Figure 7.8. How would you describe the balance of power between your trade partner and yourselves? Which strategy emerges from this position? How do you plan to develop this strategy in the short and long term?

15 What type of relationship exists with your trade partners to encourage the long-term growth of product categories as well as the success of specific brands? Are you satisfied with the degree of trust and collaboration between your trade partners and yourselves? Are the senior managers of both parties committed to category growth? Do you freely share your sources of information and areas of expertise?

16 How complete is your knowledge of your consumers as shoppers? What do you know about their purchasing behaviour and their response to promotions in your category? Could this knowledge be improved by undertaking further market research?

17 What kind of information systems do you currently use to exchange the information with your trade partners? Is the information exchange efficient and effective? Do you assess whether the data and sources used are really necessary? Have you established high-quality databases to link consumer and retail data?

18 Do all the activities within your supply chain really deliver value to consumers? Do your consumers need the new brands and line extensions offered or are they confused by the ever-increasing range? What information do you have on their reactions to promotions?

References and further reading

Anon. (1991). Value of own label at Sainsbury. *The Grocer*, 6 July, 18.

British Business (1988). DTI retailing inquiry for 1986. *British Business*, 18 March, 29–30.

Burk S. (1997). The continuing grocery revolution. *Journal of Brand Management*, **4** (4) 227–38.

Burnside A. (1990). Packaging and design. *Marketing*, 15 February, 29–30.

Caulkin S. (1987). Retailers flex their muscles. *Marketing*, 7 May, 37–40.

Davidson H. (1987). *Offensive Marketing*. Harmondsworth: Penguin Books.

Davies G. (1993). *Trade Marketing Strategy*. London: Paul Chapman.

Davis I. (1986). Does branding pay? *ADMAP*, **22** (12), 44–8.

de Chernatony L. (1987). Consumers' perceptions of the competitive tiers in six grocery markets. Unpublished PhD thesis. City University Business School, London.

de Chernatony L. and Knox S. (1991). Consumers' abilities to correctly recall grocery prices, 151–69. In *Proceedings of Marketing Education Group 1991 Conference* (Piercy N. et al, eds). Cardiff Business School: MEG.

de Kare-Silver M. (1990). Brandflakes. *Management Today*, Nov. 19–22.

Economist Intelligence Unit (1971). The development of own brands in the grocery market. *Retail Business*, **166** (Dec.), 27–35.

Euromonitor (1989). *UK Own Brands (1989)*. London: Euromonitor.

French J. and Raven B. (1959). The bases of social power. In *Studies in Social Power* (Cartwright D., ed.). East Lansing, Michigan: University of Michigan Press.

The Grocer(1988). Multiple price pressure is blamed for the 'debasement' of ice cream. 23 April, 4.

The Grocer (1991). Why the squeeze was eased. 10 August, 10.

The Grocer (1991). The ultimate proposition? Money back and replacement pack. 16 March, 10.

Harlow P. (1995). Category management: a new era in FMCG buyer-supplier relationships. *Journal of Brand Management* **2** (5), 289–95.

Henley Centre for Forecasting (1982). *Manufacturing and Retailing in the 80s: A Zero Sum Game?* Henley: Henley Centre for Forecasting.

Liebling H. (1985). Wrapped up in themselves. *Marketing*, 7 November, 41–2.

Macrae C. (1991). *World Class Brands*. Wokingham: Addison Wesley.

MacNeary T. and Shriver D. (1991). *Food Retailing Alliances: Strategic Implications*. London: The Corporate Intelligence Group.

McGoldrick P. (1990). *Retail Marketing*. London: McGraw Hill.

Moss S. (1989). Own-goals. *Marketing*, 16 February, 45–6.

Nielsen (1989). *The Retail Pocket Book*. Oxford: Nielsen.

Nielsen (1993). *Category Management in Europe: A Quiet Revolution*. Oxford: Nielsen.

Ohmae K. (1982). *The Mind of the Strategist*. Harmondsworth: Penguin.

Porter M. (1976). *Interbrand Choice, Strategy and Bilateral Market Power*. Cambridge: Harvard University Press.

Quelch J. A. and Harding D. (1996). Brands versus private labels: fighting to win. *Harvard Business Review*, Jan–Feb, 99–109.

Rapoport C. (1985). Brand leaders go to war. *Financial Times*, 16 February, 24.

Sambrook C. (1991). The top 500 brands. *Marketing*, 7 March, 27–33.

Segal-Horn S. and McGee J. (1989). Strategies to cope with retailer buying power. In *Retail and Marketing Channels* (Pellegrini L. and Reddy S., eds). London: Routledge.

Sheath K. and McGoldrick P. (1981). Generics: Their development in grocery retailing and the reactions of consumers. A report from the Department of Management Sciences, the University of Manchester Institute of Science and Technology.

Thompson-Noel M. (1981). Big time grocery brands – the beginning of the end? *Financial Times*, 9 April, 11.

Walford J. and Edwards T. (1997). Where own label is heading: a recommendation. *Journal of Brand Management,* **4** (5) 320–6.

Walters D. and White D. (1987). *Retail Marketing Management.* Basingstoke: Macmillan.

Whitaker J. (1990). Single market – multiple opportunities. Paper presented at Private Label Manufacturers Association Conference.

Winning the Brands Battle

Chapter 8

How powerful brands beat competitors

Summary

The purpose of this chapter is to review the diverse ways of positioning and sustaining brands against competitors. It explores the two broad types of brand competitive advantage – being cost-driven or value-added, and considers how value chain analysis can help identify the sources of competitive advantage. In considering the competitive scope of brands, strategies to develop different brands are reviewed. Methods of sustaining competitive advantage are described within a context of clarifying who competitors are and how their responses can be anticipated. The strategic implications from a knowledge of brand share are presented. Characteristics of winning brands are presented, along with findings about advertising activity. Issues about building or buying brands are raised and a structured approach to brand extensions is described.

Brands as strategic devices

In Chapter 2, we showed that firms interpret brands in different ways and as a consequence place different emphasis on the resources they use to support their brands. Some firms believe that brands are primarily differentiating devices and as such they put a lot of emphasis on finding a prominent name. Others view brands as being functional devices and their marketing programmes emphasise excellence of performance. Our research has shown, however, that the really successful companies adopt a holistic perspective by regarding their brands as strategic devices. In other words, they analyse the forces that can influence the profitability of their brand, identify a position for their brand that majors on the brand's unique advantages and defend this position against competitors. By adopting this perspective, the marketer does not just emphasise design, or advertising, but instead coherently employs all the company's resources to sustain the brand's advantage over competitors.

Once confident about the unique advantages of the brand, and their relevance to purchasers, brand plans will be developed and followed through to ensure that the brand's differential advantage is sustained. At this point, it is worthwhile repeating our definition of a brand from Chapter 2, which encapsulates these points

> *A successful brand is an identifiable product, service, person or place, augmented in such a way that the buyer or user perceives relevant, unique added values which match their needs most closely. Furthermore, its success results from being able to sustain these added values in the face of competition.*

The strategist subscribing to this holistic view of branding recognizes that the key to success lies in finding a competitive advantage that others find difficult to copy. Unless the brand has a sustainable competitive advantage, it will rarely succeed in the long run. Brands such as Frigidaire fridges, Sinclair Spectrum computers, and Double Diamond ale disappeared because they were unable to sustain their added values against more innovative competitors who were attentive and responsive to changing consumer needs.

In the market for overnight delivery of letters and parcels there are many competent brands to choose from, yet Federal Express proudly boasts their positioning in their advertising as, 'When it absolutely, positively has to be there overnight'.

Federal Express's ability to sustain, particularly in the USA, their competitive advantage of rapid delivery is due to their efficiency in integrating a variety of supporting issues. All of their employees are carefully selected and trained to deliver superior customer service. Everyone is committed to the dictum, 'satisfied customers stay loyal to my firm' and individuals are encouraged to be independent, resourceful and creative in helping to meet customers' requests. Logistics planning and investment in physical distribution enable the firm to have the infrastructure to provide timely delivery. Supporting systems have been carefully designed and installed to ensure total customer satisfaction. For example, information technology enables any enquirer to be rapidly informed as to the location of their parcel. By integrating all of these issues within a clearly communicated strategy, Federal Express have a powerful set of competitive advantages acting as a strong barrier to competitors.

In the industrial sector, Snap-on Tools' competitive advantage of superior service enables them to sell their tools successfully at a higher price than competitors – and sustain this position. Dealers regularly call on customers, mainly garages, with well-stocked vans. Call schedules are designed so their customers know when to expect visits. Typically, on each visit, the salesperson goes in with new products, allowing customers to try them out. Very thoroughly trained salespeople learn to understand each of their customers and are able to offer attractive credit terms. With life-time guarantees and the reputation of the salespeople, the firm stays away from competing on price.

Both of these examples show brands succeeding through having a competitive advantage and a strategy to ensure that competitors cannot easily share this position.

The first stage in developing a competitive advantage is to analyse the environment in which the brand will compete. One of the most helpful ways of doing this is to use the framework shown in Figure 2.5 in Chapter 2. This logically enables marketers to consider the opportunities and threats facing the brand from within their own organization, and from distributors, consumers, competitors and the wider marketing environment. Fully aware of the forces that the brand must face, the strategist can then start to find the most appropriate positioning for the brand.

Cost-driven or value-added brands?

Brands succeed because they are positioned to capitalize on their unique characteristics, which others find difficult to emulate – their competitive advantages. This positioning is a coherent, total positioning, since it is backed by every functional department in the firm. Everyone should be aware of what the brand stands for and they all need to be committed to contributing to its success.

everyone should be aware of what the brand stands for and they all need to be committed to contributing to its success

A brand's competitive advantage gives it a basis for out-performing competitors because of the value that the firm is able to create for consumers. Consumers perceive value in brands when:

• it costs less to buy them than competing brands offering similar benefits, i.e. 'cost-driven brands'

and/or

• when they have unique benefits which offset their premium prices, i.e. 'value-added brands'.

Cost-driven brands

The advertisement for the Mazda 626GLX Executive is a good example of a cost-driven brand.

The advertisement is making the point that if the consumer is mainly concerned about luxurious car fittings, this car offers as standard the same features as those on a BMW 735iL and a Mercedes 560SEC, but at a price which is at least £26 000 cheaper. Those consumers to whom this advertisement is targeted are likely to perceive value in the Mazda brand because it offers high specifications at a lower price. Daewoo is another example of a cost-driven brand.

3M successfully developed a campaign for their Post-it Fax notes clearly portraying this as a cost-driven brand which enabled office staff to drive down their costs. Their advertisement explained that because Post-it Fax notes replaced the cover sheet on fax transmissions, users saved paper, transmission time and money.

Cost-driven brands thrive because action is continually being taken to curtail costs. As Figure 8.1 shows, compared against the industry average, their total costs are always lower. A profit margin at least equivalent to that of other competitors can then be added, and yet still results in a selling price lower than the average competitor.

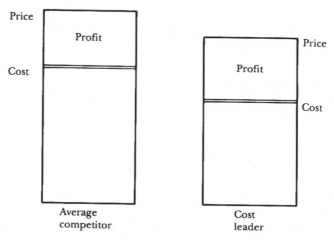

Figure 8.1   *The economics of cost-driven brands*

Some marketers shun the idea of cost-driven brands since they equate low cost with low quality. In some cases, of course, they are justified. Reducing quality standards, however, is only one way of reducing costs, but is not the recommended route to follow since it can cause consumer dissatisfaction. Some of the other ways of cutting costs are through economies of scale, gaining more experience faster than competitors, more selective raw materials scourcing, dealing only with large order customers, introducing new technology in

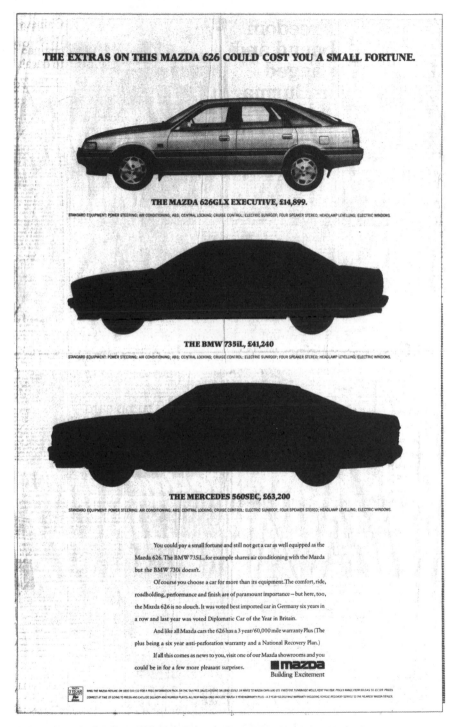

Exhibit 8.1   *Strategically Mazda is positioned in this advertisement as a cost-driven brand (reproduced by kind permission of Mazda Cars (UK) Ltd)*

by understanding
precisely what the
target market
wants, unnecessary
frills can be
eliminated and an
attractively priced
proposition
developed

production and streamlining the product range. By understanding precisely what the target market wants, unnecessary frills can be eliminated and an attractively priced proposition developed. In grocery retailing, for example, Kwik Save strives for the lowest cost position, as do its competitors Aldi and Netto, not by cutting back on quality, but by eliminating frills and services not relevant to the target market. Its low-cost competitive advantage is achieved by:

- not price-marking individual items;
- not having 'free' bags;
- not accepting credit cards and their handling fees;
- having a small number of lines;
- not stocking own labels and thus being able to negotiate better discounts from manufacturers;
- having small stores that typically cost £1.5 m to open, compared with anything up to £6 m for superstores;
- being able to open their stores in a shorter time than superstores;
- taking advantage of information technology.

Likewise in the motel sector, some of the ways Whitbread's Travel Inns are able to offer budget prices for comfortable, clean rooms to travellers are:

- making the most of spare land next to the Whitbread Beefeater restaurants;
- not having telephones or drinks cabinets in bedrooms
- being well-located close to main routes;
- not having to provide dining facilities in the motels.

Following a cost-driven branding route should not mean demotivating employees. If anything, it can act as a motivator through presenting challenges that stretch the organization and allow individual creativity. For example, to succeed against Xerox in the personal copier business, Canon set its engineers the task of designing a home copier to sell profitably at under half the price of Xerox's current range. By literally reinventing the copier, substituting a disposable cartridge for the more complicated image-transfer mechanism, they were able to meet this challenge. Without the resources of Xerox, Canon had to become more creative in cost-effectively selling its range. This was achieved by:

- distributing through office-product dealers rather than meeting head-on Xerox's massive sales force;
- designing reliability and serviceability into its range and delegating servicing to its dealers rather than setting up service networks;

If you want a status symbol
buy a Rolex with the money you'll save.

3 years free servicing, 3 years free warranty, 3 years free RAC cover.

KIA

0800 775 777

As calls are free, you can phone your Auntie Beryl with the money you'll save.
The Kia Mentor from £9,379

To find out more about the Kia Mentor range and your nearest dealer, simply complete and return this coupon to: Kia Cars (UK) Limited, FREEPOST 1226, Maidstone, Kent ME16 9BR.
Mr/Mrs/Ms _____ Address: _____ Postcode: _____
Daytime tel no: _____ Present car make & model: _____ Registration letter: _____
Car shown: Mentor SLX £9,839. All prices and specification are correct at time of going to press and include VAT, number plates, delivery and 12 months road fund licence. Free servicing for 3 years or up to 36,000 miles (whichever is sooner). Servicing includes parts and labour for routine servicing on Kia Mentor models detailed and registered between 1.5.97 and 31.8.97 excluding fleet, motability and tax-free sales. Warranty for 3 years or up to 60,000 miles (whichever is sooner). KTN/7/7

Exhibit 8.2 *Note how the cost-driven theme is coherently communicated in this Kia car advertisement*

- selling rather than leasing their machines, thus not having to administer leasing facilities.

Cost-driven brands succeed when everyone in the firm knows that each day they have to become more independent and more creative in curtailing the costs of good quality brands. Any newly-launched competitor brands are subjected to careful scrutiny to see if further cost improvements can be made. Cost advantages are not just sought from one source, but from many areas.

In common with all strategies, there are risks in developing cost-driven brands. R&D activity may result in lower cost, superior brands which some firms may short-sightedly consider give them a sustainable edge. However, technological advances need to be further developed, as others can soon emulate the technology. Another danger is that marketers fail to foresee marketing changes because of their blinkered attention to costs. A classic example of this was during the 1920s when Ford was busy improving production efficiency and achieving lower costs on models whose sales were falling because General Motors had introduced a wider range of cars, better enabling drivers to express their individuality. The days of 'Any colour, as long as it's black' were not to last that long.

Before following a cost-driven brand strategy, the marketer needs to consider how appropriate this is. For example:

- Is the price-sensitive segment sufficiently large and likely to grow?
- How will buyers respond when competitors launch low price alternatives?
- How fast can experience be gained to reduce costs?
- Is the culture of the firm geared to reducing costs?

Should there be doubts about this route, the alternative of value-added brands needs to be assessed.

Value-added brands

Value-added brands are those that offer more benefits than competitors' brands, and for which a premium price is charged. Cray Research supercomputers have the competitive advantages of huge data processing capabilities and are able to interface with any other computer equipment. They operate with software written in any language and are supported by an ever-expanding software library. There is an on-site support team that ensures users know how to use the machines effectively and which maintains virtually 99 per cent problem-free running time. At over $15 m for each computer, this brand represents the computing dream of most engineers and scientists.

value-added brands offer more benefits than competitors' brands, and for which a premium price is charged

Value-added brands do not succeed just through functional excellence; a strong image can also be a powerful competitive advantage. For example, both the Toyota Supra Turbo and the Porsche Carrera have an acceleration of 0–60mph in 6.1 seconds and both have approximately the same top speed of 150 mph. Yet the Porsche image, created by years of advertising, helps contribute to this car's price premium over the Toyota.

To produce and market a value-added brand, the firm usually incurs greater costs than the average competitor in that sector. There is something special about the brand that necessitates more work to make it stand out. By making the brand different, it is likely that consumers will notice this and, for relevant added values, they will be prepared to pay a higher price. In such a situation the marketer is able to anticipate a higher margin than his competitors and set a price which fully reflects the benefits being sold. The resulting economics of value-added brands are shown in Figure 8.2

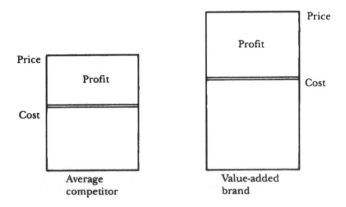

Figure 8.2   *The economics of value-added brands*

In the grocery retailing sector, Harrods' Food Hall is a good example of a value-added brand. Consumers recognize that they are always certain of high quality produce, backed by a no-quibble guarantee. They enjoy the tastefully designed environment and appreciate being served by knowledgeable staff. Furthermore, the image surrounding the well-known brand of Harrods adds further value to the grocery shopping experience and justifies the price premium.

In the potato market, Marks & Spencer transformed a cheap commodity into a value-added brand through innovative marketing. They developed this by only accepting a certain size of potato, washing its skin, cutting it, placing cheese in it, aesthetically wrapping it and proudly giving it a prominent shelf position in their stores. Through this value-adding process, they were able to charge a price considerable higher than the cost of the raw materials.

Ideally, value-added brands differentiate themselves using a variety of attributes, as can be appreciated from the way that Citibank managed to increase its business in the hostile Japanese retail banking sector. Its original six branches operated in a cartelized sector, where all banks were required by the Ministry of Finance to pay the same interest on yen investments. It originally had no automated teller machines, while many of its competitors each had over a thousand. After undertaking a situation analysis, it developed its retail banking operation into a value-added brand through a series of actions.

1   *It competed on the basis of foreign yield*   The regulations forbid offering competitive rates on yen investments, but said little about foreign currency deposits. By offering virtually double the interest on deposits in American dollars, they attracted a significant new number of customers.

2   *It advertised aggressively*   Breaking the traditional Japanese promotional approach of not having comparative advertising, they aggressively advertised the higher rates on American dollar deposits.

3   *It redefined service*   It was common for customers to have to wait to be served in banks. As such, the Japanese made their banks comfortable places to wait in. By launching a telephone banking service Citibank changed the rules of engagement by not making customers wait.

4   *It defined an image and targeted customers*   Citibank stressed its international, sophisticated image and targeted itself at clearly defined groups who traveled abroad a lot and were likely to have considerable liquid assets. These included expatriates, business executives and, following their service orientation, professionals who have little time to queue.

5   *It widened distribution*   An agreement was made with a bank in Tokyo which has a significant number of automated teller machines (ATMs) allowing Citibank customers to use their ATMs to make cash withdrawals.

6   *It expanded the product portfolio*   High interest deposit accounts were developed for other foreign currencies, as well as gold deposits.

Developing value-added brands, however, also has its risks. The price differential between the value-added brand and its lower-cost competitors may widen to such an extent that consumers may no longer be prepared to pay the extra cost, particularly when there is little promotional activity justifying the brand's more exclusive positioning. Another threat is that of competitive imitations. If the technology supporting the value-added benefits is not that difficult to copy, competitors will soon appear, at a lower price. Alternatively, buyers become more sophisticated as they repeatedly buy brands in the same product field and they start to take for granted the most recent value-added change, expecting more from the brand.

Value-added brands with cost-driven characteristics

It should not be thought that brands can only have the competitive advantage of being *either* cost-driven *or* value-added. These two scenarios represent extreme cases. Instead, it is more realistic to think of the extent to which brands have a cost-driven component as well as a value-added component. By considering which of these two components is more dominant, the marketer is able to think in terms of having a brand which is predominantly cost-driven or predominantly value-added.

By considering the contribution of cost-driven and value-added elements of branding, it is possible to classify brand types and identify appropriate strategies. In Figure 8.3, we have presented a matrix that shows the classification of brands on a strategic basis. This model of strategic brands can best be appreciated through examples of different brands of travel agents.

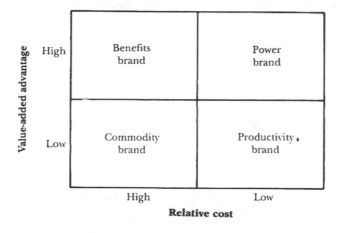

Figure 8.3   *Classifying brands on a strategic basis*

An example of a **commodity brand** would be a travel agent in a small market town, probably without any other competitors in that town and dangerously unaware of much more competitive and customer-orientated travel agents in the nearby towns. It is likely to be a small, independently run business with small offices and a cramped display in its front window. Inside the agency there is likely to be a small open-plan office, with a brochure stand restricted to only the leading travel operators. The office would be open during the weekdays from 9.00 to 5.00 and would be closed on Wednesday afternoons. It would only open on Saturdays from 9.00 to 2.00, without the full complement of staff. The staff inside the office see their role solely as that of ensuring brochures are on display and taking customers orders. Their ability to help customers choose a holiday is restricted to their own limited travel experience. With limited training, they are unable to advise customers about anything other than the brochures for standard package holidays. Questions about cheap flights, or visits to faraway obscure foreign cities, or hotels with special facilities, cannot be competently and rapidly answered. Facilities for arranging

foreign currency rarely exist and there is no service to arrange special visas. No discounts are offered. This commodity brand offers
consumers an inferior service compared with other travel agents and
its chances of surviving are not that good – particularly when a new
agency opens.

A **benefits brand** is one which is not able to offer significant
cost savings, but instead offers a particularly good service. Typical

Sainsbury's Frozen
British Grade 'A' Chicken
(Up to 4lb 8oz) 58p

39p per lb

When it comes to value, Sainsbury's lead the pecking order.
Our quality is consistently high and our prices consistently low.
Good food costs less at Sainsbury's.

SPECIAL OFFERS VALID UNTIL 24TH AUGUST 1991. ALL MERCHANDISE SUBJECT TO AVAILABILITY. SOME LINES AVAILABLE AT LARGER BRANCHES ONLY. **PRODUCTS ALSO AVAILABLE AT SAVACENTRE** THE SAINSBURY'S HYPERMARKET

Exhibit 8.3   *Attracting a lot of consumers through a range of quality goods,
Sainsbury's is able to offer competitive prices and is categorized as a power
brand (reproduced by kind permission of J Sainsbury plc)*

benefits brands are travel agents specializing in business travel. They have very good computerized systems to cope with requests, often at very short notice, to book complex itineraries for executives, arrange hotel accommodation along with taxis to and from all airports, advise and arrange visas, provide insurance and arrange foreign currency. The staff are well-trained and regularly receive information about new developments in global travel. They spend a lot of time ensuring that they have as wide a portfolio of contacts as possible with airlines, shipping firms and hotel booking agents. These travel agents tend to target their services at organizations where there is a continual demand for 'stress free' executive travel. Unless there is a sole agency agreement, they do not offer any discounts.

A good example of **productivity brands** are those 'bucket shop' operations specializing in cheap travel arrangements. They are continually scouring the market to learn where the best travel bargains are to be found. Their shop windows and press advertisements have a simple theme – low price tickets. The larger operators sell cheap travel tickets to a wide variety of destinations, the smaller firms service a narrower range of destinations. Very few services are provided by this type of operator.

Power brands are those successful brands that offer consumers many relevant extra benefits. As a consequence of high consumer satisfaction, they have a high relative share of the market, enabling them to take advantage of economies of scale and the experience effect. By passing on some of these cost savings to consumers in the form of lower prices, they are able to give their brands a price advantage over competitors and maintain a virtuous brand marketing circle. Thomas Cook, as a major travel agent, is a prime example of a power brand. It offers consumers very knowledgeable staff, a wide range of holidays to numerous destinations, long opening hours and foreign currency facilities. Its staff are well versed in their wide portfolio of holidays and can provide advice about the most appropriate destination/hotel for the concerned client. They provide attractive terms for arranging travel insurance and competitive rates when arranging currency/travellers cheques.

Commodity brands offer no advantages over any other brand and they are not particularly good value for money. Before F. W. Woolworth in the UK became part of the Kingfisher group of companies and underwent significant change, it was a commodity brand in retailing. It was unsuccessfully trying to appeal to everyone and its lack of focus resulted in a fuzzy image. It had too wide a product range, which put excessive demands on management time and tied up capital in high stocks of slow-moving lines. History has shown that the commodity brand domain is an area to be avoided.

Benefits brands succeed because they are targeted at a specific segment, with a company-wide commitment for a process which delivers extra benefits which consumers particularly appreciate. It is essential for these brands that the firm maintains regular contact with its market to continually assess satisfaction with the brand and identify ways that it could be improved. The firm will continually invest in R&D, production, logistics and marketing to ensure that the brand remains the best. Any cost-saving programme which might have an adverse impact on the brand's quality must be resisted.

Productivity brands need to be supported by a company-wide mission that stresses the need for each individual to be continually questioning 'why do we have to do it this way?'. These brands' cost advantages can only be sustained if all aspects of the business system are continually subjected to tight cost controls. Wherever possible standardization and narrowing of the product mix need to be encouraged. Potential segments which fall below a critical size must be ignored.

Power brands like Coca-Cola, Kodak, American Express, Sony and Nescafé thrive through being very responsive to changing market needs and continually trying to improve their brands, while at the same time looking for cost advantages. When North America shrugged off the appearance of small Japanese motorcycles as an event unlikely to succeed, they failed to recognize the significance of much larger Japanese motorcycles being raced on European circuits. The racing experience provided valuable learning about designing and producing larger motorcycles. While building up a volume production and selling capability in small motorcycles this quickly resulted in a cost advantage, enabling the returns to be used to invest in widening the portfolio and adding value through attractively priced larger motorcycles.

Identifying brands' sources of competitive advantage

When managers are faced with the problem of identifying their brands' competitive advantages, Porter's Value Chain (Porter 1985) can be a very useful tool. An example of this is shown in Figure 8.4. A flow chart first needs to be constructed showing all those actions involved in transforming raw material into profitable sales – the value-creating processes. This is divided into the stages:

* in-bound logistics, e.g. materials handling, stock control, receiving goods;
* operations, e.g. production, quality control, packing;
* out-bound logistics, e.g. storing finished goods, delivery, order processing;

- marketing and sales, e.g. pricing, promoting;
- service, e.g. installing, training, repairing.

The services supporting these activities are categorized into purchasing (procurement), technical development, human resource management and infrastructure. These are presented in the format shown in Figure 8.4, since each of these services can support many of the value-creating processes. For example, different departments within the firm may be buying raw materials, the skills of industrious employees, delivery lorries, creative advertisements and an after-sales support unit.

Benchmarking itself against its competitors, the firm should then identify those activities that its managers believe they do better, or cheaper. As competitive advantage is a relative concept, it is important that the key competitors are identified for that particular segment. If a firm has a brand competing in several distinct segments, it should produce value chains for each segment.

if a firm has a brand competing in several distinct segments, it should produce value chains for each segment

Within the template of the value chain, managers can start to identify their brands' competitive advantages. This may be better appreciated using the example of Ratners, the jewellers. This was a case of brilliant management of an organization that eventually fell through factors altogether unconnected with the core values of the brands.

Most of Gerald Ratner's era as Chairman saw Ratners rapidly grow to the extent that in 1991 it controlled approximately 2500 outlets, with a 31 per cent share of the jewellery market. The group operates under a series of names, such as, H. Samuel, Ernest Jones and Watches of Switzerland. A not insignificant part of its growth came from acquisition. This not only allowed its expansion into the quality end of the market, having bought H. Samuel and Zales, but also stopped the threat from these retailers moving down into its low-cost stronghold.

Its size enabled it to capitalize on economies of scale that could not be achieved by the large number of small jewellery competitors. As one of the world's largest gold buyers, it was able to negotiate very competitive prices, and in the diamond market, by dealing directly with loose stone polishers, it cut out several levels of intermediaries, resulting in further savings. With a clear vision about having the lowest priced range of jewellery to appeal to young consumers, Gerald Ratner developed a portfolio of cost-driven brands, particularly evident in its stores trading as Ratners. Each part of the value chain had been successfully managed in these Ratner stores to drive costs down.

Many executives were sceptical about whether Ratners had gone too far down the low-cost route, debasing the value buyers perceive. What they failed to appreciate is that Ratners changed the rules of

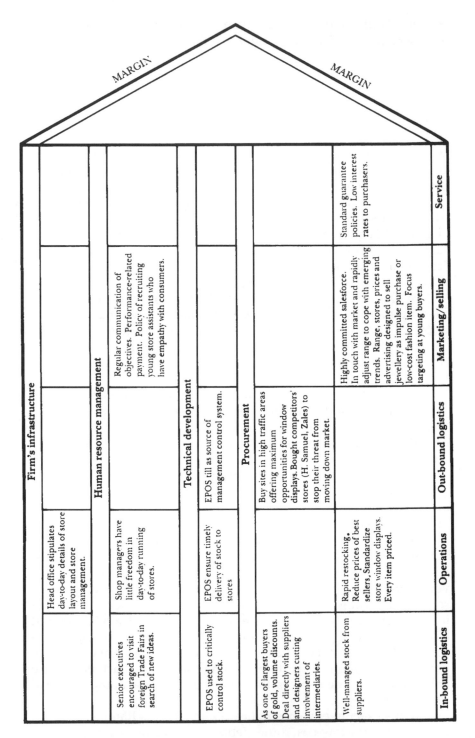

Figure 8.4   *Ratner's value chain, using Porter (1985) analysis*

engagement. Instead of positioning jewellery as a seriously considered, life-time investment, normally for middle aged and wealthy people, it targeted the young consumer seeking highly fashionable accessories to match their clothing and moods. They buy on impulse, not after a lengthy period of deliberation.

In the quest for low prices, Ratners invested in information technology and a highly efficient logistics system. Through the use of EPOS at the cash registers, order processing systems are effectively managed, as well as rapid replacement of in-store stock. Linking each of the stores' EPOS tills with the Central Management Information System provides decision makers with rapid and accurate information about sales activity. This enables them to identify the faster selling lines, which are discounted more than slower moving lines in aggressive consumer price reductions. The argument behind this selective extra discounting is that these lines are particularly responsive to price cuts. All items are clearly price marked.

The costs of the sales force are to some extent controlled by paying a basic wage, plus a bonus related to increases in turnover. Store managers spend a significant proportion of their time at the front of the shops selling, rather than at the back of the shops taking care of store administration. This is due in part to the effective use of information technology and the management control from head office stipulating details about how each individual store will be run. All stores follow a standardized layout format dictated by mock-up photographs issued on a regular basis from head office. Not only does the use of young employees enable young consumers to establish a relationship quickly during the brief sales transaction but, yet again, it contains labour costs.

Another way that Ratners can offer fashion jewellery at low prices is by getting their designers to work to a low-price objective. For example, rather than using solid gold in a necklace, they have hollow gold. As their consumers want to be fashionable, they value being able to replace or add to their jewellery accessories regularly.

Ratners set its sights on being a fashion leader, and was able to respond quickly to changing tastes. Its internal operations were structured to capitalize rapidly on new opportunities. For example, there was a great deal of interest about the type of engagement ring Lady Diana Spencer would have on her engagement to the Prince of Wales. As soon as the press had a photograph, this was rushed to their suppliers, who immediately set to work producing a similar-looking ring. Four days later, on a Friday, stock was dispatched to their stores and by Saturday they had sold approximately 10 000 pieces at £28.50 each. The original ring was estimated to be worth £30 000.

Unfortunately, to liven up his afternoon presentation at a conference early in 1991, Gerald Ratner light-heartedly referred to his sherry decanter, retailing at £4.95, as 'crap'. The considerable media coverage that then ensued did little to help Ratners. In fact, after establishing a good profit record, Ratners declared a loss of £17.7 m in September 1991, and there were comments that some of this was due to the ill-considered comment. The goodwill that had been built up over the years had been tarnished and some consumers changed their allegiance to other jewellery retailers.

Gerald Ratner's skills were in spotting market opportunities and driving his brands with low overhead costs. The problem was that he over-stretched the organization in his acquisition programme, continually appealing to the City for more cash. The £800 m acquisition programme proved a strain on the firm which, combined with the severe recession and a deterioration in consumer goodwill after he made some injudicious public comments, resulted in a lack of confidence in the Stock Market. In a year, Ratners' share price fell from over 200p to approximately 20p in January 1992. Jim McAdam subsequently accepted Chairmanship from Gerald Ratner in an attempt to refuel City and consumer confidence, as well as implementing a rationalization plan with stringent cost controls. It's one thing successfully to change the competitive rules of engagement from 'don't come in unless you're knowledgeable and want to buy something' to 'everyone, including budget shoppers, is welcome'. But, it's also important to manage a growth programme that doesn't belittle the consumer or the City.

Besides acting as a guiding framework to help managers identify *how* brands achieve a competitive advantage, the value chain also helps managers check *whether* they are reinforcing and capitalizing on their competitive advantages. This is done by considering how well-linked each of the activities are. For example, if the managers believe that the brand achieves its low-cost competitive advantage because of its unique production process, this may well be protected by buying higher priced, but better quality, raw materials. As a consequence, less time and lower-costs could result from not needing such significant quality control procedures at the goods-in stage, from smoother running of the production process and from less wastage at the finished goods stage. Coordinating internal activities should ensure that all of the processes in the value chain are optimized to give the brand the best chance of capitalizing on its competitive advantages. At Disney, for example, which prides itself on its excellence of customer service, telephones are discreetly located in its theme parks so that employees can quickly have access to advice and, if needs be, extra resources, when they spot a problem occurring.

Overlooking the linkages between any of the activities in the value chain can harm a brand. In its attempt to respond to an increasingly hostile competitive environment, EMI Medical, which had been developing different body scanners, was persuaded to let its

Margin notes:

the goodwill that had been built up over the years had been tarnished

overlooking the linkages between any of the activities in the value chain can harm a brand

North American company undertake the development research for a new generation of CT scanner. The problem was that they paid little attention to the 5-hour time lag and 2000-mile distance between the new R&D location and its Central Research Laboratory in England, where a wealth of technical expertise had developed earlier models. Communication between the two centres impeded progress and after two years many UK scientists and technologists had to be transferred to America to make up time on the much delayed programme. This was but one of the factors contributing to the demise of EMI's CT body scanner.

When considering linkages between activities, firms should not take a myopic perspective and solely consider their internal linkages. Instead, they should also identify advantages by linking their value chain back to their suppliers and forward to their customers. Clearly the better a supplier understands how their industrial customer will use their product, the more scope they have for adding more value by designing their value chain to integrate better with that of their buyers.

The value chain, however, has one major disadvantage. To be used effectively, managers need to have a good database describing the processes and economics of each aspect of every competitor's value chain. It is rare to have such a rich database. Trade journals, industry reports, sales peoples' reports, distributors' comments and Monopolies and Mergers Commission reports can help to build a database, but any remaining gaps will have to be filled by management judgement. Clearly if there are a lot of gaps in competitor analysis and if the wrong assumptions are made, any comparative analysis may well be flawed.

Focusing brands' competitive advantages

So far we have concentrated on strategic brands in terms of the two broad competitive advantages of value-added and cost-driven. But, beside the *type* of competitive advantage, marketers also have a choice about the *scope* of the market they wish their brand to appeal to. Again, drawing on the work of Porter (1985), marketers are able to refine their brand strategies further by considering whether a cost-driven or value-added competitive advantage should support their brand for either a narrow or a broad target market. The four possible generic strategies are shown in Figure 8.5.

Amstrad personal computers (PC) is a good example of a brand that followed a **focus cost** generic strategy. In the early days of PCs, Alan Sugar, Chairman of Amstrad, set his design and production engineers the task of building a PC to sell for £399 – a figure significantly lower than anything available. The new brand was targeted

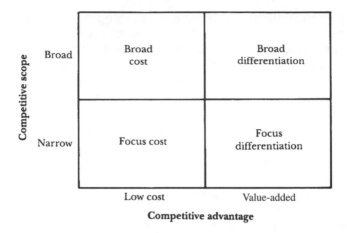

Figure 8.5   *Generic strategies for brands (adapted from Porter 1985)*

at small businesses and householders with an interest in computers. At the time of its launch it aroused a lot of interest amongst this narrowly-defined target market, because it represented very good value for money. While the features offered were rather limited, it nonetheless enabled the target market to acquire basic computing capabilities, easing the administrative problems in their small businesses or homes. Brands succeed in this quadrant because they focus solely on a clearly-defined group of purchasers who have very apparent needs, often less than the much broader needs of other groups. Any temptations to add new features which may appeal to a closely-related group are resisted, since the marginal volume gains incur significant costs.

By contrast, Fujitsu, has followed a **broad cost branding** strategy. Its good quality computers appeal to a broad range of industries and, as a global competitor, it is able to gain significant economies of scale. It markets a wide range of computers which, while not having the subtle extras of some brands, are seen as providing a more than capable facility for most users.

IBM built its brands following a **broad differentiation** strategy. It has developed a range of computers that appeal to virtually all industries. Not only does it have a significant R&D investment, giving it a basis for functional excellence, but it has also developed a strong image as a total solution provider. Broad differentiators succeed by creating value for buyers and communicating this. A heavy cost is incurred achieving a value-added positioning and, while attempts are made to hold down costs through, for example, more effective processes, the higher price is used positively to reinforce the quality positioning.

Cray Research computers is an example of a firm following a

focus differentiation strategy with their supercomputers. Offering the most powerful computers in the industry, backed by a very large R&D investment, the philosophy at Cray Research is to focus only on customers for supercomputers. Even with the advent of mini-supercomputers, Cray refused to be drawn into this related market, arguing that it would dilute its total effort and jeopardize its position. For a carefully targeted, small number of customers, they created a unique brand with many benefits, for which a significant price premium has been charged.

Sustaining a brand's competitive advantage

Having identified the sources of the brand's competitive advantages, and positioned it with the most appropriate generic strategy, the marketer is then faced with the problem of sustaining the brand's uniqueness. If the brand is successful, competitors usually work hard to understand the basis of this success and then rapidly develop and launch their own version – often with an improvement. The time before competitors develop their own improved versions of a new brand is shrinking, due in no small part to companies' understanding and appreciation of technology. For example, the 64K RAM, which first appeared in 1981, had virtually four and a half years before being superseded by the 256K RAM. By contrast, this had only two and a half years before the arrival of the one megabyte RAM.

time before competitors develop their own improved versions of a new brand is shrinking

When looking to protect their brand's competitive advantage, some managers attempt to stay ahead of competitors by concentrating, as Porter has shown, on operational effectiveness – performing the same activities better than rivals. A far more effective route to sustain a brand's competitive advantage is by concentrating on performing different activities from rivals, or performing similar activities in different ways.

It is much harder to sustain a brand's competitive advantage with the first route since usually this is technology driven and competitors soon learn to emulate this. For example, one can track over time how some firms have sought to sustain their advantage of a lowest cost sales force through the use of laptop computers, mobile phones and access to the Internet. Yet all of these, plus others such as route planning software, are soon adopted by other competitors. Furthermore, as firms become more receptive to learning about best practices from other industries, there is a trend for the players in a market to adopt operationally effective processes to enhance their brand's performance – but in so doing to cancel out competitive advantages.

Notable successes have been recorded by brands such as Southwest Airlines and IKEA which have sought to sustain their competitive advantages by undertaking different activities from rivals, or performing similar activities in different ways. Southwest Airlines is a good example of a cost-driven brand. It concentrates on short distance, low ticket price flights between midsize cities and secondary airports in large cities. While others may fly into primary airports in major cities, Southwest chooses to be different. To drive down its costs it doesn't offer in-flight meals or pre-assigned seats. It concentrates on rapid turnarounds at gates, typically of 15 minutes, keeping its planes in the air longer. Unlike others, its fleet of planes is standardized on Boeing 737s, enhancing maintenance efficiency and further driving down costs.

By following a strategy of focusing on different activities, managers need to make trade-offs. Southwest firstly decided that it would not compete on long haul routes, or offer different classes of service or fly into the primary airports of major cities. Taking a firm line in terms of what it would not do, it had in effect decided about its critical brand resources, process configurations, staff recruitment and behaviour.

Being clear about what the brand does and, equally importantly, does not stand for, managers can sustain their brand's competitive advantage through the way its activities fit and reinforce each other. These two factors are important contributors to sustaining competitive advantage. The fit between different resources and processes needs to be assessed in terms of:

*   The degree of consistency between each activity. To offer lower prices IKEA decided upon modular furniture designs enabling choice from a wide variety of potential suppliers who could easily manufacture and supply all year. Furthermore, modular designs can be transported easily and carried relatively quickly from delivery lorries into the backs of stores.
*   The degree of reinforcement between activities. For example, in order to drive costs down IKEA decided that consumers should transport the furniture kits themselves. Therefore suburban sites in big conurbations were sought since consumers would be more likely to transport their furniture kits over short distances. However, to achieve good economies of scale, these sites needed to be linked by good road systems to encourage high traffic visits. Furthermore the sites needed to be on a flat terrain, to ease the task of consumers pushing their trolleys from the store to the cars.

By looking at the whole system of activities, a more integrated investigation of fit can be addressed enabling a greater likelihood of sustaining competitive advantage.

Sustaining a service brand's competitive advantage

The challenge facing the marketer is how to sustain their brand's competitive advantage. This is a particularly difficult problem in the services sector, where competitive responses can very quickly appear. One study (Easingwood 1990) proves particularly illuminating. It analysed thirty-six successful new services that competitors had difficulties in copying. Interviews with managers associated with these brands indicated ten factors that impeded rapid competitive responses. Table 8.1 shows their views about which factors were particularly effective at slowing competitors' responses.

Table 8.1 *Factors inhibiting competitive copies (based on Easingwood 1990)*

Factor	Contribution to competitive positioning
Company reputation	4.3
Effective branding	3.9
New software introduced	3.4
Linking into existing network	3.4
Administrative and learning barriers	3.2
Access to users	3.1
New hardware introduced	2.9
Hardware already available	2.6
Software already available	2.6
Development of new network	2.1

Scores based on 5 = major contribution to competitive positioning and 1 = no contribution.

The company's reputation was regarded as presenting the most effective barrier to rapid competitor 'me-too' brands. In consumers' minds, the Automobile Association is strongly associated with services for cars and the launch of its new credit card for car-related expenditure was instantly accepted. Were the card to have come from a financial institution, it is thought that it would have had a lot more resistance to overcome.

reputation was regarded as presenting the most effective barrier to rapid competitor 'me-too' brands

The next most effective inhibitor was effective branding, i.e. logically extending the brand into a related area with the same positioning. For example, an English grocery superstore chain took advantage of attractive sites very close to the French channel port of Calais and built a superstore, attracting English day trippers interested in buying well-known drinks at lower prices.

The next most important factors impeding competitor responses were 'new software' and 'linking into existing networks'. To enhance its position as a power brand Thomas Cook developed software which, amongst other things, controlled the stock of foreign currency each outlet had and set currency rates. Other travel agents were impressed by the system and leased the software rather than devising their own version. Having a well-established distribution network enabled the National Express Bus Company to develop a new service by using its network to launch its Express Rapide coach service.

The fifth most effective blocker was felt to be the administrative and learning barriers associated with the brand. For example, one airline company which launched a service based on collecting passengers from their homes or offices, driving them to the airport and offering the same facilities after the plane had landed, had to spend a lot of time understanding and planning with the appropriate airport authorities. They argued that it would take any competitor time to learn how to replicate this service.

Other authors argue that customer service is one of the major contributors to sustaining a brand's positioning. The type of service associated with a brand is strongly influenced by the people working on it. As company employees, they share a unique company culture with distinctive values and attitudes. Disney, British Airways, Federal Express and McDonalds are all legendary in the way that they have developed training programmes to ensure that their employees give a unique type of customer service. Provided that the employees are sufficiently briefed about a new brand, their contribution to sustaining its added values can inhibit competitor responses.

One way of helping the brand remain competitive is to be the first into a market. Being the first to exploit a market opportunity leads to the cost advantages of economies of scale, and the learning curve effect. If the firm has a policy of not allowing its employees to present case studies at trade conferences, any learning is proprietary and competitors find it hard to appreciate how to gain from 'sitting on the side' and observing brand developments. Being the pioneer brand offers scope for gaining an advantage through opportunistic marketing, provided the firm monitors progress and rapidly incorporates any learning back into brand enhancements

Anticipating competitor response

One of the ways in which firms and financial analysts in stock brokers evaluate brand strength is on the basis of their market share. Strong brands tend to be market leaders who have capitalized on the opportunities from economies of scale and the experience effect. Likewise, the brand strategist is concerned with evaluating their brand's performance against key competitors. They will normally have a clear view about who are their prime and secondary competitors. As they formulate brand strategy, they will consider how they can group their competitors according to their characteristics. For example, two authors have suggested that the strategic grouping of firms in the brewing industry can be characterized by their degree of diversification and whether they are local, regional or national marketers. By modeling the competitive environment into clusters of competitors based on the degree of similarity between members of the strategic groups, the strategist is better able to evaluate competitors' strategies and anticipate responses to their brand activity. For instance, one author reported that in the early 1980s two strategic groups could be identified amongst computer chip manufacturers. The first strategic group, predominantly containing Japanese firms, was characterized by:

- being technological followers;
- having a commitment to quality, reliability and low-cost;
- being diversified firms with large computer divisions.

The second strategic group, with firms such as Motorola and Texas Instruments, were:

- technological innovators;
- leaders in process innovation;
- mainly semiconductor firms.

With such clear appreciation of the similarities of firms' strategies, it becomes easier to plan against known competitors.

Yet, while economists have historically conceived of an industry as a clearly-defined group of competitors, evidence is mounting that managers in the same firm do *not* have similar perceptions about who the main competitors are. As part of a major research programme sponsored by the ESRC to evaluate managers' perceptions of strategic groupings, de Chernatony, Johnson and Daniels interviewed senior managers in firms supplying pumps to the North Sea offshore oil industry and repeatedly found differences between members of the same management team concerning who their competitors were and the basis which they were using to form strategic groupings. When also undertaking similar interviews amongst senior managers in firms providing mortgages for the first-time homeowner market, results again showed different perceptions amongst the management teams in each firm as to the composition and nature of competition. While there was some commonality between managers concerning many competitors, several competitors were unique

managers in the same firm do not have similar perceptions about who the main competitors are

to particular managers. By debriefing the management team about their views on who are the competitors and what bases they were using to formulate their strategic grouping, a better appreciation can be gained as to how each manager is formulating their strategy and ensure a more unified approach to competitive brand positioning.

If companies are going to become more effective at formulating competitive brand strategies, managers in the same firm will need to discuss more openly amongst themselves who they perceive as their competitors and what basis they are using to group competitors. Without this debate, individual senior managers may be incorrectly directing their departments to follow diverse routes which may not necessarily best support the intended strategy.

After all those working on the brand have debated who they perceive their competitors to be and what the bases for strategic groupings are, they then need to evaluate which competitors are likely to respond fastest and in the most aggressive manner as a result of the firm's changes to its brand strategy. Attitudes can be an indicator of likely competitor response. For example, Mars, Unilever and Procter & Gamble have always striven to be leaders in their particular markets. It goes against their corporate cultures to accept that a newcomer to their market can go unchallenged in its quest to rob them of their brand shares. History may be another pointer to competitive responses. In some firms, for example, there may be a deep resentment against a particular geographical market, or type of product, because the firm tried and failed to succeed with its brand. It does not want to reopen old wounds and may well take no action when a new competitor appears to be succeeding. Alternatively, the size of investment in plant may indicate what response to anticipate. In the packaging market, Metal Box has a considerable investment in machinery producing high volume runs of standard-sized containers. It cannot afford to let its lines run slowly and any new competitor brand launches are quickly evaluated and challenged.

Brand strategists need to consider how important the market is to each of their competitors and what their degree of commitment is. Particularly when competitors have a wide variety of brands across many different markets, their interest and commitment to protecting their brands is likely to vary. For example, commitment to part of the range might be particularly high because these markets are regarded as having significant growth potential, and have historically enabled their brands to achieve healthy returns, as well as enabling them to be highly visible players, gaining spin-offs for some of their other brands. In the UK breakfast cereals market Kellogg's, with its wide range of brands, would never let its flagship brand, Kellogg's Corn Flakes, fall against other competitors. For too many consumers, this particular brand *is* the firm. Any weakening on this brand might be read as a weakening of the Kellogg's firm and, by inference, a deterioration of the rest of its range.

A considerable amount of *data* may well be held on competitors about such things as their plant capacities, labour rates, organizational structure, discount structures and suppliers used. However, we would question whether sufficient *information* is available on their brand strategy. To position a brand and anticipate competitors' responses, marketers should either know, or be able to gauge for each competitor:

- its main brands, their size, profitability, growth and the importance of each brand to that firm and its commitment to that brand;
- its brand objectives and the strategy being followed – whether, for example, they are trying to enter, improve, maintain, harvest or leave the market;
- its brands' strengths and weaknesses;
- the competitive position of each brand in terms of having either a leadership, strong, favourable, tenable or weak position.

The meaning of brand share

When marketers try to outflank competitors' brands with their own brands, they use market share data to track their performance. Unfortunately, all too often market share is used predominantly as a monitoring device rather than as a further aid to brand strategy formulation. Kenichi Ohmae's (1982) considerable experience of strategy consulting throws a lot more light on the way that brand share can help strategic thinking. Figure 8.6 shows the strategic meaning of brand share.

When a firm has achieved a presence in a market, its share of the market reflects the extent to which its brand is meeting consumers' needs better than other brands. Particularly with a high brand share, marketers are prone to complacency and, short-sightedly, do not consider the two components of market share. One element is those consumers actively competed for and won, i.e. area D in Figure 8.6. This can be regarded as **active brand marketing**. An often overlooked constituent of the brand's market share, however, is represented by area E in Figure 8.6, i.e. those consumers buying the brand who were not competed for. This component, resulting from **passive brand marketing**, may well be those consumers, for example, intent on buying Heinz Baked Beans. When doing their grocery shopping, they discover that this particular brand is out of stock and, rather than go to another store, they choose an alternative brand. The more successful the brand, the closer the ratio D:E approaches 1. Marketing research can help identify this ratio by asking buyers just before

unfortunately, market share is used predominantly as a monitoring device rather than as a further aid to brand strategy formulation

the purchase what brand they intended buying and then recording the brand actually bought. By questioning those who bought a different brand from the one intended and why they did this, marketers can develop ways of marketing their own brands more effectively.

We believe the model in Figure 8.6 can be further developed, in particular those customers competed for and won, shown in area D. In our opinion, these customers can be broken down into four further groups:

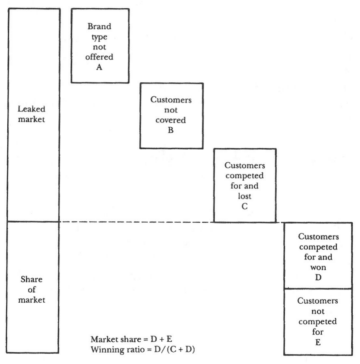

Figure 8.6   *The strategic meaning of market share (based on Ohmae, 1982)*

- D1 – Customers who are satisfied with the brand and who will actively select the same brand on the next occasion, regardless of competitive activity.
- D2 – Customers who are satisfied with the brand, but who can be enticed to a competitor's brand on the next occasion if there is an attractive incentive, such as a price discount.
- D3 – Customers who regard the brand as being adequate, but not fully satisfying their needs. They stay with the brand since it is inconvenient to switch to a different brand. An example of such inconvenience might be changing bank accounts, when all the standing orders have to be changed.

- D4 – Customers who have tried the brand, but on the next purchase occasion will switch to an alternative brand, even though this may involve more effort on their behalf.

D1 customers, the 'loyalists', need to be nurtured and frequently consulted about their views on the brand. Any dissatisfaction needs to be quickly resolved. D2 customers, the 'swingers', exist in all markets. The trade-offs they are making when choosing a particular brand need to be understood and incorporated as a further factor to consider when formulating brand strategy.

D3 customers, the 'apathetic', are offering the brand a chance for survival. If the marketer can evaluate what aspects of the brand need fine-tuning to satisfy this group, they are then better able to consider implementing corrective action rapidly. Otherwise, a competitor will find a way of taking care of consumers' perceptions of inconvenience and encourage them to switch brands. For example, some building societies marketing cheque accounts offer to take care of notifying the new consumer's employer as well as arranging the smooth transfer of standing orders from their previous bank/building society account.

D4 customers, the 'doubters', gave the brand a chance and are sceptical about whether it could be changed to meet their needs. Their perceptions about what the brand could do for them, or say about them, were not realized. The reasons for these perceptions need to be assessed and, if possible, changes considered.

Area C in Figure 8.6 (customers competed for and lost), was an important part of Sir John Egan's strategy when trying to halt the decline of Jaguar cars in the mid-1980s. Market research studies with previous Jaguar owners who had switched to a different marque indicated problems with Jaguar's quality and reliability. Changes were made to improve quality and reliability and these were communicated in a new promotional campaign.

Some brands do not fully capitalize on their capabilities as they are not available to all of the potential market, as represented by area B in Figure 8.6. This may require a more intensive distribution push to cover new areas.

Area A represents a brand opportunity, since there is a group of consumers who share needs similar to those of the core market. However, they are looking for something extra which the brand is not yet offering. For example, the novice sailor gains basic sailing skills from the stable Topper dinghy, but then switches to the more finely-balanced Laser dinghy, offering greater scope for racing. The challenge here is being able to develop new variants which capitalize on the core brand's heritage, yet which do not damage the image of the core brand.

Characterizing winning brands

The core of a successful brand is that it offers benefits to consumers in a way that other brands are unable to meet. However, profitability doesn't only result from a brand's unique competitive advantages, as research has shown.

Profitable brands are leaders

A research project was instigated in 1972 to evaluate which dimensions of strategy affect profitability. This resulted in the highly respected PIMS database (Profit Impact of Marketing Strategies). Information from approximately 3000 business units has been analysed and one of the key findings is that large share brands are much more profitable than small share brands. On average, number one brands achieve pre-tax returns on investment three times that of brands in the fifth and lower ranked position. There are many reasons why leading brands are more profitable.

Leading brands have lower-costs than followers. Economies of scale are one way that costs are reduced. For example, one source estimates that a 90 m tonnes oil refinery costs only one and a half times as much to build as a 45 m tonnes refinery. Running costs per unit of output are also lower for larger production processes. The larger refinery needs less than double the number of employees of the smaller refinery. Production efficiencies are achieved with some techniques once a critical volume level is exceeded.

The learning curve presents a further opportunity for leading brands to curtail costs. For example, production managers soon learn the best way of configuring their employees on the production line and engineers soon begin to appreciate how to better harness the new technology. Taken together, economies of scale and the experience effect cause a constant reduction in costs each time cumulative production is doubled.

Leading brands instill more confidence in risk-averse consumers. They also attract higher quality employees, who are proud to be associated with a winning brand and willing to stretch their own involvement with the brand so that it maintains its dominant position.

Profitable brands are committed to high quality

The PIMS database has shown that those brands which offer superior perceived quality relative to competitors' brands are far more profitable. Having a brand which consumers perceive to be of superior quality than other brands makes it easier for the marketer

(margin note) large share brands are much more profitable than small share brands

to charge a price premium. Part of the extra revenue should be used for R&D investment to sustain the quality positioning for future earnings. Also by committing everyone in the organization to doing their job in the best possible way there is a greater conformance to standards, which results in less rejection, less brand recalls, less re-working and, ultimately, greater profitability. Higher quality results in higher brand shares and all the benefits that this brings.

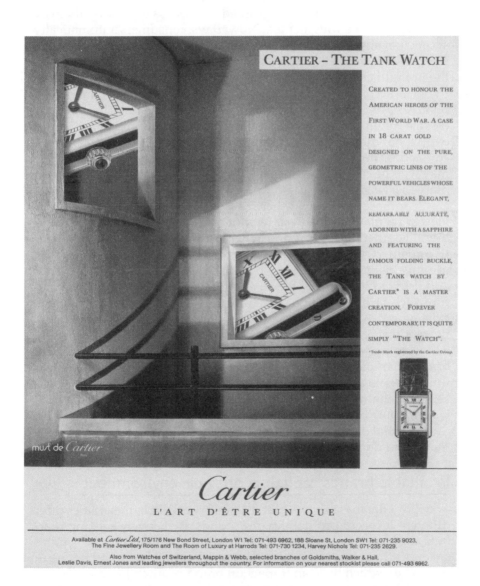

Exhibit 8.4 *Prized for its quality excellence, Cartier commands a price premium, reinforcing perceptions of quality*

Two points need to be stressed. The first is that it is *perceived* rather than *actual* quality which counts. Engineering may well set internal specifications for others to follow but, ultimately, consumers decide whether the quality meets their expectations. Furthermore, consumers are often unable to evaluate the quality of a brand and they use clues to assess its performance. The size of stereo speakers, for example, may be taken as an indication of their performance, or the price of a brand of wine as to its taste. In some product fields, they take the core benefit for granted and assess quality by the way the brand has been augmented. Nowadays, consumers automatically accept that any airline will safely transport them to their destination. They assess quality through issues such as the politeness of the staff, the in-flight entertainment, choice on the menu, etc.

The second point is that quality is assessed by consumers on a relative basis. They assess brands against other brands. The way they do this might not necessarily be the way that the marketer would expect. For example, even though McDonalds sees Burger King as a competitor in the hamburger market, to the consumer McDonalds may well be competing against Pizzaland, since their interest lies in places serving fast meals.

For these and many other reasons, consumers should be interviewed regularly to enable us to understand who they see a particular brand competing against and what criteria they use to assess relative quality. Only consumer-relevant attributes should guide quality improvement initiatives. Employees should be encouraged to go out and listen to consumers' views about their brands. A corporate culture, such as that at Honda, which encourages employees to challenge existing procedures and make improvements, can raise consumers' perceptions of quality.

Having achieved a reputation amongst consumers for a quality brand, marketers need to work continuously to improve this. Over time, there is a danger of the quality positioning eroding. As markets become more mature, competitors try harder to emulate the leader. Some organizations become complacent and underestimate the potential of new competitors. Others fail to protect their quality image and do not invest in product enhancement.

Profitable brands capitalize on their environment

The PIMS database shows that different market characteristics offer different levels of profitability for brands. By actively seeking markets that have the right characteristics, the marketer can more successfully utilize resources to nurture a profitable brand. Some of the factors which have an impact on brand profitability are:

*   market evolution – brand profitability is highest in fast growing markets and lowest in declining ones;

- markets with a high level of exports are more profitable than those with a significant import element;
- markets with frequent new product launches are subject to lower returns on investment, although this is less so in the services and distribution sector.

Winning brands are memorable

Brands win the minds of consumers because they are distinctive and stand out as having relevant added values. In other words, it is not just because they are heard above the noise of competitors, but because they are making the *right* noises. A brand could be scoring well on awareness, but if consumers abhor its brashness it will not succeed.

a brand could be scoring well on awareness, but if consumers abhor its brashness it will not succeed

Communicating a brand's added values is an essential component contributing to long-term success. A communication strategy, however, needs to be carefully devised. It is wrong to assume automatically that advertising is the prime route to follow. For example, Marks & Spencer have traditionally made little use of advertising, since they have correctly recognized that there are many other appropriate ways for brand communication. Consumers assess the Marks & Spencer brand from the locations where their stores are sighted, from their store designs, store layout, quality of goods, the way they are treated by staff, their prices and the way they handle customer complaints. Word-of-mouth endorsement is also an important ingredient in their success.

Winning brands have a supporting communication strategy which results from a deep understanding of the myriad of clues that consumers use to interpret them. For those brands differentiating themselves primarily through their unique image, advertising is invaluable. It reinforces the essential images amongst consumers and their peer group alike. By establishing the brand on a unique and highly valued pedestal, the marketer is yet again able to charge a premium price.

Levels of promotional support

The relationship between advertising spend and brand share is a complex domain, not least because the quality of advertisements and competitors' activity are but two of many other variables that influence the equation. There is a lot of evidence to show that leading brands are committed to significant advertising spends. For example, an analysis (Broadbent 1979) was undertaken of the top seventy-five brands in twenty-five packaged grocery markets for 1978. The results, in Table 8.2, show that the advertising shares of the leading brands exceeded their sterling sales shares.

Table 8.2   *Advertising and sales data for 25 grocery markets (after Broadbent 1979)*

	Sterling sales share %	Advertising share %	Advertising to sales ratio %
Brand leader	30	35	6
Number 2 brand	17	21	7
Number 3 brand	11	13	8

inference is that promotional budgets are more effective for the leading brand than for the close followers

To compensate for the fact that big brands tend to spend more on advertising than smaller brands, the advertising-to-sales ratios provide further insight. The table shows brand leaders spending less on advertising as a proportion of sales revenue than the number two or number three brands. The inference is that promotional budgets are more effective for the leading brand than for the close followers. One of the reasons for this is advertising economies of scale. The causes of this are not yet fully understood, but are probably related to an aspect of consumer behaviour in respect of leading brands which leads to above-average purchase frequencies – what one researcher has referred to as the 'penetration supercharge phenomena'.

The WPP Group has further analysed the PIMS database. Reassuringly, the findings from the late 1970s still held true. Also, high market share brands still have larger advertising spends than competitors. Their findings are shown in Table 8.3.

Table 8.3   *Advertising analysis using PIMS data (after Biel 1990)*

Advertising to sales ratio versus direct competitors %	Average share of market %	Average return on investment %
Much less	14	17
Less	20	22
Equal	25	22
More	26	25
Much more	32	32

It would seem that consistently having an advertising-to-sales ratio greater than competitors is associated with a higher brand share, which in turn enhances the probability of better profitability.

The problem facing the marketer is to decide the optimum advertising spend to maximize brand profitability in the long run. Normally, one would expect that a brand's share of market would approximate to its share of voice, i.e. its advertising share. In an analysis of data collected in 1987 for 1096 J. W. Thompson advertised brands from twenty-three countries, these were categorized as being:

- profit taking brands, or under-spenders, whose share of voice is the same as or below their share of market;
- investment brands, or over-spenders, whose share of voice exceeds their share of market.

Over half, 56 per cent, of the brands were categorized as investment brands. In other words, their owners were taking a long-term view about the benefits of advertising.

It would, however, be wrong to assume that by increasing advertising spend on a quality brand to the extent that share of voice considerably exceeded short-term share of market brand success would automatically follow. Without understanding the other brands' market shares and their shares of voice, this could bankrupt the brand.

To help appreciate what broad levels of advertising are appropriate for different brands, the matrix in Figure 8.7 is of value.

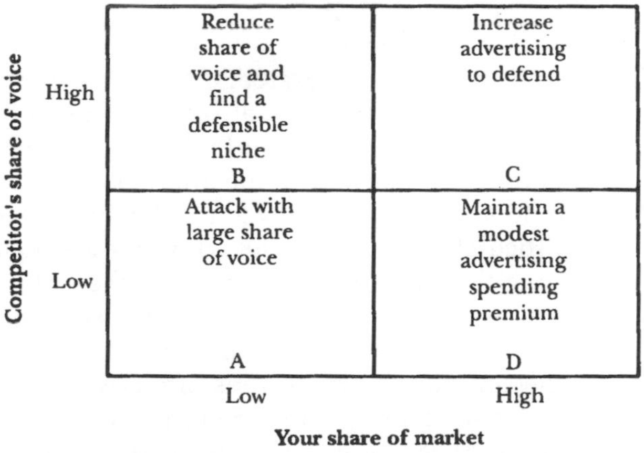

Figure 8.7   Evaluating appropriate advertising levels (after Schroer 1990)

In quadrant A there is an opportunity to increase brand share when competitors' advertising spend is low and they are slow to respond. The challenging brand must exceed competitors' advertising spending and should have a favourable cost structure to enable it to sustain continued advertising.

In quadrant B the small brand is under attack from a competitor with a much more noticeable share of voice. With its higher costs, the brand cannot realistically sustain an advertising war and it would do better to find a niche that it can defend.

By contrast, in quadrant C the brand leader is more likely to have a cost advantage because of its size, and it should increase or maintain its advertising activity to defend its position.

In quadrant D the smaller competitor has accepted the status quo and has a low share of voice. In this situation it is wise to aim for a small advertising spend premium, thereby maintaining the brand's higher market share.

Should a company build brands or buy brands?

Some have argued that the rising cost of advertising during the 1980s caused many marketers to shift their attention towards buying other firms' brands, rather than building their own. Particularly for those new brands that needed a continuous advertising presence, the time that could be afforded on television began to shrink dramatically

Another reason for the attractiveness of brand buying was the ability to extend brand leverage throughout the European Union. Where a multinational felt it to be strategically appropriate to have a particular range in each major country, it was not unusual to find a team evaluating different brand purchases and also assessing how easily the new brands could be integrated.

A brand acquisition is particularly attractive when it has built up a considerable amount of goodwill and when its value is not included on the balance sheet. With the increasing interest of accountants in brand valuations, however, it is likely to become increasingly more difficult to find companies who have not made some attempt at estimating the value of the goodwill of their brands.

brand acquisitions are often seen as a quicker way of gaining entrance to a new market

Brand acquisitions are often seen as a quicker way of gaining entrance to a new market. However, the difficulty of integrating the new brand into the company's structure is often overlooked. Furthermore, the potential for synergy can sometimes be overestimated. The takeover of the American Howard Johnson hotel and restaurant chain by the Imperial Group floundered because Imperial's knowledge of consumer markets was irrelevant to the American hotel and fast food market. This unsuccessful acquisition was sold off five years later.

By contrast, brands acquired in product or services sectors which are closely-related to the firm's current expertise stand a greater chance of succeeding under the new owner than those in sectors where the owner has little expertise. There are many stories of firms unsuccessfully diversifying this way. For example, BP bought its way into the coal minerals and information technology sectors, all of which are markedly different from its core competence in oil exploration, transportation, refining and distribution. It soon recognized the problems of this diversification route and sold off these interests.

Extending brands

If the firm finds that it is unable to penetrate the market further with its current brands, it may consider moving into a related market. It could argue that the best way to overcome consumer apathy and competitive resistance would be to stretch its existing name. While the inherent goodwill and awareness from the original brand name may help the new brand's development, however, there is also the danger that the new could dilute the strength of the original brand and convey the wrong perceptions with a consequent detrimental effect on the original brand.

The economics of establishing new brands are pushing companies more towards stretching their existing names into new markets. Daunted by the heavy R&D costs, and more aware of the statistics about failure rates for new brands, marketers are increasingly taking their established names into new product fields. Tauber (1988) reviewed a sample of 276 brand extensions to evaluate the different ways of extending brands and concluded that there are seven types of brand extensions:

- *Same product in a different form*   For example, Mars Bars extending into Mars Bars ice cream.
- *Distinctive taste, ingredient or component*   An ingredient or component of the current brand is used to make a new item in a different category. For example, Kraft extended the distinctive taste of their Philadelphia cream cheese into Philadelphia Cream Cheese Salad Dressing.
- *Companion product*   Where some products are used with others, these lend themselves to brand extensions. For example, Duracell batteries in Duracell torches.
- *Same customer franchise*   Marketers develop different brands to sell to their loyal customers. For example, the AA is primarily known for its roadside assistance service to motorists yet it markets a variety of AA products, such as books, to its customers.
- *Expertise*   Brands are extended into areas where consumers believe the original brand has connotations of special knowledge or experience. For example, Canon's perceived expertise in optics was extended into photocopiers.
- *Unique benefit, attribute or feature owned by the brand*   Some brands stand out for their uniqueness on a particular attribute, which is extended into a related field. For example, the makers of Sunkist orange drink launched Sunkist Vitamin C tablets.
- *Designer image or status*   Some consumers feel that their Saab

cars have a higher status when they know that Saab also work in jet aircraft.

benefits that come
from stretching the
name must be
weighed against
any damage that
may be done to the
core brand

When considering extending the original brand name into a new sector, the benefits that come from stretching the name must be weighed against any negative connotations with the original name and any damage that may be done to the core brand. Looking at each of these three areas in more detail, using a checklist adapted from Aaker (1990), should enable marketers to decide whether it is wise to extend the brand name.

Possible benefits from extending the brand name

1   **Awareness**. Are consumers aware of the brand name? Whirlpool, the white goods manufacturer entered into a joint venture with Philips in 1989 as part of its expansion programme into Europe. Philips was not prepared to sell its well-known name and Whirlpool employed a dual-branding policy, knowing that as a result of the contract they did not have many years before they had to drop the Philips name.
2   **Brand associations**. Will the consumer consider the extension to be a credible move? Does the name bring the right sorts of associations to mind? Cadbury's use of its name in the liqueur market brings to mind automatically an expectation about a certain type of taste.
3   **Quality associations**. Will the name stretch to give the correct perception of quality? IBM is able to use its name whenever it launches small or large systems, in part because of quality perceptions.
4   **Encourage trial purchase**. Will the name give the needed reassurance to the risk-averse consumer?

Possible weaknesses from the core brand name

1   **No value-added**. Will the name add value to the new line? Some would argue that the designer label status from the name Pierre Cardin adds little to its line extensions – particularly when it marketed bathroom tiles in Spain.
2   **Negative associations**. Will the wrong associations result? For example, Levi Strauss were known and respected for their jeans. The extension into Levi Tailored Classics suits failed because of the wrong associations.
3   **Name confusion.** Does the name imply the type of product about to be marketed?

Possible damage to the core brand

1   **Undesirable associations.** Will the image of the core brand be damaged? Black & Decker's acquisition of the small appliances range from General Electric caused much internal debate. It was questioned if the heavy duty image that Black & Decker had would be weakened by stretching their name across the new range.

2   **Perceived quality deteriorates.** Will the perceived quality of the core brand fall? With its acquisition of holiday companies Thompson's kept the original names, such as Horizon, so protecting the Thompson Holiday brand.

3   **What about disasters?** Will an unforeseen threat damage the core brand? When Persil launched Persil System 3 it did not anticipate dermatological problems and the resulting short-term market resistance.

Besides these three broad areas of questioning, it may well be wise for the marketer to address two further questions that focus on the economics of brand extensions. Are there limitations on the size of the marketing budget? If the brand marketer is constrained by company cutbacks, brand extensions may be the only viable route. However, of more importance may be the question of cannibalization. The presence of the core brand name may result in sales of the new brand coming not just from new consumers, but also from those who used to buy the core brand. While it is inevitable that some cannibalization will occur, the marketer needs to anticipate the likely extent of this.

Researchers have investigated the extent to which brands which stress functional or prestigious connotations can be extended. For example, consumers regarded Timex watches as being more associated with functional benefits, while Rolex watches have more prestigious associations. They found that **a brand name which is strongly associated with functional benefits can be more easily extended into product areas bought mainly for their functional benefits.** So, for example, a branded wristwatch, positioned primarily as offering functional excellence, could stretch its name with little difficulty into stopwatches. By contrast, they found that if the original brand name majored on the dimension of prestige it could be more easily extended into a product field known for its prestige rather than its functionality. In other words the Rolex name could more likely be extended to grandfather clocks than into stopwatches.

It was also reported that when consumers perceived a brand being extended into a product field that many firms would find relatively easy to produce, the brand extension would not be accepted.

This may be because consumers felt that in the new product field there was little difference between competing brands and that the new entrant was going to do little more than use its image to charge an unnecessary price premium. On a more positive note, where consumers perceive

- the original and extended product classes to be complementary,

and
- the firm is viewed as being able to transfer its skills and resources in making the extension,

then there is a greater likelihood of the brand extension being accepted.

Conclusions

By analysing environmental opportunities and threats, as well as thoroughly appreciating the nature of the brand's competitive advantage, marketers are able to develop strategies that position their brands to achieve the best return while being protected from competitive attacks. The lifespan of brands will depend on the sustainability of their competitive advantage.

The two broad competitive advantages inherent in successful brands are based on either delivering similar benefits more cheaply than competitors – cost-driven brands, and/or delivering superior benefits than competitors at a price premium – value-added brands. It is crucial that a decision is taken about the strategic path that the brand will follow, and that everyone is informed of this. Each of these two routes makes different demands on employees, resources and processes. With everyone in the firm aware of the branding route being followed, they can all contribute by being vigilant in cost-curtailing activities and by being creative in devising added value. Strategies appropriate for each type of brand need developing, avoiding at all costs the commodity brand domain, characterized by little added value and, frequently, no cost advantage.

A useful device for identifying the competitive advantages of brands is Porter's Value Chain. This helps managers to consider the processes and supporting services involved in transforming commodities into highly respected brands. It also acts as a check as to whether the competitive advantages of brands are being reinforced, by considering the linkages in each part of the value adding process.

A more sophisticated way of developing brand strategy is to consider both the type of competitive advantage inherent in the brand, and the competitive scope of the market it will be targeted at, i.e. a narrow or broad group of consumers. From the resulting matrix, four generic strategies were documented.

Having identified the brand's competitive advantage, and the strategic direction to be followed, the marketer then needs to anticipate competitors' responses and develop ways of sustaining the brand's advantage. An important issue is agreeing as a brand team who the competitors are and using the concept of market share to evaluate future opportunities.

Winning brands focus on adopting leadership positions in specific markets, offering superior perceived quality than competitors, taking advantage of environmental opportunities and being memorable. It is not unusual for their share of advertising spend to exceed their market share.

More recently, high advertising costs have forced many firms to look more favourably at buying, rather than building brands from scratch. Another way that marketers can save costs is by extending the core brand's name into new markets. The dangers inherent in this strategy, however, need to be carefully evaluated.

Marketing action checklist

It is recommended that, after reading this chapter, marketers undertake the following exercises to test and refine their brand strategies:

1   Write down what you believe to be the reasons why consumers buy your brand and your competitors' brands. For each of these reasons, evaluate which of the brands comes closest to satisfying consumers' needs. If this information is already available from an accurate marketing research study, it should be used instead of management judgement. On a separate sheet of paper, summarize these findings by stating for each brand which attributes it best satisfies. This is one way of identifying each brand's competitive advantage(s). Those brands which do not have any 'success attributes' are unlikely to succeed for long.

2   How easy is it for your competitors to copy any of your brands' competitive advantages? What actions are you taking to sustain your brands' competitive advantages?

3   For each of your brands separately, use the matrix of value-added advantage versus cost-driven advantage in Figure 8.3 to plot your brand and those of your competitors. Whichever quadrant your brand occupies, ask how appropriate your current strategies are. Those competitors' brands falling in the same quadrant as your brand represent potentially the greatest threat. What are you doing to protect your brand against these?

4   Using the example of the value chain in Figure 8.4, identify all
     those activities you undertake in transforming low value goods
     or services into high value, finished goods or services. Which of
     these activities do you believe you do, or could do, better than
     competitors? How do these 'doing better or cheaper' activities
     relate to the competitive advantages identified in question 1
     above? Try to assess what proportion of costs can be allocated
     to each part of the value chain for a particular brand. How do
     these cost components compare with competitors'? How well-
     linked are each of the processes and support activities on the
     value chain?

5   For each of your brands separately, use the matrix of competi-
     tive scope versus competitive advantage in Figure 8.5 to plot
     your brand and those of your competitors. Whichever quad-
     rant your brand occupies, check the appropriateness of your
     current strategy. Which competitive brands fall in the same
     quadrant as your brand? How appropriate are their current strat-
     egies? What plans have you to protect your brand against those
     brands in the same quadrant?

6   Take one of your brands and evaluate whether you are striving
     to sustain its competitive advantage by concentrating on op-
     erational effectiveness, or by concentrating on performing
     different activities from your competitors, or by performing simi-
     lar activities in different ways. If you are reliant upon operational
     effectiveness, be aware of the difficulty of staying ahead of com-
     petitors and consider how you could follow either of the latter
     two strategies. To what extent do each of the activities in your
     brand building (a) show consistency and (b) reinforce each other.
     Take your value chain and consider how you could restructure
     any of the activities to give a stronger fit and therefore greater
     sustainability.

7   For any of your brands which compete in services markets,
     evaluate which of the ten factors in Table 8.1 are most appropri-
     ate for sustaining their competitive advantages.

8   As individuals (rather than in a team), select a brand and write
     down which competitors it competes against. Then, as individu-
     als, group competitors together into discrete clusters such that
     those competitors grouped together show a similarity in terms
     of the strategy being followed. Then meet as a management team
     and discuss your rationale for the named competitors and the
     different bases for strategic groupings.

9   From question 8, which competitors did the management team
     identify as following a similar strategy to your brand? How
     much relevant information do you hold about these competi-

tors (consult the section at the end of 'Anticipating competitor response')?

10   Using Figure 8.6, which shows the components of brand share, what marketing research data do you hold to evaluate the volume of sales that is, or could be made to customers in the blocks A to E? In terms of those customers competed for and won in block D, what proportion of customers falls into each of the categories D1, D2, D3 and D4 (as outlined in the section 'The meaning of brand share')? What actions could be taken to maximize the number of customers in category D1?

11   What marketing research data is held about consumers' perceptions of the quality of your brand and those of competitors? From qualitative research, are you able to establish accurately how consumers evaluate the quality of your brand and competitors' brands? Based on these marketing research reports, what actions are needed to improve consumers' perceptions of your quality?

12   This question is only applicable if advertising is appropriate for your brands. Produce a table for your brand, and those brands against which it competes, showing each brand's share of market and share of voice, as well as each brand's advertising-to-sales ratio. For the brand that you believe your brand competes most against, use the matrix of competitor's share of voice against your share of market, Figure 8.7, to assess the most appropriate level of advertising activity.

13   On the last occasion that you followed a policy of using an existing brand name for a new addition to your range, evaluate:
   • the strengths of using the core brand name;
   • the advantages for the new line of carrying the core brand name;
   • the effect the new line had on the core brand.
   Taking all of these points into consideration, was it wise to have followed a brand extension policy?

References and further reading

Aaker D. (1988). *Strategic Market Management*. New York: J. Wiley.
Aaker D. (1990). Brand extensions: the good, the bad and the ugly. *Sloan Management Review*, **31** (4), 47–56.
Aaker D. (1991). *Managing Brand Equity*. New York: The Free Press.
Aaker D. and Keller K. (1990). Consumer evaluations of brand extensions. *Journal of Marketing*, **54** (Jan.), 27–41.
Abell D. and Hammond J. (1979). *Strategic Marketing Planning*. Englewood Cliffs: Prentice Hall.

Biel A. (1990). Strong brand, high spend. *ADMAP*, Nov., 35–40.

Broadbent S. (1979). What makes a top brand? *The Nielsen Researcher*, No. 3.

Buday T. (1989). Capitalizing on brand extensions. *Journal of Consumer Marketing*, **6** (4), 27–30.

Buzzell R. and Gale B. (1987). *The PIMS Principles*. New York: The Free Press.

Christopher M., Majaro S. and McDonald M. (1987). *Strategy Search*. Aldershot: Gower.

Clifford D. and Cavanagh R. (1985). *The Winning Performance: How America's High Growth Midsize Companies Succeed*. London: Sidgwick & Jackson.

Davidson H. (1987). *Offensive Marketing*. Harmondsworth: Penguin.

de Chernatony L. (1991). Formulating brand strategy. *European Management Journal*, **9** (2), 194–200.

de Chernatony L., Daniels K. and Johnson G. (1993). Competitive positioning strategies of mirroring sellers' and buyers' perceptions? *Journal of Strategic Marketing*, **1**, 229–48.

de Chernatony L., Daniels K. and Johnson G. (1995). Managers' perceptions of competitors' positioning: a replication study. Paper presented at TIMS Marketing Science conference. Australian School of Management, Sydney.

Doyle P. (1989). Building successful brands: the strategic options. *Journal of Marketing Management*, **5** (1), 77–95.

Easingwood C. (1990). Hard to copy services, pp. 325–36. In *Marketing Educators Group Proceedings* (Pendlebury A. and Watkins T., eds). Oxford: MEG.

Easton G. (1988). Competition and marketing strategy. *European Journal of Marketing*, **27** (2), 31–49.

Grossberg K. (1989). How Citibank created a retail niche for itself in Japan. *Planning Review* (Sept.–Oct.), 14–17, 48.

Hamel G. and Prahalad C. (1989). Strategic intent. *Harvard Business Review* (May–June), 63–76.

Johnson G. and Scholes K. (1989). *Exploring Corporate Strategy*. Hemel Hempstead: Prentice Hall.

Jones B. and Ramsden R. (1991). The global brand age. *Management Today* Sept., 78–83.

Jones J. (1990). Ad spending: maintaining market share. *Harvard Business Review* (Jan.–Feb.), 38–42.

Karakaya F. and Stahl M. (1989). Barriers to entry and market entry decisions in consumer and industrial goods markets. *Journal of Marketing*, **53** (April), 80–91.

Karel J. (1991). Brand strategy positions products worldwide. *Journal of Business Strategy* (May–June), 16–19.

Kelley B. (1991). Making it different. *Sales & Marketing Management*, (May), 52–5, 60.

Lorenz C. (1988). Unrelated take-overs spell trouble. *Financial Times*, 4 March, 22.

Ohmae K. (1982). *The Mind of the Strategist*. Harmondsworth: Penguin.

Park C.W., Milberg S. and Lawson R. (1991). Evaluation of brand extension: the role of product feature similarity and brand concept consistency. *Journal of Consumer Research*, **18** (Sept.), 185–93.

Peters T. and Waterman R. (1982). *In Search of Excellence*. New York: Harper & Row.

Porac J. and Thomas H. (1990). Taxonomic mental models in competitor definition. *Academy of Management Review*, **15** (2), 224–40.

Porter M. (1979). How competitive forces shape strategy. *Harvard Business Review* (March–April), 137–45.

Porter M. (1980). *Competitive Strategy*. New York: The Free Press.

Porter M. (1985). *Competitive Advantage*. New York: The Free Press.

Porter M. (1988). Michael Porter on competitive strategy. *Harvard Business School Video Series*. Boston: Nathan/Tyler.

Porter M. (1996). What is strategy? *Harvard Business Review* (Nov.–Dec.), 61–78.

Prahalad C. and Hamel G. (1990). The core competences of the corporation. *Harvard Business Review* (May–June), 79–91.

Schroer J. (1990). Ad spending: growing market share. *Harvard Business Review* (Jan.–Feb.), 44–8.

Tauber E. (1988). Brand leverage: strategy for growth in a cost control world. *Journal of Advertising Research* (Aug.–Sept.), 26–30.

Thornhill J. (1991). Ratner gloomy as recession drives group into £17.7m loss. *Financial Times*, 17 September.

Thornhill J. (1992). Jewellery innovator and the textile veteran. *Financial Times Weekend*, January 11/12, 6 (See also p. 1 and p. 22).

Urban G. and Star S. (1991). *Advanced Marketing Strategy*. Englewood Cliffs: Prentice Hall.

Wachman R. and Fairbairn S. (1992). Ratner steps down as sales slump. *The Evening Standard*, 10 January, 5.

Woodward S. (1991). Competitive marketing, In *Understanding Brands* (Cowley D., ed.). London: Kogan Page.

Zeithmal V., Parasuraman A. and Berry L. (1985). Problems and strategies in services marketing. *Journal of Marketing*, **44** (Spring), 33–46.

Chapter 9

The challenge of developing and sustaining added values

Summary

The aim of this chapter is to consider the challenges marketers face in developing and sustaining brand added values. The chapter begins by making the point that it is only worth developing added values if they are relevant to the target market and noticeably different from those of competitors. Any marketing activity then needs to integrate these added values and present brands as **holistic** offerings. In other words all, rather than one single aspect, of the brand's assets should be developed, enabling customers to appreciate their points of difference, the way they satisfy both functional and emotional needs, reduce perceived risk, and make purchasing easy.

One way of identifying possible added values for brands is to consider a four-level model of a brand as a **generic** product or a basic service with an **expected**, **augmented** and **potential** branding surround. We describe the development of brands using this conceptual model in both product and service sectors. Moreover we identify further ways of adding value, such as consumer participation and customization. We also consider the problem of sustaining brands' added values against imitators through trademark registration. Counterfeiting, however, is but one of the challenges facing brands. We conclude the chapter by considering some of the other challenges, for example adopting a greater strategic perspective, balancing the short-term benefits of promotions against the long-term gains from advertising, the new electronic environment, the opening of markets and the move to corporate branding – amongst other issues.

Positioning brands as added-value offerings

Brands succeed because customers perceive them as having value over and above that of the 'equivalent' commodity (if there is such a thing!), or value in excess of the sum of the price of the product's or service's constituent parts. This makes them *noticeably different* with *relevant* and *welcomed* attributes. The added value that brands bring to the purchase or consumption experience is not restricted just to consumers. For example, Airbus ran an advertisement showing a section of the globe with the Airbus A340 following a path directly from Chicago to Mumbai with competitors going via Archangel. There clearly is the added value to consumers flying with carriers who use the A340 service of not having to refuel on these routes, making their journey time shorter. Likewise there is added value to the airline purchasing A340s, since it presents opportunities for greater efficiencies in fleet management by driving down operating costs. (We first saw the Airbus A340 advertisement in late 1996/early 1997. In May 1997 we became aware of an advertisement for the Boeing 777, promoting the fact that this can fly non-stop further than any jetliner in its class. Yet another example of the difficulty in sustaining a functional added value.) IBM provides another good example of added values in business to business markets with its campaign 'Show us an opportunity you picked up and we'll show you another nine you threw away'. IBM goes beyond just selling machines, and with its decision support tools can analyse data about a client's customers, unearthing potential opportunities.

　　　Developing a brand through adding extras to enhance consumers' perceptions of more value needs to recognize that, as value 'is in the eyes of the beholder', any extras need to be greeted with joy by consumers. Continually striving to engender repeat buying behaviour, plus a more favourable consumer disposition to a particular brand, is the goal of all marketers, but from an added value perspective this presents challenges. Repeat buying behaviour means that, as consumers experiment more, so they start to gain more confidence and their expectations rise. With repeated brand buying, what is regarded as an added value by the marketer becomes an expected necessity to consumers, who start to take it for granted. The implication of this is that marketers should continually strive to add further

with repeated brand buying, what is regarded as an added value by the marketer becomes an expected necessity to consumers, who start to take it for granted value. The second issue is that any added value is judged by the consumer *relative* to competing brands. It therefore behoves the marketer to track their competitors' strategies. An interesting example of this is the development of Club Class by P&O European Ferries around the time of train services starting between England and France through the Channel Tunnel.

There are different interpretations about the meaning of added value. The perspective we have reviewed so far relates to added value in terms of providing extra benefits beyond the basic level. In some cases the consumer may not be fully aware of the extra benefits in-

The Boeing 777 can fly farther nonstop than any jetliner in its class. An impressive fact that assures your precious time is only spent getting to where you're going. (Not waiting wearily for a connecting flight.) But the perks of flying on a 777 don't end with the respect it shows for your schedule.

Exhibit 9.1   *Boeing 777 is promoted with its added value of flying longer distances without having to refuel in addition to its roomy cabin (reproduced by kind permission of The Boeing Company)*

cluded when buying the brand. For example, when signing up for an American Express card members are aware of the associated back-up services, but not their detail. American Express play on this in their advertisements showing examples of how their service representatives have responded to members' requests for assistance with stories such as getting an important drug to a member in Eastern Europe and battling against floods to get replacement travellers' cheques and a passport to a stranded member.

Another interpretation takes a slightly different slant, considering added value as being a feeling consumers have that the brand

Stretch out. Stroll around. The 777's cabin is wider and gives you more shoulder and head room than competing airplanes. So, next time you find yourself booked on a 777, remember these two rather pleasant certainties: You can reach your destination with no stops and you're bound to enjoy the ride.

Exhibit 9.1 *continued*

offers more than competitors, regardless of whether the feeling is based on a real or perceived issue. This consumer-focused interpretation draws to our attention the importance of consumers' perceptions. Thus while two financial advisers working for the same consultancy have the same technical knowledge about financial services, a high net worth consumer may prefer to deal with one of these advisers primarily because he or she feels, due to the way they get on with one of the advisers, that this adviser goes beyond their expectations to provide an outstanding service. A further implication from this interpretation is that it recognizes the way that brand personality and reputation are sources of added value. An interesting discussion of types of added values which adhere to this interpretation is provided by Jones (1986), an American professor. For example, there are added values which

added value as being a feeling consumers have that the brand offers more than competitors, regardless of whether the feeling is based on a real or perceived issue

- come from experience of the brand, due to factors such as familiarity or reputation or personality;
- come from the sorts of people using the brand;
- come from beliefs that the brand is effective, as is the case with cosmetics;
- come from the appearance of the brand or its distinctive packaging.

Another interpretation of added value blends both the consumer and managerial perspective, regarding it as satisfying consumers' needs better than competitors at an attractive price. Adding extra benefits to a brand results in extra costs and this perspective is concerned with ensuring that consumers are prepared to pay a greater premium than the cost of adding such benefits. One of the problems managers face when following this perspective is that they over-engineer the brand with non-relevant consumer benefits and the price consumers perceive to be a fair representation of its value is lower than the economic costs of developing it.

We explore later in this chapter formal models that enable managers to identify ways of adding value. However, what should not be overlooked is the fact that each department in a firm contributes to building a brand's added values and managers from different departments therefore need to be aware, and understand, how as a *total system* they all contribute to adding value. A classic problem occurred in one firm which attempted to position itself as adding value through excellent service. When any of its clients reported a product failure, an engineer was on-site within a few hours. Having diagnosed the fault, the engineer then contacted the warehouse parts staff to order a replacement part. But this was where the problem arose – the engineer spoke in terms of engineering parts, while the warehouse staff spoke about part numbers. Until a common com-

the
"how to make
every customer
feel like your
only customer"
solution

Have you ever phoned your own company, pretending to be a customer? It's an illuminating experience. Did they understand your problems or were you merely "processed"? Most importantly, did the person who answered have the power to help you? If your answer is no, then read on.

Yes, we can do that for you right now.

Our experts can set up systems that link your people to customer records, company information and powerful datamining tools. Instead of being passive message takers, they'll be able to make on-the-spot decisions based on all the facts necessary.

Fewer walls, more sales.

Actually, 95% of dissatisfied customers will return if they feel that you dealt well with their complaints. In other words, people will forgive almost anything if they get great service. Want to impress your customers? Become one of ours. Visit us at www.ibminfo.com/uk3/ or call us on 0800 675 675 (quoting STIT 1)

IBM

Solutions for a small planet

Exhibit 9.2 *IBM seeks to add value by providing services that help its customers add value to their consumers (reproduced by kind permission of IBM UK Ltd and Ogilvie and Mather)*

munication protocol was agreed, inefficiencies arose from the warehouse staff dispatching incorrect parts.

Noticeably different, relevant and welcomed added values

The conveyancing solicitor who publicizes the fact that his clerk drives papers round to clients' homes is more likely to win in the commodity conveyancing market than the undifferentiated firm of solicitors which tries to negotiate lower priced conveyancing. The winner in the commodity car hire market is the firm which can deliver the car the night before it is needed for a very long journey. The hire cars from competing firms may well be replaced every six months, but ultimately it is the smile, civility and genuine personal concern that often prove to be the real discriminators that make some firms more successful than others. These added values contribute to the brand's success because they make these two firms noticeably different on attributes that are customer-relevant and welcomed.

To be successful, it is crucial for firms to have a very clear view about precisely what added values their brands offer as well as understanding the relevance of these added values to consumers. A kitchen kits sales director perceived his brands as having the added value of 'quality'. The problem was that many of the competitors also saw quality as *their* added value. When forced to define more precisely what he meant by 'quality', he spoke about the kits not breaking when the flat packs were dropped from a height of 5 m! But, as consumers are hardly likely to test the durability of their kitchens in this manner, and are more concerned about designs, types of fascias, dimensions and delivery times, this is hardly likely to be relevant. In other words, little thought had been given to identifying *relevant* added values and his brands were not being marketed with a point of differentiation that was relevant to the consumer. Consequently, their long-term future was at risk.

Once there is a clear internal appreciation about the brand's added values, a holistic strategy then needs to be developed, integrating the added values into every part of the value chain. For example, the added value of reliability in a new brand of testing equipment starts by having good quality components and stringent testing procedures at every stage of production. This is followed through by having everyone who works on the brand committed to satisfying this goal. This means that if the testing equipment does fail in the customer's factory, there is a facility to provide a rapid temporary replacement while the instrument is being repaired. This enables the firm's brands to be differentiated from those of their competitors by positioning them in such a way that their added values are clearly appreciated.

To succeed, a holistic approach is needed when developing a brand's added values, which would need to be recognized as:

to succeed, a
holistic approach
is needed when
developing a
brand's added
values

- being **differentiated** from competition in such a way that the name is instantly associated with specific added values, as is the case of Nike sports gear, urging consumers not to be con-

17% OF TRAVELLERS WILL FORGET SOMETHING ANYWAY.

No matter how you pack, there's often that small but essential item that gets left behind. Like a toothbrush, a comb or a razor. That's why at Holiday Inns we provide those items we know our guests most often forget.

We call it our "Forget Something?" programme. It's just a small example of our big commitment to service. So next time you travel, why not give us a call? And take a load off your mind.

STAY WITH SOMEONE WHO REALLY KNOWS YOU. ❋ *Holiday Inn*®

FOR RESERVATIONS CALL LONDON (071) 722 77 55 OR YOUR TRAVEL AGENT

Exhibit 9.3 *The forgetful traveller may no doubt perceive Holiday Inn's 'Forget Something?' programme as being a welcome added value*

tent with being second but rather to aim to win, inspired by the
Greek goddess of victory after whom the brand has been named;

- having added values which don't just satisfy **functional** needs
  but also meet **emotional** needs. For example, the RAC do not
  provide only the added value of speedy roadside repairs, but
  also combine it with allaying anxiety;
- being perceived as a **low-risk** purchase, for example through
  the endorsement from Richard Branson's name on Virgin PEPs;
- making purchasing easy through being presented as an effective **shorthand** device;
- being backed by a registered trademark, **legally guaranteeing**
  a specific standard of consistency.

In other words, successful brands do not stress just one part of the
brand asset. They blend all of these components together. Furthermore, they ensure that a coherent approach is adopted, with each
component reinforcing the others.

Brands succeed because they have clearly-defined added values which match consumer needs at a particular point in time. In
Russia and China, where manufacturers' brands can take advantage
of significant market opportunities, success will probably be linked
to the way that West European brands will be repositioned to reflect
consumer needs. For example, brands of washing powder positioned
as being environmentally friendly, with bio-degradable packs, may
not be as well received as brands much more in tune with the evolving market needs to wash different types of fabrics together and to
leave the washing soft and fresh.

While these points show the need to use as many elements of a
brand's assets as possible when adding value, a consideration of some
branding approaches in our sophisticated society shows an excessive reliance on only a few or, worse still, just one component of the
brand. The most frequent branding error appears to be an undue
emphasis on using the brand name purely as a differentiating device. For example, John Cleese, in an Australian advertisement for
Planters Pretzels, does little more than introduce a group of dancers
to chant the brand's name. The advertisement is shot against a white
set and no clues are presented about what, or who, the brand represents. Tacking a name on a pack, and saying it as many times as
possible in advertisements, does little more than create initial interest. It is often quickly forgotten. Consumers look to brands as problem
solvers and in so doing need to be able to associate instantly a brand
name and a specific added value. Incantations, such as those referred
to in the Planters case, which do not facilitate associations of added
values with specific brands, can actually hinder marketing programmes.

We can draw on the work of Interbrand to appreciate how the values added to brands work together to build brands. Value is added to brands through superior technology or superior systems to give **functional** values beyond those of competitors. The problem is that competitors can emulate these. Just consider the race Intel finds itself in as it continually develops more powerful computer chips. **Expressive** values can be added to brands, enabling consumers to make statements about themselves which more clearly express aspects of their individual personality. For example, confident about Levi's functional values of toughness and authenticity, a considerable investment in advertising this brand has added expressive values such as being individualistic, freedom-loving, rebellious and, some groups might argue, sexy. The Apple Mac user may well appreciate this brand's expressive values of creativity and being personable. **Central** values can also be added to a brand, showing what the soul of the brand is. These values make it clear what the brand believes in and represent deeply-held philosophical, ethical, political and nationalistic beliefs. In the case of Nike, consumers are buying into the central value of irreverence.

Gluing together and harmonizing these three types of values, which have been added to the brand, is the brand's **vision**. The vision represents a view about how consumers can become closer to the brand, almost to the extent of the brand making the world a better place. When thinking about the Apple Computer Company's vision of man not being subservient to machines, it becomes easier to appreciate how software and hardware engineers have jointly developed easy to use functional benefits, enabling consumers to display something about their own creativity.

Identifying added values

When faced with the need to find a removal company, the home-owner may initially perceive very little difference between removers. However, when a few firms are asked to give quotations, differences start to become apparent. There are those estimators who can call at a time convenient to the homeowner, while others cannot be definite. Some will appear with a brochure describing their firms' capabilities and provide advice on how to minimize packing effort. Others will wander round the house, making comments about the difficulty of having spiral staircases and the irritation of having to wait for the key to the new home to be released. In other words, while the basic service is akin to an undifferentiated commodity, the way that it is offered is recognized by consumers as having added values superior to competitors.

By recognizing that buyers in consumer, service and industrial

buyers regard
products and
services as clusters
of value
satisfactions
markets regard products and services as clusters of value satisfactions, marketers can start to differentiate their brands by developing relevant added values. For example, removal firms can differentiate themselves by adding values such as responsiveness to unusual handling requests, politeness, the confidence they give homeowners through the care they take when packing, reliability and the guarantees they offer. All of these features present opportunities for differentiation.

As a further example, many would argue that the salt market comes close to being a commodity market, yet Reichenhaller refused to accept this and marketed its brands of salt in order to satisfy consumers' needs for either health or flavour. For example, for health-conscious consumers they launched Alpine Light Salt (sodium reduced) and No Salt (salt-free flavouring); for consumers looking for new flavours, they developed Alpine Salt With Herbs, Alpine Salt for Meat & Poultry and Alpine Salt for Fish & Vegetables.

The model in Figure 9.1 is a helpful conceptualization of the way in which further value can be incorporated into brands to satisfy consumers' needs.

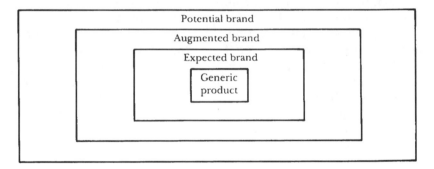

Figure 9.1   *The four levels of a brand (after Levitt 1980)*

The generic level

At its most basic, there is the **generic** product or service functionality, that enables firms to be in the market. For example, the cars produced by Ford, Vauxhall and Toyota; the home loans advanced by the Abbey National and Halifax; the computers from IBM, Dell and Fujitsu. At this level, it is relatively easy for competitors to develop 'me-too' versions – just think how many manufacturers produce a small, hatchback town car. In developed countries, the generic product or service funtionality is rarely the basis for sustaining brands since functional values can be emulated.

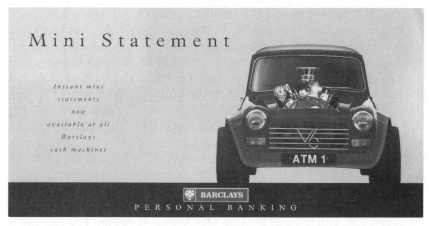

Exhibit 9.4   *Barclays have augmented their Barclays Personal Banking brand through making account statements available at Barclays cash machines (reproduced by kind permission of Barclays Bank plc)*

The expected level

Buyers and users have a perception about the minimum characteristics that differentiate competing brands in the same product field and value can be added by going just beyond this. At the **expected** level products and services are made to satisfy purchasers' minimum requirements for attributes such as name, packaging, design, availability, price, quantity and so on.

One of the most helpful ways of identifying what these characteristics should be is through depth interviews with buyers and users.

The expected level of brand competition is typically seen when buyers do not have much experience of competing brands. In such cases, they look at product attributes to assess how well different brands will satisfy their motivational needs. For example, some of the motivating reasons for having a hot drink are relaxation (Ovaltine), energy (Cadbury's Chocolate Break), stimulation (Nescafé coffee) and warmth (Bovril). Buyers consult the brand names, the packaging details, price and promotional details to form an overall assessment of the extent to which competing brands may satisfy different motivational needs. At an early stage in any market's development, it is unlikely that several brands will be perceived as being equally able to satisfy the same motivational need. The added values here again tend to be functional characteristics, reinforcing the positioning of what the brand *does*.

The augmented level

With more experience buyers become more confident and experiment with other brands, seeking the best value, and they begin to pay more attention to price. To maintain customer loyalty and price premiums, marketers **augment** their brands through the addition of further benefits, such as, for example, the inclusion of a self-diagnostic fault chip in washing machines. The chip was something that a less-experienced user might perceive as having minimal value, but as they become more dependent on the brand so they learn to appreciate the way it reduces delays by the service engineer arriving with the right spare part. To assess what types of added values would enhance their brands at this stage, marketers should arrange for depth interviews to be undertaken amongst experienced users. They should be asked to talk about the problems they have with different brands and the sorts of ways in which they could be improved.

At the augmented stage, several brands may well come to be perceived as satisfying the same motivational needs. For example, Heineken, Skol and Carling Black Label all offer refreshment. So consumers focus on the **discriminating factors**. These may be functional features such as size, shape, colour and availability, or emotional ones reflecting different brand personalities. Several different ways of positioning brands using functional discriminators are:

- with respect to use – 'once a day' for a pharmaceutical brand;
- with respect to the end user – Calpol for children, Asprin for adults;
- with respect to the competitor – the number two brand, Avis, trying to take share from Hertz, the brand leader through its campaign 'we try harder';
- with respect to a specific attribute – the long life of Duracell Batteries.

possibly an even
more powerful
discriminator is
endowing the
brand with a
personality

Possibly an even more powerful discriminator is endowing the brand with a personality. Both Ford and Renault produce similar hatchbacks, which satisfy the motivational need for cost-effective town transport, but they also have unique brand personalities that differentiate them. For example, some might perceive the personality of the Ford Fiesta as a male, not very ambitious, but conscientious and hard-working and who plays football on Saturdays. By contrast, the Renault may be a trendy, young girl who enjoys being surrounded by people, likes to make decisions on the spur of the moment and reads *Cosmopolitan*.

In effect, at the *augmented* stage, buyers have narrowed down the list of suitable brands by considering those which match their *motivational* needs, then they differentiate between these brands on the basis of *discriminators* relevant to their particular lifestyles.

The potential level

Eventually, however, buyers and users come to regard such augmentation as a standard requirement for brands. To stop the augmented brand slipping back to the expected level, where buyers would be

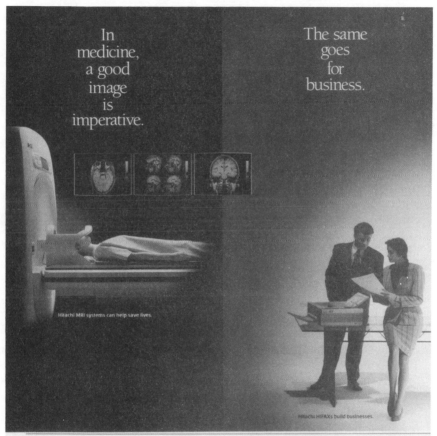

In medicine, a good image is imperative.

The same goes for business.

Hitachi MRI systems can help save lives.

Hitachi HIFAXs build businesses.

Many people think of Hitachi as a consumer electronics company. Which is true – to a point. We're also a technological leader in medicine. Business equipment. Science. Industry. Computers. Our 20,000 products include everything from TVs to image processing equipment. Such as facsimile machines and magnetic resonance imaging (MRI) systems.

Take MRI. It's the most significant advancement in diagnostic imaging since the X-ray. MRI enables doctors to detect problems early

©1991 Hitachi, Ltd. Tokyo, Japan. All rights reserved.

on and to make more accurate diagnoses.

Hitachi is a world leader in high-resolution, compact MRI equipment. What's remarkable, however, is that MRI equipment only begins to tell the story of our commitment to medicine. Our involvement encompasses clinical analysers. Electron microscopes. X-ray CT scanners. And ultrasound equipment.

Chances are you already use Hitachi facsimile machines. You'd be in good company. Our unique technological advancements enable

business people to quickly and efficiently transmit super clear images. Even very small characters come out with a remarkable high degree of precision.

Taken together, Hitachi is a people company. Responding to the wants and needs of individuals everywhere.

And that's not an advertising image. That's a fact.

◉ HITACHI

Exhibit 9.5   *Hitachi promotes itself at the potential level as the firm that has extremely broad experience of displaying high quality images*

more interested in prices, the brand marketer needs to become more innovative and develop new added values to push the brand into the **potential** phase.

This is a much more challenging task, inhibited predominantly by the creativity of the brand's team and their financial resources. One way of identifying new added values for these highly experienced buyers is to map out the channels through which the brand passes, from manufacturer to end user. At each stage in this chain of events, the brand marketer needs to appreciate exactly how the brand is used and who is using it. A sample of those individuals coming in contact with the brand should be interviewed to assess their likes, dislikes and views about improvements. The opinions of factory floor workers are just as important as those of senior managers in the chain of events.

An example of a brand that was managed from the **augmented** to the **potential** level is American Airlines (AA). With deregulation in the American air travel market, the barriers to entry for new airlines were lowered. This resulted in new airlines increasing travellers' choice, along with more price competitive routes. As a brand, AA could have slipped to the expected level, competing against the others on price. Instead, it evaluated how people used its services and identified every point where it came into contact with customers. Based on this, it identified a few areas where it believed customers and consumers would welcome new added values. It undertook a review of its in-flight service and improved its quality. It recognized the need for being on time, both when departing and arriving, and, by assessing all of the events that influence flight operations, developed systems which resulted in it becoming the most punctual airline. The problem of over-booked seats was lessened through better information technology. They also developed far stronger relationships with travel agents, who were previously regarded as an evil necessity. A computerized booking system, Sabre, was specially developed for them. This automated the booking of tickets. Through the use of its frequent flyer card, AA was able to understand the needs of its consumers more clearly and develop more tailored services for them. Finally, it communicated all of these added values to its customers and consumers.

In the mature tea market, Tetley managed to push its brand to the potential level when in 1989 it launched round tea bags. Both Tetley and the brand leader, PG Tips, are of an equally high quality, both being based on approximately 25 blends of tea. Previous marketing activity had been directed at satisfying consumers' motivational needs by differentiating brands along dimensions such as their ability to restore, revive and refresh. But, in addition to these functional characteristics, consumers also see teas as satisfying emotional needs through being comforting and soothing. It was the emotional needs that Tetley concentrated on. They discovered that consumers actually felt that round tea bags were more appropriate emotional satisfiers, besides which they overcome the problem of square bags – dripping from the edges! Cynics were critical, arguing that large teabags facilitate infusion by allowing the tea to circulate. However, the change, supported by a £4.9 m press and television campaign during 1990, helped the brand increase its market share by 25 per cent.

Eventually, competitors will follow with similar ideas and buyers will gain more confidence, switching between brands that they perceive as being similar. Yet again, the brand may slip back to the expected level unless the brand marketer recognizes that he must continually track buyers' views and be prepared to keep on improving his brand.

The problem with continually enhancing the brand is that a point may be reached at which the extra costs may not be recovered through increased sales and competitors may soon find ways of copying the change. In such cases, an audit needs to be undertaken to evaluate whether the brand has a viable future. The audit needs to look at consumers' views, competitors' activities and the firm's long-term goals. If it is not thought viable to enhance the brand further, a different strategy for its future needs to be identified. This could entail selling the brand off, freezing further investment and reaping profits until a critical sales level had been reached, withdrawing the brand or becoming an own label supplier if there is sufficient trade interest.

the problem with continually enhancing the brand is that a point may be reached at which the extra costs may not be recovered through increased sales

The problem of competitors copying a brand's added value can be better analysed if we consider the 'coding' or the building blocks that constitute the brand and its added values. For example, a restaurant owner may find that his restaurant is so successful that he wishes to open a second one and let one of his managers run it. To ensure that the new manager is effective, the owner needs to reveal all the codes that constitute the successful formula. On the other hand, he may wish to hold something back, for fear of the manager leaving with the formula, or of competitors copying it. Researchers have argued that successful brands are difficult to copy even if the nature of all the component parts are well understood, as long as secrecy is maintained about the manner in which these components are integrated. As a result of this, the owner could explain to the manager all the systems that support the restaurant, such as types of menu, the pricing policy, staff recruitment, and so on. He need not insist on always being consulted when decisions are necessary on operational issues. But the development of the restaurant's image or brand personality should be the sole responsibility of the owner. The brand personality is the unifying device that integrates the component parts and it is this that competitors find difficult to copy.

The previous four-level model can be applied to both product and service markets. Grönroos (1990) has developed a more refined version specifically for service markets, as shown in Figure 9.2.

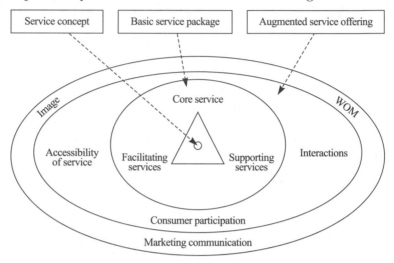

Figure 9.2   *The service offering (adapted, after Grönroos 1990)*

Grönroos' model shows the different levels on which the service can be offered. Managing the service offering requires the development of:

- a **service concept** – the company's intention and mission for being in the business;
- a **basic service package** to fulfil customer needs – the core, facilitating and supporting services;
- an **augmented service offering** – the processes and interactions between the company and its customers for the production and delivery of the service;
- a system to manage **image** and **communication** so as to enhance the perception of the augmented service offering.

In the **basic service package** the core service clarifies the main benefit being offered. For example, a hotel's core service could be lodging as opposed to catering for conferences and business meetings. Facilitating services make it possible for customers to use the core service. For instance, customers need an efficient and friendly clerk at the hotel reception or at the airport check-in desk. Supporting services can be used to increase the value of the core service. Examples are the provision of shampoos and hair-dryers in hotel rooms, and meals served at the airport lounge instead of on the air-

in the basic service package the core service clarifies the main benefit being offered

craft which allows business travellers to rest during intercontinental flights.

In the **augmented service offering** the accessibility of service depends on the number of employees and their skills, the office hours, the locations and the ease of use for consumers, all of which provide ways to add further value. Designing new, valuable systems to increase the accessibility of service is not sufficient if employees are not trained to implement or to use them. It is useless for intercontinental airline passengers to wear eye-masks with the label 'do not disturb', if the cabin staff still wake them up to serve the meal. Interactions with the service firm take several forms, all of which offer value-adding opportunities:

- interactive communication between employees and customers – how they behave towards each other;
- consumers' interactions with physical resources – vending machines, till machines, documentation;

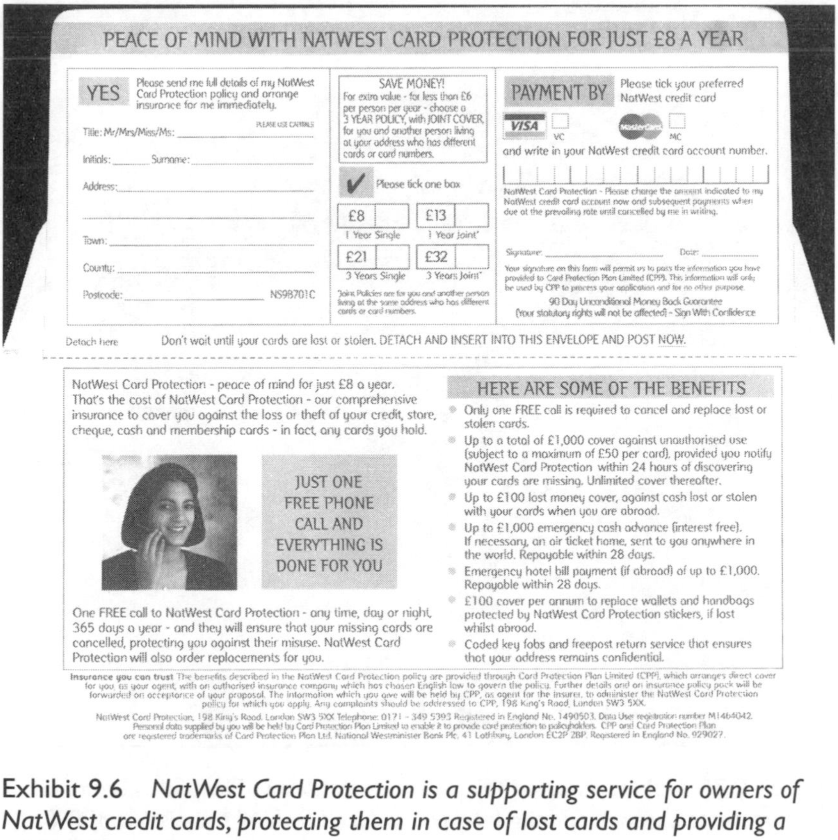

Exhibit 9.6 *NatWest Card Protection is a supporting service for owners of NatWest credit cards, protecting them in case of lost cards and providing a rapid replacement service*

- consumers' interactions with systems, such as waiting, delivery and billing systems;
- consumers' interactions with other customers involved in the process.

The correct type of customer participation is fundamental when striving to enhance the service brand. For example, at a private clinic the patient's ability to describe their symptoms correctly influences the doctor's ability to diagnose and cure their illness.

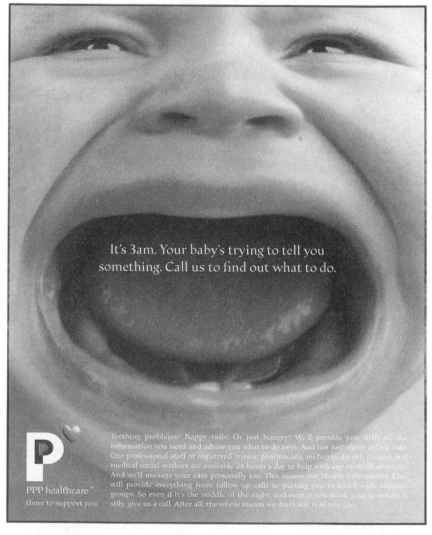

Exhibit 9.7 *PPP Healthcare major upon accessibility of helpful information at the augmented service offering level (reproduced by kind permission of PPP Healthcare)*

Using vibrant advertising creates an identity for the service brand and the resulting **image** perceived by consumers will either enhance or diminish their perception about the likely services. As they experience the brand, so they will talk to others and will start to affect their views about the service. Effective brand management should capitalize on these opportunities.

Adding value through consumer participation

In the traditional view about value creation, a firm adds value to the inputs received from its suppliers and passes them on to its customers. This approach is based on the notion that a firm 'does things' to its customers, either to another firm or to the final consumers, who are passive receptors. Within this context, the firm's strategy is based on finding the right positioning within the value chain.

A new view of value creation is evolving, whereby consumers are regarded as being actively involved in creating value and added values can be jointly tailored more closely to their needs. Normann and Ramirez (1993) proposed this new perspective, by which firms do not just add value, but rather reinvent it. This strategy focuses on a value-creating system in which economic actors (suppliers, firms, consumers) work together to co-produce value. Managers' key strategic task is to reconfigure the roles and relationships among all the actors in the value-creating system.

a new view of value creation is evolving, whereby consumers are regarded as being actively involved in creating value and added values can be jointly tailored more closely

A good example of value creation according to this view is provided by IKEA, the home furnishing retailer. The key elements of IKEA's formula are: simple, high-quality Scandinavian designs; global sourcing of components; customer kits which are easy to assemble; and huge suburban stores. The result is products offered at prices 25 per cent lower than the competition. However, IKEA's real innovation is the redefinition of actors' roles and organizational practices. This company has invented value by matching the capabilities of participants more efficiently and effectively.

IKEA involves customers in the selection, transportation and assembly of its products and designs its business system to support them. For example, clear catalogues explaining each actor's role, stores developed as family-outing destinations, measuring aids at the front door (catalogues, pens, paper, tape measures), product groupings to offer designs for living rather than the traditional product groupings, detailed labels on each item, and car roof-racks for hire or sale.

IKEA helps customers to create and then consume value. It does not aim to relieve customers of their tasks, but rather to mobilize them to do tasks never done before. With the same purpose of creating value, IKEA mobilizes 1800 suppliers around the world, chosen for their ability to offer good quality at low-cost. A chair, for example, is assembled with a Polish seat, French legs and Spanish screws! All parts are ordered electronically with EPOS systems and the warehouse functions as a logistics control point, consolidation centre and transit hub.

In this new logic of value creation, roles and relationships are redefined and the distinction between products and services disappears. A visit to an IKEA store is not just shopping, but also entertainment. The new value is more 'dense' insofar as more information and knowledge is provided with each product to allow the appropriate actors to create their own value. There are three strategic implications from this. First, the firm must be able to mobilize customers to take advantage of the 'denser' value and help them create value for themselves. Secondly, the firm can rarely provide everything by itself and should therefore aim to develop relationships with all actors. Thirdly, it can achieve competitive advantage from reconceiving the value chain as a value-creating system.

The case of Danish pharmacies illustrates that to re-invent value successfully, an organization needs to address all the actors involved. In the 1980s deregulation of the state health care allowed the Danish Pharmaceutical Association to reposition its business as a comprehensive source of health care information and services as well as supplying a wider range of pharmaceutical products. Although DPA redesigned an efficient business system and developed 'denser' offerings, its customers, doctors, hospitals and patients, regarded this innovation with suspicion and resistance. Eventually success came when the association reconsidered its partners in their respective corporate environments and built alliances with the various stakeholders.

Some brands already build on the opportunity of adding value through active participation. Unlike other makers of anti-wrinkle creams, Cheesebrough Ponds actively involves customers by providing a transparency stick to enable them to measure the dryness of their skin over time. Likewise, Miracle Whip Mayonnaise invites customers to send recipes and prints them in a quarterly newsletter. Consumers can also actively add value in service brands. They are not necessarily passive receptors of the service, but can actively perform what is required to satisfy their needs – preparing their own salad in a restaurant as opposed to being served by a waiter, or taking their own pictures of Paris instead of buying an illustrated book. In this case the producer of the service is the consumer termed the **prosumer**. In the traditional view, companies focus on *relieving* the customers of certain functions and activities, such as providing a house cleaning service. The new view shows companies targeting prosumers focusing on *enabling* them to perform particular activities. In the case of house cleaning, the enablers would be vacuum cleaners. The following equation (Michel 1996) shows how firms can add value to customers by either concentrating on supplying them with a 'reliever' or encouraging them to buy an 'enabler' and perform the activity themselves, at a time and in a way that best suits them.

$$\text{Reliever} = \text{Enabler} + \text{Prosumer}$$

There are several reasons for prosuming. It is cost effective and can save consumers time, for example using an ATM rather than queuing in a bank. More importantly, it allows consumers to control the timing, duration and pace of their own activities and by being more involved they are more likely to show higher satisfaction levels.

Adding value through customization

Companies can adapt each of their products and services to suit each individual customer's unique needs, but while this adds value it is likely to be uneconomic. Instead, a smaller variety of customized brands can be offered to different groups of customers. Using traditional segmentation variables may still result in customers in the same segment showing differences, since each one of them is in a different market, at different times, in different places. Just think of passengers flying in business class: are they travelling for business or leisure? If they are flying on business, will they have the same refreshment needs going out to their meeting (e.g. Coca-Cola, Schweppes Tonic) as when they return (for example, Bacardi and Coke, Gordon's Gin and Schweppes Tonic)? The challenge managers face is getting the right balance between adding value through a small or large degree of customization and the payback they can expect from consumers trading off extra benefits against higher costs.

the challenge is getting the right balance between adding value through a small or large degree of customization and the payback

To help managers appreciate alternative ways of customizing their brand, Gilmore and Pine (1997) have devised a useful two-dimensional matrix (shown in Figure 9.3) whereby standardized or adapted forms of the product can either be presented or portrayed in a standardized or adapted format according to four customer types. We are all aware of examples of ways of changing product forms, and additionally this matrix brings out the need to consider changing the product's representation through aspects such as its packaging, name, terms and conditions, promotional material, distribution and merchandising. From this matrix, they identify four approaches to customization – collaborative, adaptive, cosmetic and transparent.

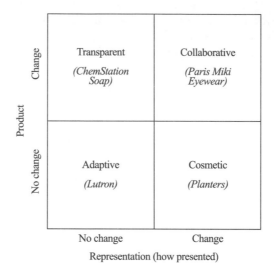

Figure 9.3   *Approaches to customization (after Gilmore and Pine 1997)*

Collaborative customizers conduct a dialogue with individual customers at the design stage to help them describe their needs and identify the best solution. The Japanese eye-wear retailer Paris Miki spends time understanding how consumers would like to look, then produces a digital picture of the consumer's face and within minutes the consumer can see how their face appears with lenses of different shape and size. Consumer and optician jointly adjust the shape and size of lenses and the type of bridges and hinges until both are pleased with the final result. A technician then grinds the lenses and builds the glasses within an hour. There is a high degree of collaboration to tailor the product and its presentation.

Transparent customizers provide products and services unique to each customer without letting them know explicitly that they have been customized. This approach is the most appropriate when customers' needs are predictable or can be easily forecast and saves repeatedly asking customers about their reorder quantities. ChemStation supplies industrial soaps and, after analysing the usage patterns of each of its customers, provides them with the most appropriate formulation in the quantity and frequency of delivery best suited. Customers do not have to reorder or specify the desired characteristics. This type of customization depends on having a good system for collecting data on individual customers and a flexible design and delivery system.

Adaptive customizers offer one standard product designed so that users can customize it themselves. The lighting systems made by Lutron Electronics allow users to programme different lighting effects for their rooms to match particular occasions, such as romantic moments or lively parties or time spent reading. The aim with this type of customization is to transfer to consumers the ability to design and use the product or service in a way that best suits them.

Cosmetic customizers present standard products differently to different customers by changing only the package and not the product itself. The Planters Company provides different retailers with peanuts packaged in different sizes, labels and containers according to their preferences. This type of customization is appropriate when the standard product satisfies almost all customers and only the presentation needs changing.

The previous four examples show how companies gained a competitive advantage by selecting the most suitable stage during which customers value an individual approach: Paris Miki customizes during the design stage, Planters during the packaging, ChemStation during both production and delivery, and Lutron lets customers do the customizing

Adding value through building relationships

As the previous sections indicate, adding value can be achieved through a variety of ways. In today's world where firms strive to build stronger relationships with customers, adding more value to the generic offering should increase customer satisfaction and more strongly bond the customer link. By delving into the pricing literature, another view on the concept of value emerges, as the ratio of perceived benefits relative to perceived costs (financial as well as non-financial). From this ratio it is apparent that brands can be perceived to have even more value when either more has been added (as has been addressed so far in this chapter) or when customers experience less cost. Thus, if the essence of the brand's benefits is not changed but costs are lowered (by, for example, reducing the ticket price, or widening distribution thereby reducing search costs, or having a famous celebrity endorse the brand thereby reducing uncertainty) customers should perceive lower costs and therefore greater added value.

brands can be perceived to have even more value when customers experience less cost

A consumer's perceptions of value are time and place specific. For example, a teenager perceives value from their Swatch because of its accuracy, but when with a group of friends perceives even more value because of its noticeably attractive design. Furthermore, as the teenager wears the watch over a number of years, they begin to form a closer relationship with Swatch. Thus, as Ravald and Grönroos (1996) would argue, we need to have an expanded concept of value, i.e.

$$\text{Total episode value} = \frac{\text{Episode benefits + relationship benefits}}{\text{Episode costs + relationship costs}}$$

If the teenager values the relationship with Swatch and is committed to its brands, they are more likely to tolerate the occasional episode problem, such as a broken strap. Positive episodes build consumers' perceptions of the brand's credibility, increase the total value of the relationship and enhance the total episode value.

When consumers judge a single episode, they consider factors such as superior product quality and supporting services. On the other hand, when they reflect on the value of the entire relationship, they normally consider whether the supplier has offered them safety, credibility and continuity. Figure 9.4 shows how the perceived value can be increased both on an episode level and on a relationship level.

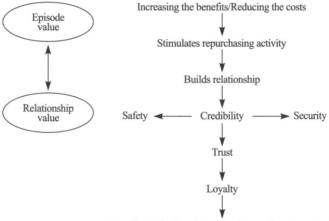

Figure 9.4   *The effect of value-adding strategies in a long-term relationship (after Ravald and Grönroos 1996)*

Often, added value is considered in terms of the extra benefits that augment the offering, but less thought is given to devising ways of reducing consumers' costs. When a customer selects a new supplier offering a better product at a lower price than competitors, the supplier needs to work on each episode in order to build the relationship by addressing ways of reducing the customer's costs. For example, providing on-time delivery and invoicing accurately reduces the user's costs, which, along with other benefits, contributes to building a cost-effective relationship.

Protecting brands through trademark registration

By blending all of the assets constituting brands, marketers are able to develop brands which build goodwill between the brand producer and the consumer. As one advertising executive at Saatchi & Saatchi commented, 'Powerful brands are just like families. They persist through thick and thin'. The goodwill that Coca-Cola has built up over the years is such a valuable asset that if all its production facilities were destroyed it could get adequate funds to rebuild them using the goodwill from the brand name as security. Likewise, even though Mars Confectionery does not own property, hires its distribution vehicles and leases its machinery, it would cost any potential acquirer hundreds of millions of pounds to buy this firm, since what is being bought is not the tangible assets, but the goodwill and reputation from the Mars name.

Unfortunately, the success of some brands has driven certain competitors to respond by developing counterfeits, that is to say, illegally-produced look-alikes, which take advantage of the inherent goodwill in brand names. It has been estimated by the Counterfeiting Intelligence Bureau that in 1995 fakes accounted for 5 per cent of world trade, and they have cost brand manufacturers in Europe approximately 100 000 jobs. Some markets are particularly prone to illegal imitators. For example, 60 per cent of software in Western Europe, 35 per cent of video cassettes in Asia and 25 per cent of audio tapes worldwide are unauthorized copies.

success of some brands has driven certain competitors to respond by developing counterfeits

Some counterfeiters have invested heavily in production facilities. When Yves Saint Laurent unearthed one illegal copier and destroyed £11 m of fake perfumes, they found production machinery valued at £33 m. Unfortunately, with such large sums to be made from counterfeiting, more sophisticated production facilities are being built. Glaxo, for example, once seized a consignment of 6000 counterfeit packets of Zantac and were dismayed to discover that the packaging was so professionally copied that only under microscopes could any differences be noticed.

To reduce the scope for counterfeiters, marketers can register their trademarks, employ firms to track down copiers and devise more sophisticated packaging and batch-numbering processes. All of these enable brand owners to halt counterfeiters legally – until they find another way of circumventing the obstacles!

Marketers in the UK can protect their brands under the Trademarks Act (1994), which follows the EC Trademark Directive intended to harmonize trademark laws throughout the European Union. The Act makes it easier for trademark owners to register and protect their marks more efficiently. It also ensures that trademarks have the same rights and test for validity everywhere in the Single Market. Moreover, the Act broadens the scope for what can be registered as a trademark. Previously only words, logos, symbols and labels were eligible. Now potentially any sign may be registered that can be reproduced in some graphic form or appears distinctive, as well as music, jingles, smells, and three-dimensional shapes such as the traditional Coca-Cola bottle. If the registration process is followed, greater legal protection is offered.

Trademark registration can be professionally expedited using trademark agents. They would first check if anyone else has registered a particular trademark, avoiding expensive and embarrassing litigation.

Anyone in the UK can submit an application for the registration of a trademark or a service mark. These applications are examined in the Trademarks Registry of the Patent Office to see whether the goods and services proposed are eligible for registration. There are a variety of reasons why some brand names cannot be registered. For example, it is prohibited to register brand names that are descriptive of the character or quality of the goods and which other traders or businesses may legitimately wish to use in relation to their own goods or services. Furthermore, names that are generic, deceptive, disparaging, confusing or conflicting with others, cannot be registered. When evaluating new brand names, legal advice has to be balanced against marketing needs. For example, lawyers argue that firms' existing trademarks are the most protectable legal option. When IBM first entered the personal computer market, it did not develop a new brand name. Instead, it launched the 'IBM PC'. Not only did it have sound legal protection, but also it deliberately wanted to take advantage of its image as being the most dependable computer manufacturer. In IBM's case, there was little danger of the brand's equity being diluted.

A balance also needs to be struck between the distinctiveness of the name and the extent to which it describes the goods that the brand name stands for. The more it describes the goods, the more difficult it is to register it. PaperMate is a good example of a company getting the balance right between the brand name's communicability and its suitability for registration. Late in the 1970s it launched an erasable ballpoint pen in Europe, branded Replay. This was felt not to be so descriptive of the product, and it was protectable.

Once the trademark has been successfully registered, it should be used as soon as possible and implemented with care. If sufficient attention is not paid to promotional details, there is a danger of the brand name lapsing into a non-protectable generic term. In its advertising copy, the Otis Elevator Company did not insert the line, 'Escalator is a registered trademark of the Otis Elevator Company',

balance also needs to be struck between the distinctiveness of the name and the extent to which it describes the goods that the brand name stands for and in a subsequent court case the registration of its 'Escalator' trademark was cancelled.

To ensure that the brand name is not being infringed, some firms employ their staff to monitor retail activities. For example, Coca-Cola employees visit outlets that do not stock Coca-Cola and, without identifying themselves, ask for a Coca-Cola. If they are served a drink which is clearly not Coca-Cola without any comment, a sample is sent for chemical analysis, and if it is not the actual brand, the outlet is asked to refrain from this action. Failure to comply results in legal action.

An alternative way of policing the brand is to use private investigators, such as Carratu International. Particularly when there is evidence of a very sophisticated channel being used by counterfeiters, as was the case with Caterpillar parts, this is a very effective way of blocking imitators. Some firms are now so concerned about brand infringements, that detectives and legal costs are a significant expenditure. For example, 0.5 per cent of Givenchy's turnover is spent on this.

A further route whereby brand owners can protect themselves from retailers' look-alikes is by invoking the Dispute Resolution Procedure, an advisory code developed by the Institute of Grocery Distribution in 1996. Major brand owners and retailers, such as Tesco, Sainsburys and Safeway, signed the code and agreed to call discussions at the operational or, if required, at the director level to settle disputes on look-alikes. Some brand owners, however, have questioned the validity of the code, as it only focuses on discussion and cannot prevent the launch of look-alikes.

Some firms are trying to make the copying of their brands much harder. Glaxo started printing holograms on its packets of Zantac drugs to deter copiers, but it is only a matter of time before counterfeiters become more sophisticated. In some markets, such as car parts, it is much more difficult to apply an inexpensive security device.

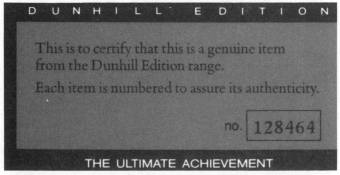

Exhibit 9.8 *The box containing Dunhill After Shave also includes a certificate of authenticity in an attempt to fight counterfeiters (reproduced by kind permission of Alfred Dunhill Ltd)*

While the Internet offers new opportunities for brands it can also create legal problems. The geographical and jurisdictional boundaries that limited the legal concept of trademarks do not apply to the global communication system of the Internet, facilitating communication among millions of independent users. These users rely entirely on their unique Internet name, i.e. their domain name, for registration and identification. Currently a user can choose any domain name, provided it has not yet been registered, almost regardless of the fact that this might be an existing brand name. A check is done to ensure that the domain name is unique but no check is done as to whether the user is entitled to use the name. For example, Harrods sued opportunists who had registered the domain of 'harrods.com' to profit from this famous brand. Fortunately the court applied existing legal rules to the Internet and ordered the user to hand over the domain name. However, companies should not merely rely on time-consuming legal measures with often unpredictable outcomes, but should proactively register their corporate and brand names as Internet addresses.

Whilst counterfeiting is likely to pose a continuing threat to manufacturers, it is only one of the many challenges that face marketers, who must continually devise added-value strategies to succeed. Some of the other challenges are reviewed in the following section.

The challenges to brands

In order to develop the right sort of brand added values, marketers need to be aware of some of the factors which can affect their future. Some of these are:

The shift from strategy to tactics

With the increasing pressure to generate ever-improving profitability, it is often considered a luxury for managers to develop long-term strategic plans. This is further exacerbated by short-term goal setting, which is frequently designed primarily for the convenience of the financial community.

short-sightedness is dangerous, since successful brands have evolved through long-term commitments to brand support

A consequence of this is that organizations adopt a 'crisis management' attitude. This short-sightedness is dangerous, since successful brands have evolved through long-term commitments to brand support. Furthermore, it illustrates a rather naive managerial style which is incapable of responding appropriately to crises.

The shift from advertising to promotions

As a consequence of the increasing pressure on brand managers to achieve short-term goals, there is a temptation to cut back on advertising support, since it is viewed as a long-term brand-building investment, in favour of promotions which generate much quicker short-term results. This can be problematic, as is best summarized by Broadbent's analogy: If a pilot cuts his plane's engines, believing it could cruise adequately without them (as indeed it would, for a while), one would question his sanity. When the plane subsequently goes into freefall and the engines are switched on, and then off again several seconds later because they were not making that much difference, he would be regarded as a suicidal maniac. Broadbent's analogy exemplifies the accepted view that advertising builds up a 'stock' of brand goodwill in consumers' minds. This takes time, however. If advertising is subsequently stopped, there may be only a small reduction in sales for several months while the stock of goodwill is depleting, but then there will be a rapid fall in sales. Furthermore, a disproportionately large spend is needed to raise a fallen brand back to its original position.

With such high advertising costs encountered in the launch of new brands, many brand marketers are questioning whether they have fully exploited the potential of their old brands before embarking on risky new brand development. There is increasing caution about new brand development. This can be appreciated from an analysis Tesco did of their top 100 lines. Only twelve of these were launched in the past ten years. Only eighteen were launched in the past twenty years. Horlicks, which was launched in 1883, is a good example of old brand development. It was originally promoted as a warming food drink to help elderly people to sleep. In the 1970s a marked reduction in sales was noted due to demographic changes, warmer homes and later eating. Rather than withdrawing the brand and following an expensive strategy of launching a new brand, Horlicks was successfully repositioned in the late 1970s to a much broader target market as the natural way to relax. Some of the many examples of successful old brand development are Equitable Life, with their focus on Personal Pensions, and Lucozade, repositioned from being a health tonic for the sick to a refreshing energizer.

On-line shopping

Current research predicts that at least 20 per cent of all trade transactions will be on-line by 2006. On-line shopping is different from traditional mail order because:

- brands are available all the time and from all over the world;

- information and interactions are in real-time;
- consumers can choose between brands which meet their criteria, as a result of selecting information which is in a much more convenient format for them, rather than the standard catalogue format.

This poses threats to brands, since some components of added value, such as the agent or the retail outlet which originally added value by matching consumers with suppliers, may well be eliminated. The brand's values will be exposed more explicitly. However, brands will still have a key role, regardless of how much on-line shopping will grow. In any kind of remote purchasing they can offer customers a guarantee of quality and service and will act as a powerful way of facilitating choice in a world of ever-increasing data.

Brand advertising on the Internet

the Web encompasses a new sales channel as well as a new form of advertising and allows new forms of customer relationship and sponsorship

Marketers face new challenges as they attempt to leverage the opportunities offered by the Internet. The Web encompasses a new sales channel as well as a new form of advertising and allows new forms of customer relationship and sponsorship. Many brand owners believe in the advertising opportunities available on the Internet. While in 1995 only \$42.9 m was spent on banner advertising on other companies' sites, Internet-based advertising is predicted to grow into a multibillion dollar market.

Why should consumers want to access the advertising messages on the Web and why should they access the Web in the first place? Using the Web is different from watching television or reading a newspaper: people use it in the same way as they decide to 'go places' or visit a new town. These tourists-consumers choose to stay, shop, look around or entertain themselves according to how they feel or how much time they have. As such in 'WebTown' commercial on-line shops need to offer distinctive advantages, such as a wider product range or more entertainment than traditional competitors, if they want to become popular 'sightseeing' sites.

The model in Figure 9.5, devised by McWilliam and her colleagues (1997), illustrates the interactions between the level of involvement experienced in relation to the advertising medium, the message and the brand. It enables us to appreciate how Web advertising might work.

The first figure applies to conditions of high involvement, such as the purchase of a car or white goods, in which consumers pay great attention to the content of the brand message and how it is communicated. They are likely to think about the advertisement in this situation. The second figure relates to traditional advertisements used for FMCGs, where consumers pay little attention, show little

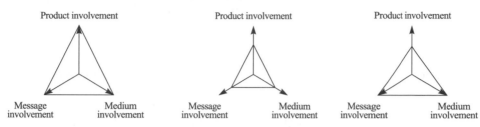

Figure 1 – An interplay of high involvement, irrespective of media (e.g. cars, white goods)

Figure 2 – Traditional media: low involvement in FMCGs

Figure 3 – The Web: high involvement for many FMCGs

Figure 9.5 Levels of involvement and different media (after McWilliam et al. 1997)

involvement and therefore the advertisement needs to be repeated frequently. The third figure illustrates the high involvement context of FMCG advertisements on the Web. As 'going to the Web' is a deliberate action, it is generally highly involving. Advertisers can be more confident that visitors will pay more attention to the information displayed on their Web sites and consumers are more likely to evaluate any claims. Marketers therefore need to beware of dull or poorly-developed sites, as visitors are more likely to ignore the brand or form negative impressions, if they had not been adequately 'entertained'.

Successful sites offer the opportunity to transform trial visits into lasting relationships by providing constant challenges and stimulating visitors' attention. Companies aware of the strategic potential of the Internet have realized that success also depends on involving many parts of the business in the design and management of their Web site.

Retailers' names as brands

An examination of advertisers in 1995 reveals that Procter & Gamble was the top advertiser, with over £100 m media support for its numerous brands, all of which have different brand names. By contrast Sainsbury, though the twelfth biggest advertiser, promoted its name with just over £40 m. The challenge many brands face, particularly when not strongly associated with their parent corporation, is that while they receive advertising support, this does not match the significant sums major retailers spend developing a clear proposition for their stores and their own brands. With over three-quarters of packaged grocery sales going through multiple retailers, the challenge to manufacturers from powerful retailers' own brands is indeed daunting. Furthermore, retailers such as Boots, Laura Ashley, Marks

& Spencer and Sainsbury have a particularly innovative policy of developing new products under their own names.

The challenges of the Single Market

Pan-European buying groups are becoming more common with re-tailers forming alliances to exploit opportunities jointly. This has resulted in buying groups with considerable power. For example, it was estimated in 1993 that Associated Marketing Services (AMS) had a grocery buying power of ECU 45 bn and the European Retail Alliance of ECU 18 bn. One consequence of this is that these groups are able to source brands at the lowest price. In grocery retailing, manufacturers' brands will face increasing price pressures from these alliances.

The Single Market currently consists of a community speaking nine different languages with strong nationalistic preferences. Eventually, there will be a more homogeneous community, as consumers recognize the advantages of powerful Euro-brands such as Kellogg's and Nescafé. More emphasis on visual identifiers will help overcome linguistic differences within the Single Market. Examples are the distinctive shape of Jif Lemon, the Perrier bottle and the VW badge. It is more likely that brands will be developed at the outset to appeal to consumers in many different countries. For example, Chee-tos, a cheese flavoured snack from PepsiCo was developed and tested in the USA and subsequently extended to fifteen other countries with little change.

more emphasis on visual identifiers will help overcome linguistic differences within the Single Market

Strong brands have richly complex personalities, enabling them to adapt and appeal to consumers in different countries by, for example, sharing the same language or adhering to a country's cultural norm. Yet at the same time successful international brands have a core set of values which remain constant across countries. International brands which remain true to their core values, but have these enacted in different ways in different countries, are admired, since they show respect for their host countries. The well-travelled consumer appreciates international brands which remain true to their core values, since in a foreign land these brands act as havens of reassurance about guaranteed consistency – albeit presented slightly differently.

The larger brand manufacturers are moving cautiously into Europe. Some are doing this by acquiring other firms. Examples of the more notable recent acquisitions are Grand Met buying Pillsbury, Philip Morris buying Jacobs Suchard and BSN buying RJR Nabisco, Galbani and HP Foods.

Other brand manufacturers are identifying product fields which are less subject to national taste differences, such as the confectionery and petfood product fields, for which they are developing pan-European strategies. Mars changed the name of its confectionery bar Marathon to Snickers as part of its pan-European approach and in the petfood sector, Cesar has replaced Mr. Dog.

Coca-Cola, Benetton, Kodak and Camel are good examples of strong brands gaining strength by taking advantage of more open markets. Brand positionings have been developed and fine-tuned to appeal across Europe. For example, Coca-Cola is the drink for friends in any situation and in the financial services sector American Express developed the positioning of being the known and trusted person with a pan-European campaign, 'You recognize me'.

To expand across Europe, brand manufacturers need to assess whether their brands will be used in the same way as they are in the UK. For example, United Biscuits recognized that in Italy some consumers eat biscuits with milk at breakfast just as British consumers eat breakfast cereals. With their Italian company, they reformulated one of their British brands and developed an advertising campaign positioning it more as a cereal.

Opportunities from technology

Brand marketers are now more able to take advantage of technology to gain a competitive advantage through time. Technology is already reducing the lead-time needed to respond rapidly to changing customer needs and minimizing any delays in the supply chain. General Motors in the USA, for example, implemented a computer controlled system, 'Saturn', which significantly reduced the order-delivery time. Furthermore, as a result of the dealer inputting customers' requirements for colour, trim and other accessories, the system is able to ensure not only that cars are tailored to customers' needs, but also that they are delivered more promptly. Another example is the way home builders in Japan use rapid response to customer needs to differentiate themselves. Potential home buyers visit estate agents and describe their ideal home. Equipped with a unique CAD-CAM program, the agent sketches a design on a computer screen in front of the prospective purchaser. The program instantly tells the cost of building the new home, and if this is too high, it enables the home dimensions to be scaled down until an acceptable price is reached. If the purchaser then wishes to buy the new home, the agent confirms this in the computer program and the builder usually offers completion six weeks later.

To succeed, marketers are going to have to use technology to stay ahead of competitors. For example, global brand manufacturers such as Unilever have well-conceived marketing intelligence systems that rapidly inform relevant divisions in different continents of any new competitive launches in any part of the world. In some markets it is now realistic to anticipate responses to new brand launches within a week – in the financial services sector it is only a matter of hours.

With new technology, brand marketers are also likely to be served by better marketing intelligence systems. The vast amounts of data in company databanks will be filtered so that decision makers will be presented with key information to help formulate and evaluate brand strategies. The emphasis will be on smaller *quantity* but higher *quality* information.

New technologies such as computers, flexible factories and rapid distribution should enable brand marketers to become more effective at micro-marketing. Rather than having to dilute marketing resources by directing campaigns at broad consumer groups, information technology is enabling marketers to target their activities more accurately. As firms build more powerful databases with knowledge of their customers' buying behaviour, so database marketing should enable them to start to think more about developing more profitable one-to-one relationships.

In the biotechnology sphere, Genetech, a company acquired by Roche, helped its brands grow through a deliberate policy of encouraging everyone to take advantage of technology. For example, its sales representatives were all issued with laptop computers, initially to send and receive electronic mail, file reports and place orders. However, it was quickly realized how these could give the firm a competitive advantage by transforming their sales staff into marketing consultants. Doctors valued the way that the reps used their laptops to access the latest medical articles and technical reports and in so doing could keep them up to date. When unable to answer complex medical questions, the reps also used their laptops to send questions through electronic mail to their internal specialists and rapidly respond to doctors' requests.

More sophisticated buyers

In business to business marketing, there is already an emphasis on bringing together individuals from different departments to evaluate suppliers' new brands. As inter-departmental barriers break down even more, sellers are going to face increasingly sophisticated buyers who are served by better information systems enabling them to play off brand suppliers against each other.

Consumers themselves are also becoming more confident and sophisticated. They expect higher standards from brands and appreciate brands that deliver real values. But the values being sought are not just functional ones. In fact, in an ever-changing and increasingly turbulent environment, they seem to prefer consistent brand personalities which provide some stability and help them better understand their social environments.

Consumers are becoming much more marketing literate and are

increasingly critical of advertising. Nonetheless, the danger for some brands is that advertisers make assumptions about consumers' involvement with advertisements and exceedingly 'clever' approaches are developed. For example, there was a move towards cross-fertilizing advertising ideas and blending different campaigns together. Polo mints used the Perrier approach in the 'Refreshing Poleau' advertisement, using the slogan, 'The mint with the heaule', while Canon adopted the slogan 'Some things in life are as reliable as a Volkswagen'. There is a danger that, without a good appreciation of consumers' perceptions, weaker brands may well lose out with these clever approaches.

consumers are becoming much more marketing literate

The growth of corporate branding

With media costs inhibiting individual brand advertising, there is a trend towards firms putting more emphasis on corporate branding, stressing the company as the brand through corporate identity programmes. In this way functional aspects of individual brands in the firm's portfolio can be augmented, enabling consumers to select brands through an assessment of the values of competing firms.

For example, in the affinity credit card market and the financial loans market there are many competing organizations. To differentiate themselves, Beneficial Bank have a core set of values and they use their corporate name to communicate these. These values are summarized by the mnemonic CREDO, i.e. *C*are and *R*espect for customers and staff, *E*ffective and always determined, *D*iversity amongst staff and *O*ptimize returns for shareholders. Firms which have developed powerful corporate identity programmes have done so by recognizing the need first to develop their internal corporate values, from which flows employee attitudes and specific types of staff behaviour, and then, secondly, to devise communication programmes for different external audiences. Emphasis is placed on explaining to staff the corporation's values and encouraging a particular type of culture to support this. For example, in 1997 when British Airways launched a new corporate identity, with 50 different aircraft tail designs, it first undertook an internal communication programme directed at all its employees. It explained the changes in brand strategy and only when all staff were aware of this did it then launch the new identity to the public. Successful corporate identity programmes are underpinned by clear values and when properly managed this can be a fearsome challenge to those firms who have individual line brands which make little attempt to draw on corporate values.

Corporate branding is based on a well-devised corporate identity programme which provides a clear vision about how the firm's brands are going to make the world a better place, has a well-thought-through set of core values, is communicated to staff and which gives them a better feeling of involvement and belonging. Well-devised programmes engender pride amongst staff who become even more committed to working hard in order to play their role in delivering brand benefits. They are more likely to become inspired to take new initiatives, as 3M found. All the goodwill generated through its individual lines is connected through corporate branding, giving rise to much greater customer respect. In view of the strategic nature, and benefits, of a powerful corporate identity, this should be the responsibility of senior managers, if not the CEO. As we discussed in Chapter 5, an aspect of a good corporate identity programme is its visual representation, but this should be regarded as reflecting the firm's vision and values.

in view of the strategic nature, and benefits, of a powerful corporate identity, this should be the responsibility of senior managers, if not the CEO

Once a firm has undertaken an audit to understand how it is perceived by its different stakeholder groups and has clarified its values and its vision for a better world, it can then start to consider the most appropriate brand architecture. Wally Olins (1995) and the corporate identity agency he was involved in building, Wolff Olins, provide helpful advice on this. They identify, and have worked with numerous clients on implementing, three broad brand structures – monolithic, endorsed and branded.

The **monolithic structure** is one where the firm's name is used across all its portfolio, for example, Sainsbury, Shell and Virgin. The same message is carried across all the firm's lines – for example, Virgin championing the consumer's case in such sectors as airline travel, financial services, drinks and music. It should reflect a consistent culture across all its internal departments, promise the same values across different products or services, and if properly enacted, facilitate the transfer of goodwill and offer significant promotional economies of scale.

In the **endorsed structure**, the corporation clusters its products or services into particular groups which are recognized as being part of the corporation, yet which offer different benefits. For example, Forte Crest Hotels offer a different level of service from Forte Travelodge, but they are all part of Forte Hotels. This type of structure is common when the firms have grown by acquisition, such as, Nestlé with brands like Nestlé KitKat and Nestlé Shreddies. Adopting this type of structure provides greater flexibility for developing different types of propositions. There is, however, a danger of overstretching the credibility of the corporate name. The extent to which the firm endorses its brands can be highly visible, as with P&O, or can be more subtle, for example, in much smaller letters stating that the brand is part of a particular corporation.

In the **branded structure**, the firm uses a series of brand names showing no apparent relation to each other, or to a corporation. Procter & Gamble and Unilever provide good examples of this. The argument for this is that using highly effective segmentation and targeting they can capitalize on segments that are not very dissimilar. However, the rising costs of following this route are reducing its attractiveness.

Conclusions

Brands succeed because they have real added values which are relevant to the target market and which the market welcomes. The longer it takes competitors to develop an equivalent, if not better, added value, the longer the brand has to capitalize on the goodwill it builds with customers and consumers. Added values are not about superficial, one-off issues such as a smile or the greeting, 'have a nice day'. Instead, they are about integrating relevant ideas into every point of contact the brand has with consumers. So, for the car hire company differentiating itself through customer concern, it means such things as checking each car before the hirer is given the keys, recruiting staff with a genuine interest in consumers, training staff, manning a 24-hour breakdown recovery service and making car reservations as simple as possible. All aspects of the brand's assets are employed to communicate rapidly the point of difference from competition, so that the consumer instantly associates the brand with functional reliability, and 'no hassle' administration, reinforcing the car hire service as a low-risk event that only the firm with this specific logo can provide.

> added values are not about superficial, one-off issues they are about integrating relevant ideas into every point of contact the brand has with consumers

One of the problems marketers face is finding added values which are relevant to the brand's stage of development. Even if the marketer erroneously thinks they have a commodity, it can still be developed as a brand through the way it is offered to consumers. The sorts of added values appropriate for both young and mature brands can be identified by considering a brand as growing from being solely a generic product, to being a product surrounded by an expected, an augmented and a potential layer. The generic product is the commodity form which enables firms to compete. The same considerations apply to services, which can be developed from a basic concept into an augmented service offering.

The expected brand represents the minimum criteria needed for purchasers to perceive sufficient added value to warrant a price premium in excess of the commodity costs of producing the brand. Here, the added values tend to be functional, reinforcing what the brand can do. For example, a new type of petrol could be positioned as kind to the environment, or as being able to help cars develop more power. As consumers gain more experience, they expect more from competing brands. To satisfy this, brands are augmented with added values that new consumers would not necessarily appreciate.

A strong brand personality can be an effective added value at this stage. Over time though, competitive activity and consumers' variety-seeking behaviour necessitates new added values to push the brand to the potential level. Once at the potential level, a time will be reached when consumers become disenchanted with the brand. At this stage, an audit is needed to evaluate whether the brand has come to the end of its useful life, or whether there is scope for the future through introducing a new added value. Value can also be added to a brand in the following ways: by stimulating customers to participate in the value-creating activity, by offering the most appropriate degree of customization, and by building long-term relationships with customers.

If the brand augmentation is successful competitors may try to develop similar versions, so marketers need to protect their brands against blatant imitators. Trademark registration provides a legal route to protection, but necessitates continual vigilance to discover the first signs of counterfeiting.

Brands face other challenges, however, besides those of imitators, so marketers need to anticipate these. In this respect, some of the issues that need to be addressed are:

- resisting the temptation of short-term tactical thinking;
- adopting a commitment to continually communicating brand benefits;
- understanding the different requirements of on-line shopping and the Internet;
- recognizing the support retailers are placing behind their own brands;
- developing strategies to capitalize on the opportunities of the Single Market;
- integrating new technologies;
- responding to more sophisticated buyers;
- building on the assets of the company brand.

Marketing action checklist

To help clarify the direction of future marketing activity, it is recommended that the following exercises are undertaken:

1   List the added values you believe your brands have. Evaluate the strength of these added values by undertaking interviews with your customers and consumers to assess how relevant and unique they are, and how much people appreciate these values compared with those of your competitors.

2   Scan your company brochures and check whether you use very broad terms to describe your brands' added values. For example, 'quality', 'dependable', 'caring'. If you have some of these all-encompassing added-value terms, get your team together and clarify amongst yourselves what you mean. Once you have reached a consensus, evaluate the strength of these added values and incorporate the most appropriate new added values in your brochures.

3   Map out all the main groups of people who are involved with each brand as it evolves from raw material entering the factory, right through to the point of consumption. Check the extent to which each group knows about each brand's added values. Has any of these groups ever been asked for their comments about how their task could be changed to better contribute to the brand's added values? Do the tasks of all of these groups contribute to the brand's added values?

4   For each of your brands, assess the extent to which your marketing programme incorporates these added values in order to
    • differentiate you from competition;
    • satisfy customers' functional and emotional needs;
    • reduce customers' perceptions of risk;
    • aid rapid selection;
    • be backed by a registered trademark.
    If your assessment shows an excessive reliance on only one of these points, consider the relevance of developing a more balanced programme.

5   If there is a view in your firm that you are competing in a commodity market, evaluate the differing needs of the channels that your brand passes through and consider ways of tailoring your offerings to better satisfy the needs of each group.

6   For each of your brands, identify from the model shown in Figure 9.1, the level on which each brand is competing. Have you a clear view about the motivational needs that your brands satisfy and the discriminators people use to differentiate between you and your competitors? How have each brand's added values developed? What plans do you have to enhance your brands when customers become more demanding and competition becomes more intense?

7   Do customers purchase your product or service to be relieved of undertaking particular tasks or because they want to use the product or service themselves, enjoying the task? How could the brand be modified to reinforce its relieving or enabling function more strongly?

8   For each of your brands, compare the extent to which they are

customized against your customers' requirements. With your colleagues, assess whether all of the different variations are really necessary and whether fewer variations would satisfy customers' needs as efficiently. Alternatively, is there a need for a greater degree of customization that consumers would welcome? What are the cost implications of any changes and how do these compare against the different prices you could achieve?

9   Consider the list you have already prepared, from the first question, of value-adding factors associated with your brand. Assess whether these solely focus on 'adding' benefits to customers or whether they look at reducing customers' sacrifices. With your team, analyse each of your major customers' value chains and identify opportunities to provide benefits, and reduce customers sacrifices, that affect the long-term relationship with your customers.

10   What systems do you have to identify when another firm is illegally copying your brand?

11   With your colleagues, go through 'The challenges to brands' section of this chapter and for each of the challenges, consider the implications for your brands and identify what types of actions are most appropriate.

References and further reading

Anholt S. (1996). Making a brand travel. *Journal of Brand Management*, **3** (6), 357–64.

Anon (1990). Coke's Kudos. *The Economist*, 15 September, 120.

Bidlake S. (1989). Reaching across the seas. *Marketing*, 5 October, 31–2.

Bidlake S. (1990). Levi's changes course for 90s. *Marketing*, 7 June, 9.

Bidlike S. (1991). Coca-Cola changes ad strategy to bolster its spin-off brands. *Marketing*, 7 Feb., 4.

Blois K. (1990). Product augmentation and competitive advantage. In *Proceedings of the 19th annual conference of the European Marketing Academy* (Muhlbacher H. and Jochum C.eds). Innsbruck: EMAC.

Brownlie D. (1988). Protecting marketing intelligence: the role of trademarks. *Marketing Intelligence and Planning*, **6** (4), 21–6.

Cohen D. (1986). Trademark strategy. *Journal of Marketing*, **50** (Jan.), 61–74.

Davidson H. (1987). *Offensive Marketing*. Harmondsworth: Penguin Books.

Davies I. (1995). Review of the Trademarks Act. *Journal of Brand Management*, **2** (2) 125–32 and **2** (3), 187–90.

Davies I. (1997). The Internet: some legal pitfalls. *Journal of Brand Management*, **4** (4) 273–7.

de Chernatony L. and McWilliam G. (1989). The varying nature of brands as assets: theory and practice compared. *International Journal of Advertising*, **8** (4), 339–49.

Doyle P. (1989). Building successful brands: the strategic options. *Journal of Marketing Management*, **5** (1), 77–95.

Drucker P. (1990). *The New Realities*. London: Mandarin Paperbacks.

Gilmore J. H. and Pine B. J. (1997). The four faces of mass customization. *Harvard Business Review* (Jan.–Feb.), 91–101.

Grönroos C. (1990). *Services, Management and Marketing*. Lexington: Lexington Books.

Hemnes T. (1987). Perspectives of a trademark attorney on the branding of innovative products. *Journal of Product Innovation*, **4**, 217–24.

Johnson M. (1991). Brewing up an all round alternative. *Marketing*, 2 May, 19.

Jones J. (1986). *What's in a Name? Advertising and the Concept of Brands*. Lexington: Lexington Books.

King S. (1991). Brand-building in the 1990s. *Journal of Marketing Management*, **7** (1), 3–13.

Kochan N. (ed.) (1996). *The World's Greatest Brands*. London: Macmillan Business and Interbrand.

Leadbeater C. (1991). Moles unearth spare part scam. *Financial Times*, 14 March, 1.

Levitt T. (1980). Marketing success through differentiation of anything. *Harvard Business Review* (Jan.–Feb.), 83–91.

McKenna R. (1991). Marketing is everything. *Harvard Business Review* (Jan.–Feb.), 65–79.

McWilliam G., Hammond G. K. and Diaz A. (1997). Going places in Webtown: A new way of thinking about advertising and the Web. *Journal of Brand Management*, **4** (4) 261–70.

Michel S. (1996). Prosuming Behavior and its Strategic Implications for Marketing. The 9th UK Services Marketing Workshop. Stirling: Stirling University.

Midgley D. (1990). World brand leaders. *Campaign*, 21 November, 39–40.

Mitchell A. (1990). Back to basics. *Marketing*, 26 July, 26–7.

Moore K. and Andradi B. (1997). Who will be the winners on the Internet? *Journal of Brand Management*, **4** (1), 47–54.

Normann R. and Ramirez R. (1993). From value chain to value constellation: designing interactive strategy. *Harvard Business Review* (July–Aug.), 65–77.

Olins W. (1995). *The New Guide to Identity*. Aldershot: Gower.

Peters T. and Austin N. (1985). *A Passion for Excellence*. Glasgow: William Collins Sons & Co.

Porter M. (1985). *Competitive Advantage*. New York: The Free Press.

Ravald A. and Grönroos C. (1996). The value concept and relationship marketing. *European Journal of Marketing*, **30**, (2), 19–30.

Sambrook C. (1991). The top 500 brands. *Marketing*, 7 March, 27–33.

Thomas T. (1990). A new golden gate for great pretenders. *The European*, 19 Oct., 24.

Chapter 10

Brand planning

Summary

This chapter considers some of the issues in brand planning. It opens by stressing that consumers welcome consistency and as such the brand's core values should not be tampered with. Understanding the core values of the brand is essential, but managers should also consider how these synergistically blend together to form a more holistic brand. The use of bridging is described as one way of enabling managers to take a more holistic perspective on brand building. We show that consumers evaluate brands primarily by the extent to which they satisfy functional and representational needs. Through an appreciation of brands' functional and representational characteristics, we consider how best to invest in brands. We review some of the issues in developing and launching new brands and address the problems of managing brands during their growth, maturity and decline phases. The financial implications of these different phases are considered. Finally, we look at ways of rejuvenating 'has been' brands.

Maintaining the brand's core values

In previous chapters, we stressed the point that brands succeed because marketers have a good appreciation of the assets constituting their brands. By recognizing which aspects of their brands are particularly valued by consumers, marketers have invested and protected these attributes, sustaining their value and maintaining consumer loyalty. Any pressures from accountants or factory managers to cut support for these core values have been strenuously resisted.

Over time consumers learn to appreciate the core values of brands and remain loyal to their favourite brands since they represent bastions of stability, enabling consumers confidently to anticipate

their performance. It therefore behoves companies to have a statement of their brand's values which is given to any manager working
on the brand, whether internal or external to the firm, in addition to
all of the most senior management team. There needs to be a mechanism in place whereby any marketing plans for the brand are carefully
considered against the statement of core values to ensure that none
of the core values are adversely affected by any planned activity. It is
common for companies to regard brand management as a good training ground for junior managers. They would typically work on a
brand for around three years and then seek promotion. As a consequence of their junior positions and their focus on achieving
improvements in short periods, there is a danger that their concern
with short- rather than long-term horizons results in them changing
some of the brand's values. In effect they are driven more by building short-term market share rather than by building brands. Where
there is a system in place whereby any brand plans have to be checked
against the statement of core values, there is a greater likelihood of
the brand thriving over a longer horizon.

behoves
companies to have
a statement of
their brand's
values which is
given to any
manager working
on the brand,
whether internal
or external to the
firm

Having a statement of core brand values ensures that changes
in advertising agencies, aimed at breathing new creative life into the
brand, will be in a direction consistent with the brand's heritage. It
can also act as a 'go-no-go' decision gate when managers are faced
with the need to respond to an increasingly hostile commercial environment. In the first half of the 1990s Lever's brand of washing
powder, Persil, faced increasing challenges from Procter & Gamble's
brands, such as Ariel. Little innovation was evident until Lever's
research laboratory developed a revised formulation for Persil with
a manganese accelerator. Up until this innovation, one of Persil's
values was that of a caring brand, caring about whiteness, skin, washing machines and mothers' reputations. One might question whether
this technological enhancement reinforced the caring value, but faced
with an aggressive competitor Lever decided to change Persil's formulation. To get Persil Power to market as quickly as possible, only
very limited field trials were undertaken. Alas, problems were discovered with Persil Power which Ariel used to their advantage. Lever
pulled back from Persil Power and with New Generation Persil it
returned to its core values. Clearly managers have to respond to short-
term threats, but referring back to the statement of brand values
should help identify strategies which build, rather than diminish the
brand's core values.

A further advantage of having a statement of brand values is
that it enables managers to check their interpretation of the brand
against the agreed view. By so doing they can then evaluate the appropriateness of their planned actions. Managers wisely concentrate
on matching their target market's needs and are rightly concerned
about not letting their brand fall against competitive actions or chang-

ing consumer needs. However, what is often overlooked is the question 'do all of the brand's team have the same views about the brand's values?' Brands don't just die because of the external environment – their life can be shortened by a lack of consistent views amongst the brand's team. In a study amongst the senior management teams of firms operating in financial services markets, de Chernatony and Took (1994) found that amongst the twelve firms interviewed, while there were many managers in each team sharing similar views about the nature of their brand, in all of the firms there were managers who had idiosyncratic views about particular aspects of their brand. Bearing in mind that these interviews were undertaken with senior managers responsible for staff and significant resources, idiosyncratic views could result in different departments almost pulling against each other as they separately enact the brand's strategy. Not only is it worth having a widely circulated statement of brand values, but on an annual basis, when brand plans are being prepared, an independent party should audit all members of the brand team about their interpretation of their brand's values. Where individuals have diverse views about aspects of the brand, these should be pointed out and through discussions any issues resolved.

Any plans to cut back on investments affecting the core values of the brand should be strenuously opposed by strong-willed marketers. By ensuring that everyone working on a particular brand is regularly reminded of the brand's values, an integrated, committed approach can be adopted, so that the correct balance of resources is consistently applied. Checks need to be undertaken to ensure that any frills which do not support the brand's values are eliminated and that regular consumer value analysis exercises, rather than naive cost-cutting programmes, are undertaken to ensure the brand's values are being correctly delivered to consumers.

Want to keep it looking like new?
Keep a can of WD-40 handy.
Just a squirt protects surfaces against
corrosion and rust. You'll take a shine to the
can that keeps a shine on things.

THERE'S ALWAYS ANOTHER USE

Exhibit 10.1   *Over many years WD-40 has always remained true to its core values (reproduced by kind permission of WD-40 Company)*

Bridging the brand's values

There is a danger that, when guarding the consistency of their brand's core values over time, managers become too focused on considering their brand in terms of its individual values. Whilst this is an important part of brand analysis, it should be recognized that brands are holistic entities whereby the individual values are integrated into a whole whose strength comes from interlinking parts. Managers therefore need to consider how their brand's component values are synergistically integrated to form a more powerful whole. A branding consultancy, Brand Positioning Services, has developed a technique (1987) which enables managers to appreciate how bridging between these parts makes the brand stronger and enables it to attain the optimal positioning.

managers need to consider how their brand's component values are synergistically integrated to form a more powerful whole

Brand Positioning Services conceptualize the brand as being composed of three components. The **functional component** characterizes what the product or service does. The **psychological component** describes which of the user's motivational, situational or role needs the product or service meets and the **evaluative component** considers how the brand can be judged. The brand, as Figure 10.1 shows, can then be considered as the integration of these three components.

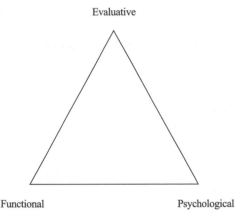

Figure 10.1   *The integrated brand (after Brand Positioning Services 1987)*

Consumers do not consider any of these three components in isolation. When a brand of soft drink is described as being functionally full of energy, consumers' perceptions of the brand may evoke thoughts of a healthy lifestyle. Thus the functional component of the brand is assessed within the perspective of its psychological associations. For an integrated brand both the functional and psychological components need to work together. When this is the case they are regarded as bridged and a single word should describe the benefit both these components satisfy.

When developing a brand of toothpaste, there are many functional needs it could satisfy, such as the desire for white teeth or to fight bacteria. Colgate Palmolive decided that their brand, Colgate Toothpaste, would focus on fighting bacteria, thereby reducing the likelihood of problems such as cavities, plaque, tartar and bad breath. Psychologically, some consumers are worried by the prospect of regular visits to dentists and the social embarrassment of bad breath. Analysis indicated that Colgate Toothpaste could be positioned in terms of protection, since this word bridged the functional and psychological needs, leading to an integrated brand. Likewise Comfort Fabric conditioner is about softness, which bridges the functional and psychological components.

Several competing brands may be able to meet consumers' needs in a particular category. To give the firm's brand a lead over competition managers need to suggest to consumers how to judge competing brands and encourage evaluation along a dimension that their brand excels on. This is the third component of the brand, the evaluator. It was decided that Colgate Toothpaste should be about *trusted* protection and that Comfort Fabric Conditioner should be about *loving* softness.

A unique two-word statement for each brand – the evaluator plus the bridged need – not only defines the brand's positioning but also enables managers to consider their brand as a holistic entity. While it is laudable to understand the core values constituting the essence of the brand so that they can be protected over time, these need to be integrated to produce a holistic brand. The procedure that Brand Positioning Services have developed is a helpful way of getting managers to think beyond the component parts to arrive at the integrated whole.

Since a brand is the totality of thoughts, feelings and sensations evoked in consumers' minds, resources can only be effectively employed once an audit has been taken of the dimensions that define it in the consumer's mind. To appreciate this planned use of resources, it is therefore necessary to consider the dimensions that consumers use to assess brands.

Defining brand dimensions

When people choose brands, they are not solely concerned with one single characteristic, nor do they have the mental agility to evaluate a multitude of brand attributes. Instead, only a few key issues guide choice.

our attention is drawn to people buying brands to satisfy functional and emotional needs

In some of the early classic brands' papers, our attention is drawn to people buying brands to satisfy functional and emotional needs. One has only to consider everyday purchasing to appreciate this.

For example, there is little difference between the physical characteristics of bottled mineral water. Yet, due to the way advertising has reinforced particular positionings, Perrier is bought more for its 'designer label' appeal which enables consumers to express something about their upwardly mobile lifestyles. By contrast, some may buy Evian more from a consideration of its healthy connotations. If consumers solely evaluated brands on their functional capabilities, then the Halifax and Abbey National, with interest rates remarkably similar to other competitors, would not have such notable market shares in the deposit savings sector. Yet the different personalities represented by these financial institutions influence brand evaluation.

This idea of brands being characterized by two dimensions, the rational function and the emotionally symbolic, is encapsulated in the model of brand choice shown in Figure 10.2. When consumers choose between brands, they rationally consider practical issues about brands' functional capabilities. At the same time, they evaluate different brands' personalities, forming a view about them which fits the image they wish to be associated with. As many writers have noted, consumers are not just functionally orientated; their behaviour is affected by their interpretation of brand symbolism, as was shown in Chapter 4. When two competing brands are perceived as being equally similar in terms of their physical capabilities, the brand that comes closest to matching and enhancing the consumer's self-concept will be chosen.

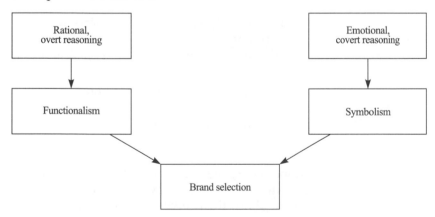

Figure 10.2   *Components of brand choice (after Lannon and Cooper 1983)*

In terms of the functional aspects of brand evaluation and choice, consumers assess the rational benefits they perceive from particular brands, along with preconceptions about efficacy, value for money, and availability. One of the components of functionalism is quality. For brands that are predominantly product-based Garvin's work (1987) has shown that when consumers, rather than managers, assess quality they consider issues such as:

- **performance**, for example the top speed of a car;
- **features** – does the car come with a CD stereo system as a standard fitting;
- **reliability** – will the car start first time every day it's used;
- **conformance to specification** – if the car is quoted to have a particular petrol consumption when driving around town consumers expect this to be easily achieved;
- **durability,** which is an issue Volvo majored on showing the long lifetime of its cars;
- **serviceability** – whether the car can go 12 months between services;
- **aesthetics** which Ford's KA majored upon in its launch;
- **reputation** – consumers' impressions of a particular car manufacturer.

For predominately service-based brands, Parasuraman, Zeithaml and Berry (1988) developed the SERVQUAL instrument to assess consumers' perceptions of service quality. They found that the five core dimensions of service quality are:

- **tangibles**: the physical facilities, equipment and appearance of staff;
- **reliability**: the ability of staff to perform the promised service dependably and accurately;
- **responsiveness**: the willingness of staff to help consumers and provide prompt service;
- **assurance**: the knowledge and courtesy of staff and their ability to inspire trust and confidence;
- **empathy**: the caring, individualized attention provided to consumers.

At a more emotional level, the symbolic value of the brand is considered. Here, consumers are concerned with the brand's ability to help make a statement about themselves, to help them interpret the people they meet, to reinforce membership of a particular social group, to communicate how they feel and to say something privately to themselves. They evaluate brands in terms of intuitive likes and dislikes and continually seek reassurances from the advertising and design that the chosen brand is the 'right' one for them.

The de Chernatony–McWilliam brand planning matrix

Building on the previous section, we see that when consumers choose between competing brands, they do so in terms of a low number of dimensions. Further support for this is provided by Sheth and his team's work on values (1991), which we reviewed in Chapter 4, where they found evidence of brand choice being influenced by functional, social, emotional, conditional and epistemic values. In fact, even this could be conceived in terms of fewer dimensions, since by focusing on a given situation for regularly purchased brands (i.e. holding the conditional value constant and where there is no novelty or epistemic value), brand choice behaviour is influenced by functional value and the social and emotional values. If we regard the social and emotional values as describing a consumer's personal expression needs, or representationality, we can describe brands in terms of their functionality and representationality.

There is notable evidence supporting the view that consumers choose between brands using two key dimensions. The first dimension is the rational evaluation of brands' abilities to satisfy utilitarian needs. We refer to this as functionality. Marketing support is employed to associate specific functional attributes with particular brand names, facilitating consumers' decision-making about primarily utilitarian needs such as performance, reliability and taste. Brands satisfying primarily functional needs are Castrol GTX, Formica and Tipp-Ex. The second dimension is the emotional evaluation of brands' abilities to help consumers express something about themselves, for example, their personality, their mood, their membership of a particular social group, or their status. We call this dimension representationality. Brands are chosen on this dimension because they have values which exist over and above their physical values. For example, Yves Saint Laurent neckties and Chanel perfume are very effective brands for expressing particular personality types and roles, with a secondary benefit of inherent functional qualities.

These two dimensions of brand characteristics are independent of each other. Furthermore, consumers rarely select brands using just one of these two dimensions. Instead, they choose between competing brands according to the *degree* of functionality and representationality expressed by particular brands. It is possible to use these two dimensions to gain a good appreciation of the way consumers perceive competing brands. For example, Audi cars are perceived as being very effective brands for communicating status and personality issues, and at the same time also reassuring consumers about design and engineering excellence.

through qualitative
market research
techniques, it is
possible to identify
the consumer
attributes
reflecting the
dimensions of
functionality and
representationality

Through qualitative market research techniques, it is possible to identify the consumer attributes reflecting the dimensions of functionality and representationality. Then, by incorporating these into a questionnaire, a large sample of consumers can be interviewed to gauge their views about the competing brands in a particular product field. Statistical analysis of these questionnaires enables the marketer to characterize each of the competing brands in terms of their functionality and representationality. By knowing the scores of each brand on these two dimensions, a spatial display of the brands can be produced by plotting the brand scores on a matrix, whose two axes are functionality and representationality, as shown in Figure 10.3. From this matrix, the marketer is able to consider how resources could best be used to support their brand. The reader interested in the detail of undertaking this market research is referred to the paper by de Chernatony (1993) in the 'References and further reading', at the end of this chapter.

Strategies from the de Chernatony–McWilliam matrix

If the marketer is satisfied with the quadrant within which the brand is located, as would be Rolls Royce in the high representationality–high functionality quadrant, then the brand strategy needs reinforcing. If, however, the brand is not perceived by consumers in the quadrant desired by the marketer, a strategy appropriate to the desired quadrant should be enacted. To sustain the brand in a particular quadrant, the following strategies are felt to be particularly appropriate.

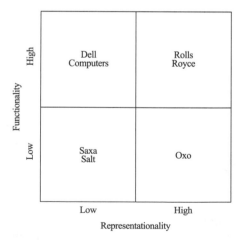

Figure 10.3   *An example of the de Chernatony–McWilliam matrix*

High representationality–high functionality

Brands in the top right quadrant of Figure 10.3 are perceived as providing functional excellence and, in the consumer's mind, to be very good vehicles for non-verbal communication about themselves. Qualitative market research needs to be undertaken to appreciate the lifestyle that users wish to project through the brand and a posi-

Exhibit 10.2 *On the de Chernatony–McWilliam matrix, Isle of Jura Single Malt Whisky is positioned as high on functional excellence, with a small amount of representationality supported by the image aroused from the topographical advertisement (reproduced by kind permission of Invergordon Distillers)*

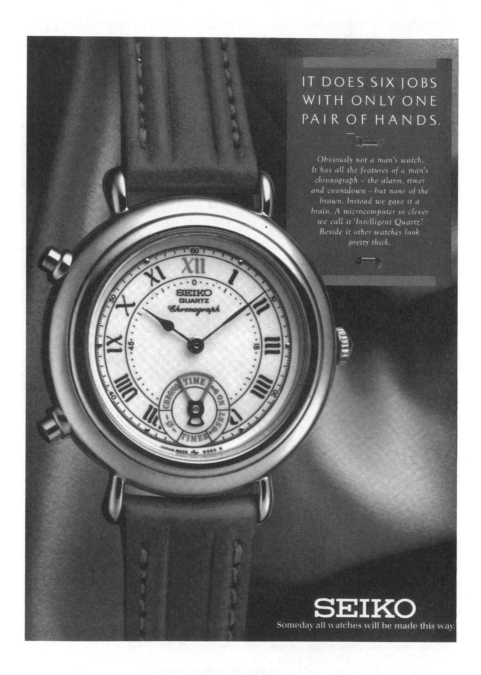

Exhibit 10.3 *On the de Chernatony–McWilliam matrix Seiko would appear to be positioned as low representationality–high functionality (reproduced by kind permission of Seiko UK Ltd)*

tioning objective subsequently defined and satisfied through the appropriate marketing mix. A creative strategy that reinforces consumers' lifestyle requirements should be developed (for example, using reference group endorsement, appropriate mood and tone of advertising etc.) and communicated through selective media channels. A continuous promotional presence is essential to reinforce users' brand choice and to communicate symbolic meaning to those in contact with brand users. The quality of the brand needs to be maintained through high standards of quality control and continuous product development. Regular consumer surveys need to assess users' views on product performance and any negative comments investigated. Availability of the brand should be restricted to quality distributors. A strict audit of the way distributors interact with the brand is required and they would need to be dissuaded from any activities which may undermine the brand's value.

Low representationality–high functionality

These brands are in the top left quadrant of Figure 10.3. They are sought by consumers because of a high utilitarian need and a less pressing drive to communicate something about themselves. Product superiority needs to be maintained. Continuous R&D investment is particularly necessary here, since it will be vitally important for the company to maintain functional advantage over the competition. 'Me-tooism' will always be a potential threat to these brands. Promotional support is important in communicating the functional benefits of the brand. The creative strategy would probably focus upon 'product as hero' in the advertising.

High representationality–low functionality

Consumers are primarily concerned about using brands in the bottom right quadrant of Figure 10.3 as symbolic devices and are less concerned about satisfying functional needs. They would probably recognize that there are small differences between brands in product performance, but they would believe that the representational issues are of more importance. The role of advertising for these brands is either to gain their acceptability as 'part of the culture' (e.g. the Oxo Family), or to reinforce a lifestyle (e.g. Martini). A continuous advertising presence would be needed here. Product development issues would be less crucial compared with those brands which satisfy high functional needs. The product's strategy, however, must ensure a coherent approach to satisfy the positioning objective. More reliance needs to be placed upon the results of branded, rather than blind product-testing against competition.

Low representationality–low functionality

Brands in the bottom left quadrant of Figure 10.3 are bought by customers when they are not particularly concerned about functional needs. The development of Spar as a 'convenience store' epitomizes this type of brand – a limited range of groceries that satisfy consumers who realize they have run out of a grocery product and whose sole concern is replacing the product regardless of brand availability. In general, brands in this quadrant must have wide distribution and be very price-competitive. To be able to fight on price, the producer needs to strive for cost-leadership in the industry. This entails being an efficient producer, avoiding marginal customer accounts, having long production runs and continually monitoring overhead costs. Brands in this quadrant are vulnerable to delisting and to succeed, the supplier must be able to justify an attractive price proposition to the distributor and consumer. It is quite possible for manufacturers to deliberately launch 'fighting brands' into this sector, the purpose of which, for example, would be to complete a range of products or as an offensive attack against a particular competitor, or as part of a segmented approach to their market.

Managing brands over their life cycles

So far, this chapter has focused on clarifying what combination of marketing resources best supports a particular type of brand, *at a given point in time*. It needs to be appreciated, however, that the returns from brands depend on where they are in their life cycle. Different types of marketing activities are needed according to whether the brand is new to the market, or is a mature player in the market. In this section, we go through the main stages in brands' life cycles and consider some of the implications for marketing activity.

Developing and launching new brands

Traditional marketing theory, particularly that practised by large fast-moving consumer goods companies, argues for a well-researched new product development process. When new brands are launched, they arrive in a naked form, without a clear personality to act as a point of differentiation. Some brands are born being able to capitalize on the firm's umbrella name, but even then they have to fight to establish their own unique personality. As such, in their early days, brands are more likely to succeed if they have a genuine functional advantage; there is no inherent goodwill, or strong brand personality, to act as a point of differentiation. One of the problems with the innovative excellence of Sir Clive Sinclair was that his new techno-

when new brands are launched, they arrive in a naked form, without a clear personality to act as a point of differentiation

logical brands came to market without sufficient bench-testing or anticipation of consumer usage. Several of his brands could not deliver on the functional benefit claimed by the promotional support. Miniature televisions stopped working after twenty minutes, due to overheating, and the batteries in the Sinclair digital watches only lasted for about a month, due to the number of times users wanted a time display.

New brand launches are very risky commercial propositions. To reduce the chances of a new brand not meeting its goals, many firms rightly undertake marketing research studies to evaluate each stage of the brand's development amongst the target market. Sometimes, however, very sophisticated techniques are employed, lengthening the time before the new brand is launched. While such procedures reduce the chances of failures, they introduce delays which may not be financially justified. It is particularly important that delays in the development programmes for technological brands are kept to a minimum. For example, it was calculated that if a new generation of laser printers has a life cycle of five years, assuming a market growth rate of 20 per cent per annum, with prices falling 12 per cent per annum, delaying the launch of the new brand by only six months would reduce the new brand's cumulative profits by a third.

Virtual reality techniques provide a means to cut market research time by using 3D computer simulations to immerse consumers in new environments and experience new products. Several new techniques have evolved which overcome some of the limitations of respondents having to make the mental leap from concept statement to visualization. Urban and his colleagues (Urban *et al.* 1994) developed the Information Accelerator (IA) technique. Respondents are placed in a virtual buying environment in which they are first accelerated into a future time period, experience the new product and then are allowed to choose information sources by which they wish to evaluate the new product. Raymond Burke (1995) developed a system that created the look and feel of an in-store environment on computer screens. Using a computer mouse, respondents 'walk' down shopping aisles removing and examining brands which they either return to the shelves or put in their trolley. Store environments can be realistically created and the simulation can be relatively quickly set up. This system provides information on consumer decision-making which is usually difficult to obtain.

Marketers launching new technological brands need to adopt a far more practical approach, balancing the risk from only doing pragmatic, essential marketing research against the financial penalties of delaying a launch. The Japanese are masters at reducing risks with new technology launches with their so called 'second fast strategy'. They are only too aware of the cost of delays and once a competitor has a new brand on the market, if it is thought to have potential, they will rapidly develop a comparable brand. A classic example of this was when Sony launched the very successful CCD TR55 camcorder. This weighed 800 grams and had 2200 components shrunk into a space which was a quarter of that of the conventional camcorder. Within six months, JVC had an even lighter version, soon followed by Sanyo, Canon, Ricoh and Hitachi. Likewise in the 35 mm single-lens-reflex camera market, Minolta launched the first autofocus model. Realizing the potential in this new development, Canon underwent a crash research programme and shortly afterwards launched an improved model, which halved the autofocusing time.

It is less common for Japanese companies to test new brand ideas through marketing research to the extent seen in Western Europe. One report, for example, estimated that approximately 1000 new soft drinks brands were launched one year in Japan, with 99 per cent failing. In both low and medium cost goods, more emphasis is placed on testing through selling. In part, this reflects the Japanese philosophy of not just passively listening to the customer, but of more actively leading them. Few purchasers have the ability to envisage futuristic new products such as the NEC dream of the telephone that can translate different languages, or Motorola's desire for telephone numbers attached to people rather than places. The greater emphasis on testing new products through selling reflects the Japanese view that this enables their managers to get much more experience of new markets much faster. The importance of understanding new markets resulted in one Japanese car manufacturer sending its design team to live in the country where their new brand was being targeted to appreciate the environment within which their car was to be driven. Time was taken to drive around towns, observing how consumers used their cars. They took photographs of people driving and queuing to really get to know their new consumers.

New product failures should not be seen as a hunt for a scapegoat. Instead, analysis is needed to learn from the failures and these results rapidly fed back to improve the next generation of products. Just as the archer's arrow rarely hits the centre of the target the first time, but does so on the second trial, so the analogy of using learning to further refine new brand concepts needs adopting.

just as the archer's arrow rarely hits the centre of the target the first time, so the analogy of using learning to further refine new brand concepts needs adopting

There are several benefits from being first to launch a new brand in a new sector. Brands which are pioneers have the opportunity to gain greater understanding of the technology by moving up the learning curve faster than competitors. When competitors launch 'me-too' versions, the innovative leader should be thinking about launching next generation technology. Being first with a new brand that proves successful also presents opportunities to reduce costs due to economies of scale and the experience effect.

Brands which were first to market and are strongly supported offer the opportunity for consumer loyalty. Almost without thinking about it, customers ask for the brand which has become generic for the product field. Xerox copiers have been so well-supported with their innovative developments, that they've become part of everyday terminology.

Being the first with a new brand sets habits which are difficult to change. For example, in the drugs industry GPs prefer to prescribe medication with which they've become confident. To listen to a sales representative talking about a 'me-too' version takes time and introduces uncertainty about efficacy in the GP's mind.

When launching new brands in technological markets, marketers are only too aware of the high costs they are likely to incur. As such, the successful firms look at launching a new technology into several product sectors. For example, Honda's development work on multivalve cylinder heads with self-adjusting valves was extended across motorcycles, cars, lawn mowers and power-generation equipment.

One of the nagging doubts marketers have when launching a new brand is that of the sustainability of the competitive advantage inherent in the new brand. The 'fast-follower' may quickly emulate the new brand and reduce its profitability by launching a lower-priced brand. In the very early days of the new brand the ways in which competitors might copy it are through:

- design issues, such as, colour, shape, size;
- physical performance issues, such as quality, reliability, durability;
- product service issues, such as guarantees, installation, after-sales service;
- pricing;
- availability through different channels;
- promotions;
- image of the producer.

If the new brand is the result of the firm's commitment to functional superiority, the design and performance characteristics probably give the brand a clear differential advantage, but this will soon be surpassed. In areas like consumer electronics, a competitive lead of a few months is not unusual. Product service issues can sometimes be a more effective barrier. For example, BMW installed a software chip in their engines that senses, according to the individual's driving style, when the car needs servicing. Only BMW garages have the ability to reset the service indicator on their cars' dashboards. Price can be easy to copy, particularly if the follower is a large company with a range of brands that they can use to support a short-term loss from pricing low. Unless the manufacturer has particularly good relationships with distributors that only stock their brand, which is not that common, distribution does not present a barrier to imitators.

Finally, if the firm is prepared to give the new brand promotional support, they can take advantage of the halo effect from any positive associations through the firm's image and generally develop a strong brand personality. Promotional support helps communicate the new brand's point of difference and can sustain its competitive edge.

Managing brands during the growth phase

Once a firm has developed a new brand, it needs to ensure that it has a view about how the brand's image will be managed over time. The brand image is the consumers' perceptions of who the brand is and what it stands for, i.e. it reflects the extent to which it satisfies consumers' functional and representational needs.

At the launch, there must be a clear statement about the extent to which the brand will satisfy functional and representational needs. For example, Lego building bricks, when originally launched in 1960, were positioned as an unbreakable, safe toy, enabling children to enjoy creativity in designing and building. Using the earlier brands matrix, this brand was positioned as high on functionality and low on representationality.

As sales rise, the brand's image needs to be protected against inferior, competitive, look-alikes. The functional component of the brand can now be reinforced, either through a problem-solving specialization strategy, or a problem-solving generalization strategy. If the specialization strategy were to have been followed, Lego would have been positioned solely for educational purposes. It would have been targeted at infant and primary school teachers. The problem with this strategy is that in the long term competitors may develop a brand that meets a much broader variety of needs. By following a product-solving generalization strategy, the brand is positioned to be effective across a variety of usage situations. This was the route that Lego actually followed.

The original approach to supporting the representational component of the brand needs to be maintained as sales rise. For example, for those brands that are bought predominantly to enable consumers to say something about themselves, it is important to maintain the self-concept and group membership associations. By communicating the brand's positioning to both the target and non-target segments, but selectively working with distributors to make it difficult for the non-targeted segment to buy the brand, its positioning will be strengthened.

Managing brands during the maturity phase

In the maturity part of the life cycle, the brand will be under considerable pressure. Numerous competitors will all be trying to win greater consumer loyalty and more trade interest. One option is to extend the brand's meaning to new products. A single image is then used to unite all the individual brand images. This strategy was successfully employed by Polycell in the DIY home improvements

Exhibit 10.4   *The Land Rover is an example of a brand which has been well-managed during its impressively significant maturity phase (reproduced by kind permission of Land Rover and WCRS Ltd on behalf of Max Forsythe (photographer))*

market. It established an image of DIY simplicity and reliability with its original range of wallpaper paste, then extended this image across such products as fillers, double glazing and home security. When following this strategy in the maturity stage, the firm must continually question whether a new addition to the product range will enhance the total brand image. If the new line has brand values inconsistent with the parent brand, serious consideration should be given to launching the new line without any associations of the parent organization.

Where the brand primarily satisfies consumers' functional needs, these functional requirements should be identified and any further brand extensions evaluated against this list to see if there is any similarity between the needs that the new brands will meet and those being satisfied by an existing brand. Where there is a link between the needs being satisfied by the existing brand and the new needs fulfilled by a new brand, this represents an appropriate brand extension. For example, Black & Decker's proposition is that of making DIY jobs easier with the use of high performance, electrically-powered tools. Their extension from hand-held electrical drills, to lawn mowers and car vacuum cleaners, was entirely consistent with their original brand image. By contrast, when the brand primarily satisfies representational needs, these should be assessed and taken as an essential criteria for future brand extensions. For example, the quality Gucci range of fashion wear and accessories says a lot about the chic and discerning tastes of a sophisticated person. Their range is successfully expanding by building on this representational dimension, showing how the consumer's lifestyle is more complete with further Gucci brands.

Managing brands during the decline phase

As brand sales begin to decline, firms need to evaluate carefully the two main strategic options of recycling their brand or coping with decline.

When the brand is recycled the marketer needs to find new uses for the brand, either through the functional dimension, or the representational dimension. A good example of functional brand recycling is the Boeing 727 aircraft. In the late 1960s, rising oil prices made this aircraft less attractive to airline companies and sales fell. Boeing refused to let this brand die and redesigned the 727, making it more economical on fuel. Sales of the brand recovered between 1971 and 1979 with this functional improvement. Guinness is a classic example of how a brand was repositioned to capitalize on demographic change, with marketing activity focusing on representationality. Spearheaded by a novel promotional campaign, Guinness was successfully repositioned in the 1980s away from an ageing consumer group to younger drinkers.

Should the firm feel there is little scope for functional or representational brand changes, it still needs to manage its brands in the decline stage. If the firm is committed to frequent new brand launches, it does not want distributors rejecting new brands because part of the firm's portfolio is selling too slowly. A decision needs to be taken about whether the brand should be quickly withdrawn, for example by cutting prices, or whether it should be allowed to die, gradually enabling the firm to reap higher profits through cutting marketing support.

Financial implications of brands during their life cycle

According to the stage in the brand's life cycle, so it needs to be managed for long-term profitability. In the early stages of its life, the brand will need financial support, while in the maturity stage it should generate cash. The matrix in Figure 10.4 shows these financial implications.

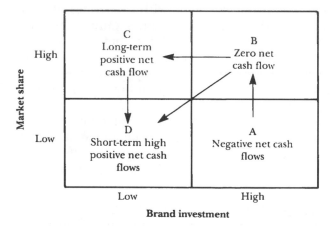

Figure 10.4   *Financial management of brands (after Ward et al. 1989)*

In its introduction stage, the new brand will be fighting for awareness amongst consumers and will depend heavily on the skills of the sales force to win the trade's interest and stock the new brand. Company executives must resist the temptation to try to recoup the large R&D brand investment by saving on promotional support; all this will do is to prolong the period of slow sales. On the matrix in Figure 10.4, the very early days of the brand are represented by quadrant A, where there is a need for large cash resources, with only a small market share resulting. At this stage, the new brand is a drain on company resources.

As consumer and retailer acceptance grows, sales rise and the brand moves into quadrant B. Satisfied consumers talk to their friends and more retailers stock the brand as they begin to appreciate its

in its introduction stage, executives must resist the temptation to try to recoup the large R&D brand investment by saving on promotional support potential. Higher levels of sales begin to cover the continuing brand investment and eventually the brand revenue begins to balance the costs being incurred. This stage represents the transition from marketing investment being required to develop the brand, to that of maintaining the brand.

At this crossroads in its career, the brand can then fall into quadrant D, or be nurtured into quadrant C. Where marketers are obsessed with short-term gains, brand investment will be cut very quickly after the brand begins to show a net positive cash flow, the argument being that there is sufficient awareness and goodwill amongst consumers. However, the brand will glide along for a short time, without any driving power, but like most non-powered aircraft will then go into rapid freefall.

Long-term benefits can be accrued by maintaining marketing support and keeping the brand in quadrant C. As the rate of market growth slows down and competitors become more aggressive, a maintenance strategy should be directed at sustaining, if not increasing, the brand's leadership position. With economies of scale and the benefits of the experience effect, the brand should generate healthy profits. Eventually though, the firm will feel that the market for the brand is less attractive, for reasons such as more aggressive competitors, or falling consumer interest. Brand support will be cut, market share will fall and for a short time the brand will be in quadrant D, prior to being withdrawn.

From time to time, brands are not sufficiently nurtured and they lose their leading market position. This is not an inevitable feature, but should the brand experience a worsening position there may well be a need to put new life into it. This is discussed in the next section.

Rejuvenating 'has been' brands

The cynic within the overly-cautious marketer would argue that from the moment a new brand is launched it becomes a wasting asset. The technology to produce the brand soon becomes outdated, demography changes and competition becomes intense. The market research for the new brand concept may well have been conducted in the most thorough manner, but it investigated attitudes, beliefs and social norms *at a specific point in time*. If the brand is to succeed, it usually has a short time to prove itself. Yet, even with hostile forces fighting against brands, many not only survive but thrive. The reason for their success is a strong internal commitment to brands, based on a solid belief that they have unique characteristics which consumers value sufficiently to buy. Well-thought-through brand plans have been prepared, documenting realistic objectives and viable strategies to counter competitive threats. Brand successes abound. For example, brands such as Gillette, Hoover, Schweppes, Colgate, Black Magic and Hovis have pedigrees going back over fifty years.

It would be naive to assume that the great brand successes have not had problems, as Coca-Cola's reformulation exemplifies. What is clear about brands which have a long history, is that they have been subtly adjusted to keep them *relevant* to changing market conditions. For some brands, this has resulted from continually tuning their pack designs to keep them contemporary. In other instances, it has been a case of putting the brand's core values in a different context. Lucozade, for example, used to be about providing a revitalizing source of energy for ill people. Between 1974 and 1978 sales fell by 12 per cent. This prompted more analysis, which showed that there were fewer 'flu epidemics and a trend to a healthier population. A decision was taken to present the brand as a source of energy for highly active people. The brand was taken to a much wider audience through the introduction of different pack sizes, the use of cans and plastic and its extension to Lucozade Glucose Tablets.

Brands which have successfully stood the test of time have built up a considerable amount of goodwill with their consumers, so much so that when sales start to fall it should not be automatically assumed they are in a terminal state and investment must be cut. It is often less expensive to revitalize an established brand than it is to develop and launch a new brand. Furthermore, consumers are less likely to try a new, unknown brand than a name that they are very familiar with. When years of activity have engendered such strong consumer trust in brands like Kellogg's Corn Flakes and Horlicks, it is almost an abdication of marketing responsibility to ignore the potential for revitalizing old brands.

The task of revitalizing old brands is less difficult when the core values of the brand have been protected and consistently presented to consumers. It is likely that the main task will be to update the way that the brand is presented. For example, when Black Magic was launched in 1934 it was positioned as the luxury plain chocolate assortment. It has always been associated with romance. This successful brand still conveys the same symbolic message between two people, albeit with television advertising that reflects contemporary views. The packaging has been changed to keep the brand up to date. The distinctive dominance of the black pack and the key-line motif on the diagonal corners have been subtly changed to reinforce the brand's modernity.

task of revitalizing old brands is less difficult when the core values of the brand have been protected and consistently presented to consumers

Brands sometimes need rejuvenating when they have not adapted to different social situations. One has only to think of the trainers market, where the leading players are continually monitoring and anticipating changes in social and cultural trends to fine-tune their brands to keep them fresh and relevant.

A systematic procedure for revitalizing brands

When looking to revitalize old brands, one way of progressing is to follow the procedures shown in the flow chart in Figure 10.5.

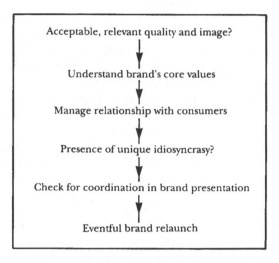

Figure 10.5   *Stages in rejuvenating brands (adapted from Berry 1988)*

A considerable amount of data has been collected by the Strategic Planning Institute (Buzzell and Gale 1987), looking at those factors that are strongly related to profitability. One of the key findings was that superior quality goes hand-in-hand with high profitability. But, it is not quality as defined from an internal perspective but from consumers' perspectives relative to the other brands they use. The slamming of a car door and the resultant 'thud', says more to many consumers about a car's quality than does a brochure full of technical data. The first stage in any revitalization programme should, therefore, investigate what consumers think and feel about the brand. This can be done using a minimum of ten depth interviews, where consumers are presented with the firm's and competitors' brands and their perceptions of relative strengths and weaknesses explored. It is particularly important that this be done using qualitative research techniques, since this identifies the attributes that are particularly relevant to consumers. The findings can then be assessed with more confidence by interviewing a much larger sample of consumers with a questionnaire incorporating the attributes found in the depth interviews.

The qualitative market research findings will broadly indicate how the physical characteristics of the brand are perceived, such as product formulation, packaging, pricing, availability, etc. They should also provide guidance about emotional aspects of the brand, such as the type of personality that the brand represents. The sorts of issues here may lead to questions such as, is it old fashioned? is it 'fuzzy'? is it relevant? is it too closely linked to an infrequently undertaken activity? Also by investigating changes in demography, social activities, competitive activity and distribution channels, the marketer should then be able to identify what changes might be needed for the brand's positioning.

With ideas beginning to evolve about positioning and personality changes, the marketer needs to consider how these would affect what the brand has always stood for. Managers need to be clear about their brand's core values. Any changes from the first part of the process need to be considered against the brand's core values. Marlboro stands for dominance, self-esteem, status, self-reliance and freedom. As it faces an increasingly hostile environment, any changes to make it more acceptable should not go against these core values.

The marketer needs to consider what type of relationship their brand has had with consumers and whether this is still relevant. For example, it may well have adopted an 'authority figure' relationship, treating the consumer almost as an inexperienced child. Without sufficient knowledge of the product field, the consumer may well be content to abdicate responsibility to the brand since it offers an almost paternalistic reassurance. However, as buyers become more experienced they will be looking for a 'husband–wife' type relationship, where they are treated as an equal, and with some respect. If the marketer has not allowed the brand to recognize the more mature nature of the consumer the wrong type of relationship may impede brand sales.

if the marketer has not allowed the brand to recognize the more mature nature of the consumer the wrong type of relationship may impede brand sales

Brands succeed because people recognize and value their personalities. But, just as people are not perfect, so brands need to have some idiosyncratic element to make them more human. If the brand needs revitalizing, one way to bring it more alive is to add an idiosyncratic element. Examples of this are the Hathaway man with the eye-patch advertising shirts.

Once a view has been adopted about possible changes, these must be carefully coordinated to ensure that each element of the marketing mix supports the new proposition. What is then required, is a promotional launch that rapidly gets the message across about the rejuvenated brand.

Conclusions

Once a brand has been launched, with core values that consumers appreciate, it is important that these core values are clearly communicated to all the people working on the brand and any differing perceptions amongst the brand team about the brand's values should be identified and addressed. Any attempt to change its core values over time should be strongly resisted. There may well be a need to update the brand's presentation, but its new design should still communicate that the brand represents those values which consumers have grown to respect and welcome.

Managers need to recognize that while they analyse brands in terms of details about their core values, consumers do not undertake such detailed assessment and when they choose between brands only a few issues are considered. It is therefore important for managers to consider how the component parts of a brand are synergistically integrated into the brand as a holistic entity. By considering the bridged need satisfied by the functional/psychological components of the brand, then thinking about the evaluator consumers can use to judge their brand, a more holistic brand is likely to succeed with a clear positioning.

When consumers choose brands, there are two broad dimensions that are primarily assessed in each situation. They consider the extent to which the brand satisfies their **functional** needs. For example, when wind surfing, they gauge whether certain brands of watches accurately tell the time regardless of how often they are immersed in water. They also evaluate the effectiveness of different brands in communicating something about themselves. In other words, they take into account how well different brands satisfy **representational** needs. The wind surfer may well consider the extent to which different brands of watches imply that he or she is agile and experienced.

In any product field, it is possible to evaluate the extent to which different brands satisfy functional and representational needs. By plotting competing brands on a functional–representational matrix, it is possible to assess, from consumers' perspectives, which brands are close substitutes for each other by identifying groups of brands that cluster together. Investment strategies to sustain brands can also be developed from this matrix.

An understanding of brands' functional–representational characteristics enables marketers to plan resources at a particular time. A longer-term planning process, however, needs to anticipate resource requirements over brands' life cycles. During the development stage of the brand, it is crucial that the functional characteristics of the brand are able to meet the expectations raised by any awareness campaign. To ensure that it is functionally superior, consumer testing is needed. However, the marketer needs to be aware of the high costs incurred by delaying the launch due to over-sophisticated testing procedures. The advent of virtual reality techniques should enable consumer assessments without much delay. Being first to market with a new brand which catches consumers' interest offers several attractive benefits.

As sales of the brand start to grow, its image should be reinforced, enabling consumers to recognize precisely what the brand represents and in which functional situation it is particularly effective. In early maturity, when it starts to become a cash generator, its high brand share needs to be guarded to ensure that long-term profitability accrues. Short-sighted marketers may be inadvisably tempted to cut brand support and enjoy only a limited period of brand profitability.

After a healthy period in its maturity phase, the brand may show a sluggish fall in sales. Rather than incorrectly assuming that the brand is in terminal decline, analysis should be undertaken to evaluate why its popularity is waning and whether it is viable to inject new life. New brands are very expensive to launch and their future is very uncertain. By contrast, revitalizing brands may well be a less-expensive route to follow, with a greater likelihood of success. Good analysis should show how the brand's well-established core values can be presented in a way more in tune with developing consumer expectations.

in early maturity, when it starts to become a cash generator, its high brand share needs to be guarded to ensure that long-term profitability accrues

Marketing action checklist

To help clarify the direction of future marketing activity, it is recommended that the following exercises are undertaken:

1   Is there a document within your firm which, at the birth of each new brand, states what each brand's core values are? What systems are in place to stop any of your management team changing the brand's core values? Do you have an annual monitor of each individual manager's views about the core values of the brands they are working on and do you provide feedback about instances where their views are dissimilar from the central statement of core values?

2   Take one of your major brands and write down the most important functional consumer needs it satisfies. What are the most important psychological needs being satisfied? Are these needs interlinked? What one word bridges the key functional and psychological benefit of this brand? What evaluator encourages

consumers to judge the brand? From this analysis how could your brand be better positioned?

3   For a particular product field, reach a consensus view with your colleagues about the functional attributes consumers consider when choosing brands. You should not have more than five attributes. Give a score to your brand and to your competitors' brands, according to the consensus view about how well each brand satisfies consumers' functional needs. Do this on a scale where 10 represents 'excellent satisfier of consumers' functional needs' and 1 represents 'extremely poor satisfier of consumers' functional needs'. What could be done to improve your brand's positioning on this dimension? What is the brand leader doing particularly well on the functional dimension?

With those colleagues who have been with your firm for some time, repeat the exercise, but this time for a period 12 months ago. Compare the historical and current scores for all the brands on the functional dimension and evaluate why these movements took place.

4   Amongst your colleagues, form a consensus view about what consumers are trying to say about themselves when they buy brands in your product field. Identify no more than five attributes describing this representational dimension. Score your brand and competitors' brands according to the consensus view about how well each brand satisfies consumers' representational needs. Do this on a scale where 10 stands for 'excellent satisfier of consumers' representational needs' and 1 represents 'extremely poor satisfier of consumers' representational needs'. Are there any improvements that will help your brand's positioning on this dimension? What is the brand leader doing particularly well on the representational dimension?

With long-serving colleagues, repeat the exercise for a period 12 months ago. Compare the historical and current scores for the brands on the representational dimension and evaluate why these movements took place.

5   From the results you now have from questions 3 and 4, plot your brand on the functional and representational dimensions of the de Chernatony–McWilliam brand planning matrix. Knowing within which quadrant your brand is positioned, how appropriate is your strategy to support this brand?

6   Using the approach from questions 3 and 4, with your colleagues plot on the functional and representational dimensions where your competitors' brands are positioned. Focusing on those competitors who are in the same quadrant as your brand, evaluate

the strengths and weaknesses of their strategies. What could you do to better defend your brand?

7   Undertake an audit of all the new brands which your firm has launched in the past five years. Focusing on those brands that have since been withdrawn, and those which are regarded as doing badly, identify the reason for their poor performance. Does any one reason continually appear?

8   For any one of your more recently-launched new brands, get your marketing research department to produce a timetable detailing the amount of time taken for each piece of marketing research. Does any one piece of marketing research appear to have consumed a lot of time? Are there any reasons why this took so long? How much time elapsed between the completion of fieldwork for each project and the presentation of results? How long could it have taken to a brief 'top line' finding, where only the results on each question are presented, without any detailed cross-analysis and without any written report? Are there any implications about how time can be saved on future marketing research reports?

9   How effective is your firm at bringing together groups of people from different functional backgrounds to form a new brand project team? Are there any barriers within your firm that impede the formation of new project teams?

10 Do your brand plans consider how each brand's image will be protected as they pass through their life cycles?

11 For any recent brand extensions, evaluate whether there is a natural link between the functional, or representational, needs satisfied by the brand extension and the original brand. Where there is only a weak link, it is worth considering severing any association between the two brands.

12 Using the matrix shown in Figure10.4, plot where each of your brands currently resides. If there are no brands in quadrant C you should question what has to be done to secure your firm's future over the next three years.

13 Undertake an analysis of the brands in your firm's portfolio and identify any brands which are showing sluggish sales performance. Are there any changes in the external environment that have gradually been impeding these brands' performance? Using the flow chart in Figure 10.5, how could new life be put back into these rather staid brands?

References and further reading

Alcock G. and Batten C. (1986). Judging the worth of brand values. *Marketing Week*, 25 April, 58–61.
Anon (1991). What makes Yoshio invent. *The Economist*, 12 January, 75.
Berry N. (1988). Revitalizing brands. *Journal of Consumer Marketing*, 5 (3), 15–20.
Brierley S. (1994). ASA document slams P&G ads. *Marketing Week*, 2 December 7.
Brierley S. (1995). Lever drops 'accelerator' formulation. *Marketing Week*, 20 January 5.
Brierley S. (1995). Making way for New Generation. *Marketing Week*, 24 February 23–4.
Brand Positioning Services (1987). *Positioning Brands Profitably*. London.
Burke R. (1995). Virtual shopping. *OR/MS Today*, Aug., 28–34.
Buzzell R. and Gale B. (1987). *The PIMS Principles – Linking Strategy to Performance*. New York: The Free Press.
Clifford D. and Cavanagh R. (1985). *The Winning Performance: How America's High Growth Midsize Companies Succeed*. London: Sidgwick & Jackson.
Connor B. (1986). How oldies go for black. *Marketing*, 20 Feb., 39–43.
Cooper R. (1987). *Winning at New Products*. Agincourt, Ontario: Gage.
de Chernatony L. (1993). Categorizing brands: evolutionary processes underpinned by two key dimensions. *Journal of Marketing Management*, 9 (2), 173–88.
de Chernatony L. and McWilliam G. (1989). Clarifying how marketers interpret 'brands'. *Journal of Marketing Management*, 5 (2), 153–71.
de Chernatony L. and McWilliam G. (1990). Appreciating brands as assets through using a two dimensional model. *International Journal of Advertising*, 9 (2), 111–9.
de Chernatony L. and Took R. (1994). Team based brand building: questioning the current marketing research role. In *Proceedings of Building Successful Brands*, 265–78. Amsterdam: European Society for Opinion and Marketing Research.
Gardner B. and Levy S. (1955). The product and the brand. *Harvard Business Review*, 33 (March–April), 35–41.
Garvin D. (1987). Competing on the eight dimensions of quality. *Harvard Business Review*, 65 (Nov.–Dec.), 101–9.
Hamel G. and Prahalad C. (1991). Corporate imagination and expeditionary marketing. *Harvard Business Review*, 69 (July–Aug.), 81–92.
Hoggan K. (1988). Back to life. *Marketing*, 3 March, 20–2.
Interbrand (1990). *Brands – An International Review*. London: Mercury Books.
Jones J. P. (1986). *What's in a Name?* Lexington: Lexington Books.
Katz D. (1960). The functional approach to the study of attitudes. *Public Opinion Quarterly*, 24 (Summer), 163–204.
Kim P. (1990). A perspective on brands. *Journal of Consumer Marketing*, 7 (4), 63–7.
Landon E. (1974). Self concept, ideal self concept and consumer purchase intentions. *Journal of Consumer Research*, 1 (Sept.), 44–51.
Lannon J. and Cooper P. (1983). Humanistic advertising: a holistic cultural perspective. *International Journal of Advertising*, 2, 195–213.
Lawless M. and Fisher R. (1990). Sources of durable competitive advantage in new products. *Journal of Product Innovation Management*, 7 (1), 35–44.
Munson J. and Spivey W. (1981). Product and brand user stereotypes among social classes. In: *Advances in Consumer Research*, Vol. 8, (Monroe K. ed.). 696–701. Ann Arbor: Association for Consumer Research.
Nevens T., Summe G. and Uttal B. (1990). Commercializing technology: what the best companies do. *Harvard Business Review*, 68 (May–June), 154–63.
Olshavsky R. and Granbois D. (1979). Consumer decision making – fact or fiction? *Journal of Consumer Research*, 6 (Sept), 93–100.
Parasuraman A., Zeithaml V. and Berry L. (1988). SERVQUAL: A multiple-item scale for measuring consumer perceptions of service quality. *Journal of Retailing*, 64 (1), 12–40.

Park C., Jaworski B. and MacInnis D. (1986). Strategic brand concept-image management. *Journal of Marketing*, **50** (Oct.), 135–45.

Rosenberger III P. and de Chernatony L. (1995). Virtual reality techniques in NPD research. *Journal of the Market Research Society*, **37** (4), 345–55.

Saporito B. (1986). Has-been brands go back to work. *Fortune*, 28 April, 97–8.

Sheth J., Newman B. and Gross B. (1991). Why we buy what we buy: a theory of consumption values. *Journal of Business Research*, **22** (2), 159–70.

Solomon M. (1983). The role of products as social stimuli: a symbolic interactionism perspective. *Journal of Consumer Research*, **10** (Dec), 319–29.

Urban G. and Star S. (1991). *Advanced Marketing Strategy*. Englewood Cliffs: Prentice Hall.

Urban G., Weinberg B. and Hauser J. (1994). Premarket forecasting of really new products. Massachusetts Institute of Technology unpublished paper.

Ward K., Srikanthan S. and Neal R. (1989). Life-cycle costing in the financial evaluation and control of products and brands. *Quarterly Review of Marketing* (Autumn), 1–7.

Weitz B. and Wensley R. (1988). *Readings in Strategic Marketing*. Chicago: Dryden Press.

Wicks A. (1989). Advertising research – an eclectic view from the UK. *Journal of the Market Research Society*, **31** (4), 527–35.

Chapter 11

Brand evaluation

Summary

The purpose of this chapter is to examine the concept of brand equity and provide useful guidelines to managers who need to measure the health of their brands. We open this chapter by considering the dynamic nature of brand equity. With the aid of theoretical and commercial models, we then explain how growth in brand equity can be achieved.

The definition of brand equity we propose recognizes the richness of this concept. This interpretation links three components of brand equity: the characteristics of a brand, how they affect its strength which is in turn reflected in its financial value. We investigate these three components, considering ways of assessing the well-being of brands. The chapter concludes by considering alternative ways of financially valuing brands.

Growing brand equity

The previous chapters in this book have considered how resources can best be employed to develop and sustain powerful brands. Once managers have been successful in using these resources for branding purposes, they will need to monitor the health of their brands. In order to be able to sustain their brands' strengths they require a method of regularly monitoring performance. Managers are particularly interested in measuring the equity that has been built up by their brand. Delving deeper into this issue of measuring brand equity reveals that it is a multi-dimensional concept, which we discuss in this chapter.

One of the challenges managers face when attempting to measure brand equity is that there are numerous interpretations of this concept, each leading to a different set of measures. For example, two independent groups of academics in the USA (Farquhar 1989

brand equity is a multi-dimensional concept

and the work of Simon and Sullivan 1990) adopt a financial perspective, regarding brand equity as the incremental cash flow resulting from associating a brand name with a product. By contrast, Aaker and Biel (1993) take a value-added perspective, conceiving brand equity as the value added to the core product or service by associating it with a brand name. Keller (1993) takes more account of consumer behaviour, regarding brand equity as the result of consumers' responses to the marketing of a particular brand which depends on their knowledge of that brand. We were impressed by a particularly well-thought-out exposition developed by Feldwick (1996), and adapted this further. We concluded that:

> *Brand equity consists of the differential attributes underpinning a brand which give increased value to the firm's balance sheet.*

Not to put too fine a point on it, brand equity only exists if income streams over and above the average for the sector or segment result from putting a particular brand name on a product or service.

Later in this chapter we show how this interpretation enables a multi-dimensional measuring procedure to assess the brand's health. Regardless of the measures selected, it is essential that managers track their brand equity on a regular basis since, as outlined in Chapter 10, managers are continually striving to fine-tune their strategies over the brand's life-cycle. To effectively measure brand equity, managers need to appreciate that brand equity is a dynamic concept and thus it needs tracking.

Readers can begin to appreciate the dynamic nature of brand equity from a particularly helpful evolutionary model developed by Gordon and his colleagues (1994), shown in the Figure 11.1.

When a new brand is developed, it initially exists only through its physical characteristics. For the brand to be **born**, two decisions

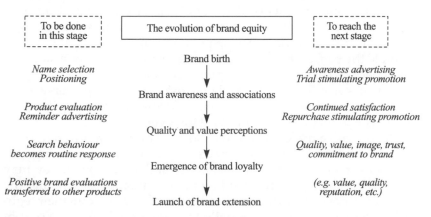

Figure 11.1   *The evolution of brand equity (after Gordon et al. 1994)*

must be taken: a brand name and a positioning strategy must be agreed. The former is critical because it contributes to the brand identity and can also communicate information about the product performance or ease of use. For example, the brand name 'Netscape Navigator' clearly states the function of the product, a guide to visitors to the Internet, and underlines its characteristics of user-friendliness and reliability. Likewise, Post-It Notes were given a very explicit brand name in order to make clear what the function of the product was in its early days. Positioning is critical because it determines the brand's desired competitive set and it is against these, if consumers' perceptions also concur with managers', that relative brand strength will ultimately be measured. At this stage, bipolar maps of the functional attributes of competing brands are very useful to appreciate similarity/dissimilarity.

When the brand is launched, managers have three objectives: the attainment of brand awareness; the development of favourable associations; and the involvement of consumers so that they will want to try the new brand and purchase it. To achieve these goals managers need to skilfully blend the elements of the marketing mix.

As consumers are repeatedly exposed to the brand, they become more familiar with it. Their degree of **brand awareness** depends on their ability to recall any promotional messages and the brand's availability. At this point, marketers need to focus on efficient communication and gaining distribution. Once consumers become familiar with the brand, their perceptions of it become more detailed. Managers aim at this stage to ensure that consumers include the brand in their consideration set.

The long-term success of a brand, however, is influenced by **consumers' perceptions of its value**, which are often based on functional and psychological attributes. There is a greater likelihood of success when marketers create some unique performance characteristics which appeal to a sufficiently large number of consumers. Consumers' judgements of the brand's quality are based on both objective measures, such as performance and fitness for use, and subjective criteria, such as past experiences and associated cues, for example the packaging colour. Past experiences can have a substantial impact on consumers' perceptions of quality.

Price is an indicator of the relative risk consumers perceive when they choose one brand over another, particularly when they have no previous experience of the brand. However, consumers are generally faced with a reasonably wide choice of brands at different price levels. While the competing brands may contain identical ingredients, consumers' perceptions of quality and value for money may differ. Their choice is influenced by their evaluation of whether the price difference justifies the risk incurred in switching from their regular brand to a new one. Eventually the new brand becomes part of

their choice is influenced by their evaluation of whether the price difference justifies the risk incurred in switching from their regular brand to a new one

the consumer's brand repertoire. At this stage, they rarely compare competing brands, automatically choosing their preferred brand for particular situations. Their behaviour shifts from searching for information in order to choose between brands to a routine response, which in many cases leads to loyalty towards particular brands.

Brand loyalty is a measure of a consumer's attachment to a specific brand and is a function of several factors such as the perceived quality of the brand, its perceived value, its image, the trust placed in the brand, and the commitment the consumer feels towards it. Committed consumers guarantee future income streams as well as facilitating brand extensions by transferring any positive associations to new brands.

The last stage in the evolution of brand equity enables firms to strategically exploit any equity the parent brand has built up. **Brand extension** allows companies to further grow brand equity by gaining loyalty for related brands from existing consumers and existing channels.

Commercial models of brand equity growth

Models, such as the one just described, have also been developed by commercial organizations. Young & Rubicam have their own interpretation of the brand equity growth process. According to their model, brand equity growth is achieved by building on four brand elements: differentiation; relevance; esteem; and familiarity.

Differentiation represents the starting point of the growth process, as the brand cannot exist in the long run unless consumers can distinguish it from others. To attract and retain consumers, the brand needs to convince them that it is **relevant** to their individual needs. As competition increases, marketers wisely protect their brand and show consumers that it delivers what has been promised. The next challenge for managers is to ensure that consumers have regard and **esteem** for the brand's capabilities. If the brand has established itself as distinctive, appropriate and highly-regarded, its ultimate success will depend on **familiarity**, that is whether the brand is truly well-known and is part of consumers' everyday lives. Familiarity does not solely depend on advertising, albeit this is a notable contributor, but also results from consumers recognizing that the brand provides more value than other brands.

brand equity growth is achieved by building on four elements: differentiation, relevance, esteem; and familiarity

Young & Rubicam's empirical analysis indicates that scores on relevance and differentiation provide an assessment of the brand's potential for growth, and they refer to this as 'brand vitality'. Furthermore, scores on esteem and familiarity measure the brand's current strength, its 'brand stature'. By plotting these values on the matrix, shown in Figure 11.2, it is possible to consider the equity the brand has achieved and identify appropriate strategies for its future growth.

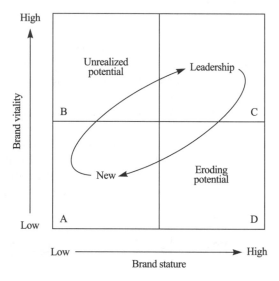

Figure 11.2 *The strategic direction of brand strength* (after Young and Rubicam 1994)

Initially a brand begins its life in quadrant A with low scores on all attributes. For the brand to move upwards into quadrant B and gain more vitality, managers need to invest in attaining higher levels of differentiation and relevance. Once brands have reached a higher level of 'vitality', brand owners have two options – maintenance by establishing them as niche brands, or investing in building the brand's esteem and encouraging growth into quadrant C. The top right-hand quadrant is home to strong brands which have achieved remarkable brand equity growth, though they still may have potential for further growth. By maintaining the brand's stature and creatively managing its vitality, managers can look forward to the brand having a long lifetime. However, without sufficient maintenance of the brand's vitality, its differentiation and relevance fall, resulting in the brand increasingly selling on price promotions and declining to quadrant D. In such a situation, the brand becomes vulnerable to price wars. As firms lose confidence in a brand's future, they cut marketing support, resulting in familiarity and esteem falling. Consequently brand equity falls as the brand slips back to quadrant A.

The framework by Young and Rubicam helps managers to understand the concept of brand equity and highlights which aspects of the brand (differentiation, relevance, familiarity and esteem) need attention over the short and long term. Moreover, by comparing the

Newton

Apple MessagePad 2000
eMail, Fax, Internet
access, Word processing,
Spreadsheets,
GSM communications...

For further information
call free on: 0800 639 866
or visit our web site at:
http://www.euro.
apple.com/newton

Now you can
travel light
and pack heavy.

Give your dreams a chance.

The new Apple™ MessagePad™ 2000 weighs less than 700 grams and fits in your palm, yet offers almost every feature you'd expect to find on a desk-bound computer. Diminutive in size it may be, but it certainly packs a punch. Not only is the 160MHz processor in the MessagePad 2000 ten times more powerful than its predecessor, but the battery offers continual use for a full 24 hours – without recharge. It also comes with all the applications you need to get started built-in and you can connect it to your PC (Windows® or Macintosh™) in moments, to download information or simply to synchronise your diaries. Connect a GSM mobile phone to a MessagePad 2000 and the world is your oyster – you can send faxes, eMail and even connect to the Internet. So next time you're packing for the airport, why not take the MessagePad 2000 along for the ride. On your return, you might even find space for an extra bottle of duty free.

Exhibit 11.1 *To many business people who have grown to value the productivity gains they have personally achieved, the Apple brand has a high score on familiarity (reproduced by kind permission of Apple Computer UK Ltd)*

position of the company's brands with that of competitors' brands, the model suggests appropriate strategies to increase brand equity and protect it against competition.

consumers' value of a brand grows from a distant to a closely-bonded relationship

Millward Brown International have devised a helpful diagnostic tool which, like the Young and Rubicam approach, enables managers to appreciate the basis for their brand's equity compared with competing brands. Their BrandDynamics™ pyramid model is shown in Figure 11.3, portraying the way consumers' value of a brand grows from a distant to a closely-bonded relationship.

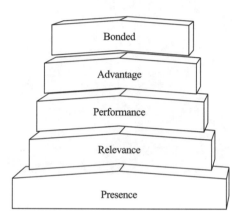

Figure 11.3 *The criteria to assess the strength of a brand* (after Millward Brown International 1996)

To be considered for purchasing a brand must have a presence, both physically in terms of availability and psychologically in terms of awareness. Should people find the promise inherent in the brand to be relevant to their particular needs, they are more likely to progress to trying the brand, forming a view about its performance. Evaluation of the brand's functional and emotional performance capabilities, relative to other brands, leads consumers to a view about its relative advantages. If these advantages are particularly strong they are likely to continue buying the brand and over time a bonded relationship results.

The benefit of this diagnostic is that by interviewing consumers about competing brands in a market, their profiles can be assessed on these pyramids. Through comparing these profiles, strengths and weaknesses can be identified, enabling appropriate strategies to be devised.

Measuring brand equity

As this book has sought to clarify, brands are complex concepts which can be characterized by several dimensions. Therefore, evaluating the health of a brand by measuring its brand equity necessitates taking several different measures along several different dimensions. We next provide guidance about some of these measures.

Our view about the meaning of brand equity is more embracing than that of other authors. We adopt a broad perspective because it recognizes the complexity of the brand and the different roles man-

DIANA MORAN AGED 58.

What does Ulay's new moisturiser give
mature skin apart from extra moisture?

PROTECTION.

NEW REVITALISING PROTECTIVE FLUID

As your skin matures it needs extra protection, because as well as being drier, it's more vulnerable to UV damage such as age spots. That's why Ulay's new Pro-Vital fluid combines vitamins, SPF15 UV filters and extra Ulay moisture to help protect mature skin from further damage, leaving it looking fresh and healthy. And the name? New Pro-Vital Fluid from Oil of Ulay.

OIL of ULAY
WE CAN PROVE YOU CAN LOOK YOUNGER

Exhibit 11.2 *The Oil of Ulay moisturiser is striving to communicate its performance capability (reproduced by kind permission of Procter & Gamble)*

agers and consumers expect brands to play. The umbrella nature of our definition supports several different measures, which managers can tailor to their own environment, since according to the extent to which a brand draws on functional or representational characteristics (covered in Chapter 10) so perceived performance or image measures are particularly relevant. The measures we review are comprehensive, although the practitioner may prefer to use just a few of them. Wisely selected, a few dimensions should enable managers to appreciate the state of health of their brands.

Our interpretation of brand equity is heavily influenced by Feldwick's insightful review (1996) of the literature on brand equity along with the work of Aaker (1996) and Keller (1993). We have adapted Feldwick's model and regard brand equity as 'the differential attributes underpinning a brand which give increased value to the firm's balance sheet'. An important word in this definition is **differential**, since consumers usually evaluate a brand relative to the brands they perceive it competing against. The definition can be understood in terms of the causal model shown in Figure 11.4.

brand equity as 'the differential attributes underpinning a brand which give increased value to the firm's balance sheet'

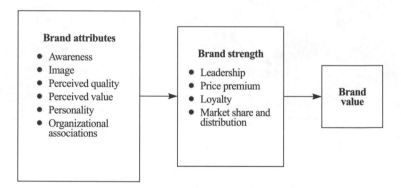

Figure 11.4 *The causal nature of brand equity* (adapted after Feldwick 1996)

In essence, the relative attributes of a brand will affect its strength and this in turn will be reflected in the financial value of the brand. Measuring brand equity should therefore involve an investigation of these three components. Drawing on the published literature about the different types of measures, managers are able to choose from the following ways of evaluating each of the linkages.

Brand attributes

The response by a consumer to a brand will, as Keller (1993) so cogently argued (1993), depend on their favourable or unfavourable knowledge about it. Their brand knowledge results from their level of awareness and the images they have about the brand. Thus, these two core components are at the heart of any brand attributes.

Brand awareness reflects the salience of a brand and facilitates consumers' abilities to identify the brand with a specific product category. Aspects of brand awareness can be measured through the following ways:

- *Brand recognition* – This refers to the consumer's ability to recall previous exposure or experience with the brand. For example,

Having cancer scared the hell out of me, and then the doctor brought in a specialist.

She's a Macmillan nurse. A specialist in cancer care who complements the work of doctors by dealing with her patients' physical and emotional needs from diagnosis onwards. She needs your support.
To make a donation please call free on 0500 800 111.

Macmillan
cancer relief

Exhibit 11.3 *Macmillan Cancer Relief have a well-respected image of caring for cancer sufferers*

'Have you seen this brand before, or not?'.

- *Brand recall* – This refers to the consumer's ability to retrieve the brand from memory when given the product category as a cue. For example, 'What brands of lager are you aware of?'.
- *Brand dominance* – This identifies the most important brand in a specific product category. For example 'Which brand of lager do you drink most often?'.
- *Brand knowledge* – This evaluates the consumer's interpretation of the values linked to a brand. For example 'To what extent do you agree or disagree that the following cars have high accelerations?'.

Brand image reflects consumers' perceptions of a brand's characteristics and can be gauged by the associations they hold in their memory. The different types of brand associations can be grouped according to: their level of abstraction; the amount of information held; whether they are product-related or non-product-related; and whether they refer to attributes considered essential by consumers. There are different tools to measure the brand image:

- *Projective techniques* are helpful when consumers are unable or unwilling to express their feelings. These techniques include: sentence completion – 'When I buy a personal computer, I look for...'; brand personality descriptors – 'The typical driver of a Ford Fiesta is ...'; and picture interpretation – there may be a picture of a man driving his new BMW into a golf club's car park and two golf players are looking on – what would they say to each other about the driver?
- *Qualitative techniques*, such as free association, are used to explore possible associations along with further investigation during group discussions or depth interviews.
- *Ratings of evaluations and beliefs* are suitable to capture consumers' views on key attributes and the strength of their associations with particular brands.
- *Comparison of brand associations* with those of competitors identifies the relative strengths and weaknesses of the brand. For example, 'Of the fruit juice brands that you identified earlier, which one do you believe to be the best? Why is it better than the other brands? What don't you like about it compared with the other brands?'.

Aaker's work (1996) enables us to delve deeper into measuring a brand's attributes and its strength as we explore. **Perceived quality** is an important brand attribute and can be measured by comparing the brand with its competitors, using scales such as:

- above average, average and below average;
- consistent quality and inconsistent quality.

To measure perceived quality, consumers should first be asked which category they perceive the brand to be in and against whom it competes. Without asking this, there is a danger that inappropriate competitors might be specified by managers which are not relevant to consumers.

Perceived value indicates the extent to which the brand meets performance expectations, given its price. It can be measured by considering value for money and the reasons for purchase, for example:

- 'Do you think that the Toyota Corolla represents good value for money?'
- 'Why did you buy the Toyota Corolla rather than another car brand?'

The brand's **personality** is a useful metaphor to appreciate the brand's values and this shows the brand's emotional and self-expressive capabilities. This is particularly useful for brands which have only minor physical variations and are conspicuously consumed, for example brandy. In these instances, very few consumers can distinguish between the taste of different brands and the brand is used to make a statement about the user. The brand's personality can be identified through questions such as:

- 'If brand X came to life, what sort of person would it be?'
- 'If brand X were to die, what would be written on its tomb stone?'
- 'What type of person do you think would use this brand?'
- 'If brand X were a famous person, who do you think it would be?'

Organizational associations refer to the perceptions of a brand that consumers derive from its parent organization. This dimension is appropriate when the organization is particularly visible (as in a service business), or a corporate branding strategy is being used, such as Ford. Positive associations provide a valuable basis for differentiation. Measurements focus on how consumers consider the organization, for example:

- 'Do you trust this brand, knowing it comes from…?'
- 'How do you feel about this organization?'
- 'How would you describe the people that work for this organization?'

Brand strength

As a consequence of its attributes, the strength of the brand can be gauged. Another set of measures needs to be used to assess brand strength.

Leadership not only identifies the most successful brand, but also whether it is technologically or socially innovative within its category. This dimension can be measured, besides using market audit data, with questions such as:

* 'Do you regard brand X as being a leading, rather than following brand?'
* 'Is brand X the first to break with tradition?'
* 'Does brand X offer you the latest technological development?'
* 'Is brand X a fashion leader in its category?'

The **price premium** reflects the brand's ability to command a higher price or to be less price sensitive than its competitors. This measure needs to be defined relative to those brands consumers consider as substitutes. A brand's price premium can be identified by informing consumers of the price of competitors' brands, then asking consumers how much more, or less, they would pay for the brand. A more involved, albeit some argue a more reliable method, is to use trade-off analysis. A simpler way of assessing the price premium of the brand is employed by Intel who regularly interview potential customers, asking how much discount they would require before they would accept a PC without 'Intel Inside'.

Price premium is not a suitable measure in markets with legal restrictions which prevent companies from charging a premium price. Also, it is not appropriate for strong brands, such as Swatch, that intentionally charge lower prices to keep competitors out of the market, or for brands such as Mars Bars, that have no direct substitutes for their products.

there are numerous measures of loyalty

There are numerous measures of **loyalty**, for example measuring actual purchasing behaviour over time which reflects the degree of satisfaction existing customers have with the brand. Loyalty can also be gauged asking questions such as:

* 'Next time you buy this product category, would you buy this brand again?'
* 'Thinking about the few brands of this product category that you often buy, is this brand one of your more frequently bought brands?'
* 'If someone were thinking of buying this product, which brand would you recommend?'

Buy yourselves the time to leave the fast track and get back to a freedom you both can enjoy. Lighter, faster and easy to ride, the new Pioneer Jaguar range takes classic design and turns it into a 21st century proposition.

New technology, the latest comfort features and proven Raleigh quality, combines to create a new breed of bicycles to suit every cyclist's style.

Lightweight, anatomic frame designs add to comfort and control.
While the latest gear and brake specifications make the going easy in town or on a country trail.

With a range of models starting from as little as £150, isn't it time you splashed out on a Raleigh Pioneer?

- LIGHTWEIGHT SEMI OVERSIZE JAGUAR SERIES CROMOLY FRAME
- SHIMANO 18 SPEED GEARING WITH EASY USE GRIPSHIFT ROTATIONAL SHIFTERS
- DUAL PURPOSE ON/OFF ROAD AQUA TREAD SKINWALL TYRES
- EXTRA COMFORT SPRUNG SADDLE ● FULLY ADJUSTABLE REAR ALLOY CARRIER

PIONEER JAGUAR 18 | **£249.99**

WHEN WAS THE LAST TIME YOU SPLASHED OUT ON EACH OTHER?

The Pioneer range, £150 to £350. For a full Raleigh range catalogue and details of your nearest stockist call 0345 056006. http://www.raleighbikes.com
All prices quoted Recommended Retail Prices

Exhibit 11.4 *With a notable heritage, Raleigh bicycles are perceived as being good quality machines (reproduced by Raleigh Industries Ltd and Cross Hill Conwill)*

Managers should be aware that the responses to these questions may reflect past behaviour rather than intended future behaviour and that the favourableness of replies may be more a reflection of brand size than loyalty.

Another method of measuring loyalty is provided by the concept of 'Share of Category Requirement' (SCR). The SCR for Ski yoghurt is all Ski yoghurt volume expressed as a share of all yoghurt bought by consumers who purchase Ski yoghurt during a defined period, such as a year. An alternative is to define loyalty by considering consumers' purchasing patterns over time and estimating the probability of their buying the brand on the next purchasing occasion. However, this analysis should also include data on price variations, as most patterns are strongly influenced by promotions.

Market share and **distribution** data indicates brand strength without recourse to consumer surveys. To obtain realistic results, however, marketers need to define the market and the competitor set from consumers' perspectives and recognize that market share indicators are often distorted by short-term price and promotional activities.

The financial value of brands

Debate still continues about whether brands can be included in the balance sheet and views are split on financially accounting for brands. Does the balance sheet with an inclusion of the value of brands represent a subjective appreciation of the brand's real value or should the balance sheet reflect a more objective assessment including completed financial transactions only when brands are bought?

to be acceptable in financial accounting terms, any brand valuation method should apply to both acquired and internally-created brands

To be acceptable in financial accounting terms, any brand valuation method should apply to both acquired and internally-created brands. One of the problems is that there are different perspectives on the value of a brand at any one time. For example, prior to market bids Rowntree was worth around £1 bn to its shareholders, yet a few months later was worth £2.4 bn to Nestlé. Although the value of a brand becomes much more apparent at the time it is acquired by another company, there remains uncertainty about the firm's annual valuation of its brands and consequently it has been rare up to now to include the value of created brands in published accounts. In the absence of a generally accepted standard for brand valuation, the internally-calculated value is subject to various interpretations.

At the acquisition stage, the brand's value depends very much on the purchaser, who will probably value it more if the acquisition is expected to bring synergy to the company, as was clearly the case with Nestlé's purchase of Rowntree. The issue of separability of the brand is best illustrated by the words of John Stuart, former Chairman of Quaker Oats Ltd: 'If this business were to be split up, I would be glad to take the brands, trademarks, and goodwill, and you could have all the bricks and mortars. And I would fare better than you.' He is certainly right! However, a brand's value is not automatically transferable and the purchase of the brand could negatively affect its value. When the acquired brand becomes part of a new firm, it is divorced from the previous firm's management, culture and systems and, without the flair and networks the previous owners had, it may lose its consumer base. Any sales are strongly influenced by promotions and shelf visibility, but more importantly there is also the goodwill from the corporation. In new hands, with a different corporate halo, the brand might not be as strong. Brands with unique functional qualities may not be manufactured in the same way by the purchaser of the brand. For example, a new company could not easily offer to consumers of BMW cars the same guarantee of engineering excellence and reliability without the BMW support.

Valuing brands is fraught with different assumptions. For ex-

Exhibit 11.5 Boots Advantage Card has been developed to encourage consumer loyalty (reproduced by kind permission of Boots the Chemist)

ample, the valuation of a marketing consultancy at 8 in the morning when few staff are there is different from its valuation at 11 in the morning. How do you account for a consultant working out his notice who was particularly successful at winning new business? In view of the difficulties in valuing what are essentially clusters of mental associations recognizable through a name, some companies question the usefulness of valuing brands for balance sheet purposes. Nevertheless, the overall trend shows that more companies believe there are benefits in valuing their brands and have accepted this challenge.

It has been argued that valuing brands is a worthwhile exercise because it draws attention to the long-term implications of brand strategies. By including brand values in the company accounts, managers are forced to identify the long-term effects of their marketing decisions. Moreover, being forced to consider long-term effects counterbalances the pressure that usually drives managers who focus on policies to achieve short-term profits, but which pay lip service to brand building. Brand valuation therefore encourages managers to think more about building brands than market share. Where managers' performance is evaluated on an annual basis by changes in their brand's equity, they are more likely to emphasize decisions that are beneficial to the long-term growth of their brand and are less inclined to accept quick-fix solutions, such as price-off promotions, or brand extensions which become too remote from the core brand and may undermine the value of the parent brand. The brand represents a major marketing investment which it would be unwise not to evaluate, despite the fact that the assumptions underpinning the brand valuation process affect the resulting figure.

the value of the brand also differs according to whose perspective is considered

The value of the brand also differs according to whose perspective is considered. From a firm's point of view, a brand's value is derived from the incremental cash flow resulting from associating the brand with a product. For example, in a television factory once jointly owned by Hitachi and General Electric, Hitachi was able to sell the same product as GE but labelled Hitachi with a £50 premium, and at twice the volume. A brand brings three competitive advantages to the firm: it provides a platform from which to launch new products and licenses; it builds resilience in times of crisis as seen by the quick sales recovery following the incident when Tylenol was tampered with; and it creates a barrier to entry, for instance, formidable barriers are present through names such as Nike, Rolls-Royce and Chanel. From a trader's perspective, the value of a brand lies in its ability to attract consumers into their stores. From a consumer's point of view, the brand has value since it distinguishes the offering, reduces their perceptions of risk and reduces their effort in making a choice.

To manufacturers, retailers' and consumers' brands have value and therefore it is right that some attempt be made to quantify this. While one might argue whether Marlboro's 1996 valuation of \$44.6 bn is precisely correct, the issue really is that this is a multi-billion dollar asset and regular tracking is needed to assess how different branding activities are affecting its value.

The debacle at Saatchi & Saatchi illustrates how the value of a brand is heavily dependent on the intangible goodwill inherent in the brand's associations which can fluctuate over time. In 1994 Maurice Saatchi was ousted as chairman of this famous advertising agency after the share price had fallen from £50 in 1987 to £1.50. At the time of his departure the company re-branded itself as Cordiant. As a direct result of his leaving the company, it lost business worth £50 m and during the following six months its market value decreased by another third. However, the Saatchi brand came to life again in the new company founded by Maurice Saatchi, called M&C Saatchi, which benefited from 'Saatchi' intangible assets such as their creative employees and the clients he had taken with him.

Methods of measuring the financial value of a brand

We will now review five methods used to measure the value of a brand.

The first approach aims to calculate the brand's value on the basis of its **historic costs**. These are the aggregated investment costs, such as marketing, advertising and R&D expenditure, devoted to the brand since its birth. However, an assumption is being made that none of these costs were ineffective. By virtue of little more that its heritage, a 100-year old brand is more likely to have had more investment than a 20-year old brand. The management team need to agree how the historical costs should be adjusted for past inflation. Since several years have to pass before it is evident whether the brand is successful, when should a company start to include the brand value in its balance sheet? Another drawback of this method is that it ignores qualitative factors such as the creativity of advertising support. The value of a brand also depends on unquantifiable elements, such as management's expertise and the firm's culture. Finally, there is also the question of financially accounting for the many failed brands that had substantial sums spent on them, out of which experience the successful brand arose. Overall this approach to brand valuation raises many questions and without well-grounded assumptions could be problematic.

Another approach is that of comparing the **premium price** of a branded product over a non-branded product: the difference between the two prices multiplied by the volume of sale of the branded product represents the brand's value. However, it is sometimes difficult to find a comparable generic product. For example, what is the unbranded counterpart of a Mars Bar? This method also assumes that all brands pursue a price-premium strategy. It is clear that the brand value of Swatch or Daewoo for example could not be assessed on this basis when equivalent competitive brands are sold at a higher price.

The valuation of a brand based on its **market value** assumes the existence of a market in which brands, like houses, are frequently sold and can be compared. However, since such a market does not yet exist there is no means of estimating a market price other than putting the brand up for sale on the market. Moreover, while the price of a house is usually set by the seller, the price actually paid for a brand is determined by the strategy of the buyer, who may plan for the brand to play a very different role from its existing one. For example, Unilever paid £70 m for Boursin just to gain shelf-space for its expansion plans for other parts of its brand portfolio.

Some have proposed valuing brands on the basis of various **consumer-related factors**, such as recognition, esteem and awareness. These are all important elements of brands and high scores on these are indicative of strong brands. However, it is very difficult to derive a relationship from an amalgam of these factors to arrive at an objective valuation. For example, most consumers are aware that Rolls-Royce is a famous brand, but what value should be placed on it? Worst of all, however, is the fact that there are many famous brands, such as Co-op, with very little value attached to them.

another way of valuing a brand is to assess its future earnings discounted to present-day values

Yet another way of valuing a brand is to assess its **future earnings discounted to present-day values**. The problem, however, with this method is that it assumes buoyant historical earnings levels, even though a brand may be being 'milked' by its owners. One of the most widely-accepted ways of assessing the brand value is provided by Interbrand (Birkin 1994). In order to determine brand value, a company must calculate the benefits of future ownership, i.e. current and future cash flows of the brand, and discount them to take inflation and risk into account. The Interbrand approach is based on the assumption that the discount rate is given by a 'brand multiple', representative of the brand strength. For example, a high multiple characterizes a brand in which the firm is confident of a continuing stream of future earnings and consequently represents low risk for the company. This also translates into a low discount rate.

The Interbrand method is similar to deriving a company's market value through its price/earnings (P/E) ratio. This provides a link between the share capital and the company's net profits and thus the brand multiple can be applied to a single brand within the company to calculate its value. Just as the P/E ratio equals the market value of the company divided by its after-tax profit, likewise the brand multiple equals the value of the brand divided by the profit generated by this brand, i.e.

$$P/E = \frac{Market\ value\ of\ equity}{Profit} \qquad Brand\ multiple = \frac{Brand\ equity}{Brand\ profit}$$

To calculate the brand value, we multiply the brand profit by the brand multiple:

$$Brand\ profit \times Brand\ multiple = Brand\ equity$$

When calculating the brand profit several issues need to be considered. A historical statement of the brand's profit is first required since as a good approximation tomorrow's profits are likely to be similar to today's, provided there is no change in brand strategy. The brand profit should be the post-tax profit after deducting central overhead costs. There may be instances where the same production line is used for both the manufacturer's brand and several own labels. Where this is the case, any profits arising from shared own label production need to be subtracted.

The next stage in arriving at a realistic assessment of the brand's profit is to deduct the earning that do not relate to brand strength. For example, a firm may market two brands of bread. One competes through major grocery stores against other branded breads, and the other may be sold to a few distributors who sell this with related products through door-to-door delivery. Both brands may show similar brand profits, yet the profit of the first brand is heavily influenced by the strength of branding, while the profit of the second brand is much more dependent on the few distributors with their distribution systems. To eliminate the earnings which do not relate to branding the most common approach is charging the capital tied up in the production of the brand with the return expected from producing a generic equivalent.

When looking at historical profits, to reduce the effect from any unusual year's performance the previous three year profits are averaged. Following the logic of other forecasting systems, the more recent profits are likely to be more indicative of future profits. Therefore, a three-year weighted average is used, applying a weighting of three to the current year, two to the previous year and one to the year before that. These aggregated profits are then divided by the sum of the weighting factors, i.e. six in this case. If though a change in strategy for the brand is envisaged these weightings need to be reconsidered. Finally, each year's profits should be adjusted for inflation.

Interbrand argue
that a brand's
strength can be
found from
evaluating the
brand against
seven factors

Having calculated the brand's profit, the brand multiple then needs to be calculated. This is found through evaluating the brand strength since this determines the reliability of the brand's future earnings. Interbrand argue that a brand's strength can be found from evaluating the brand against seven factors:

- *Leadership* – There is well-documented evidence showing a strong link between market share and profitability, thus leading brands are more valuable than followers. A brand leader can strongly influence the market, set prices and command distribution, thus these criteria must be met to score well on leadership.
- *Stability* – Well-established brands, which have a notable historical presence, are strong assets.
- *Market* – Marketers with brands in non-volatile markets, for example foods, are better able to anticipate future trends and therefore confidently devise brand strategies than marketers operating in markets subject to technological or fashion changes. Thus part of the brand's strength comes from the market it operates in.
- *Internationality* – Brands which have been developed to appeal to consumers internationally are more valuable than national or regional brands because of their greater volumes of sales and the investment to make them less susceptible to competitive attacks.
- *Trend* – The overall long-term trend of the brand shows its ability to remain contemporary and relevant to consumers, and therefore is an indication of its value.
- *Support.* The amount, as well as the quality, of consistent investments and support are indicators of strong brands.
- *Protection* – A registered trademark protects the brand from competition and any activities to protect the brand against imitators augers well for the future of the brand.

The brand is audited against these seven factors, with the maximum scores for each factor shown in Table 11.1. By aggregating these seven scores, the brand strength can be calculated.

Table 11.1 *Maximum scores for the seven strength factors* (after Interbrand, Birkin 1994)

Strength factor	Maximum score
Leadership	25
Stability	15
Market	10
Internationality	25
Trend	10
Support	10
Protection	5
Total score	100

The higher the brand strength score the greater its multiple score. Interbrand argue that there is an S-curve relationship between the multiple and the brand strength score, as shown in Figure 11.5. Thus having calculated, for example, a brand strength score of 71, from Figure 11.5 this gives a multiple of 16, i.e. the brand's value is 16 times its three-year weighted average profit.

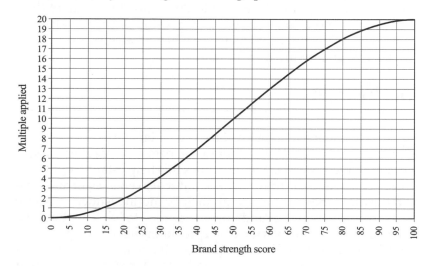

Figure 11.5   *The relation between brand strength and multiple*

Several questions have been raised about the Interbrand method. Although Interbrand has derived the data for the S-curve from the multiples involved in actual brand negotiations, market multiples may not necessarily be a correct indicator of the brand strength. All these multiples have been derived from the final transaction figures and may be inflated because market prices for brand acquisition often include an element of overbid. As the S-curve ignores this additional factor, the brand equity resulting from such a multiple might be over-valued.

A slight variation in the multiple can modify the value of the brand significantly. For example, in the case of Reckitt & Colman a one-point variation in the multiple corresponds to £54 m difference in brand value.

Interbrand argues that a new brand grows slowly in the early stages, then it increases exponentially as it moves from national to international recognition and then slows down as it progresses to global brand status. However, experimental analysis shows that the development of a brand is susceptible to threshold effects. It gradually acquires strength with consumers and retailers in different stages, but beyond a certain point its rate of growth is much greater. Research has found that brands achieve respectable spontaneous awareness scores only after a high level of prompted awareness has been achieved. Therefore, the relationship between brand strength and brand multiple may be better represented by a less regular pattern.

Despite these limitations, the Interbrand method is a popular method amongst firms valuing their brands and is being adopted by more companies as a practical way to determine the value of their brands. Furthermore, firms have growing historical brand valuation databases enabling managers to assess which strategies are particularly effective at growing their brands.

Conclusions

Effective brand management involves a considerable use of resources and we believe that it is important for managers to regularly assess the health of their brands. Not only does this help establish a library of those strategies that drive success, but it also enables firms to assess the returns they are getting on their brand investments. Before starting to evaluate their brand, managers need to be clear about the concept of brand equity. Various interpretations have been proposed to explain the concept of brand equity, each one leading to a different set of measures and valuation methods. Our suggestion is that managers should tailor their monitoring system to best suit their environment.

Brand equity is an evolutionary, rather than static, concept. Understanding the dynamics of this concept enables managers to consider strategies to help grow their brands. As different strategies are particularly suited for different stages, managers need to constantly monitor progress and be continually alert to the need for new strategies.

We have presented a definition of brand equity that encompasses several factors. This allows managers to tailor their particular interpretation of brand equity to ensure it fully reflects the nature of their market. We regard brand equity as consisting of three components: attributes; strength; and brand value. Investigating each component provides diagnostics about the well-being of the brand and indicators for future actions. The brand attributes component can be gauged from considering characteristics relating to: brand awareness; image; perceived quality; perceived value; brand personality; and organizational associations. These affect the strength of a brand, which in turn can be measured by dimensions such as: leadership; price premium; loyalty; market share; and distribution. The third component of brand equity relates to the brand's value.

This chapter highlighted some of the conflicts raised by striving to value brands for balance sheets. While problems remain about measuring brand value, some tracking is necessary to identify trends. This should provide a greater opportunity for maintaining the brand's strength and provide insightful information that can help grow brand equity. The precise valuation process needs to be carefully considered and we believe that brand valuation should be part of any good monitoring system.

Marketing action checklist

To help clarify the direction of future brand marketing activity, it is recommended that the following exercises are undertaken:

1   With your marketing team, review the stages in the life cycle of your brands. Then assess how successful your brands have been at each stage. If you have not devised any system to measure the brand's success, consider which milestones marked the growth of each brand. Now consider the future of the brands. How do you plan to keep track of their development? Establish some benchmark figures to help you assess the growth of the brand. Do your short- and long-term strategies support the achievement of these goals?
2   With your colleagues select one of your firm's brands and go through the four factors that Young and Rubicam argue contribute to brand building (differentiation, relevance, esteem and familiarity), assigning a score on each of them. Compare your responses with those of your consumers, which may necessitate a customer survey. Any discrepancy between your and consumers' views is an indicator of a possible performance gap and corrective action should be considered. With the results of

the consumer survey, determine the brand score on vitality and stature. Analyse, using the same procedure, the brands of your competitors. Finally, plot your brand on the matrix shown in Figure 11.2 together with the brands it is competing against. What conclusion can you draw from this comparison? Does your marketing programme protect your brand's position? Does the programme reflect your long-term objectives or does it primarily focus on achieving short-term results?

3   Using the model in Figure 11.3, profile your brand against competitors. What strategies have led to these profiles? Does your marketing programme take the lower layers for granted? What marketing activities could you devise to improve your brand's profile.

4   From the list of attributes shown in the first box of brand equity in Figure 11.4, identify those that would best apply to your brands, making explicit the reasons for including or disregarding any attribute. What market research data do you have to assess these attributes, both for your brand and your competitors? If your data is based on research undertaken more than twelve months ago, it is advisable to consider commissioning new market research.

5   For each attribute you have selected in the previous exercise (brand awareness, image, perceived quality, perceived value, personality and organizational associations), how is your brand performing? What improvements will help the brand on each attribute?

6   Selecting the brand strength dimensions from Figure 11.4 most appropriate to evaluating your brand, how strong is your brand? By considering its weaknesses, consider possible routes to improvement.

7   Assess how appropriate and realistic it would be to value your brands solely on historic costs. With your colleagues, discuss how to attribute costs to that specific brand and identify those intangible elements that were important for the development of the brand. How could these intangible elements be valued?

8   Following the Interbrand method, score your brand on the seven factors listed in Table 11.1. How could you improve performance on each of these seven factors? How well do your scores reflect consumers' perception of your brand? Repeat this exercise considering the scores your brand would have received one, then two years ago. Has the brand's value grown over time? What strategies have you followed to encourage the growth? Are they still valid and appropriate for the future? Are any others more suitable?

9   From the material covered on brand valuation techniques, consider with your colleagues the valuation process that would be most suitable for your brands.

References and further reading

Aaker D. (1991) *Managing Brand Equity.* New York: The Free Press.

Aaker D. (1996). *Building Strong Brands.* New York: The Free Press.

Aaker D. (1996). Measuring brand equity across products and markets. *California Management Review,* **38** (3), 102–20.

Aaker D. and Biel L. (1993). *Brand Equity and Advertising.* Hillsdale, New Jersey: Lawrence Erlbaum Associates.

Barwise P. (1993). Brand equity: snark or boojum. *International Journal of Research in Marketing,* **10** (1), 93–104.

Barwise P., Higson A., Likierman A. and Marsh P. (1989). *Accounting for Brands.* London: London Business School and the Institute of Chartered Accountants.

Birkin M. (1994). Assessing brand value. In *Brand Power* (Stebart P. ed.) Basingstoke: Macmillan.

de Chernatony L. (1996). Integrated brand building using brand taxonomies. *Marketing Intelligence & Planning,* **14** (7), 40–5.

Farquhar P. (1989). Managing brand equity. *Marketing Research,* **1** (Sept.), 24–33.

Feldwick P. (1996). What is brand equity anyway, and how do you measure it? *Journal of the Market Research Society,* **38** (2), 85–104.

Gordon G., di Benedetto A. and Calantone R. (1994). Brand equity as an evolutionary process. *The Journal of Brand Management,* **2** (1), 47–56.

Kapferer J.N. (1992). *Strategic Brand Management.* London: Kogan Page.

Keller K. (1993). Conceptualizing, measuring and managing customer-based brand equity. *Journal of Marketing,* **57** (Jan.), 1–22.

Millward Brown International (1996). *The Good Health Guide.* Warwick: Millward Brown International.

Murphy J. (ed.) (1991). *Brand Evaluation.* London: Business Books.

Simon C. and Sullivan M. (1990). The measurement and determinants of brand equity: a financial approach. Working Paper, Graduate School of Business, University of Chicago.

Young & Rubicam (1994). *Brand Asset Valuation.* London: Young & Rubicam

Index